SCHOOL OF
ORIENTAL AND AFRICAN STUDIES
UNIVERSITY OF LONDON

London Oriental Series
Volume 32

Group at Viceregal Lodge, Simla, 1918. *For key, see Contents page.*

LONDON ORIENTAL SERIES · VOLUME 32

THE GOVERNMENT OF INDIA AND REFORM

POLICIES TOWARDS POLITICS AND THE CONSTITUTION
1916–1921

BY

P. G. ROBB

*Lecturer in Modern South Asian History
at the School of Oriental and
African Studies*

OXFORD UNIVERSITY PRESS
1976

Oxford University Press, Walton Street, Oxford OX2 6DP

OXFORD   LONDON   GLASGOW   NEW YORK
TORONTO   MELBOURNE   WELLINGTON   CAPE TOWN
IBADAN   NAIROBI   DAR ES SALAAM   LUSAKA   ADDIS ABABA
KUALA LUMPUR   SINGAPORE   JAKARTA   HONG KONG   TOKYO
DELHI   BOMBAY   CALCUTTA   MADRAS   KARACHI

ISBN 0 19 713590 0

© P. G. Robb, 1976

Printed in Great Britain by
William Clowes & Sons, Limited, London, Beccles and Colchester

TO MY PARENTS

London Oriental Series

* These volumes are out of print.
† These volumes are obtainable only from the School of Oriental and African Studies.

LONDON ORIENTAL SERIES

* These volumes are out of print.
† These volumes are obtainable only from the School of Oriental and African Studies.

PREFACE

THIS book was originally a Ph.D. dissertation of the University of London. I received financial support from the Commonwealth Scholarship Commission for three years, and later visited India with a Fellowship from the School of Oriental and African Studies, London. Publication has been made possible through the generosity of the Publications Committee of the School of Oriental and African Studies, to whom I am pleased to express gratitude.

I am glad to acknowledge the help and co-operation of many friends and colleagues; of Martin Daly, Publications Officer at the School of Oriental and African Studies; and of the directors and staffs of the India Office Library and Records, the National Archives of India, the Scottish Record Office, and the University of Birmingham Library.

Most of all, I am grateful to Professor K. A. Ballhatchet of the School of Oriental and African Studies. Both as the supervisor of my thesis and subsequently as a colleague, he has helped me immeasurably with his tactful but unfailing advice and encouragement.

I thank my wife for having typed most of the final draft of this book, and for having given me much support during a period of what she came to regard as endless revision.

P. G. R.

December 1973.
School of Oriental and African Studies,
University of London.

CONTENTS

CONTENTS

Left to right, in front: W., B., Margaret, R. and D. Thesiger; *1st row:* **Gait**, **O'Dwyer**, Mrs Maffey, **Ronaldshay**, **Meston**, **Pentland**, Lady Chelmsford, **Chelmsford**, **Montagu**, Mrs Thesiger, **Willingdon**, Mrs Verney, Mrs Mackenzie; *2nd row:* Miss Hogg, Gould, Donoughmore, Bridget and Anne Thesiger, W. Thesiger, **Duke**, Slocock, **Seton**, **Robertson**, **Vincent**, Gourlay, Basu, Joan Thesiger; *3rd row:* **Marris***, **Maffey***, Vaux, Mackenzie, Austen-Smith, Bayley, Earle, Halliday, **Gwynne**, Kisch, **Crerar**, Greenway, Lovelace, Money, Charles Roberts (obscured); *4th row:* Carnegie, Alexander, Freeman-Thomas, Denny, Parsons, Franey, Akbar Ali Khan, Holland-Hibbert, Baring, Verney. (Reproduced by permission of the Director, India Office Library and Records. For identifications see Mss. Eur. D. 523/44. Those marked* have been superimposed from other contemporary photographs.)

ABBREVIATIONS

ACP	Austen Chamberlain Papers (with ref. no.)*
AD	Army Department
C	Confidential
CC/	Chief Commissioner of
CD	Commerce Department
C&ID	Commerce and Industry Department
CID	Central Intelligence Department
CP	Chelmsford Papers (with vol. no.)*
ED	Education Department
FD	Finance Department
F&PD	Foreign and Political Department
G/	Governor(s), Government(s) of (I = India)
HD	Home Department
H.Police	HD (Police) Proceedings No. (with date)*
H.Poll.	HD (Political) Proceedings No. (with date)*
H.Public	HD (Public) Proceedings No. (with date)*
ILA	Imperial Legislative Assembly
ILC	Imperial Legislative Council
IOR	India Office Records (with ref. no.)*
LD	Legislative Department
LG/	Lieutenant-Governor of
MP	Montagu Papers (with vol. no.)*
PS (PSV)	Private Secretary (Viceroy)
RD	Reforms Department
RO	Reforms Office
RP	Ronaldshay Papers*
Speeches	Speeches of Lord Chelmsford (with vol. no.)*
S/S	Secretary of State for India
V	Viceroy

NOTE

Home Department Proceedings have been consulted in both London and New Delhi. To distinguish the sources, citations are without indication of series in the former case (where all are A series), and with in the latter; thus: *H.Poll.*10, Jan. 1917 (consulted in London), but *H.Poll.* A10 (or B10 or Dep. 10), Jan. 1917 (consulted in New Delhi). In the latter case 'k.w.' indicates papers kept with a file; 'Dep.' stands for 'Deposit'.

* See Bibliography for details.

A CHRONOLOGY OF MAJOR EVENTS

1916   5 April, Lord Chelmsford Viceroy
April, Tilak's Home Rule League formed
September, Besant's Home Rule League inaugurated
24 November, Government of India reforms despatch
December, Congress-League reforms scheme agreed at Lucknow

1917   March, differential cotton duties
—, unilateral ban on indentured emigration
April, Gandhi in Champaran
—, Indian members in Imperial War Conference and Cabinet
May, Chelmsford endorses demand for policy declaration
15 June, Besant and associates interned
20 July, Edwin Montagu Secretary of State
2 August, Cabinet accepts King's Commissions for Indians
8 August, Chelmsford declares policy declaration 'imperative'
20 August, Montagu Declaration promises responsible government
September, Hindu-Muslim riots in Shahabad, Bihar
17 September, Besant released
19 September, O'Dwyer forced to apologize to Imperial legislature
19 October, India Office reforms despatch
10 November, Montagu arrives in India
10 December, Rowlatt's Sedition Committee appointed

1918   January, heads of government's conference
27 March, Home Rule deputation refused passports
April, Rowlatt Committee reports
—, Montagu leaves with Montagu–Chelmsford report
—, Delhi War Conference
16 April, Home Department restricts use of Defence of India Act
June, Central Publicity Board formed
8 July, Montagu–Chelmsford Report published

1919   Llewellyn Smith's Secretariat Committee formed and reports
January, five governors agree on their own reforms scheme
6 February, Rowlatt bills introduced
30 March, riot in Delhi
6 April, Gandhi calls *hartal* in Rowlatt protest

8 April, Chelmsford orders firm but sympathetic policy
9 April, Kitchlew and Satyapal deported from Amritsar
10 April, firing in Lahore
13 April, Jallianwala Bagh, Amritsar massacre by Dyer
15 April, martial law orders in the Panjab
18 April, Gandhi suspends civil disobedience
5 May, war with Afghanistan
14 May, Cabinet approves introduction of reforms bill
September, Indian Arms Amendment, and Indemnity, Acts
October, Hunter's Disorders Inquiry Committee appointed
15 October, all restrictions on Gandhi lifted
23 December, Government of India Act receives royal assent

1920 March, Gandhi calls *hartal* in Khilafat protest
May, harsh peace terms offered to Turkey
26 May, Hunter Committee Report published
28 May, Central Khilafat Committee adopts non-co-operation
July, *Hijrat* movement
September, Special Congress Session, Calcutta
19 October, Gandhi's arrest considered after Lucknow speech
November, government proclamation on non-interference

1921 January, Nagpur Congress
—, reforms scheme operative
—, disturbances in Rai Bareli
March, Home Department urges local prosecutions of agitators
10 March, Repressive Laws Committee appointed
2 April, Lord Reading Viceroy

INTRODUCTION

'Micro-studies provide insights while macro-studies yield perspectives, and movement from one to the other is essential'—M. N. Srinivas[1]

TOO often books of this kind have purported to be histories not of government but of India. This is not one of them: in its own way it is a microcosmic study. It examines the emergence of a reform policy and its impact on the political stance of the central government.

The argument of the book is simple enough. The claim is that during 1916 the Government of India became committed to a goal of Indian self-government and that, because this commitment was deliberately linked to practical reforms, it began slowly to have repercussions on political policy in general.

I have deliberately limited my interest to this aspect of central affairs. Provincial or district matters did not concern me, except in so far as to suggest that officials at these levels did not generally share the central government's attitudes nor always obey its orders. I have also not attempted to analyse the character of Indian politics, being content in the main merely to report the views and information known in the central government.[2] To have dealt with all these questions, in our present state of knowledge, would have been too great an undertaking.

My concern with aspects of central policy is no doubt unfashionable, but I make no apology for it. Detailed studies of Indian nationalism are in progress and will need to be complemented by detailed understanding of government policy. Events at the centre are in themselves as valid a subject of inquiry as any other, provided they do not pretend to be the whole jig-saw puzzle. They are only a few pieces of it.

This book is not, then, comprehensive even as an account of Lord Chelmsford's viceroyalty. It is not organized chronologically, but as an analysis of those aspects of policy which reflected the changing approach of the government. It begins in 1916 because Chelmsford's first Council meeting can be taken as a starting

point for the shift in policy. It ends in 1921 because by then this
policy was firmly established, and to have continued the story
would have meant only further examples complicated by the
presence of a new Viceroy, a new constitution, and three Indian
members of Council—a situation which was in many ways the
product of the shift which had already occurred. How that shift
progressed and how it fared in later years is really the subject for
other books.

This is not an account, either, of Chelmsford's own role, though
inevitably (I think) it calls for a reassessment of his term of office.
His personal contribution does not often emerge very clearly, for
reasons that will be explained, and the collective responsibility (the
government acting as a whole) is the central character of the book.
This is more the case than may appear at first sight, for, in so far
as government is often carried on in the name of the chief executive, many opinions or actions attributed to Chelmsford in this
book, as a convenient short-hand, will have been of course the
work of the Governor-General in Council.

It is argued that for this government, in its political approach,
the period marks a watershed. The Indians' desire to rule themselves had long been regarded by many of the British as an aberration—it had unaccountably appeared in a nation they had created.
During the First World War the aberration proved startlingly con-
tagious. The government itself was not immune; and the infection
spread even from one sphere of official activity to another. The
reform policy gave rise, in government, to a politics of reform.

Some of this has long been recognized. Most general histories
begin or divide their narratives between 1917 and 1919. H. V.
Hodson, endorsing an historical truism, explained firstly how 'The
advance was towards a . . . concept . . . that it was . . . the political
duty of an imperial power to grant self-government', and secondly
how 1918 was the year when this became 'a question of time and
method, not of ultimate objective'.[3] But this book asks what precisely was the nature of this change. Within its general conclusion,
it suggests two new things: that the Government of India were
more closely involved than has been thought, and that underlying
their policy was a coherent idea.

Examination of the reforms discussions demonstrates firstly
that there was commitment to ultimate self-government coupled
with practical steps towards it (and this for the first time) in the

Government of India's reforms despatch in 1916, and secondly that when others extended those practical steps to include partial legislative responsibility they did so within this context, and with Government of India consent. That government, it is claimed, effectively set the limits to the practical advance: the corollary of this is that they accepted the steps which were proposed, and that their acceptance was reflected in other aspects of their political policy. It is true that after providing the impetus they were usually a restraining influence. It is not suggested that they were liberal or enlightened. But their conservatism, whatever its roots in habits of paternalism and autocracy, does not diminish the importance of their change in approach. The caution was no doubt in individuals the result of an emotional attachment to the past certainties of British rule; but the psychological breakthrough had nonetheless been made, in India, and within officialdom. Self-government (of a sort) had been accepted as the goal, preparation for that day had become the stated purpose of British presence, and practical steps had been taken, as never before, which relinquished certain powers to Indians, as a deliberate stage on the way to an Indian take-over of the administration. And the validity of this change was shown by complementary changes in other spheres.

The coherent idea underlying the policy was formulated in India from the government's enunciation of the goal of Indian self-government within the Empire. The government had decided that they must begin to resolve the contradictions between bureaucracy and Indian advancement, and give positive expression to their acceptance of the goal. Thus, it will be shown, they themselves worked through collective responsibility in consultation with local governments and (to a lesser extent) legislators and public— as befitted their changing role. They attacked racial discrimination, internal and international, as inappropriate to the Indians' future status. In spite of the dangers of popular activism, they evolved a tactic of non-interference with national politicians, partly because of an admission that Indian aspirations, if not methods, were basically legitimate. They repressed political 'crime' and disorders, but saw them as exceptional and as counter-productive to Indian progress; and, though the repressive habit persisted in the 'Rowlatt' Act, the atrocities of 1919 were a local aberration which they repudiated. Finally, they presided over constitutional reforms in which they tried for the first time to prepare for a future transfer of power.

All this recognizes different influences on policy, limitations to the vision, and the exceptional unpopularity of Chelmsford's rule. The failures are not disputed, but positive achievements are also presented for scrutiny.

2

Lord Chelmsford arrived in India when the world was at war; he left as the subcontinent faced internal disruption. In India the war and its aftermath had brought a few people wealth, confidence and ambition; to many more it had brought hardship and disease. India had lost much and been promised much. Chelmsford had to remedy the deprivation and redeem the promises. He sought change, and was overtaken by it. He had to govern in the years when the war seemed long, and in those, after the war, when the rewards seemed small.

His viceroyalty saw the worst disturbances since the Mutiny, and what was perhaps the most important initiative in the history of the British Indian constitution. His name is associated with repression of a brutality rarely seen before in British times, and with a report which rivals that of Durham in its contribution to Commonwealth evolution. Under Chelmsford the British officially recognized that India's future belonged to the Indians, and tried to ensure that its present remained firmly in British hands. Probably no earlier period had seen such rapid shifts in the British position, but perhaps never before was that position so rigorously challenged. Chelmsford's five years coincided almost exactly with the period in which national leadership was assumed by Mahatma Gandhi. In Chelmsford's time the Indian National Congress and the nationalist movement as a whole changed almost beyond recognition. They emerged with new weapons—not only Gandhi's *satyagraha*, but the Home Rule League's powers of popular appeal and permanent concerted opposition; not only a new discipline within the Congress, but an unparalleled co-operation with the Muslim League; not only powerful slogans and ideals, but a fusion of religion and politics and a common cause in demanding *swaraj*. Change, readjustment, instability, progress were all the hall-marks of this period. Under Chelmsford the course of British history in India was altered.

On all sides we are told that the alteration had nothing to do with Lord Chelmsford or his government. Leading Indian and British scholars have been unanimous on this point. R. C. Majumdar has told us that 'Chelmsford cannot be regarded as an able administrator or a successful Viceroy in any sense. He lacked personality and independence of judgment and was more or less a tool in the hands of the bureaucracy'. Percival Spear has claimed that Chelmsford 'was more nearly an agent, and less of a policy-maker than any other Viceroy in the last period of British rule'. Chelmsford's colleagues have been almost alone in having any doubts. Edwin Montagu, often grudging in his assessment, told Chelmsford he would be 'one of India's foremost Viceroys'. In 1921 the official *Moral and Material Progress Report* enumerated the achievements of the viceroyalty, and stated that, by the end of Chelmsford's term,

India's future within the Empire no longer remained undefined; she could look forward to Responsible Government as an entity of Dominion status. She was actually operating a progressive scheme leading directly to Self-Government, a scheme holding out before her infinite possibilities of advancement. In token of her changed position, many of those anomalies which aroused such bitter feeling had been removed. The racial stigma was gone from the Arms Act. Indian soldiers were holding King's Commissions. Indian youths were being trained for Sandhurst. ... In industrial and educational spheres, steady and substantial progress had been achieved, while local self-government had made notable advances. In brief, as a result of the labours of Lord Chelmsford and his Government . . ., the face of India was changed in half a decade.

The report had summed up Chelmsford's contribution thus: 'To few Governors-General has it been given to accomplish so much towards the enduring welfare of their great charge; to fewer yet has the meed of praise and appreciation been so scantily rendered'.[4]

The latter remains true: contemporary vilification has run deep. It continues on the original basis—discounting of Chelmsford's role as a reformer, accompanied by abhorrence at the repression in the Panjab during the disturbances of 1919. Sachchidananda Bhattacharya, in his *Dictionary of Indian History*, though inaccurate in details, epitomizes the orthodox view, beginning with the usual disclaimers: 'Lord Chelmsford had little initiative of his own and he had little influence on the framing of the Indo-British policy which led to the famous announcement made on August 20, 1917 . . . Lord Chelmsford also had little to do with the framing of the Government of India Act, 1919 . . .'. Then the entry concentrates on the Panjab repression: 'Lord Chelmsford who was aware of all these enormities did little to stop the barbarities . . . failed to repress effectively and immediately the official criminals, . . . and thus alienated Indo-British feelings more deeply than any other viceroy since the Sepoy Mutiny'. Negative elements are emphasized: thus verdicts have been partly emotional. In the *Dictionary*, rather oddly, Chelmsford is criticized first for having done nothing, having played a 'passive part in the dynamic politics of India', and then for having created a desperate crisis, by handling the political situation 'very clumsily'.[5] Indignation at Chelmsford and his government is still partly a product of Indian grief and British shame.

Chelmsford governed in a period of great and fundamental change; the consensus is that he played no part. The government had to meet a major challenge and severe problems; the consensus is that they handled them badly. It is now time to examine the record. By using the documentary evidence now available, we can look behind the public personality of the Viceroy, and seek a way through the emotions the period aroused. We will concentrate on the twin spheres of politics and reform—on precisely those spheres, of nationalist agitation and the constitution, on which the traditional interpretation has been based. But first we shall look at the system within which Chelmsford and his government had to work, and at some of the methods they employed.

Part One

REFORM

I CONSULTATION

Chapter 1. The System

IN 1916 the system of government in India bore all the traces of a
mixed evolution. At the top the Viceroy ruled, at least in name. On
the one hand he was the sole representative in India of the King-
Emperor. On the other hand he was a British government nominee,
responsible to the Secretary of State for India, who was in turn
responsible to the Cabinet and to Parliament. The Secretary of
State was also advised by the Council of India (a body of retired
dignatories with a few suitably anglicized Indians) and assisted by
the India Office, a branch of the British civil service having no
formal link with its Indian counterparts. The Viceroy was advised
in some, though not all, matters by his Executive Council, comprising the Commander-in-Chief, who also enjoyed certain
independent rights, and a group of officials who were each thought
of as representing one of the great departments of the central
government, departments which nevertheless through their Secretaries maintained their own independent relationship with the
Viceroy, departments which, moreover, were each more or less a
compendium of diverse interests and responsibilities. Below this
central structure came a confusion of subordinate authorities. The
most important were the Presidency Governors of Bengal, Bombay
and Madras, who with their own Councils exercised sway over
semi-independent empires, theoretically subject to the Viceroy,
but usually appointed from outside the Indian services and
guarding a right of independent communication with the Secretary
of State. These governors communicated with the Viceroy, as it
were, as government to government; nevertheless' the Government
of India was able to exercise control, mainly by a right of financial
scrutiny and veto.

Beside the governors stood the Lieutenant-Governors, promoted from the Indian Civil Service, and sharing in some cases the
independence of the Presidency governors, in others subject to the
closer control exercised over the next and lesser breed, the Chief
Commissioners. These were in charge of areas of greatly differing

importance but were all responsible directly to the Government of India. In a not dissimilar situation (except where they dealt with local governments) came the multitude of Indian princes and chiefs, varying enormously in power, independence and influence, subject to a great profusion of treaty rights and obligations. Thereafter, in the British system, followed hierarchies of minor officials—divisional commissioners, revenue collectors, district officers, judges, magistrates, police, medical officers, inspectors of education—each organized slightly differently (often with further variations between provinces) and subject to the appropriate department of the local government. The Government of India or the Viceroy also exercised some quite separate powers of supervision at this level—over Calcutta University (a legacy from Calcutta's days as the capital), over the Anglican church, over the railways, in some respects over the judiciary and the revenue collection. In most departments, the Indian services were divided into two sections, imperial and provincial, and of all of these the Indian Civil Service was the greatest, or at least the most exclusive. The system was a distended bureaucracy; its methods autocratic.

But the British had also tried to make this machine the vehicle for liberal gestures towards Indians. At one level this had meant attempts to include Indians in the bureaucracy through the progressive indianization of the services. To some extent, in so far as limited practical power and opportunities for initiative rested on district officers and depended upon their diverse enthusiasms, this did mean real opportunities for Indians to take over some of the affairs of their country. But it was never suggested that it was necessary to change the system and not merely to include Indians in it. Yet the system was paternalistic not only in its role and traditions, but in its structure—devised for alien administrators who were intended to rule (not to advise), combining executive and judicial powers, separate, authoritarian. Thus too there was talk of giving Indians commissions in the Indian army; but there was no suggestion that the army might also have to modify its role as the ultimate weapon of an occupying power or its structure as a great imperial force, unified with other imperial forces, designed (or was it inflated?) as an expensive instrument for imperial policies decided in London.

On other levels, it is true, there were attempts which looked like the beginnings of modifications in the system. There had been

high sentiments and rather less noble efforts expended on experiments in local self-government, involving Indians to various
degrees, though seldom in very much responsibility. The local
governments were all great advocates of the devolution of power,
but they usually had in mind their own standing *vis à vis* the
Government of India (who in turn looked for concessions from the
Secretary of State); there was less practical enthusiasm for
devolution of responsibility to local and district boards. More
important, legislative councils had been tacked on to some governments and were planned for more. But they did not really fit into
the system, and were often regarded as a wilful irrelevancy which
twice a year interrupted official business. They had been improved
in size by a series of reforms; the latest of these had even made
possible non-official majorities. But the numbers were tiny; the
minority of members who were not nominated by government was
chosen by cumbersome machinery of indirect election, involving
a few hundreds out of the millions; and the councils had not
advanced from their original purely advisory role. Of course a few
Indians had also been included in what were in name the highest
posts of government, memberships of the Executive Councils.
Both these intrusions and the handfuls of Indians in the legislatures were in fact to be of enormous importance in changing
British attitudes, advancing them further than the stage which
these concessions themselves represented. Not always—perhaps
seldom—will real influence strictly follow the lines of formal
responsibility. But nonetheless the liberal aspects of the Indian
constitution in 1916 looked like, and in some senses were, a show-
case and a sham.

Progress had been piece-meal. But the heyday of incoherent and
often inconsistent expedients was almost over. What was needed
was a wholesale re-evaluation of the entire system. It had to be re-
designed to fit the liberal purpose which some of the British had
long professed to be the object of their rule. The new direction had
to come from the top; and it was too great a task for one man or one
viceroyalty. But pre-war promises and wartime pressures were
bringing matters to a crucial stage. The process of rationalization,
as yet uncomprehended, was already underway. It was inherent
(though vehemently denied) in Morley and Minto's reforms; they
had created legislatures which, though strictly advisory in conception, had become such self-conscious vehicles for Indian

opinion and guardians of Indian hopes—all this perhaps in the person of G. K. Gokhale alone—that already it was natural that one day they would be replaced by responsible parliaments. The same process could be discerned in ideas put forward by Chelmsford's predecessor, Lord Hardinge, for future remedial measures—even though they were conceived as appeasements for Indian opinion and not as a coherent plan to reform Indian government. Chelmsford was presented with the increasingly urgent need to reconcile the two halves of the system, the apparently immovable bureaucracy and the yet unformed democratic alternative.

We shall be considering this dichotomy further, in the specific context of attitudes to political agitation. Before leaving the topic for the moment, however, it is worth remarking that the same division may be discerned at the personal level as at the institutional. Thus the local governors in Chelmsford's time reflect the contradictions we have observed in the system itself. Sir James Meston in the United Provinces embodied one impulse, the 'liberal'; Sir Michael O'Dwyer and Lord Pentland, in the Panjab and Madras, embodied the other, the 'conservative'. The remainder fell somewhere in between. But we should not assess the division too simply. O'Dwyer and Pentland were vilified by politicians, but in some ways their positions were unexceptionable—Pentland for example had opposed further press restrictions in 1914 (on the grounds that it would be 'a first-class political blunder' to ascribe to sedition something 'due to ignorance')—and their administrative abilities, especially in the case of O'Dwyer, and their dedication to India, in their own terms, cannot be doubted. It was their perspective that was narrow. They were suspicious of change and appreciative of the workings of the autocratic system. They had little sympathy with those elements in which Indians had begun to count. Such men were paternalists, not only in their manner and their instincts, but in the exclusion from their ideas of government of any commitment to Indian involvement. When asked why Indians did not participate, they replied it was because Indians had no experience. When asked why they had no experience, they replied it was because they did not participate. When asked why this state of affairs was allowed to continue, they referred to the virtues of British rule.

Thus this attitude was expressed chiefly during the discussions on constitutional reforms. O'Dwyer argued that an elected majority in the legislature was out of the question, and begged that at least the Panjab should be saved from this fate; Pentland opposed any discussions of reforms during the war, objected strongly to the terms of the Declaration of 20 August 1917, dissented from his own Council in refusing any transfer of responsibility, and obstructed the work of the committees set up under Lord Southborough to fill in the details in the proposals of Montagu and Chelmsford. But this attitude was not confined to the reforms; it affected all aspects of policy—determined priorities and the assessment of what was reasonable. And thus both O'Dwyer and Pentland were suspicious, even outraged, when the politicians made (as they thought) impossible demands, and both believed such irresponsible nonsense should be put down with a firm hand; both concentrated their attention and bestowed their good will on those Indians who supported the *status quo* or those who were inarticulate but acquiescent, and both were dedicated to measures which would benefit such people. And it should not be forgotten that in 1916 these categories undoubtedly comprised the majority of the population, and that there was some credibility in the paternalist demand that the British must continue to rule as the sole impartial element amongst the divisions of Indian society. Indeed, 'liberalism' was no guarantee of popularity among Indians. O'Dwyer was made the subject of effusive and affectionate eulogies during the course of his governorship—until the 1919 disturbances he was thought of as a popular administrator, and there were public meetings in his support even after the tragedy.[1]

There can be no clear division, then, according to the degree of commitment to particular policies. Sir James Meston favoured a conciliatory approach to agitators and was one of the most important positive influences on the Government of India, but he too could adopt a conservative stance, as in his early exposition of the impossibility of divided responsibility at the provincial level, or his reluctance to see the transfer of higher education to Indian control. Again, Lord Ronaldshay in Bengal espoused a sympathetic understanding of Bengali terrorists, but was perhaps the prime mover in the decision to take executive powers to repress them. Sir George Lloyd in Bombay, though sceptical of 'dyarchy', supported constitutional reforms as a pressing need, while being at best luke-warm in his advocacy of political conciliation. Lord Willingdon, in Bombay and then in Madras, by and large supported

rapid constitutional change, but did not envisage any diminution
of his own influence: his 'liberalism' was the product of a confidence
in his ability to lead Indians, not of a readiness to step aside. His
approach is neatly summed up by his own description of it, written
from Madras:

The Dravidian is a terribly difficult person to deal with. He has no
sense of honour, no public spirit, & I get little help from leading citizens
in any form or way. Still I go blundering on telling them what I think.
They hate this, but in years to come it may improve their moral sense.
They are clever devils too . . . but I beg of you not to make too much of
them or trust them too far.[2]

The problem was that the means which had earlier given Willingdon success in Bombay had now become anachronistic. He professed to intend participation, but his means were paternalistic:
the latter was a contradiction of the former. Not surprisingly, he
too favoured a strong line with those politicians who demanded
more than he offered. Thus attitudes varied: what remained the
same was the philosophy behind them. It is at this point that the
line between governors can safely be drawn. Administrators in
India came to different conclusions on specific issues, but each had
a concept of British rule and a view of its purpose. The division
was between those whose aims (however expressed) were primarily
paternalistic, and those whose aims were primarily educative.
Thus the men mirrored the contradictions of the system.

But at the personal level also the contradictions had to be
resolved. It is instructive to look briefly at the appointments made
under Chelmsford. Sir Edward Maclagan, a man of more flexible
mind, followed O'Dwyer in the Panjab. Willingdon replaced
Pentland in Madras. Meston, singled out by Chelmsford for confidence and advancement, joined the Government of India with a
special responsibility for reforms. Sir Reginald Craddock, a 'conservative', was replaced as Home Member by Sir William Vincent,
who was considered *'persona grata'* with Indians; O'Dwyer
had been considered, but on his own admission was disqualified
by his lack of rapport with Indian politicians. Finally, Lord Sinha,
the first Indian governor, replaced Sir Edward Gait in Bihar and
Orissa. The trend is plain. Increasingly the first criterion for
judging administrators was not their administrative ability (the
qualities of the old paternalism) but their attitude to Indians and to

constitutional reforms. Thus the school of Pentland and O'Dwyer was gradually discredited; and central in this process had been their failure to adapt to the reforms and to accept the policy of non-interference with politicians—the explosion of 1919 delivered the *coup de grâce*. Newer men—in the tradition of Meston—gained in influence, accepted by Government of India and Secretary of State as the most articulate, subtle, able and reliable of their subordinates. The 'liberal' Willingdon on the other hand, though respected (and a personal friend of Montagu), was thought rather old-style in method. His credibility and influence declined accordingly—thus he was ruled out of consideration as Chelmsford's successor, an advancement he had rather expected.[3]

It would be going too far to suggest that this trend in appointments was smooth or even deliberate. After all, Willingdon did eventually become Viceroy. Moreover it remains ambiguous what the appointments, even Sinha's, represented in the eyes of the government and, equally, of the Indian politicians. Nonetheless a trend existed—because it was an inevitable concomitant of Indian participation that the British would appoint officials with whom participation would be possible, and because it was unavoidable that a reforming administration would advance those who agreed on first principles and would support its changes. And of course Indian participation increased in this period: officials had to be appointed who would not only work with Indians, but also accept them as colleagues and equals, be prepared to be outvoted by them, even take orders from them. Thus the future had begun to assert itself.

Chelmsford's appointment may have foreshadowed this in one sense at least. He was selected by Asquith as a liberal conservative with a respectable proconsular record. He was chosen from among men of his own type, and in replacement of Hardinge who had been ruled out for a second term because Austen Chamberlain, the Secretary of State, believed he was becoming impatient of control and feared that an extension of his term would lead to 'very unfortunate friction'. Thus to some extent Chelmsford was thought of as a man who would be easy to work with, and who would not create difficulties during the war. But he was also (it was presumed) to be the Viceroy after the war, and thus, in so far as it was recognized that changes would then be needed, his appointment was deliberately as a safe man who could be trusted to be flexible and

open to ideas but not to countenance anything drastic or revolutionary.[4] Yet Chelmsford was chosen solely on the merit he had
shown as a governor in Australia, for he had no other relevant
public service. It would be absurd to suggest that Asquith therefore had in mind a Dominion-type of governor for India; but it is
true that the colonial governor's experience was relevant in the
sense that, as Indian administration developed, it was becoming
more and more desirable for the Viceroy to be the leader of a team
rather than a despot. It was certainly inadvertent on Asquith's
part, but Chelmsford, safe, co-operative and constitutional, had
some qualities which fitted him for the necessary re-thinking and
re-shaping of British Indian administration. In his method and
also his acceptance of the goal of Indian self-government, Chelmsford was strongly influenced by his experience as a constitutional
governor, especially in New South Wales where he had helped
shepherd the first Labour government through its early years.

Of course Chelmsford was to put his name to proposals far
beyond what a liberal conservative would have allowed himself in
1916, but this does not mean that Asquith and Chamberlain had
been wrong in their assessment. Perhaps they had not altogether
understood their man, whom neither of them knew personally; but
Chelmsford's policies as Viceroy in no way represented concealed
radicalism coming out of hiding. The strongest force moving him
was always the force of events, and logic, of changing situations,
increasing needs, burgeoning demands. Thus Chelmsford leant
towards that side of Indian government which we may call the
side of the future, but was not necessarily committed to it in all its
forms: his was the liberalism of the pragmatist not the doctrinaire.

Edwin Montagu's appointment as Secretary of State, made by
Lloyd George, was a quite different matter. He was known for his
energy and enthusiasm—some would have called him unreliable
and unstable. Lord Islington, the Under-Secretary of State, a man
in Chelmsford's mould, refused to work with the new Secretary
(until persuaded by the Prime Minister and the urgent need to
continue Chamberlain's policies). On 12 July 1917, in the House of
Commons, Montagu had denounced the Government of India,
calling it 'too wooden, too iron, too inelastic, too ante-diluvian,
to be of any use for the modern purposes we have in mind'. The
speech had caused a sensation. On 20 July Montagu was Secretary
of State for India: the dragon-killer made keeper of the dragon.

Whether this was calculated or not is uncertain—it was true for example that only the prize of India would have brought Montagu into the coalition in betrayal of Asquith. But, if Lloyd George was not conscious of the significance of his choice, and of the excitement (or alarm) it would create in India, then we can only conclude that he showed remarkable insensitivity to the consequences of his actions.[5] Chelmsford's appointment had taken into account the fact that change was necessary; Montagu's could only be a declaration of intent to begin at once.

It is tempting to relate this to the trend we have noticed in appointments. It would be neat to assume that Montagu was the driving force introducing change, and Chelmsford the conservative restraint ensuring that change was acceptable to Parliament and the Government of India. But the facts deny this simple pattern. Most of the changes introduced in this period were under consideration before Montagu took office; and in some respects, notably in the response to Gandhi's *satyagraha* after 1920, Montagu tended to lend his weight towards an active, repressive approach rather than a passive one—this in spite of his suspicion of the police and their attitude to Indian politics. It is better, in these circumstances, to note the difference in temperament, but to judge the respective contributions to policy separately as each case arises. The point which immediately strikes us is that in 1916, quite apart from native inclination, Chelmsford was faced with a situation in which it was apparent at once that the whole administrative system would have to be reviewed—both for the war effort and for postwar changes. The point was reinforced in 1917, when the Mesopotamia Commission reported on the bureaucratic incompetence and over-centralization of the Indian army administration. Austen Chamberlain resigned, and admitted that he would have had to recall Lord Hardinge if he had still been Viceroy. In 1916, therefore, Chelmsford had had to begin by reorganizing the Army Department to relieve the burden on the Commander-in-Chief and to assert the collective responsibility of the Viceroy's Council. The army remained his personal daily concern until Sir Beauchamp Duff was replaced by a new Commander-in-Chief, C. C. Monro.[6] In the reaction to these circumstances, we shall find, finally, that in terms of philosophy Montagu and Chelmsford were fundamentally on the same side. We must conclude that change had to occur because the world war was a crisis for the bureaucracy faced with democratic alternatives, as well as for the Indian society and economy.

Chelmsford was in charge of a complex system subject to two contradictory impulses. As an outsider, with a methodical, lawyer's mind, his obvious response was to try to impose some order on the muddle. Before his arrival, some of his senior colleagues had been thinking along similar lines. The attack was to be on several fronts. In the course of the viceroyalty, the attention of the government was to be forced to centre increasingly on the problem of and responses to political agitation. Chelmsford's own preference would have been to carry out positive reforms in industry, education, the public services and local self-government—reforms consciously directed towards a slow modification of the British role in India, and seeing the European administrators as trustees preparing India for self-government. The increasing militancy and strength of Indian political movements made this slow progress impractical, and time and energy (among a seriously depleted cadre) were diverted to the pressing need for constitutional concessions and to the immediate problem of Indian unrest. But, if events overwhelmed the government's cautious and systematic approach, the main directions of their policy remained more or less clear. If bureaucracy and Indian involvement were to be reconciled, both of them would have to be changed. The administrators would have to adapt to a new role, in which they were not autocrats but aides; and the legislators would have to be prepared for the time when they would choose and control their rulers and not merely rail impotently against them. The Viceroy himself would also have to change, in his relations to the legislators and the people, but also, just as important, in his functioning as the head of the bureaucracy. Of course Chelmsford and his Council did not see all this at once, though circumstances were forcing the recognition upon them. Their first moves were exploratory. The first task seemed to be to open lines of communication on the main issues that were crowding in on the government. In some cases this led to substantive changes—we shall consider these in due course. First, we shall look at the mode of operations within the system.

Two points about the administration immediately made themselves evident. The first was native caution, qualified by an energetic concern for concerted advance planning. The second was an insistence upon consultation as a means of decision-making.

Both may be related to the changes needed in the Indian government.

In general, Chelmsford's view was that the war should not be used as an excuse for procrastination. Under Hardinge a moratorium had been placed on controversial questions, and Chelmsford found that this had been interpreted as meaning a postponement of any advance planning. 'To my mind,' he reported to Chamberlain, 'this is the moment when the Government should consider the future legislative proposals; I have pressed this course on Members and Secretaries, and I am glad to say they agree'.[7] Thus the Foreign and Political Department soon found itself considering a scheme for a Council of Princes; the Industries and Commerce Department began to be reorganized, with the Munitions Board and later in 1916 the Indian Industrial Commission, with a view to the better prosecution of the war and the eventual advancement of Indian industry;[8] the Education Department was soon to embark on a major review, in particular with the Sadler Commission on Calcutta University;[9] the Home Department was faced with the very large questions of constitutional reform, future measures against 'anarchism', and changes recommended by the Public Services Commission. In 1916, Chamberlain wrote to Chelmsford claiming to have seen, in his administration, 'such evidence of energy and activity as only great industry and keenness could produce'.[10]

The Viceroy's Council had been disposed to show caution. Thus changes in the public services were not taken up with the directness later shown over the Indian Industrial Commission—and this promoted from Montagu what Chelmsford called 'an excellent homily' on delays. But even in this case Chelmsford was able to reply: '. . . if I had adopted Hardinge's policy, acquiesced in by the India Office, the Report would still be in my safe locked up from prying eyes'.[11] In June 1916, only one local government had recommended publication of the Public Services Report, but the Government of India had advocated early consideration. This typified the new approach: they had wanted to have proposals for advance ready when they would rightly be expected, at the end of the war.[12]

In 1918 Montagu, returning from the discussions on constitutional reforms, wrote to Chelmsford calling for reforms in the public services, the Arms Act, the Criminal Investigation Depart-

ments, the Native States' treaties, the Press Act, separation of
judiciary and executive, and legal procedure. He hoped also for the
establishment of a Propaganda Department, and for the encouragement of better relations between Hindus and Muslims. This, he
wrote, was an illustrative not an exhaustive list. Later he called
for an enquiry on the railways.[13] Chelmsford was able to report
that many of the matters were being considered; but on legal
procedure he wrote, 'Lord preserve me!'—this was a matter for a
new viceroy. But the record of the viceroyalty does not support the
view that caution expressed itself in an inability to begin projects of
reform. In addition to normal work, Chelmsford, for example, had
four major reports to deal with at the time of Montagu's letter—
on the public services, 'anarchism', constitutional reforms and
Calcutta University. There was not really any prospect of quicker
progress.[14]

But Chelmsford has not been remembered as a strong Viceroy.
One reason is that he practised a form of leadership unfamiliar in
India. This brings us to the second characteristic of Chelmsford's
style: he preferred consultation and worked through collective
decisions. He expected his colleagues to co-operate and express
their opinions forcefully.[15] His policies were therefore consensus
policies—he claimed he wished to administer according to wisdom
or unwisdom, not according to 'weak' or 'strong' principles; he
tried to walk down the middle and was attacked from both sides.[16]
With the growth in the volume and complexity of business,
accelerated by the war, a viceroy had little choice but to delegate
responsibilities; but Chelmsford was convinced, he claimed, by his
experience as a constitutional governor, that 'the Council should
be consulted on all possible occasions'. 'My methods', he wrote to
Montagu, 'are not of the *sic volo sic jubeo* order. I deliberately lay
before myself the policy of constitutional practice. . . . I am more or
less indifferent to personal credit and only want to get things done.
We have a creaky and lumbering machine to work, and I believe
with present conditions it can best be worked only by minimizing
the friction . . .'.[17] This method was sneered at by more traditional
administrators and disapproved of by Montagu;[18] but it was the
method of the future rather than the past, of devolution rather than
autocracy.

Constitutionally, at least since the days of Sir Charles Wood and
the reforms of 1861,[19] the Government of India were required (as

restated in 1904, after the disputes of Curzon and Kitchener) to operate on 'common responsibility', 'rendered effective by frequent personal conference and discussion', in spite of departmental divisions.[20] But this ideal had seldom been realized. Curzon's autocracy was notorious. Even under Minto, the Council had been seriously divided, with Fleetwood Wilson claiming that he was never consulted and saw too little to be able to judge the situation (on policy towards agitation)—the Council, he claimed, are 'summoned in hot haste, treated to chips out of letters, told that Lord Morley favours a strong policy and after desultory conversation dissolve into nothing'.[21] Wilson believed only palatable advice (that is, from Adamson and Risley) was acceptable to Minto.[22]

Chelmsford, on the other hand, tried to obtain the 'best considered views' of the whole Executive Council on all matters of importance. He had regular Council meetings except when he or most members were on tour. When he was away, members who were considering important matters were instructed to consult their colleagues personally, and send the file and their comments to the Viceroy. Chelmsford also introduced a new practice of meeting each member informally once a week—a privilege formerly confined to departmental secretaries. At these weekly meetings Chelmsford discussed with each member the problems of his department and any matters of general interest—in Minto's time, Fleetwood Wilson had reported, 'the whole Govt. is in the hands of the Secretaries. They see him [Minto] once a week and it seems to me that they do just what they like with him, which is bad for India.'[23] In Chelmsford's own department, the Foreign and Political, all telegrams were circulated to other members as soon as they were printed.[24] Chelmsford also kept himself and his colleagues informed, on a longer view, by instituting an annual review of important decisions—formerly undertaken only at the end of a viceroyalty—and after 1917 by maintaining a personal collection of important despatches.[25] During his viceroyalty, Chelmsford claimed, the Government of India was 'that of the Governor General-in-Council, not only in spirit but also in letter.'[26]

Consultation meant delays. Chelmsford sought to minimize these by working as far as possible through personal meetings and not by written memoranda.[27] He believed members of Council should be the thinking part of the government, leaving routine matters to the secretaries.[28] He was willing to see, in these routine matters, some centralization and consolidation where necessary—as when he suggested a Chief of the Administrative Staff for the army, and when a Food Controller for India was appointed during the shortage of 1918.[29] A certain flexibility also helped. The head of the Publicity Board, Sir Stanley Reed, who had been ready to criticize the bureaucracy as editor of the *Times of India*, wrote to Chelmsford in 1919 after experience at Simla:

My conviction is that there is nothing wrong with the system on which the Government of India is organised, and that it is manned by devoted and able officials. I have been agreeably surprised to find that when little difficulties arose, which might have been accentuated by a rigid adherence to rules, there was no tendency whatsoever to adhere to rules; but always a desire to get the thing done.

In fact the traditions and shortcomings of the Simla bureaucracy were not so easily overcome—and Reed himself, though satisfied with the system and its flexibility in routine, remained worried at the non-constructive spirit in the administration and the failure of decisions to 'come from the top'.[30]

Chelmsford proposed that the machinery for routine consultation should be improved; and he sought to do this, in characteristic fashion, by appointing a committee of enquiry. He had suggested this early in 1917, but the Home Department, severely understaffed, had preferred to wait until after the war.[31] A Secretariat Committee, under Sir Hubert Llewellyn Smith, Permanent Secretary at the Board of Trade, was eventually appointed in 1919. Its terms of reference were to examine the allocation of business among the departments, and to report on how the system could be made more efficient. Each department was to provide the committee with full information on its methods; and members and secretaries were to testify on existing staff deployment and delegation of responsibility, and on possible improvements.[32]

As a result of these deliberations, certain changes were introduced in secretariat instructions during the last quarter of 1920. Some hope was offered of relieving the shortage of staff by a scheme to re-employ suitable officers on a temporary basis during the first ten years of their retirement, provided they were still under sixty-five.[33] Consultation was made more expeditious. It was generally to be personal, with results recorded on the file; and it was to be conducted simultaneously, if possible, when more than two departments were involved. Consultation with local governments was to be confined in general matters to the major administrations, and on special matters to the governments involved. A definite time limit was to be stated, and after this time the departmental secretary was to decide whether to proceed without waiting for any outstanding replies.[34] In another attempt to secure co-ordination, it was provided that an officer would normally be placed on special duty to secure government action on any recommendations of committees or commissions of enquiry.

The Executive Council was also given attention. Telegrams were being used increasingly in the interests of speed, and this tendency was encouraged by rules which tended to raise the status of the telegraphic communication—it was provided that all Council members should simultaneously be sent copies of important telegrams, those which, if sent by post, would have been in the form of a despatch.[35] There had also been an earlier rationalization in 1917, when telegrams were divided into three classes: departmental, departmental marked for attention of the Viceroy or the Secretary of State, and private (for personal information only).[36] Such prior classification could save time generally, and other ways of doing this were introduced or revitalized in 1920. Letters rather than despatches were sent to the Secretary of State when, in the opinion of the departmental secretary, the matter did not express a government opinion or was not of importance. Such matters were not referred to the Executive Council. Also in 1920 a division of financial references into those of greater and lesser importance (with the latter able to issue directly to the Secretary of State from the spending department) abolished the Finance Department's old and time-consuming monopoly in this area.[37] The Executive Council was also able to deal less with routine, by having the Governor General make necessary orders on unimportant matters, and was to waste as little time as possible on controversy, by considering only final recommendations, after departmental discussions.[38] Some steps were thus being made to free the Viceroy's Council and to make it a more effective governing device. In all the measures collective responsibility was protected, but attempts were made to limit the delays it involved.

Towards the end of the viceroyalty, Chelmsford was also concerned with the question of the proper division of subjects among

Council members and departments. In December 1920 there were
eight members of Council corresponding to the departments—
Foreign and Political (the Viceroy), Army, Home (which had a
separate Reforms Office between December 1919 and March 1921),
Finance, Legislative, Commerce, Industry (then as a Board but
formally a department after February 1921), Education, and
Revenue and Agriculture (including Public Works). This embodied some of the reallocations recommended by the Secretariat
Committee,[39] but Chelmsford believed that the arrangements were
not entirely satisfactory. He wanted to see banking concentrated
under Finance, instead of being shared with Commerce, and
believed railways and ports inseparable from Commerce and
Industry, as was certain research then under Agriculture. In
March 1921 he suggested to Lord Reading, who was about to
become Viceroy, that he set up, in addition to Foreign and
Political, Army, Home, Finance, and Legislative, three new
departments—Commerce and Industry, including agriculture,
railways and ports; Education and Public Health and Revenue,
including local self-government, excise and salt; and Public Works,
Post and Telegraphs, including emigration.[40] To Chelmsford this
seemed at once more efficient and better directed to progress—it
concentrated the main areas in which he hoped to see advance. The
Commerce and Industry Department would supervise all economic
improvements, including public intervention in industrial projects
encouraged by the war and favoured by Chelmsford. (The
argument now was that, as agriculture, commerce and industry
were inseparable for purposes of economic advance, a single
department would be better, provided Commerce were shorn of
non-commercial responsibilities: the combined department would
be the new Industries Department writ large.) The Department of
Education, Health and Revenue would deal with the central aspect
of all local and provincial affairs, including all questions of public
welfare and broadly covering the experiment in self-government
and the associated area of financial devolution. The Public Works
and Posts Department would control, as a service to other departments, mainly technical and routine matters, but also those where
the state undertook construction and improvements—emigration
was included, less consistently, to avoid associating such a controversial subject with the Foreign and Political Department under
the Viceroy. These rationalizations were not carried out by

Reading,[41] but the principle behind them was preserved. The Council was to work as a cabinet, each member having a more or less coherent sphere of activity to represent in joint discussions and to which independently to direct his energies.

The Viceroy's relations with his governors were clearly as important as his relations with his Council. In these too Chelmsford tried consultation. In 1916 he had written to all heads of provinces asking them to write to him personally on any matters which concerned them.[42] More unusually, he attempted, on the advice of Edwin Montagu, to begin a tradition of governors' conferences.[43] Some heads of government favoured the idea. O'Dwyer in the Panjab and Sir Benjamin Robertson in the Central Provinces found many topics to suggest for discussion in January 1919; in Bombay, Sir George Lloyd expressed keen disappointment when a serious mill strike prevented his attendance. Willingdon in Madras was less enthusiastic. Before the conference of 1920 he confessed to Montagu that he could not see what they had to discuss.[44] In general, participation was not enthusiastic—and Chelmsford did not succeed with his governors as he had with his Council.

It was largely a matter of temperament. Willingdon, in 1920, characterized the Viceroy as 'cold and calm', and wished he could see in him 'a spark of enthusiasm'. He had long been convinced that Chelmsford had a 'personal feeling' about him, which prevented them from co-operating.[45] In the same year, Montagu had to write to Lloyd admitting that Chelmsford's coldness could be disconcerting, but stressing his good qualities—his strength, patience and loyalty.[46] In February 1919, Lloyd had written of the Viceroy:

Personally I like him a good deal but he is a curious intangible personality. Just as you think he is going to become quite human he eludes your touch and leaves you wondering. He had been represented to me as being tired and anxious. I did not find him so. I thought him clear-minded and determined to pursue his course . . .

In September, he added:

I'm afraid the Viceroy is getting very unpopular in India. I have always got on well with him, but I fancy some other governors find it hard to do so. I don't quite know what it is. Mainly I think his cold manner and lack of any evident human sympathy. Some of the letters he writes one make one very angry, but I value his loyalty and the straightforward way he deals with things . . .[47]

With the bureaucracy unreformed, the Viceroy still had a co-ordinating role as its symbolic head, a role in which Chelmsford failed. He claimed his Council had been 'a very happy family' in 1917;[48] and G. S. Barnes had written in 1916: 'It would be difficult to find a more delightful man to work for and with, and this I think is the view of all the members of his Council'. Later Sir James Meston complimented him on his 'patience and con-sideration' and his 'Spartan courage'. Thus Chelmsford's per-sonality seems to have been effective in the committee room and in prolonged contact; but not in occasional conferences or at a distance. He took his Council with him on constitutional reforms; he was unable to convince the governors.[49]

Montagu diagnosed a further reason, which no doubt magnified Chelmsford's disability. He suggested that the problem was due to the course of events—firstly to the war in which the central government used wider authority while their staff was short-handed, over-worked, and 'tending to be snappy' in corres-pondence; and secondly to the 1919 disturbances during which local governments drew closer to their officials, while the Govern-ment of India, 'from the continued effort to get a grip of the situa-tion as a whole', tended to draw away.[50] To this must be added, as the evidence of antagonism is strongest after 1920, a factor which Chelmsford himself hinted at early in his term. 'In fairness to my subordinates,' he wrote, at the height of the criticism of the army administration, ' . . . I feel bound to point out that they are becoming gravely discouraged under the shower of criticism which is pouring down on them, and their work will inevitably suffer from the feeling that whatever they do, however hard they work, blame will be their portion'.[51] It was the system not the personnel that had broken down.[52] In the deluge of criticism which followed the 1919 disturbances and accompanied Gandhi's non-co-opera-tion campaign, and with the strains concomitant upon a funda-mental shift in the declared functions of the bureaucracy, it was inevitable that there should be some sensitivity and ill-feeling between and within different parts of the administration.

Chelmsford also attempted consultation on a wider scale. The whole tendency of his administration, while it became more and more unpopular, was nonetheless increasingly to profess to be

paying attention to Indian opinion. And of course the largest task
undertaken during the viceroyalty was to seek ways of improving
the degree and character of this contact through the legislatures.
Chelmsford welcomed the Imperial Legislative Council in spite of
the burden its sessions imposed. He remarked: 'We, as the
Government of India, live a very detached life, aloof from the
troubles which beset the administrator in his district and even
Local Governments in their provinces, and anything which brings
us up against concrete facts is to be encouraged'. He encouraged
this further after 1917 by removing the restriction preventing the
discussion of contentious matters at the Simla session of the
legislature. But it was doubtful how useful or relevant the legislators' opinions could be before the reforms. There was at the
centre only a handful of members from each province, and too
often it was tempting to ignore or underestimate the advice of such
a tiny group. Perhaps too the image which was projected was
from an age that had passed; this description of the Simla session
is pertinent: 'Sir William Vincent always had a twinkle. Sir G.
Lowndes after dropping his jaw in the most mouce [*sic*] trap
manner would very delightfully wipe the floor with any antagonist.
. . . Sir W. M[e]yer I so detested that I could not watch him with
any calm! Sir Claude Hill looked ill. . . . The Chief got angry once
and the Council cheered him to the echo. A dear old Sikh looked
like a man and spoke like one. The Viceroy was always just one's
ideal of a very knightly Englishman. But somehow the whole
thing never got to the country—the newspaper reports were dull to
a degree.'[53]
    It is true that in an enquiry undertaken in 1918 into the working
of the Morley-Minto councils (in Madras, Bombay, Bengal, the
Panjab and Bihar and Orissa) when it was found that non-official
members, nominated as well as elected, tended to vote solidly
against the government whenever there were divisions, it was
pointed out that divisions were infrequent and occurred only on
contentious issues; and most local governments considered that
legislative business, which had increased enormously in the
preceding years, had not absorbed official energies to the detri-
ment of efficiency, and all of them welcomed the extra contact
with Indian opinion. They considered that legislators had been
useful and influential in changing bills before or after introduction,
in putting forward resolutions especially on local questions, and

in a minority of cases by use of the right to ask questions.[54] But perhaps the governments had written what they thought they were expected to write. The reality, as in the Government of India, was less comfortable. The changes introduced in bills or government policy were admittedly in details and never 'material'. Several governments singled out with some asperity the one or two occasions in a decade when they had been inconvenienced by having to accommodate their will to the legislature; they made no allowance for the frustrations among the legislators at being faced time and time again with the impossibility of enforcing their wishes on the government. Chelmsford set himself 'from the very beginning to . . . win the co-operation of the educated classes in India'.[55] But the machinery of the legislative councils was so much in need of re-thinking, until it was reformed at the end of the viceroyalty, that it could not be used to create this feeling of partnership. While he was involved in remedying the situation, Chelmsford still had to suffer the disabilities of the past. With legislators as with local governments, the breakdown and contradictions of the system were the heart of the problem.

Thus isolation was a factor in the government's unpopularity. Chelmsford could state the liability and try to chip it away, but he remained distant from political as from commercial and rural India. Calcutta and Bombay, each considered by its inhabitants to be the centre of Indian affairs, were both far away. 'Simla and Delhi,' Chelmsford told Montagu, 'are merely artificial conglomerations of officialdom'. He used this argument to justify the refitting of a viceregal residence in Calcutta—'I do not want to see myself and my successors', he wrote, 'condemned to be dwellers in the limbo of things'.[56] He became increasingly aware during 1917 that conditions were changing rapidly in India—and this too made it even more difficult to keep in touch.[57] He encouraged his Council members to go on tour, and found they returned with 'minds enlarged and broadened'.[58] He argued that governors too should be allowed leave from their provinces—he was 'in favour of men getting away from their surroundings and rubbing shoulders with other people'.[59] The Home Department of course subscribed to all the important newspapers as well as receiving regular provincial reports and press abstracts.[60] In May 1918 the Panjab Government wanted to prosecute one Sarala Devi for remarks she had made in a private letter to the Viceroy; Chelmsford demurred—'It would

be most unfortunate,' he explained, 'if people were to be deterred
from writing freely to the Viceroy'.[61] But good intentions did not
solve the problem.

Moreover isolation was not only the product of circumstances
beyond Chelmsford's control. In one sense it was peculiarly his
own responsibility. For he failed in the viceroy's task of mitigating
the autocratic and bureaucratic nature of the system. As Willingdon wrote: ' . . . the atmosphere of Delhi is most depressing.
Chelmsford and his lady lead a very lonely life and I am really
sorry for them. They don't seem to be able to unbend and
be friendly . . .'.[62] Willingdon, who thought the Viceroy had
treated him badly over his sumptuary allowance, was perhaps not
the most impartial judge; but probably the isolated atmosphere of
the seat of government was partly of Chelmsford's own making.
He severely underspent his entertainment allowance because of
the war, and recommended reductions in the increase—more than
double—which Montagu proposed for Reading.[63] Chelmsford was
not easy in large social events. He was not more successful in
popularizing himself with legislators and politicians than with
governors. His speeches were correct but seldom aroused enthusiasm. Occasionally, as in the uncompromising reply to a
deputation against the Press Acts, they aroused anger.[64] Montagu
remarked to Sir George Lloyd, the Governor of Bombay, that,
throughout the debates on the 'Rowlatt' bill, Chelmsford made no
speech himself—surely, he wondered, 'a public meeting, an appeal,
might have had a great effect'. Lloyd in reply was sceptical of the
value of such speeches.[65] But Montagu had urged on Chelmsford
'the vital necessity of teaching and instructing Government
officials to explain themselves and the policy of the Government';[66]
and it was plain that Chelmsford himself did not have this
ability. His government sought consultation and responded to
public opinion, but was never fully political, never comfortable in
this new role. Montagu wrote in 1917 to report that he had heard
that the government had never been more unpopular than at that
moment.[67] It was to become still more unpopular by 1921.

One of the responses to this situation was to hope the government could project a more favourable image by propaganda. The
Government of India, declared Chamberlain in 1917, must 'not
only do right, but persuade people that it is right'. They could not
rely on press support, and had to prepare public opinion them-

selves. But they did not do so: 'Wherever public opinion is
stirred . . . the Departments exclaim "Say nothing! Do nothing!
Pray heaven if we are quiet, the storm will pass over our heads . . .".
I am sure this will not do . . . it will lead to a growing estrangement
between Government and the governed . . .'.[68] Montagu, in
August of the same year, also called for a 'new angle of vision'; the
government, he thought, 'should learn to a greater degree than
ever the methods of political life'. In his view 'publicity and frank-
ness' were the 'remedy for most Indian evils'.[69] He encouraged
Chelmsford to call a conference to improve the war effort,[70]
and at first propaganda was conceived in this narrower sense, as a
need arising out of the war.

In April 1918, a War Conference, of provincial delegates and
mostly non-officials, was convened in Delhi. It was followed by
provincial meetings of a similar type. The purpose was twofold: to
help create an enthusiastic and loyal attitude towards the war
effort, and to encourage practical steps to help. Thus the Delhi
Conference, over three days, consisted in public sessions for fine
speeches and loyalty resolutions, and private committees for
practical suggestions. Gandhi had arrived in Delhi intending to
boycott proceedings on 'various high moral grounds' relating to
the exclusion of B. G. Tilak, Annie Besant and other nationalist
leaders who, in Chelmsford's view, disagreed with the government
on first principles. Chelmsford persuaded Gandhi to attend, and
he made a short speech in support of the loyalist resolution. Chelmsford thought the conference had been a success as an exercise in
public relations.[71] In the provinces, except in Bombay, where
Willingdon provoked a walk-out of Tilak and other Home Rulers,
the conferences passed off without incident, or, arguably,
results.[72]

The Delhi Conference recommended the formation of publicity
bureaux, and had led to the appointment of a War Resources
Committee to co-ordinate activities. In June 1918, a Central
Publicity Board was appointed, with instructions to establish
similar boards in every province. They were to 'vivify Indian
interest in war and intensify co-operation'.[73] A library was formed
for use in preparing pamphlets, and in July a liaison officer for
publicity was appointed at the India Office.[74] At the head of these
developments was the former editor of the *Times of India*, Sir
Stanley Reed, now appointed President of the Central Publicity

Board—and happily seeing himself, according to Chelmsford, as 'Northcliffe Asiaticus'.[75]

The government believed that Indians, except those in recruiting districts and perhaps the educated classes, were ill-informed about the war. It was necessary to impress on them its gravity, and also to disseminate accurate news and contradict rumours. The work was to be done locally, by largely non-official committees with financial assistance from the central government, and through posters, lectures, advertisements, newspaper articles and cinema showings. The Central Board was to co-ordinate and assist these efforts. The suggestion, in this form, was sent to local governments in a circular letter of May 1918.[76] The response was enthusiastic in some provinces, notably the Panjab where publicity work centred on the government newspaper, *Haq*, and the United Provinces where this example was followed by a successful *War Journal*. But not all the provinces were active. Assam and Bihar and Orissa underspent their budgets, and Bengal, although exceeding its estimates on furniture and establishment, severely underspent its budget for printing and devoted almost no funds to schemes originally proposed for using religious societies and taking newspaper editors on factory tours. The publicity movement was strongest in those provinces where the central government had suggested it was needed least, namely in the recruiting tracts. Its political success was thus limited.[77]

Nonetheless this wartime expedient of the publicity boards represented one of the first institutionalized attempts by the government in India to influence public opinion by propaganda.[78] Some of the boards had already taken on more political functions during the war;[79] all of them were intended to explain general and not only wartime policy; and when the war ended there was widespread agreement that the boards should be made permanent. A meeting of the Central Publicity Board in March 1919 unanimously recommended that organized publicity work should continue. Sir Stanley Reed suggested the formation of a small Department of Publications under the Home Member, to advise the government on the use of existing newspapers for meeting unfair criticism, to popularize government reports and publications, and to act as an information bureau.[80]

The Home Department took up this idea, admitting that the Government of India was 'perhaps of all civilized Governments the worst equipped' for propaganda. They suggested, however, a Director of Publications rather than a department which they thought might be open to public objection.[81] Reed expressed himself rather surprised at the strength of the feeling in the government that the work of the Publicity Board should continue.[82] The Home Department had already decided on Chamberlain's advice that the *Moral and Material Progress Report* presented annually to Parliament should be improved so as to 'secure the wider purpose of interpreting the activities of the Government to the outside world'. They wanted it printed in octavo not foolscap, widely distributed at a low price (about Rs.1.00), divided by subject not provinces, 'narrated in a popular style', and brought up to date. The issue for 1917–1918 dealt with events until December 1918, the time of preparation, whereas hitherto it would have stopped with the official year at the end of March. It was prepared by an officer on special duty in the Home Department—Professor Rushbrook Williams, seconded from the Allahabad University. Formerly the report had been compiled in the Home Department, in addition to ordinary duties, and mainly from materials sent in by local governments. Thus, when the Central Publicity Board was disbanded, the government already had the beginnings of a small publicity organization within the Home Department. They decided to expand it, and give effect to Reed's suggestion by appointing Rushbrook Williams as Director of Publicity. He was to be under the Home Department, with special rights of access to the Viceroy and heads of departments. In February 1920, Williams was sent on deputation to study propaganda methods in Great Britain and America.[83]

The main publicity burden, however, was to be provincial. The wartime boards were to be replaced, preferably by voluntary agency. The publicity newspapers were continued in the United Provinces and the Panjab (where *Haq* was thought to be 'a power in the land'). By the governors' conference of January 1920, when the question was discussed, only Bengal, the Central Provinces and the Northwest Frontier Province were without some permanent organization.[84] After the disturbances of 1919 the Home Department had called for 'systematic and widespread action on a wide scale for the purpose of contradicting false rumours and reports', and had promised that the central government would provide leaflets for local distribution. Rushbrook Williams suggested that he should start sending such information directly to district officers. This idea was approved; the first leaflet distributed in this way was on Bolshevism, and came in two forms, one of which was for general use. This scheme was most popular in those provinces where local publicity organization was weakest, and therefore to some extent provided a substitute for local efforts.[85]

But printed propaganda was limited in effect. Thus, in their circular of May 1919, the Home Department suggested that local and district officers should be instructed to become concerned in propaganda, mainly through private interviews. Local governments agreed, and the idea had been endorsed generally in the Montagu–Chelmsford Report. The problem was that the Government Servants' Rules of Conduct expressly forbad participation in political movements. On 9 December 1920, in order to facilitate proposals from the Panjab and Madras seeking to permit officers to 'organise opposition' to Gandhi's non-co-operation, the Government of India asked the Secretary of State to permit officers to defend and explain government policy in public, provided that they avoided personal references and confined their criticisms to refuting mis-statements or disloyal propaganda. The Secretary of State gave his consent.[86]

This change was not very great, or probably very useful.[87] But an old principle had been breached nonetheless, and it was probably remarkable enough that the Government of India should have taken formal concern over publicizing themselves. A chief characteristic of British government in India—one of the reasons it distrusted Indian co-operation and ᶜor its isolation and unpopularity—was that it was government in secret. When Sir Sankaran Nair joined the India Office, after resigning from Chelmsford's government, M. C. Seton, assistant Under-Secretary, remarked, 'Yet S of S *knows* that everything that was said in secret conclave in Delhi that winter was known to Malaviya a few hours later. I suppose it is statesmanship . . .'.[88] The greatest offence was to reveal the ideas and actions of the executive, kept concealed far beyond what was needed for official confidentiality. This could not disappear overnight. Yet at last the autocracy had to begin to talk to the people.

Chapter 2. Public Opinion

THE government paid attention to public opinion in order to woo the educated classes. In some quarters the interests of the masses were canvassed, mostly as an argument for conservatism. But under Chelmsford the emphasis was placed on the need to placate that small minority whose discontent, Chelmsford believed, was bound to infect the bulk of the population. What India needed, he thought, was twenty years of patient rule—and his task was to enlist the co-operation of the educated elite.[1]

A section of this class, as Chelmsford recognized, was influenced by growing nationalism and alienation from the government. The unique characteristic which distinguished the 'extremist' party was not its desire for *swaraj*, but its unwillingness to come to terms with the British government. Some of the leaders were 'irreconcilable'. Thus, while the central government tried to influence all public opinion, their attempts inevitably were directed mainly to the uncommitted. It was not difficult for conciliation to become an attempt to encourage moderate opposition to the extremists. In Bengal Lord Carmichael diagnosed the main need of his government in 1916 as to win the 'confidence of the ordinary law-abiding Indians':[2] this aim, with its preconceptions (in 'ordinary' and 'law-abiding'), was not identical with Chelmsford's. In a few isolated cases the Government of India sought the formation of a moderate or pro-government party. But, as a rule, they placed little faith in this version of *divide et impera*, preferring to pursue policies which, in other circumstances, might have commended themselves equally to extremists as to moderates.[3]

In several celebrated cases the government undermined their own propaganda. They placed an officer on special duty to help the defendant and otherwise meddled in a private litigation in England between B. G. Tilak and Sir Valentine Chirol over alleged libels in the latter's book, *Indian Unrest*. Official intervention had been approved by Hardinge and was perhaps inevitable owing to an original failure of discretion when Lord Sydenham, then Governor of Bombay, had allowed Chirol access to confidential files for use in the writing of his book. Under Chelmsford a conference (Vincent and the Secretary, J. H. Du Boulay, from the Home Department; G. R. Lowndes, the Law Member; and L. Robertson, Bombay's Political and Judicial Secretary) discussed the question and came to more or less proper conclusions: Chirol was not to be assisted in such a way as would prejudice his defence if the facts became known; Tilak was to be afforded the right to examine any documents specified by him but not to inspect records generally; no pressure was to be put on witnesses to appear for Chirol, and government pensioners were to be told that there was no objection to their giving evidence on either side. But there was no doubt about the verdict wanted; and Chelmsford also showed lack of tact—at the height of the controversy and to the intense indignation of Tilak's paper, *Kesari*—when he had Chirol to stay at Government House in Delhi.[4]

In another incident the government tried to be more diplomatic. Tilak and other members of a Home Rule deputation had wanted to visit England, and were allowed passports. The government had no reason to favour the deputation—indeed their response was likely to be more than usually sour when they discovered an attempt to present Tilak as a tribune of the people by having him showered with farewell telegrams, ostensibly spontaneous but in fact (it was believed) laboriously solicited. But equally the government had no reason to be sorry that Tilak was to be out of the country. The Home Department wired to the India Office that it would be 'inexpedient' to withhold permission for the deputation, even though 'military or other authorities may regard their presence in England as objectionable or dangerous'. The War Cabinet, however, ordered that the passports be withdrawn. The Bombay Government, the Government of India and Chelmsford himself protested at this 'highly embarrassing' decision, and Tilak's party were allowed to proceed in the hope that the orders would be modified. But the Cabinet remained adamant, and the travellers were recalled. Five had reached as far as Gibraltar; the Home Department requested that they be treated 'with every consideration and not held in custody'. Montagu, who had been in India, persuaded the Cabinet on his return to allow Tilak to travel to England for his libel case on condition that he abstained from politics. Tilak gave an undertaking and left for England.[5] A similar restriction was placed on Dr. T. M. Nair of the Madras Justice Party and an opponent of the reforms; later both restrictions were

removed.[6] In September 1918, when the question of reforms
deputations was raised again, the Government of India asked for
instructions, and were directed to state that the question could not
be considered at that stage. They promised that assistance would
be given in the following year when a reforms bill would come
before Parliament. Chelmsford had objected to the ban, calling
Montagu's suggested excuse 'too thin for anybody' and arguing
that the only real answer would be 'bluntly to say that the em-
bargo is "not ours but yours"'. He thought a deputation would be
wise on all grounds, and hoped Montagu would be able to disabuse
his colleagues 'of the awfulness of this imaginary bogey'. He was
disappointed.[7]

The impression thus far is of clumsiness and insensitivity—
although with the deputations this was almost wholly the responsibility of the London authorities. In other matters the
Chelmsford administration had more success. Chelmsford had
indicated his interest in public opinion even before assuming the
viceroyalty. He wrote to Hardinge that he had decided to visit
Calcutta as soon as possible 'to remove any soreness resulting
from the change of the Capital to Delhi'.[8] There were two consistent and intermixed motives in his response: he sought both
to conciliate or forestall agitation, and to right recognized failures
or abuses. In some cases there was also a desire to reward Indians
for wartime loyalty or services.

In 1917, for example, Gandhi had started elaborate enquiries into
the grievances of the peasantry in Champaran, Bihar. Many of the
grievances were justified—particularly an arrangement enforcing
the growing of indigo at a time when prices were falling, and a
certain amount of extortion and intimidation by the landlords.
Thus, when the local Commissioner had Gandhi arrested, the
local government pronounced this a 'very serious mistake of
judgment' and ordered the Commissioner to give Gandhi 'every
reasonable facility for obtaining the information desired by him'.[9]
Similarly, when the local government themselves decided to
require Gandhi to stop his enquiries, arguing that there was a
danger of violence and that Gandhi had broken a promise to
restrict his activities (he had in fact refused to give such a promise),
the Government of India intervened and ordered that Gandhi
should on the contrary be invited to join a formal committee of
enquiry into the situation. Chelmsford stressed that he had to take

a wider view and insisted that a purely official enquiry as proposed by the local government would not meet the needs of the situation. There would be a danger that Gandhi would not agree with the decision and would force the government to take action against him—it would be impolitic to risk a storm on such a matter, especially when genuine grievances existed. A public enquiry would satisfy outside opinion, and a prompt announcement might settle the unrest within Champaran. (It is fair to say that, contrary to the usual view, Gandhi's contribution in Champaran was not in arousing the peasantry, who were already active, but rather in forcing the involvement of the Government of India and thereby securing a settlement against the opposition of the local government.)[10] A similar policy was followed over river works at Hardwar, after Chelmsford had received anxious memorials, including one from the All-India Hindu Sabha, about the interruption of the sacred Ganges. He directed that the question should be re-negotiated; a compromise was eventually agreed whereby a new channel would be constructed to provide uninterrupted flow. The Home Department recognized that the changes would be expensive and might impair the efficiency of the canal works, but Chelmsford insisted that it was worth the extra trouble and money to avoid a 'big religious row'.[11]

The centre did not always intervene of course, for strictly they believed such matters fell within the purview of local governments. Thus, when Gandhi supported the campaign in Kaira for non-payment of land revenue after crop failures, the Revenue and Agricultural Department made no move to interfere with Bombay's handling. It was noted that Willingdon, the Governor, had personally met the leaders of the campaign and given a press conference on the subject with his full Council. The conclusion was that intervention would not help Bombay; and—'nor have we reason to believe, as we had in the case of Champaran, that the local Govt. is aloof & unsympathetic.'[12]

Concern for public opinion also expressed itself in positive measures. Chelmsford believed that one of the basic problems in India was the racialist attitude of the European community. He had once stigmatized that 'typically Australian' tendency to look on Indians (in Fiji) as 'an inferior race', and he was determined to rid India of this attitude—particularly what he called that 'carping and sneering at the capacity of the educated Indian which cuts like a lash of a whip'. Other people agreed. Montagu worried at the ill effects on Indians of their present subordination; Willingdon thought the 'real bed rock' of their problems was the 'arrogant superiority' adopted by the English—if this did not change it might lose them India.[13] The behaviour of officials could be improved and the position of Indians enhanced: most of the positive measures under Chelmsford can be interpreted in these terms.

His government sought to improve Indian standing on two main fronts—by improving India's international status and by removing internal discrimination. The war had provided an opportunity for interested people, notably the Round Table group and Lord Hardinge's government, to press for a modification of India's inferior or 'subject' role in the Empire. In September 1915 Hardinge's government, with the Secretary of State's approval, accepted a resolution of the legislature recommending Indian representation at Imperial Conferences. Under Chelmsford the idea was put forward officially in a Home Department despatch, and in 1917 three Indian members, Sir James Meston, Sir Satyendra Sinha and the Maharaja of Bikaner, were admitted to the Imperial Conference and to meetings of the Imperial War Cabinet. Sir Robert Borden and W. F. Massey, Prime Ministers of Canada and New Zealand, moved at the Conference that India should be represented in future. Of their admission to the War Cabinet, Philip Kerr wrote to Lionel Curtis: 'It would have been impossible to have recognized the status of Indians more completely than to have admitted them to the most secret conclaves of the British Empire'. In 1918, however, the question of Cabinet membership was still considered open; and Islington, Under-Secretary of State for India, urged that one full member should be admitted and a representative of the Indian states should attend whenever Prime Ministers were to be accompanied by other ministers. The Colonial Office wanted Indians represented only as 'assessors' and by invitation. The Viceroy protested at this retrogression, and argued that the precedent of Bikaner and Sinha could not be abandoned without disappointment. The War Cabinet accepted Islington's compromise of allowing only one full representative, but in the event the Native States' representative was invited to most of the meetings.[14]

There can be no doubt that the personal qualities of Bikaner

and Sinha played a large part in securing this foothold; but credit
for the policy must go to Hardinge and Austen Chamberlain, and
for its defence to Montagu and Chelmsford. The practical results
were not great—at the 1917 Imperial Conference the Indian
representatives secured agreement for the Government of India's
scheme to end discrimination against Indian travellers by establishing a principle of reciprocity in the treatment of the nationals
of all countries of the Empire;[15] but on the other hand Sinha's
presence did nothing to deter a committee of the Imperial War
Cabinet from resolving in 1917, contrary to the wishes of Indian
Muslims regarding the suzerainty of the Caliph over Mecca, that
'No restoration of Turkish sovereignty or suzerainty should be
permitted' in Arabia after the war. Yet the principle of Indian
representation *was* important.[16] It established the right of India to
behave towards the Dominions as if she shared their independent
status. The admission of India to imperial councils was illogical in
that she was still a subject nation: this, like her later admission to
the Paris Peace Conference and her founder membership of the
League of Nations, arose out of her contribution to the war; but
the anomaly should nevertheless be interpreted as a recognition
that India must eventually come to play a fuller part in her own
affairs.

Lord Minto, years before, while writing of the strategy to be
adopted to preserve his government's position *vis-à-vis* the Secretary of State, had foreseen the development which had to come:
he believed that with the growth of Indian interests, and 'the
development of economic and political factors which only local
knowledge can satisfactorily direct', the relative strength of the
Government of India must increase.[17] This process had begun
indeed, and by Chelmsford's time was coming into the open.

The India which was privy to imperial conferences soon
demanded to be allowed to behave with similar independence and
self-respect towards Britain. Predictably, that conflict came to a
head first over the cotton duties. Indians and British officials in
India had always resented the obvious subservience to Lancashire
interests represented by a system which kept taxes upon internal
cotton manufacture on a level with import duties—and as other
countries began to raise import duties to protect their own
industries, the contrast became more obvious and galling to Indian
sentiment. Lord Hardinge, with the unanimous and emphatic

support of his Council and the local governors, had attempted to raise the cotton duties to 5 per cent while leaving the excise (on local manufactures) at $3\frac{1}{2}$ per cent. Sanction was refused on the grounds that raising the question in wartime would be 'little short of disastrous'.[18] Chelmsford, keenly interested in developing Indian industries, expressed a forceful view of the cotton excise: it was, he wrote to Chamberlain, 'an open political sore'; it was clearly imposed to protect British industry; it fell most heavily on the poor who bought the coarser Indian cloth; and it might be used in future as a precedent for measures against any Indian industry which showed signs of competing with British products. Its abolition, he declared, would be a *sine qua non* of Indian participation in any scheme of imperial preference. Inclusion of these sentiments in an official despatch brought a strongly worded objection from Chamberlain; the despatch was toned down in deference to his remarks, but Chelmsford defended himself to Montagu on the grounds that his government were bound to put forward their position.[19] The position they put forward, significantly, was an Indian one in opposition to that held in the United Kingdom.

In view of the rejection of Hardinge's overtures, there was little that Chelmsford could do. During 1916, however, discussions had taken place in the India Office, following a suggestion by Lord Hardinge, on the size of the contribution which India might be expected to make to the cost of the war. A consensus was eventually reached at a top figure of £50 million, which Chelmsford and his Council agreed could be undertaken after the war, subject to deductions if there were expensive frontier operations in the interim. The Army Department also pointed out that India had already made large contributions and that there were limits on the extra taxation that would be possible or just while India remained 'a dependency, won—and in the last resort held—by military power'. Privately Chelmsford warned that 'every additional obligation . . . will increase India's expectation of the benefits she is to derive from the war'. Nevertheless the Chancellor of the Exchequer named £100 million as the sum which would be well received.[20]

Chelmsford and his Council replied that they could agree to such a contribution if they were permitted to raise a loan in India, place a super-tax on high incomes, perhaps increase the export

duty on jute, and dispense with a surplus which they had accumu-
lated by economies on civil expenditure. But they could not take
these steps unless they were allowed to raise cotton duties to
$7\frac{1}{2}$ per cent, to provide a margin and pay for beneficent expenditure. They would also want an undertaking that they would be
allowed to raise the general tariff above $7\frac{1}{2}$ per cent, and to abolish
cotton excise (now $3\frac{1}{2}$ per cent) as soon as they could afford the
loss in revenue. Privately Chelmsford urged that India was poor,
her government was not democratic, additional taxes might be fuel
for agitators, and other avenues of taxation were closed—it would
be undesirable to have special exactions from landowners, or to
increase the salt tax and thus the burden on the very poor.[21] It was
implicit in these remarks that the enhanced cotton duties were not
only financially necessary, but essential to reconcile Indians to the
large contribution.[22] Chelmsford later reported that, although in
his belief a considerable body of opinion shared Malaviya's view
(embodied in a resolution later withdrawn) that the contribution
was too high, the politicians had 'exercised a remarkable restraint'
—without the cotton duties, he explained, there would have been
no 'ready acquiescence' in the £100 million.[23]

Chamberlain had taken the point, and decided that he could
carry the Cabinet. He telegraphed to Chelmsford asking him to
place special stress on the link between the cotton duties and the
war contribution, in order to strengthen his hand in England.[24]
To the Cabinet he echoed Chelmsford's phrase, and explained that
increased cotton duties were the *sine qua non* of the offer. On these
terms, the Indian proposal was accepted.[25] Chamberlain defended
the increase as a necessary war measure to a deputation from
Lancashire cotton interests and to the House of Commons.[26] At
one time he thought a government defeat possible if Liberal, Irish
and Lancashire interests combined; but Lloyd George remained
firm, and, as Asquith did not try to use the controversy, the
Commons vote gave the government a substantial majority.
Chelmsford had telegraphed warning that if the opposition were to
succeed 'the demand for Home Rule would receive a great, and
who could say unjustifiable, stimulus'.[27]

To the British in India the solution was ideal. The loan created
goodwill for India[28]—it was a showy gesture, which Hardinge
wished had been made in his time.[29] But it was obvious also that
Chelmsford was finding in the war an excuse to do what he wanted.

Perhaps more important, the increase in cotton duties introduced into India's relations with the United Kingdom that same principle of national interest, that same contradiction of India's inferior status, which appeared in this period also in the relations with the Empire. Chelmsford had promised the Imperial Legislative Council that his government would offer the 'most strenuous opposition' if any attempt were made to reintroduce the protection of Lancashire interests. In any postwar fiscal arrangements, he declared, India's interests would have to be considered.[30]

A reversal of old public attitudes to India and Indians also meant an end to indentured emigration. Nothing perhaps was more indicative of India's subservient role within the Empire than the way her people were shipped around the various colonies to provide labour, often under poor conditions and with unfair contracts. Lord Hardinge had publicly defended Indian rights in South Africa. He had also agreed that indentured emigration must end.[31] Chelmsford preferred bureaucratic methods, but was not less devoted to the cause—it was no longer practical for any Indian government to refuse sympathy on these issues. At first, however, delay was unavoidable because Hardinge and Chamberlain had agreed to negotiate with other governments before indentures were banned.[32] Chelmsford had to refuse the introduction of bills in the Imperial Legislative Council on the subject of emigration, in 1916 and again in February 1917. He disliked having to do this; he stressed that the government sympathized with the Indian view and were on very weak ground, and asked the Secretary of State to urge the colonies to accept the position.[33] Indian indignation became greater with the revelation of an agreement, made but not announced by Hardinge, whereby a maximum delay of five years was to be allowed before a final abolition. About the same time the government heard details of the degradation, including stories of sexual horrors, suffered by Indian women in Fiji. Chelmsford privately expressed his alarm at the possibility of the Fiji stories becoming widely known.[34] Unaware of Hardinge's agreement to the five year limit, he criticized the delays that had been allowed to 'creep in'; he insisted that agitation was 'very serious' and that 'the time for palliatives' was past.[35] The Commerce and Industry Department alleged that the Secretary of State did not realise the gravity of the situation, which had 'all the potency of a moral crusade'. Gandhi announced that he would try by force to prevent the recruiting of indentured labour, placing the government in the odd predicament of perhaps having to prosecute for interference with a system which they had publicly condemned.[36]

In the midst of this debate the Army Department requested that assisted emigration be prohibited under the Defence of India Rules in order to encourage army recruiting. Chelmsford decided that in this he had found 'an opportunity of finishing a vicious system'— if it were once banned, he believed, 'hard facts' would 'prevent its reinstitution'. He pointed out that the Secretary of State could not claim he had not been warned of the growing agitation.[37] Chamberlain considered some of the alarm hysterical; he was not an admirer of Hardinge's policy on South Africa, and thought Chelmsford had no justification for adopting a similar approach when the colonies were not intransigent—Meston and Sinha, in a separate negotiation during the 1917 Imperial Conference, were able to secure agreement that the system must be ended.[38] But Chamberlain's hand was forced; habitually he was unwilling to interfere with the government's discretion when it meant asking them to accept responsibility for an important policy of which they disapproved and on which they might be thought to be better informed—the scandals of the Mesopotamia campaign, then under investigation and attributable mainly to over-centralization, could only have increased his reluctance. The Government of India, by invoking the twin arguments of agitation and the war, succeeded indirectly in prohibiting indentured emigration.

In reply to Chamberlain's criticism, Chelmsford explained that he did not fear agitation except when it was strengthened by a moral issue; this came near to an admission that he had decided on the ban, not in the interests of order or the army, but because, as with the Lancashire cotton protection, he personally agreed that the system should be changed.[39] Chamberlain had also complained that Chelmsford had sacrificed negotiations and provided no alternative. But in a telegram of 19 March the Government of India had set out a scheme for safe-guarded free emigration,[40] and moreover the conference organized by the Colonial Office continued its work in July and recommended a scheme which was rather less liberal than the Government of India had wanted but which still provided, as Montagu urged, unprecedented advantages for Indian colonists.[41] The conclusions were, however, largely academic, as the Government of India refused to consider the introduction of any new scheme until Indian opinion had begun to ask for one.[42] They continued to look after Indian rights overseas, sending deputations to Ceylon, Fiji and the Malay States, and attacking discriminatory legislation in South and East Africa— Chelmsford considered that he had pledged himself 'in the most unmistakable way to stand up for Indian rights in Crown colonies'.[43]

At the end of 1920 the emigration controversy was reopened when C. F. Andrews reported on further terrorization of Indians in Fiji. Towards the end of January, the government, having sent yet another deputation to investigate in Fiji, decided to introduce a bill on emigration both because the Defence of India Act was due to expire and because renewed public interest made it necessary for them to formulate their policy. Chelmsford had already insured that there would be no return to the indenture system— at the time of the ban he had announced to the Imperial Legislative Council and to a women's deputation that, in his view, reintroduction was impossible. The government, therefore, proposed to prohibit all assisted emigration to countries where Indians did not enjoy the same political rights as other British subjects, to permit and even encourage other free emigration, and to appoint agents in appropriate countries to protect the interests of Indian settlers. Their bill permitted the emigration of skilled workers under certain conditions, except to any country specifically excluded; and prohibited the emigration of unskilled workers except to any country specifically approved.[44] Thus India had asserted her right to pass laws, against the interests of other parts of the Empire, without any prior agreement having been reached. The eventual legislation may not have violated the understanding reached with the Colonial Office, for it was open for certain countries to be approved for emigration; but, like the Indian policy which preceded it, the new law made such London-based agreements irrelevant. The Government of India were taking the sort of action normally taken only by independent nations.

They were willing also to consider the removal of racial discrimination in internal policies. As Indians participated more, and more equally, in government, certain adjustments were inevitable. Obvious steps, however, were not always easy. Throughout Chelmsford's viceroyalty, for example, the Government of India tried to persuade the Secretary of State and the Council of India to modify the rule forbidding British officials to receive presents from Indians—in many cases this rule was now absurd, embarrassing to the British and offensive to Indians. But the London authorities refused to change—the best Montagu could do was advise Chelmsford to do a little 'judicious rule-breaking'.[45] But in other more important matters the response was less wooden and bureaucratic.

The Arms Act, prohibiting the bearing or ownership of arms by any except specially exempted Indians, was one great source of discontent.[46] In Hardinge's time, the Government of India, admitting that the racial distinction—no European was subject to the Act—was 'invidious', proposed an all-inclusive licensing system, with moderately high fees except for persons required to carry arms in the course of their employment. Local governments generally approved the proposal, but the Government of the Panjab and later, in London, the Council of India pointed out that there would be ill-feeling if all *Indian* exemptions were abolished. Under Chelmsford the Government of India agreed to retain some personal as opposed to racial exemptions. This decision made delays inevitable,[47] and the Home Department had recorded that local government replies had generally strengthened their belief that a complete licensing system would be preferable. The decision to allow some exemptions was in fact made under pressure from London—Chamberlain had endorsed the Council of India's interpretation and urged it upon Chelmsford.[48]

The Home Department began by consulting local governments on the exemptions to be retained. They suggested two categories for consideration: full exemption for a limited number, including heads of governments and great zamindars; and exemption from enquiry before receipt of a licence for persons gazetted by name at the discretion of the local government.[49] Five provinces, Bombay, the United and the Central Provinces, Burma and the North-west Frontier Province, continued to support total licensing, but the remainder were unwilling to see hereditary privileges taken away—there was a feeling that they should not risk disaffecting a loyal class in order to appease politicians.[50] The Government of India, after considering these replies, produced a third plan, a compromise which moved as far as possible in the direction of full licensing while still retaining an element of the former privileges. They suggested, in July 1918, an even smaller number of full exemptions, but a very wide class of persons to whom licences would be issued without investigation. The proposed list was generous to Indians, although not to officials—it included all princes, title-holders, Coorgs, various local notables, but only senior executive officers.[51] The aim was clearly to introduce a licensed system with the least possible inconvenience to those who might be offended at the loss of their privileges. There was little concern about European sensibilities—the government ignored the more fundamental complaints from the European Association of Calcutta, and later were unmoved by criticisms in the Anglo-Indian press.[52]

After two years the government had produced what seemed like a workable and sensible plan. There remained the need to render it acceptable and to reassure any doubts about their intentions. At the second session of 1918, the question of the Arms Act was referred to a committee of the Imperial Legislative Council, with which official representatives of the provinces were associated.[53] A year later new regulations were issued.[54] Chelmsford explained that they were governed by three principles—racial discrimination was ended; arms were readily available to suitable persons; and they were kept from the unsuitable.[55]

Another outstanding grievance, of deep political significance, concerned the Indian army. Many of the attentions lavished on the army under Chelmsford—improvements in pay and conditions, land grants and pensions for discharged soldiers, even the establishment of a school for the sons of officers—were essentially in the nature of rewards for services.[56] The most important innovation, however, was a political gesture in answer to public opinion. Under Chelmsford, the racial barrier within the army was breached for the first time, and Indians were permitted to hold King's commissions. The decision was political also in its repercussions: if India was to be held by force, then the ultimate control of the Indian army had to be retained in British hands; alternatively, if Indians were to govern their own affairs, they would have to be admitted into partnership in the leadership of their own army—whether European officers liked it or not.

Commissions for Indians were not a new cause. Minto had strongly supported the proposal; Hardinge had given it prominence in his famous memorandum on postwar questions. Under Hardinge, however, there had been disagreement on details—the Commander-in-Chief and a minority of the Council and the local

governors being more cautious than the Viceroy.[57] Chelmsford
recognized that while divisions continued in India there was little
hope of convincing the military authorities in London. He considered asking the army to place one or two men on special duty
to formulate a plan.[58] In the meantime progress had been blocked
in London. The Secretary of State had suggested a few immediate
commissions as a provisional measure; even this had been turned
down by the War Office. The Cabinet were too busy to consider
the question.[59] In February 1917, however, Chamberlain was
ready to try again. He thought he could convince the War Office
if he confined his proposal to commissions for a few Indians of
'unquestionable suitability'.[60] But by this time the Indian army
plan was complete; the Army Department suggested four lines of
advance. In future, for suitable, educated and well-born Indians,
there should be ten places a year reserved at Sandhurst; for promising Indian soldiers, there should be a non-commissioned officers'
school established in India—exceptionally brilliant graduates
might also be awarded British commissions. For the present,
Indian officers of distinguished service would be granted British
commissions, and honorary commissions, with increases in pay
and pensions, would be awarded to one or two Indian officers
from each unit.[61] The India Office was at first unhappy about the
suitability of Sandhurst training for the posts which, in their
view, Indians would be likely to hold; but the Government of
India insisted that only Sandhurst education would mean equality
for Indian officers and prevent any exacerbation of racial feeling—
British and Indian officers were to consider themselves part of the
same cadre. Chamberlain accepted this view and placed it before
the War Office. It was rejected. Chamberlain prepared a minute
to take the matter to the Cabinet.[62]

At this point Chamberlain resigned as a result of the findings of
the Mesopotamia Commission. Edwin Montagu, on taking up
office, found Chamberlain's minute and circulated it with his
support.[63] In the Cabinet, Balfour supported the principle but
undermined this by stressing the 'trouble' likely to be caused.
Derby, the Secretary of State for War, backed predictably by Sir
Edward Carson, was strongly opposed, chiefly on the grounds
that British officers and men would not join the Indian army if
they had to serve under Indians. Montagu argued that the racial
bar was already hampering recruitment in India. And the majority

—Curzon, Islington, Bonar Law, Smuts, Milner, Henderson and Barnes—outvoted Derby and Carson, mainly because (as Bonar Law put it) the Government of India had come to a decision: this (as Milner said) they could not oppose; as Curzon argued, it was 'quite impossible for the Cabinet to refuse the concession'. Chelmsford had been right about the importance of unanimity in India. On 2 August 1917, the Cabinet accepted the principle of commissions for Indians, Derby and Carson dissenting. Nine named officers were to receive immediate commissions under one part of the Indian army scheme.[64]

However, the remainder of the recommendations was still in doubt. The Army Department sent a despatch embodying a full version of their proposals. Most of the cadets were to be educated at Dehra Dun, on public school lines, before being sent to Sandhurst; on gaining commissions, they were to be able to elect to join the Indian army (after one year's service with a British regiment), thus bypassing the Unattached List, from which permanent commissions were awarded in strict seniority or by place at graduation.[65] The War Office prepared to fight a rearguard action against anyone schooled in India and against the admission of Indian officers to any but the Indian army. But the Government of India accepted their objections to Dehra Dun, and, although they reacted sharply against any formal 'colour bar', pointed out that the War Office could refuse any posting to the British army on their own discretion.[66] In April 1918, after a conference between the India and War Offices, agreement was finally reached along these lines. The total number of commissions, from Sandhurst and in promotions from the ranks, was not to exceed twenty in any one year. The Government of India had asked that no limit be stated.[67]

Chelmsford had never expected that the proposals would satisfy 'vocal politicians', but he knew that greater concessions were unlikely from the War Office.[68] The decision in 1918, however, following on the expectation raised by the first nine appointments of the year before, seemed particularly inadequate. Chelmsford at first decided he would make no special announcement, unlike in 1917. He wrote to Montagu: 'It is useless to display a crumb and say "gentlemen, believe me, this is really a loaf" '.[69] The Army Department, on the other hand, suggested that they should be allowed to announce, in addition to the permanent changes, that up to two hundred temporary wartime commissions would be awarded. The Cabinet, while accepting the permanent measures, rejected this proposal, and then asked for more information. Their position was uncertain—and Sir T. W. Holderness at the India Office believed that a difference of opinion was revealed in the different tones of the private and official telegrams reporting the decision to India. The Prime Minister, in the words of his own addition to the private telegram, was chiefly 'anxious to have a fuller statement' of the military reasons, whereas Curzon and Chamberlain had expressed 'more decided disapproval'.[70] The ambiguity was to prove useful. Montagu, who was in India, launched a vigorous memorandum asking for reconsideration. He claimed that the two hundred commissions were essential to India's recruiting efforts, in which the home government had recently asked to see improvements.[71] The Government of India also protested, and promised up to half a million new recruits if they were allowed to offer the stimulus of the temporary commissions—they had in mind about fifty of these every six months. They insisted that there would be no lowering of standards; and they rejected a suggestion that the Indian Land Force cadre might be revived as an alternative—this, they held, would merely perpetuate an irritating racial distinction.[72] Lord Curzon rounded on these pleas with a strident Cabinet minute. This meant, he claimed, that commissions were to be used as 'political rewards'; this was not the type of officer they wanted; this would discredit the whole commissions scheme.[73] The question came before the Cabinet after Montagu's return. Chamberlain, irritated by Curzon's interjections, became a vigorous supporter, while the War Office, according to Montagu's description, tried to get a hearing but were routed. The Cabinet's main fear on the commissions—that British cadets would be discouraged from applying—did not apply to the temporary arrangement. The two hundred commissions were approved. There was one rather important proviso, imposed for fear of unduly raising Indian hopes. The concession was not to be published—presumably the effect for the benefit of recruiting was to be gradual.[74]

One of Curzon's objections had had more than immediate significance, and its rejection by the Cabinet was of far greater importance than the immediate decision. Curzon claimed: 'The more you hand over the civil administration of India to the Indian, the more you will have to depend in the last resort for the stability of the British connection upon the prestige and authority of the army.' It was precisely this belief that the policy of Indian commissions had sought to contest; it was precisely this view of the British raj which the whole tenor of Chelmsford's positive measures sought to deny. The question was how India was to be held. The logic of Chelmsford's policy—and the issue of army commissions now formed part of a consistent whole—was that India should be held not by force but by partnership and transfer of power.

All these positive measures Montagu related directly to public opinion and constitutional reform, calling them 'lubricants'. He wanted rather more of them than one overworked and understaffed administration could have tackled. Chelmsford and the Government of India placed more emphasis on the virtues of each measure in itself. Chelmsford identified three major concerns of his policy in 1917—to reward the Indian army; to remove all Indian grievances, whether material or sentimental; and to define the goal of British rule, mapping out the roads which would lead to it.[75] The first two of these could have been espoused by any benevolent government; the last, as interpreted under Chelmsford, imposed a view of the British raj as a preparation for Indian self-government. Thus it is not suggested that the positive reforms were new, for many had been under consideration for years; nor that earlier administrations had never put Indian considerations before British interests; nor that Chelmsford's administration put India first in all matters. Rather, it is suggested that the development of India and her public opinion had reached a crucial stage when even foreign autocrats had to modify their approach. Thus what was genuinely new was that under Chelmsford the removal of grievances and the definition of the goal were always interrelated: causes of discontent which were admitted to be material, could be put right only in ways which did not contradict a general idea of the British role in India—they were part of the mapping out; they provided some of the roads. Chelmsford told his Legislative Council in 1916: 'these preoccupations [with the war] do not and will not prevent the Government of India from giving their earnest attention to the problems of this great Empire. The growing self-respect and self-consciousness of her people are plants that we ourselves have watered, and if the blossom is not

always what we expect, it is not for us to blame the plant.'[76] The
concern with the response of public opinion, the assertion of
India's role, and the denial of racial superiority, were not only
appeasements, for all the paternalism of Chelmsford's tone. They
were part of an imperial purpose, and led to imperial partnership.

Yet relations with the influential and articulate classes worsened
steadily under Chelmsford. He had emphasized the value of
educated support and the dangers that a minority could infect the
masses; as opposition gained a wider basis, his predictions were
proved correct. He had tried to counter Simla's slowness and isolation by introducing consultation at every level of his administration, and his government had attempted to use modern methods
of publicity and propaganda; his and their unpopularity grew re-
gardless. The problem was partly that Chelmsford's personality
was different from Hardinge's; it was perhaps more that all Hardinge's promises had matured in Chelmsford's time—the time had
come when fine speeches had to be given a definite form, and inevitably that form turned out to be a disappointment, under
Chelmsford as it would have under Hardinge. Nevertheless the
most cogent reason for the unpopularity was probably the current
belief that there was a contradiction in government policy. Much of
that part of the population which was truly political, by tradition
and by resources in publicity and education, presented itself to
the government as unalterably opposed to their 'alien rule'. The
disaffected people recognised that some of the government measures were beneficial; but they consistently doubted the government's good faith. They were not impressed by what Montagu
rather ominously called 'lubricants'. They suggested that each
concession merely sweetened the next indignity. The cry of Tilak,
that home rule was more important than good rule, had been
sharpened by the belief that 'good rule' was invariably tempered
with repression.

But more than this, perhaps Indians were right to suspect the
government's policy. When they helped improve India's status
or espoused Indian causes against British or imperial interests, it
was because they believed that the Indian government should try
to reflect the will of the people; when they agreed to remove racial
disabilities, it was because they believed the government should
treat Indians as equal citizens not as subject peoples; when they
urged army commissions for Indians, even if the change had to be

forced on British officers, it was because they thought full participation by Indians in all aspects of their country's life was both
desirable and inevitable. But these were still limited aims. It does
not seem that these things were done to help create a wholly independent India, or an independent wholly Indian army. 'The
question was how India was to be held': Chelmsford's aim was
conservative, his dispute with reactionaries over the means of
preserving British supremacy. He postulated partnership for
Indians and ultimately a drastic reduction in British involvement,
but alongside the continuance of British Empire. He looked forward to the transfer of power, not of sovereignty. In practical terms
the distinction was meaningless, but this was just what was alarming—for might not the reservation of sovereignty be used in
practice, as it was in the 1919 reforms, to limit the transfers of
power which had been conceded in principle? Thus, although the
suspicion may not have been formulated precisely at the time,
the limit to Chelmsford's imagination was perhaps crucial for the
reaction to his policies. It affected his presentation of his approach;
it qualified his promises; it made his intentions seem suspect.
Perhaps altogether it helped jaundice his reception; we shall be
considering this question again. Certainly, as far as public opinion
was concerned, it is clear at least that any success claimed by the
Government of India was hedged in: it had to stand against a
growing and seemingly inevitable tide of nationalism, uncompromising and ethnocentric.

II THE CONSTITUTION

Chapter 3. The Goal

THE 1919 reforms were a response to agitation—largely of Western-educated Indians, though, as Meston was to tell the Lords, 'What lies behind and below the whole of the political difficulties of India . . . is the spirit of nationalism . . . spreading rapidly through all ranks and classes of Indian society.'[1] More important, however, to explain why such reforms were introduced how and when they were, is to understand that they represented a deliberate attempt to make the Indian constitution conform to an evolutionary concept of British rule.

It is probable that during his briefing in London Chelmsford had been advised to take up the question of reforms. Hardinge had sent in a memorandum in 1915 of steps to appease Indian opinion, questions which, in his opinion, 'the conclusion of peace must find us ready to consider'; Lord Curzon had also reminded Chamberlain that the new Viceroy would have to be responsible for postwar policies; and, since about 1912, the Round Table group, with whom (as we shall see) Chelmsford had contacts, had been discussing the question of India's constitutional status. Chelmsford, however, later wrote as if the initiative had been his. He claimed that some time in 1915, while in India with his regiment, he had decided that British rule was 'aimless', characterized by a 'hand-to-mouth policy of giving Reforms piecemeal in response to agitation'; and that he saw that another advance would have to be conceded shortly and believed it should conform to some general idea of British rule. His view was reinforced when S. P. Sinha, in his Congress Presidential address of December 1915, called for a declaration on the intentions of the British with regard to Indian self-government. Chelmsford adopted Sinha's questions: at his 'very first Executive Council' the new Viceroy asked: (1) what is the ultimate goal of British rule in India? (2) what are the first steps on the road to that goal? From the first, under Chelmsford, lines of advance were considered in terms of an attempt to plan coherently.[2]

Chelmsford's Executive Council, augmented by Sir Michael O'Dwyer, the Lieutenant-Governor of the Panjab, discussed Chelmsford's questions at informal weekly and later twice weekly meetings. The Councillors were being asked to rethink their ideas, for they had been consulted by Lord Hardinge when he was formulating his memorandum in 1915.[3] Under Chelmsford, however, they were being given a different starting-point, the question of the goal. Each member, as he was ready, separately summarized his ideas in a rough note which was then circulated among the other members. For three weeks Chelmsford held discussions with individual members on their own views, and towards the end of May 1916 asked Sir George Barnes to try to find common ground. There was more agreement than Chelmsford had expected: the Council agreed to a formula stating that the British goal was 'to endow India . . . with the largest measure of Self-Government compatible with the maintenance of the supreme authority of British Rule'. One Councillor, Sir Sankaran Nair, the Education Member, had argued that the goal should be 'good government . . . according to Western ideals' and that at present self-government was incompatible with Indian caste and class feeling and the low status of women. The other members—the British—all included some form of self-government and some degree of British suzerainty among their objectives.[4]

In the qualification 'compatible with the maintenance of the supreme authority', the term 'British Rule' had been introduced by Chelmsford himself, as a replacement for the words 'King-Emperor'. Sir T. W. Holderness of the India Office pointed out that this formula would be interpreted as a retreat from Hardinge's position: it appeared, unlike Hardinge's remarks, to hint that complete self-government would never be obtained.[5] This had not been Chelmsford's intention. He meant to demonstrate that complete independence was not feasible. He had preferred the words 'British Rule' and had rejected 'King-Emperor' on the grounds that the latter seemed to him to involve 'Colonial Swaraj', a form of government which was 'wholly inapplicable to the conditions of India'. The qualification was intended, therefore, to rule out one form of government, not (as Holderness had thought) to place a limit on the extent of the self-government. Thus, in the first

place, it is clear that Chelmsford's government had not even considered a goal involving an end to British suzerainty. Self-government, for them, meant transfer of power to Indians under some
continuing British control—a constitutional position similar, presumably, to that which might have been thought then to apply,
theoretically, to existing British Dominions. At this stage, Chelmsford explained to the Secretary of State, Austen Chamberlain, they
should emphasize that, while they sought 'a gradual extension of
self-government', they were determined not to abdicate their
position—that would be for their successors. In the second place,
as this last phrase reveals, this formula was not after all an ultimate one. Even with regard to 'Colonial Swaraj', Chelmsford said
no more than that he was 'not prepared to agree at the present
moment'.[6]

This initial version was also in no sense final. As Chelmsford
explained later in reply to Holderness' criticism, it had 'served its
purpose . . . in clearing our minds and enabling us to see where
we stand. . . . It represented a stage in our discussion from which
we advanced to further stages'.[7] Accordingly, in the final draft,
the government removed the ambiguity remarked on by Holderness, but without in any way extending what they proposed.
Chelmsford had consulted Sinha, who convinced him the original
would not be satisfactory from the Indian point of view. 'The goal
to which we look forward,' the government stated, in the despatch
which they sent to the Secretary of State in November, 'is the
endowment of British India as an integral part of the Empire,
with self-government, but the rate of progress . . . must depend
upon the improvement and wide diffusion of education, the soften-
ing of racial and religious differences, and the acquisition of political experience'. They contemplated India's gradual progress towards a larger and larger measure of control by her own people,
'the steady and conscious development of which will ultimately
result in self-government'—though in a form 'regulated by the
special circumstances of India' and not altogether on Dominion
lines. In the view of Sir Claude Hill, expressed later in 1917, he
and the other Council members were safeguarding themselves, as
bureaucrats, even in this last reservation—in fact, he claimed,
everyone contemplated that India would receive responsible
government as in the Dominions except for modifications in
detail.[8] But this meant, as we have seen, some idea of a continuing

British presence, of India 'as an integral part of the Empire'. And, as we shall see, this was true of all plans put forward in this period, whether by Hardinge, Holderness, Chelmsford, Montagu or even the Indian leaders.

The next question was how to take a definite step towards this goal. The Council discussions postulated three roads of advance: they were rewards for war service, the removal of grievances, and political progress. There was unanimity on the first two of these.[9] Indeed in these areas the recommendations showed virtually complete continuity between Chelmsford's and Hardinge's policies: in both Hardinge's memorandum and the Government of India despatch of November 1916 the emphasis was placed upon rewarding the army through commissions, pay increases and various benefits, and upon answering grievances on matters such as the Arms Act, indentured emigration, and the cotton excise duties. Sinha, too, had stressed almost exactly these improvements in his Presidential address to the Congress.

There was substantial agreement also that two of the lines of political advance should be the increased employment of Indians in the higher branches of the public services, and the development of local self-government. Hardinge had supported these lines too— for him the latter was 'the safest and most natural line of development' which would 'diminish the force of demands for Colonial Self-Government and other such claims which are neither understood nor really wanted'. Sinha, while regretting that Hardinge had not agreed to complete internal independence for local boards, also believed that local self-government was the way for Indians to gain *swaraj*. Under Chelmsford the Government of India were prepared to go further. They enunciated similar principles for both local self-government and the public services. For both the object was to be 'to train the people in the management of their own ... affairs'; the rule for both was to be that 'education of this sort must take precedence of mere considerations of departmental efficiency'.[10]

For the public services the increased employment of Indians in higher and more responsible posts was held to be 'essential to the progress of India towards the goal'. There had been disagreement in the Council on one point, the emphasis to be placed on the possibility of going beyond what the Public Services Commission had recommended—Craddock, supported by O'Dwyer and the

Commander-in-Chief, Duff, was unwilling to commit the government; Meyer, Lowndes, Hill and Nair insisted that it was necessary to admit that the situation had changed since the Report.
Barnes remained uncommitted, and Chelmsford awaited the local
government reaction before making a decision; the Council later
agreed to state that the recommendations would be put into effect,
subject to modification and extension where there were new circumstances. The guiding principle was to be to allow 'Full opportunity for Indians to qualify themselves for the more important
posts in the public services, and to demonstrate . . . their fitness
for still more responsible duties'. Progress was to be set anew 'on
sound and generous lines'.[11]

In local self-government, it was decided the 'local bodies must
be as representative as possible', 'their control . . . should be real
and not nominal', and 'they must not be kept in leading strings
but must learn by making mistakes and profiting by them'.
Government policy had already been announced on 28 April
1915 in a resolution on the report of the Decentralization Commission. In a memorandum of June 1916, however, the new Viceroy
circulated to the local governments a revised version: he confirmed that the resolution in Hardinge's time 'usually saw the right
path', but stressed that now the Government of India were no
longer 'content to let the local governments travel by it or not as
these saw fit'. For municipalities, his government had decided that
the Commission's proposal for substantial elected majorities should
be accepted and urged on local governments, with the corollary
that the franchise should be sufficiently low to include the body of
the rate-payers. Chairmen should normally be elected non-
officials. For rural and district boards, where the Commission
had recommended elected majorities with an official chairman,
the Viceroy now urged that the local governments should begin
the experiment, wherever possible, of non-official and preferably
elected chairmen. Powers for local boards should also be increased.
Municipalities, unless indebted, were to be quite free to impose or
alter local taxation; under Hardinge this right had been subject to
the local government power to vary any tax, a reservation which
Chelmsford's government considered to render the right 'nugatory'.
In 1915 also the government had been reluctant fully to accept
the principle that where a local board paid for a service it should
also control it; the Viceroy now insisted on going the 'whole way'

with the Decentralization Commmission—local boards were to have control, subject to general principles of conduct, and the local governments were instructed not to interfere on details. In particular, the compulsory reservation of parts of local funds for specified purposes was to be abolished, and unnecessary control over capital works was to be relaxed. Thus, Chelmsford's government had introduced three main changes: they had asked that the rate of progress should be increased, they had refused to leave certain matters to the discretion of the local governments, and they had enunciated a general rule that local bodies were to be subject, as in Britain, to 'ultimate powers of intervention' but not to day to day supervision.[12] They had accepted, however, a point which was made later by Chamberlain—that it was also necessary to provide safeguards through permanent officials.[13] In 1918 Edwin Montagu was to claim that no official chairman should be 'let near' any local body: the Government of India had already accepted this ideal in 1916.[14] They stipulated, as Chelmsford was to point out in 1918, only that the pace of development should not be so greatly enhanced 'as to bring about a fall'.[15]

Chelmsford's government were divided on the question of legislative reform. Chelmsford had 'studiously avoided pressing any opinion', as he was anxious to obtain the considered views 'of those whose experience would justify them in having strong convictions'.[16] He was trying most of all to secure a unanimous despatch, for that alone would carry weight and conviction in London. But on legislative reform Craddock, who, as the member mainly responsible, could not be ignored, was again ranged with O'Dwyer and Duff, against Meyer, Hill, Lowndes and Nair. Craddock's group opposed any increase in the powers of the legislative councils. In Hardinge's time, Craddock had pointed out that the British were 'at the parting of the ways' in India—the main question was whether or not they were 'to convert the non-official Members from being representatives of interests . . . to being representatives of a self-governing people entitled to control the executive'. To Chelmsford he insisted that the government must continue the representation of 'classes and interests' and not introduce territorial constituencies; he advocated the replacement of district board constituencies (which tended to return lawyers) with electorates of landowners and commercial interests; and, if Muslim representation was to be retained, he favoured narrowing

the franchise to bring it into line with that in the general electorates.[17] The opposing group, on the other hand, favoured statutory
changes for the legislative councils so as to increase their financial
and administrative powers and develop the elective principle.
Meyer and Hill argued, with some individual variation, for large
territorial constituencies, non-official majorities in the provinces,
and for some means of associating members with the government, for example as advisers on the budget. Their views were not
identical, as becomes clear in 1917 when Hill is found arguing for
extensions of the government's proposals to include greater powers
for provincial legislatures, while Meyer insists that 'the first
essential towards such a possible development is to make them more
really representative'.[18] In 1916, however, these differences were
subsumed in a consensus on limited and general principles opposed
to those advanced by Craddock.

Hill was the most progressive thinker in the central government.
He claimed it was a note of his which had prompted Hardinge to
write the memorandum of 1915. By 1916 he had refined his ideas,
in conjunction with Lowndes. 'I must warn you,' he told Malcolm
Seton, Secretary of the Judicial and Public Department at the
India Office, 'that you will think I go too far & too fast: Craddock
is frightened to death.' The main principle he set before himself
was that they 'must give wider representation'. To achieve this
aim they must, in his view, 'increase provincial autonomy . . .
make proper representative control (within limits) a living
reality: & . . . face & put up with the fact that we shall, by these
measures, sacrifice a measure of efficiency.' To argue that they
must wait until India was 'fully fitted to control herself' was
practically to 'refuse to surrender any control indefinitely: for, . . .
India . . . can only learn by experience'.[19]

Chelmsford remained uncommitted. He was certainly disposed
to be cautious—it might have seemed that he was likely to favour
the viewpoint of Craddock whose judgment and knowledge he
respected. In November 1916 he told a conference which was discussing the prospect of a permanent council for the Indian
princes and chiefs, 'I would beg you to give time to development
and growth, and the motto I would ask you to place before your-
selves is *Festina lente*'. He was inclined to apply the same principle
to reforms in British India. He told the Imperial Legislative
Council that 'progress must be circumspect and on well considered

lines'; he informed the Agra municipality: 'There can be no better
school for training the political sense than that of Municipal
administration'.[20] Thus there were changes which Chelmsford
refused to contemplate at least as first steps. In October 1916, a
majority of elected members of the Imperial Legislative Council
put forward a scheme advocating large elected majorities and complete legislative control (subject only to veto) for all legislative
councils. A nominated member Zulfikar Ali Khan, described this
notion (known as the Nineteen Members' scheme) as 'fantastic
and visionary'. Chelmsford agreed: he thought it 'preposterous'.[21]
Craddock's case was reinforced also by his intention of reducing
the predominance of lawyers in the councils—Sir James Meston of
the United Provinces had drawn to Chelmsford's attention the
grievances among landowners and had argued that this problem
should have a 'very close bearing on the method of representation
in the elective institutions of the future'.[22] For his part, the Viceroy was also ready to endorse the traditional axioms of paternalism:
he told the Bengal Landowners' Association that 'one of the most
pressing needs of India' was 'the uplifting of the actual tiller of
the soil'.[23] There was finally on Craddock's side some political logic.
As W. S. Marris, while temporarily seconded to the United Provinces,
had pointed out in a letter which Meston sent to Chelmsford,
elected Indian majorities could mean a paralysis of government—
one could not 'dis-sever legislation from administration'.[24]

But, for all this, Craddock's conservatism was untenable.
Meston had replied to Marris that they could not stand still, and
wrote to Chelmsford that if they were only 'sufficiently courageous'
they need not fear 'the passing of sovereignty'. Chelmsford replied
that he 'very much agreed' with the view that they could not stand
still.[25] Craddock, at 'the parting of the ways' and refusing to contemplate turning the legislators into the 'representatives of a self-
governing people', was undoubtedly trying to stand still. Privately,
in spite of his caution and his desire for compromise, Chelmsford
had already decided between the logic of Marris and the optimism
of Meston—and between Craddock's fears and Meyer's and Hill's
concessions. He explained to Lowndes that he valued his contributions in representing the 'non-official view on questions with
regard to which the I.C.S. members are bound to have an official
view', and in being 'sane, impartial and sympathetic'—chiefly,
we may assume, over what Lowndes' ally, Hill, called 'certain

measures in the direction of making Leg. Cls. more representative and responsible'. Chelmsford wrote to Chamberlain in August 1916: 'I have come very definitely to the conclusion . . . that we must take a step forward on the political side'.[26] He was confident of the support of the majority of his colleagues. Chelmsford's starting point, first asking what was the goal, had implied that the Morley-Minto constitution would have to be reconsidered.

The 1916 despatch, embodying the government's reforms proposals, was nevertheless a conservative document. It reflected inevitably a careful papering over of the differences in the Executive Council. For the legislative councils there was to be no increase in powers—Meyer's group had had to give way. Against Craddock's advice there were, however, to be elected majorities and a wide extension of the franchise so as to create 'really large constituencies'. The division had crystallized about the issue of territorial electorates—Craddock wanted them forbidden, and Nair insisted that they should be obligatory. Chelmsford agreed to allow the type of constituency to be at local discretion. This was no solution, and Craddock still wrote a minute of dissent to the despatch. At the last moment Nair, who had agreed to everything in Council, suddenly decided to dissent as well; Chelmsford was convinced that he had yielded to political pressure.[27] The Viceroy's tactics had been to attain unanimity: they had failed.

But even disagreements and compromises could not obscure the nature of the change which had been introduced. In most matters the despatch had been greatly influenced by the earlier suggestions of Hardinge and Sinha. Indeed Hardinge was 'very satisfied' with the proposals and suggested that they were based on his memorandum.[28] But in the changes to the legislative councils Chelmsford's government had introduced a new factor. Craddock had argued that territorial electorates were the crucial point at issue—if they were conceded there would be no retreat from a parliamentary system and the British would find 'further compulsory advances thrust' upon them.[29] The despatch had left this question undecided; but, in a memorandum to the local governments, Chelmsford had revealed the majority's views—he proposed to 'sweep away this complicated and anomalous system of class interests' and 'to substitute large constituencies primarily based on recognized territorial units, such as districts, and with a franchise pitched sufficiently low to admit of considerable bodies of voters'. Under his proposals no constituency would be considered satisfactory with fewer than three thousand voters. Moreover, even when electorates of interests and classes were to be retained, election was henceforth to be direct and not indirect—for example the body of the graduates and not the governors would elect any university representatives. The memorandum containing these views was appended to the reforms despatch, so that neither Whitehall nor the local governments were left in any doubt about the Viceroy's preferences. What was evident also was that Craddock was wrong to think that the postponement of the question of territorial electorates had prevented any commitment to a parliamentary system. The changes agreed for the franchise ensured a large increase in the number of the voters. And large electorates were seen as a definite step of preparation for self-government. The despatch explained that they were a first stage necessary before the legislatures could be allowed financial and administrative control.

The government had concluded that the preconditions for self-government did not exist in India. They thought the Indians needed more unity and greater political experience: the 1916 proposals were directed consciously towards creating these conditions. There were to be efforts to widen and improve education, and to reduce racial and religious intolerance. The immediate channels were to be the public services and local self-government. A few Indians were to gain experience in the executive councils—half of all members (apart from the governors) were to be Indians. But the legislative councils were also to be slowly developed. They were not to have control—although with elected majorities in the provinces their influence was to be more effective. The time for control, the government believed, might 'come at some later stage': it would come presumably when the experiment of wider representation had created working electorates. The intention of the 1916 proposals, cautious as they were, was deliberately to 'pave the way for an ultimate enlargement of the constitutional powers of the provincial legislative councils'.[30]

In 1888, Lord Dufferin, arguing for the introduction of the elective principle, did not suggest that it would involve any real representation of the people: the association of qualified Indians with the government was intended as a means of improving British administration—decisions would be better informed. Lord Lansdowne and the Government of India's despatch of 26 October 1892 supported this view; and in 1907 Minto's despatch of 21 March had stressed that the government were 'no advocates of representative Government for India'—the 1909 reforms were an advance, therefore, 'in the direction of associating the people of India' with the British for the operation of legislation and administration. Kitchener, by giving it extreme expression, had summed up the attitude of Minto's time: 'large advisory councils', he asserted, 'are absurd—I am not sure that any are necessary as there is nothing to prevent a Lt. Gov. from obtaining any outside advice he may want.'

Lord Hardinge, in his memorandum of October 1915, had advocated the modification of the legislative council regulations, and had argued that if the British had any intention of raising India to self-governing status they would have to concede 'some measure of real popular control, especially in provincial questions as contrasted with questions of wide Imperial concern'. A transition certainly begins with Hardinge. But what did he mean by 'real popular control'? In August 1911, his government had put forward rather confused ideas for provincial self-government under a central government permanently British; this suggestion had been in effect repudiated by the statements made by Lord Crewe in the House of Lords on 22 February and 24 June 1912. In the 1915 memorandum, moreover, Hardinge envisaged no more than changes in regulations to allow elected provincial majorities. His contribution was a massive endorsement of at least provincial self-government, as an idea; but his proposals were not a step towards this goal. He did not suggest that the Morley-Minto reforms should be upset; the result of his memorandum would have been no more than to improve existing machinery for consultation.[31]

As Chelmsford explained in July 1916, Hardinge's memorandum had dealt with isolated problems; in Chelmsford's view the British now needed to pursue 'the consideration and promulgation of a definite policy' and to accompany it with definite action.[32] This chiefly distinguishes the proposals of 1916 from those preceding them: it should not be lost sight of in the fact that in 1916, as previously, Indian independence was not considered. Georges Fischer has suggested, about the qualms over the universal applicability of British institutions, which were one element in the government's caution in 1916: 'Il semble, en réalité, que l'impossibilité de transplanter le modèle métropolitain est utilisé comme un argument pour refuser des réformes politiques substantielles.'[33] It might be argued, therefore, that Chelmsford and his Council were merely continuing a practice which Morley, Minto and Crewe had all endorsed. But the second and more important aspect of the policy of 1916 gives the lie to this: Chelmsford had not only suggested reforms, he had begun with a goal of self-government and then proposed steps towards it. This was quite different from 1909. And, though Chelmsford's proposals may look like those of Hardinge, on closer inspection they are revealed to have started from a more theoretical position: not how to appease Indians, but how to move towards self-government. The result, in the 1916 despatch, was that already some proposals— the abandonment of the non-representative ideas of electorates— indicated a new direction in policy; the greatly widened franchise was not thought of as a better method of consulting Indian opinion; it was deliberately designed to help create suitable electorates for a future (though distant) transfer of power to Indian Councils.

Thus, though in the details of the 1916 despatch Hill had had to give way, the spirit of his proposals remained. It was agreed that the British must give 'wider representation', 'increase provincial autonomy' and, 'sacrifice a measure of efficiency'. Proper 'representative control' was not a possible proposal from a group which included Craddock, but it was a logical extension of the suggestions which *were* put forward. Indeed, it seems to have been Hill who set out the principles which the Government of India were consistently to advocate: as he put it privately, first 'education in the wider responsibility of adm[inistratio]n . . . by means of expansion of the system of representation in the provinces'; second, 'a large devolution of financial autonomy, from home to us, & from us to the provinces', in order to 'make the advance a reality'; and third, letting 'courageous & substantial' provincial advance 'bear fruit over a number of years' before the framework of the central government would be touched.[34]

The India Office received the reforms despatch in January 1917. Austen Chamberlain, the Secretary of State, wanted time to consider the proposals carefully. He was personally, at this stage, disposed to favour Chelmsford's compromise on the extension of the elective principle in the Councils; but he was doubtful of his ability to decide such questions. He formed a committee of the

India Council under Sir William Duke to consider the despatch. In March Sir James Meston, who was in London on deputation with Sinha and the Maharaja of Bikaner, representing India at the Imperial War Conference, reported privately to Chelmsford that the committee had not got beyond shaking their heads over the reforms despatch.[35] He was wrong; a few days later the committee made their report. With a few reservations they supported all the Government of India's proposals, but argued that the political changes did not 'constitute a coherent and well thought out plan of reform'. In terms of function the councils were being left unchanged and this would 'perpetuate and aggravate a vicious system' of representation without responsibility. The territorial electorate would merely return more of the already over-represented educated classes, who would manipulate their legislative majority, whatever the safeguards, to make the government's position intolerable. Thus the increase in representative character would be no advantage until the councils were given 'some degree of responsibility' for policy.[36] The committee had introduced a very important new idea.

Chelmsford insisted that the fault of the Morley-Minto reforms was that they did not attempt to create representative institutions on which responsibility could be devolved. The fact was that they had created a system in which there was no possibility for growth. Chelmsford had argued that they had skipped a whole stage in evolution, and that this had to be undergone before the grant of further powers.[37] But this idea, although it methodically prepared for future development, made no attempt to deal with the present faults of the Morley-Minto system. The India Council committee, while broadly accepting the Government of India idea of the goal and agreeing that the councils should be made properly representative, argued that they would have to be reformed at the same time. Their disabilities demanded this; so did the political situation; so did the Government of India's own argument about the need to educate the Indians in politics—what was the use of the councils, if all that the members learnt was to criticise and obstruct the executive?

Chamberlain accepted the committee's arguments. He explained to Chelmsford, in May 1917, that he had been convinced that they must be ready for 'bold and radical measures'. He had consulted Sinha who had urged that the reforms must give 'increased responsibility to the elected representatives' and that a mere increase in numbers was not progressive. He had been made aware of an important letter from W. S. Marris arguing that to give elected majorities without conceding other powers to the legislature was 'a hollow & indecisive advance along a false path'— for they would be allowing Indians a stranglehold on provincial legislation, relying themselves on the veto or the Government of India, to neither of which would it be politically practical to have resort.[38] It was not possible, Chamberlain decided, to continue with a system which made it the 'main function of the Legislative Councils to oppose and criticise the Government while remaining completely free from responsibility for the results of their action'. Chelmsford had introduced a new criterion when he related the proposed reforms consciously and directly to the goal of future self-government; now this same criterion was being used against the caution of his proposals. The implication of such arguments as Marris's was that it was not feasible to concede legislative control without also conceding executive responsibility. Chamberlain had agreed that they must train Indians in self-government, but had argued that it was not enough to train only public servants, local administrators, and electors. They had to train legislators as well, by investing the councils with 'some definite powers and with real responsibility for their actions', including greater authority over provincial budgets 'or some part of them'.[39] Chamberlain gave no indication of how 'some' (but not all) powers and 'real' (but not complete) responsibility could be given. But, by postulating popular control over 'part' of the budget, he made what was probably the first authoritative endorsement of the idea of a division of powers, the direction in which his thinking was to lead. On 22 May he explained to Chelmsford that the 'kernel' of the problem was 'the devolution of power and responsibility within such limited spheres as may at present be practical and safe'.[40] The first question, however, was how to proceed.

The Government of India originally envisaged a fairly rapid response to their proposals. But the war dragged on, and the prospect for an early advance grew more remote. At the beginning of May 1917, Chelmsford suggested to Chamberlain that he visit India and consult directly with the government on the measures to be taken. 'You realize, I am sure,' Chelmsford wrote, 'how big the question is and how a visit from the Secretary of State would impress [the] imagination of [the] people.'[41] Chamberlain did not favour this idea. He did not wish to leave England, on public grounds, and he was worried that a visit by the Secretary of State might be embarrassing to the Government of India and prejudicial to their authority. He had been considering appointing a committee to visit India.[42] Some form of investigation was clearly necessary. The India Office had decided that the Government of India proposals did not go far enough, and also had noted that official opinion in India spoke with a great number of different voices—the disagreements were to be carefully summed up, as arguments for an impartial enquiry, in an India Office memorandum written towards the end of May. Earlier in that month suggestions had been made for a parliamentary committee to consider the problems and report on the merits of the different schemes. Lord Islington, the Under-Secretary of State, favoured an authoritative committee of enquiry of about five persons.[43] Sinha, who at one stage, until dissuaded by Meston, had thought of raising the question at the Imperial War Conference, was now urging free and public discussions of any reforms scheme before it was approved.[44] Chamberlain, having received this advice, decided on a small mainly private enquiry sitting in India for not more than one cold season. He explained to Chelmsford that he believed it was necessary for the impulse for change to come from outside the government—no bureaucracy would ever transform itself into self-government: the very virtues of bureaucrats, he claimed, 'are inimical to a Parliamentary system, and it is inevitable that they should magnify the difficulties and the dangers of any change'. The Secretary of State could not provide this independence—if he were in India moreover, 'all eyes would turn . . . to him, . . . and he would be regarded as superseding' the Viceroy.[45] Chamberlain put his proposal before the British War Cabinet.[46]

The Government of India were vehemently opposed to this idea. Chelmsford explained that the need was for speed—a committee would mean delay. It would also probably comprise people who were 'impartial', that is, Chelmsford claimed, 'people of definite political views but no experience of India'. How would they find members acceptable both to them and to Indian opinion? There would be an outcry if the committee recommended less than the government; but it would be even worse if they recommended more—only the Secretary of State could do this as he was even more responsible for India than the government. The questions to be decided, Chelmsford asserted, were questions of policy and not of fact. The decision could not be transferred away from those responsible. Similar arguments appeared when Meston suggested a conference on reforms with Indian political leaders. Chelmsford's Council were opposed—unanimously with the possible exception of Nair who was equivocal. Meyer thought Meston was up in the clouds, and Sir William Vincent (now Home Member) found the idea objectionable on at least half a dozen counts, political and constitutional, although he thought the government should consult the legislatures or a committee of all shades of opinion. Hill produced a long minute of substantial proposals intended (though at rather a bad moment tactically) to avoid both a reactionary and too sudden an advance; but he too rejected Meston's conference.[47]

Meston had written also to recommend that Chelmsford should 'accept a Commission and make sure of the *personnel*'—in the India Office, he reported, the atmosphere was 'very conservative'.[48] Chelmsford went so far as to discuss the terms of such an inquiry: if there had to be one, he argued, it should sit in India, as a small body of officials and non-officials, consulting records and privately hearing witnesses, and reporting to the Government of India. The president and a third of the members should be non-officials appointed by the Secretary of State, and the remainder should be Indians and officials selected in equal numbers by the Government of India.[49] But even to such a committee Chelmsford would still have had the strongest objections. His disapproval was shared by Vincent, and endorsed by the Executive Council.[50]

Chamberlain asked, what was the alternative? He had become even more convinced that it would be wrong for him to visit India as Secretary of State, and it was impossible to take the decision by mail. In June 1917 his resolve was strengthened by the report of the Mesopotamia Commission which, in investigating the reasons for the failure of the Mesopotamia campaign against the Turks, had criticized 'Hardinge's attitude to his Council' and challenged 'the constitutionality of his proceedings'—Chamberlain observed that this had brought suspicion on the Government of India as a whole, so that there was likely to be a demand for an enquiry even without reforms proposals.[51] Chelmsford continued to oppose the plan, but concluded, as he admitted to Chamberlain,

that he was 'flogging a dead horse'.[52] It seemed probable at this
stage that a committee of enquiry would be appointed.

From a very early stage there had been a second element in
the reforms discussions. In June 1916, Lord Willingdon, the
Governor of Bombay, had called for a statement on government
policy. He wanted it to stem the advance of the Home Rule
movement, which he called the only 'live policy' before the country.
He continued his pleas in July, when they were joined by those of
Lord Pentland, the Governor of Madras, who wanted a statement
that India's interests were not being jeopardized by the postponement of reform discussions during the war.[53] Chelmsford recognized that the intention was that the declaration should tell
Indians that immediate or early Home Rule was out of the question;
Chelmsford was opposed to this 'non possumus' approach. He
wanted to be able to say: 'You cannot have that, but I will give
you this.' Thus, in his view, nothing short of full disclosure of the
government's plans would be useful.[54] Chamberlain agreed. He
thought it would be impossible to make a declaration which would
satisfy the public Willingdon had in mind and yet not be open to
a wide range of interpretations: the British should deal with discontent, he suggested, by introducing practical reforms not by
coining new phrases.[55] He had some doubts momentarily in
November, when he was faced by suggestions that, without a
declaration, the moderates would be swept away at the next
Congress session. He was not convinced, but asked Chelmsford if it
would be helpful to announce, without defining how the policy
would be fulfilled or what shape self-government would take, that
in future Indians would be increasingly associated with government,
and that the Civil Service would have to learn to persuade and
not command.[56] Chelmsford remained sceptical; he replied that he
was 'doubtful whether any statement . . . would be of any value
unless it specifically stated [the] advance which we were prepared
to make'.[57]

His government intended of course that a formula based on their
suggestions should be announced shortly as just such a prelude to
specific reforms. But Chelmsford's idea of the 'value' of the
announcement differed from Willingdon's. It was not to be one in
the old style, a sop to Indian opinion made with no clear intention
of actually doing anything. For the Viceroy and his Council—as
for Sinha—the announcement was primarily a stage in practical

reforms; for Willingdon it was primarily a means of controlling agitation. Thus Chelmsford was not immediately swayed by developments among Indian nationalists. In December and January the 'extremists', as Willingdon had predicted, captured the Congress in session at Lucknow. They decided to formulate, with the Muslim League, a joint reforms scheme and a draft bill to amend the Government of India Act; they proposed to undertake large-scale propaganda in India and Great Britain, to collect a 'National Fund' of three lakhs of rupees, and, at the appropriate time, to send a deputation to petition Parliament.[58] Meston thought this 'united front' created a serious situation, and, adding his voice to Willingdon's and Pentland's, reported the suggestion of A. C. Mazumdar, the Congress President, that there should be a formal proclamation recognizing the ideal of self-government.[59] Indeed it might have been expected that the entente at Lucknow would have had an immediate and decisive impact on government thinking. Among the lower reaches of officialdom, Hindu-Muslim co-operation seems to have been regarded—in the Panjab during the 1919 disturbances for example—with a mixture of suspicion, alarm and scepticism. But in the early months of 1917 Chelmsford continued to insist that the government could combat agitation only by formulating their own policy. His persistence emphasizes that discussions on reforms started before the nationalist upsurge and not in response to it.

Chelmsford went on believing that the declaration should be made by the Secretary of State so that it would be 'final and authoritative'. Later he was to admit: 'Perhaps if I possessed Hardinge's gift of honeyed phrase, which I do not, I might have staved off agitation for a while'; but he remained convinced that any statement he could have made would have been condemned as vague and taken on appeal to the Secretary of State.[60] He believed also that 'piecemeal publication' would not satisfy opinion but would give rise to demands for action on whatever was omitted —and give the impression, when further steps were announced, that the government were giving way under pressure and could be 'squeezed'.[61] A decision of the British Cabinet was therefore needed on the whole question of the reforms. Willingdon's approach would be both bad propaganda and bad policy. It was agreed in India that an announcement should be the first stage; but it was advocated for more or less different purposes.

In May 1917, when they heard that Chamberlain planned a committee of enquiry, the Government of India decided unanimously that it would not be safe to wait any longer for an announcement. The Russian Revolution had had an effect on India; and the Home Rule agitation was winning attention and raising expectations among those hitherto of less advanced views. To avoid further moderate defection, the Government of India asked the Secretary of State, in a telegram of 18 May, for permission to publish the explanation of the goal given in the 1916 reforms despatch. They proposed to announce that they intended to institute real and immediate reforms in local self-government and the public services, and to take steps towards the ultimate enlargement of the powers of the legislative councils. The intention was to recognize 'self-government within the Empire as a legitimate and praiseworthy aspiration deserving all encouragement', but to warn against 'revolutionary changes or rash experiments'. The government admitted that there 'must be honest differences of opinion as to the rate of progress', but wanted to oppose those who, in the official view, were unscrupulously placing 'before an ill-informed public a political programme impossible of early attainment'.[62]

The government had simplified their demands on the British Cabinet, but they had not been converted to Willingdon's idea of a declaration merely to combat agitation. They were not suggesting a *non possumus* statement: the goal was specifically to be linked to immediate advance in certain directions. But they were willing, as they had not been before, to announce the goal and the lines of advance at a time when for details they could only add (as they proposed to do) that proposals were being considered by the Secretary of State. Until May the government had been ignorant of the India Office reactions to their despatch—seven months had passed with little sign of progress—but they had expected a reply in the near future and therefore resisted local government demands for an announcement without details of reforms. Early in May, however, they were faced with the prospect of Chamberlain's committee of enquiry, and it became obvious that, if they continued to insist on announcing the goal and the reforms together, there would be no announcement for a long time, probably for several years. Thus, although the government did not like the Willingdon approach and had not abandoned their objectives,

they decided that they would have to issue a statement as a temporary stop-gap.[63] Thus, though the new agitation had not
prompted the official initiatives in 1916, it began to influence the
Government of India in the following year: they were alarmed in
that they could make no substantive response to 'extremist'
demands. Moreover, Indian expectations, which of course *had*
been one of the impulses behind the reform discussions, were in
danger from the current agitation of being raised unduly high,
for British purposes—it was necessary to keep them within limits
which bore some relation to what the government expected to be
able to concede. Chelmsford was aware that in detail the 1916
despatch was no longer adequate: 'I can only say,' he wrote to
Chamberlain early in May 1917, 'that having regard to the pace
the world is moving, it almost appears to me reactionary'.[64]
Clearly if the reforms were delayed too long, and the world continued to move, there would be little prospect of satisfying
Indian hopes.

After his wavering in 1916, the Secretary of State had remained
firmly opposed to any announcement of the goal. In April 1917
Meston had reported that the King was personally opposed to a
Royal Proclamation, feeling that he had been pestered enough as a
result of the last one in 1911; in addition the India Office was
apprehensive about *any* declaration.[65] Chamberlain shared the
view of an India Office memorandum, that 'Issues of high policy
must be settled before the formula can be touched'.[66] Thus he
refused to allow a unilateral declaration by the Government of
India; he insisted that the home government had to consider
the issues first. But at the same time, on 22 May, when first
putting forward his suggestion for a committee of enquiry, he
asked the British Cabinet to consider making 'some general
statement of . . . policy'.[67] He had begun to accept, faced with
entreaties from India, that a declaration was necessary—he had
been finally and, he said, 'reluctantly' converted to the idea. The
government's telegram of 18 May had apparently made up his
mind; he had also discussed the question with Meston, who
urged an announcement in a note of 21 May.[68] But Chamberlain
still did not favour an elaborate formula, believing this would
stimulate controversy. He wanted one to deal with policy not
the goal of government, and stipulating that the stages of any
advance must be at the discretion of the British. He had con-

sulted with Sinha, who had seemed willing to accept this last condition.[69]

In the following months Chelmsford repeated his demands, which became more and more strident. Early in June he urged an immediate announcement, if necessary along the lines of Chamberlain's proposal.[70] (He did not consider Chamberlain's formula to be very different from that of the Government of India—although he had hoped that the Secretary of State would find it easier to express the necessary qualifications in language 'which holds out a hope but which is free from ambiguity'.)[71] Chelmsford was ever more conscious of the rapidity of political change; early in July he wrote: 'It is at least doubtful now whether the proposals in our telegram of 18th May, which would have been effective six weeks or two months ago, are suitable under present conditions'.[72] The local governors were by now unanimous in demanding an early announcement. The internment of Annie Besant had resulted in an unexpected upsurge in the Home Rule movement;[73] in India, as in England, it was recognized that the report of the Mesopotamia Commission had had a 'disastrous' effect on the government's prestige. Meston reported that 'the air has never been thicker with suspicion'; he believed that 'the anti-Government and almost the anti-British feeling among the advanced party is stronger than I have ever seen it. Everything that we do is misrepresented. . . . The misunderstandings are spreading into wider circles . . .'.[74] For his part Chelmsford had clearly become very irritated at the delays in London. Almost a year later he reacted with irony to the memory of this period: Montagu had told him that Chamberlain regarded himself as the 'father and mother' of the reforms; Chelmsford was glad to hear it—perhaps, he suggested, it was 'the exercise of this dual function' which had prolonged 'the period of gestation almost to danger point'.[75]

Chamberlain circulated Chelmsford's repeated telegrams to the the Cabinet and urged immediate discussion of his own proposals.[76] The question went twice before the Cabinet (only once in the presence of the Prime Minister), but no decision was taken. By 5 July Chamberlain had abandoned hope of an early solution. He reported to Chelmsford however, that Lord Curzon, who at first had concurred in the suggestion of a committee of enquiry, at the second Cabinet had argued that Chamberlain had been too hasty in rejecting the Viceroy's invitation to visit India. Chamberlain had again argued against a visit by a Secretary of State, but had expressed his willingness to resign in order to become chairman of a commission. He had also expressed reluctance to take on himself the whole burden of such a momentous decision. Curzon had then pointed out that, if he went as Secretary of State, he would still have advisers associated with him—and the other members of the Cabinet, Chamberlain reported, had seemed to favour this idea.[77] Chelmsford was 'delighted' at this prospect.[78] But at the same time he set out a full account of his position. The home government, he insisted, should either give the Government of India a free hand, or state clearly that the solution of Indian problems must wait until after the war. He explained to Chamberlain in a letter of 7 July:

I would have made this suggestion before, but it never occurred to me that after our proposals were made, days would slip into weeks and weeks into months without a decision being reached. You must forgive me if I write strongly, but it is only natural that we should feel the position in which we are placed. We are a Government which does not govern, and inasmuch as I took up this question some 15 months ago with the very object of not being caught napping, it is the irony of fate that, when the crisis comes, I have perforce to remain silent. I hold strongly to the principle that you and I must be in complete accord and I have acted loyally on that principle, but from the public point of view I think it would have been almost better that I should have spoken out on my policy at the risk of being censured or recalled than that the Head of the Supreme Government here should appear in a position of hopeless indifference.[79]

Chelmsford now proposed a new formula for a declaration. He telegraphed to the Secretary of State suggesting the following wording:

His Majesty's Government, having considered the proposals of the Government of India, concur in the view of the Government of India that self-government within the Empire is the ultimate goal of British rule in India, but His Majesty's Government, in view of their many grave preoccupations arising out of the war, are unable at present to give consideration to the steps to be taken on the road to that goal. In these circumstances His Majesty's Government would impress on Indian politicians the desirability of patience and abstention from agitation, having in view the fact that the Empire is at the present moment in the throes of a great war.

At the request of the Viceroy, Mr. Chamberlain will visit India in the course of the next cold weather for the purpose of conferring with the Government of India and with representatives of different shades of opinion.[80]

In May the most likely prospect had been for a declaration on policy followed by a commission of enquiry. Now, once again, there was a chance that the procedure would be, as the Government of India wished, a declaration on the goal followed by a visit by the Secretary of State.

In July Chamberlain resigned as a result of the strictures of the Mesopotamia Commission on maladministration for which the Secretary of State was ultimately responsible. Chelmsford, both to Chamberlain and to the Prime Minister, immediately expressed, in addition to his regret, his concern for the fate of his policy. To Edwin Montagu, Chamberlain's successor, he offered his congratulations and at the same time stressed his hopes for an announcement and renewed his invitation to the Secretary of State to visit India. In August he reported a 'positive increase in urgency' and suggested yet another formula for a declaration—it followed roughly the lines proposed in July, expressing 'sympathy' for India's aspirations, but excluded any mention of the Secretary of State's visit. Chelmsford had modified his original stand: the positive advance, which had once been *sine qua non*, was now reduced to a promise to examine the first steps, postponed because of the war, 'at the very earliest opportunity'.[81] In effect his government were urging that the India Office should abandon their preferred order of procedure, and decide on the declaration before the policy. At the end of July a joint session of the Congress and the Muslim League under the presidency of Surendranath Banerjea, the 'moderate' leader, had endorsed a scheme of reforms calling for full legislative powers and elected majorities to be conceded to both the provincial and the imperial legislatures at the end of the war. They had also demanded a pronouncement on the goal of British policy, the publication of the Government of India proposals of 1916, and the reversal of the policy of repression (to be symbolized by the release of Annie Besant).[82] Opinion was coalescing against the government, and Chelmsford accordingly tried to streamline his demands in the hope of an immediate decision by the

British Cabinet. His government still maintained their view—as they explained on 12 August, 'A mere pronouncement as to the goal . . . would not . . . now meet the requirements of the case unless accompanied by some indications that an investigation will be undertaken as to the steps proposed in the immediate future for the attainment of the goal'.[83] In Chelmsford's formula these indications had appeared at their simplest, in the minimal form acceptable to the government, as a promise of 'the very earliest' examination. The government had moved a long way in their efforts to extract an announcement from the British Cabinet.

Chelmsford had asked Montagu, on 8 August, to impress on the Cabinet that political agitation made it 'imperative' to have an announcement before the end of August. The Viceroy's patience was at an end. His telegram, when read in conjunction with his letter of 7 July to Chamberlain (which would have been due to arrive in the India Office), was in essence an ultimatum. He explained further in a letter to Montagu on 7 August: if Montagu did not make 'some announcement . . . in the course of this month', Chelmsford warned, '. . . I shall have to speak very fully on our policy when I meet my Council'—the deadline was the opening of the imperial legislature on 5 September. 'I have endeavoured to act in strict loyalty to the Secretary of State and His Majesty's Government,' Chelmsford went on, echoing the passage in his letter of 7 July when he had written of speaking out at the risk of censure or recall, 'and I think I have a right to ask that we should not in consequence be left in the lurch.' Of course this fuller explanation did not arrive in London until after the Cabinet decision; but Montagu had already taken the point. He wrote to Curzon: 'I have had another telegram from Chelmsford and seen a pathetic letter from him to Chamberlain dated July 7th. It is really serious.'[84]

By the beginning of August the new Secretary of State had 'come to be eager' that the Cabinet would consent to his visiting India; and, pointing to the urgings of Indian officials, he sought to reverse the Cabinet decision that it was impossible 'in the midst of a great war to give adequate time and thought' to Indian reforms. 'I feel,' he wrote, 'that our duty to the Viceroy requires that he should be put in possession of a definite policy with which he and his Government can meet . . . the growing Indian "opposition".' 'We must endeavour,' he went on, 'to find some immediate announcement without prolonged discussion . . . or efforts to solve vastly complicated questions.'[85] Thus he endorsed the demand implicit in Chelmsford's pleas, and sought to reverse the India Office's order of procedure. He found the Cabinet 'awfully pre-occupied' and had to resist at least one attempt by Curzon to postpone discussion.[86] At last, however, on 14 August, the War Cabinet approved both a declaration and a visit to India. Montagu had accepted Chelmsford's view and strongly advocated a visit rather than a commission—he indicated how 'abhorrent' the latter would be by citing draft terms of reference which Chamberlain had suggested. (Chamberlain now agreed.) Montagu had supported the India Government also by arguing that the declaration must include some promise of immediate action. His proposed formula had included some words of Chamberlain's, 'the gradual development of free institutions', but otherwise was based broadly on the India suggestions; and, though the Cabinet changed the wording, they accepted Montagu's proposals in substance.[87]

The Government of India did not of course figure prominently in this final stage, but there can be little doubt that their protests (once allied with Montagu's advocacy) played an important part in persuading the Cabinet to act. Moreover, because of Montagu's reversal of the usual order of precedure, only the wording, not the principle of the declaration was debated. Two important ideas were stressed. First, the words 'responsible government' were introduced. Though 'responsibility' had been emphasized already in various senses by many who were party to the discussions (Chamberlain, Lord Islington, Philip Kerr and Montagu), the term in the declaration could have only one meaning: government by ministers who commanded a majority in the legislature. Yet the Cabinet used the words to cover (as Lloyd George explained) what Curzon had meant by self-government in one of his minutes. Curzon had accepted that, after 'the area in which self-government exists' had been extended 'step by step', there would come a time when 'Indian opinion, trained and moulded by experience, will have a predominant influence in the administration of the country'. What he did not mean was that India would ever be 'a single autonomous . . . political unit, in which Indians will be universally substituted for British administrators'.[88] Thus, the Cabinet were promising self-government but not independence and to make this clear they spoke of 'responsible government', which, being by ministers and necessarily (they thought) in smaller areas, would allow a permanent British suzerainty. The Cabinet were virtually repeating the idea put forward from India in 1916.

Second, the Cabinet promised the 'progressive' realization of this goal. Thus they endorsed Chelmsford's insistence on immediate first steps, but also by implication the India Office interpolation that there should be a partial transfer of responsibility. It is very unlikely that this is what the Cabinet intended: it was a product of Montagu's mode of procedure. The word 'progressive' was an unconsidered addition in the dying stages of the meeting. But Chelmsford, in particular, concluded that it could imply some temporary division of provincial responsibilities; Montagu, believing such an advance desirable, did nothing to disabuse him. He professed to believe that the formula probably committed the British to 'some form of Parliamentary institutions', though he did not point this out to the Cabinet. Curzon hoped that in India Montagu would 'not in any way give away the show', whereas Montagu by his own interpretation did not see that he had any choice.[89]

If there were ever any doubt that 1917 had seen (in Craddock's phrase) 'the parting of the ways', it was to be dispelled in 1918, when Chamberlain pointed out in a Cabinet minute that the Declaration had been a revolution: he explicitly repudiated the earlier stance of the British in India, and declared, of Crewe's statement of 1913, that 'no more shortsighted declaration of policy was ever made unless it be Lord Morley's expressed belief that the reforms associated with his name offered a permanent resting place for the Government of India'.[90] Craddock also saw to the heart of the matter in 1918; he wrote to Curzon, as Montagu and Chelmsford were completing their report based on the Declaration, 'Nothing hitherto done gave away *control* though it afforded opportunities for advice and, incidentally, for opposition'.[91]

On the reforms, therefore, the main effect of the Declaration was to consolidate and continue the change already admitted by Chamberlain. By his suggestion that it was essential to invest Indian representatives with 'some real responsibility for their actions', Chamberlain restricted the manner in which the legislative councils could be reformed, and ruled out most of the current suggestions for advance. G. K. Gokhale, in his 'political testament', recommended an arrangement whereby the Government of India would relinquish much of their control over the provincial governments, which would be reconstructed so as to give a greater voice to the tax-payers: each local government, made up of an appointed executive of governor, three Europeans and three Indians, would have independent financial powers and complete charge of the province's internal administration; each legislative council, four-fifths elected, would have to pass all legislation including the provincial budget—the governor would retain a power of veto, and reserve legislative powers would be invested in an enlarged 'Legislative Assembly of India' in which the official majority would be retained. But the government would not be responsible to the legislature, so that elected members would have greater powers but still no responsibility—this scheme did not satisfy Chamberlain's criterion. Neither did the Nineteen Members' or the Congress-League schemes, which were based on Gokhale's proposals.[92]

One of the current suggestions did meet Chamberlain's requirements. It had been evolved by the Round Table group; this, founded by members of Milner's 'kindergarten' to study imperial problems, had turned its attention to India after the 1911 Durbar, with a view to deciding how India could be accommodated in a scheme for imperial federation.[93] In 1915 Lionel Curtis had completed the first two volumes of his study of the 'Imperial Problems' and had begun to draft chapters on the future of India. With the permission of Chamberlain, he had discussions with friends of official experience; a group of these agreed to work out a constitutional scheme. In March 1916, Chelmsford, who had returned to Britain before taking up the viceroyalty, made contact with Curtis and his group through Philip Kerr, who was a Round Table member and later one of Lloyd George's secretaries. Chelmsford himself had known at least one of the Milner kindergarten at All Souls, Oxford, years before.[94] At Chelmsford's request in 1916 the group had showed him the results of their discussions, and indeed his initial policy may have owed something to this meeting, if we are to believe Curtis's account rather than Chelmsford's—for Curtis claimed that there was 'a notion current' among the members that a pronouncement on the goal should be accompanied by 'certain definite steps' taken at once. Curtis, too, changed his mind as Chelmsford did, and by May

1917 was urging a separate announcement at the earliest possible
moment. He too envisaged some permanent British control; he
spelt out that it should concern the frontier.[95]

Certainly the Round Table group had an intimate and continuing influence on policy-makers, especially Chelmsford and
Meston. Kerr sent the Viceroy in May 1916 an amplified version
of the memorandum which it was proposed to circulate among
Round Table members. Chelmsford asked that it should not be
circulated, in view of his government's discussions, but he did
present it to his Council for consideration and sent it confiden-
tially to all local governments.[96] The novel aspect of the Round
Table plan was the idea of 'dyarchy', of dividing the administration on the basis of reserved and transferred subjects, the former
to be handled in the old way, with the legislature only advising,
and the latter to be handled in a parliamentary way, with direct
legislative control. Two governments—two separate types of
administration—would then exist side by side. When he first
encountered this idea, Chelmsford found it 'singularly fascinating'.
But the Government of India did not favour it. Chelmsford
claimed: 'I only realized its difficulties when I listened to the
scheme being riddled by the criticism of my colleagues'.[97]

But when Sir William Duke, himself a Round Table member,
introduced the idea into official circles, and first Chamberlain and
then (indirectly) the War Cabinet endorsed it, the whole perspective rapidly changed. Obviously the Indian legislatures could
be given responsibility as well as power only if their resolutions
were made binding on a government whose members were drawn
from and responsible to them. But it was not thought feasible to
grant them such control over the whole spectrum of provincial
administration. A half-way position had to be found; and this
meant 'dyarchy' or some other form of governmental dualism.
After the Declaration, the officials, who had 'riddled' the Round
Table scheme with criticism, promptly ordered forty extra copies.
During 1917, therefore, the Curtis plan gained support. It already
had its advocates, of course, and had influenced Chamberlain's
thinking. Sinha, when Chamberlain consulted him in May before
making his suggestion, had endorsed the dualist principle by suggesting that certain heads, such as education, public works or
forests, should be placed under the control of reorganized pro-
provincial councils which would also retain advisory functions

in matters reserved to the government as 'vital to the safety of India'. In April Sinha had spent an evening discussing Indian problems with Meston, Bikaner and a Round Table group.[98] About the same time, Islington had sent Chamberlain a letter which had been written in March by Bhupendranath Basu and which also suggested 'a division of functions' and a partial change-over to ministerial government if a total transfer of the provincial administration were not possible. Basu had not advocated this at the end of 1915. He had been talking to Lionel Curtis in Delhi.[99]

Chamberlain's suggestion was, therefore, a hesitant step to-wards the endorsement of dualism as presented to him by Duke, Sinha and Basu. Other people began to consider alternative ways of meeting his conditions. Meston favoured an idea, which was advocated in slightly different forms also by Kerr and Curtis—a true 'dyarchy' whereby some responsibility would be devolved upon new legislatures for areas smaller than the present provinces, with the existing governments and councils retained for reserved subjects.[100] Lord Islington, the Under-Secretary, caution taking him in another direction, suggested that it might be sufficient to associate the Indian representatives with the government, perhaps by Standing Committees for different departments, and to intro-duce responsibility in some informal way by the proper choice of two Indians among a total of four Executive Councillors, and by placing the onus upon the legislature for any policy change made in deference to its wishes.[101] This sort of thinking, once it had to be translated into a specific proposal, could only lead nearer to the suggestions of Sinha and Basu.

Arguments for the partial delegation of powers met with a re-sponse also in the Government of India. Chelmsford had admitted that the Round Table proposals, although opposed by his Council, did reach the 'kernel' of the problem as presented by Cham-berlain.[102] Moreover, as early as June 1917, Sir Claude Hill, who from the first had advocated some transfer of power over the budgets and the inclusion of one elected member in the provincial Executive Councils, had recommended giving 'certain real powers of control, in some of the provinces, to responsible Ministers selected from among the elected representatives' as the persons most likely to command a following. He did not approve of dyarchy proper, the suggestion of the Round Table that the government itself should be divided, the ministers taking responsibility only for transferred subjects: Hill felt that the executive council would have to act collectively and that a minister, although put in control of certain departments, would have to resign if he could not support government policy in regard to any department. Hill proposed that the budget would be voted on by the legislature, subject to a power of veto and to the maintenance of appropriations for essential services. He suggested that an additional safeguard might be provided by the establishment in the advanced provinces (where the changes were proposed) of second chambers, one third nominated and two-thirds elected, enjoying the same rights as the legislative councils except for budgetary control, and providing a role for aristocratic and conservative interests otherwise underrepresented in terms of their importance.[103] It might have been argued that such chambers would also have reassured the landed classes and their friends among the officials—as Chelmsford reported in August 1917, zamindari associations in Madras, the United Provinces and Sind had passed resolutions which reflected the fear that they were about to be handed over to *Vakil raj*.[104]

Undoubtedly, and quite apart from Chamberlain's dictum, the Government of India by the second half of 1917 were ready to contemplate further advances, not necessarily as suggested by Hill, but certainly in the direction of further concessions to the legislative councils. In May Chelmsford reported his colleagues steadfast in the view of the 1916 reforms despatch, that the sphere of advance should be in local self-government and the public services.[105] Early in August he wrote to Montagu that 'what would have satisfied six months ago will not give satisfaction now, and similarly what will suffice now will be useless six months hence': the reason, he claimed, was the situation created by political agitators.[106] In that month a majority at a conference of forty-three Congress delegates, foreshadowing Gandhi, voted in favour of the immediate adoption of passive resistance—the withdrawal of all non-official Indians from all forms of public work connected with the government.[107]

There were of course objections to the sort of advance that was being contemplated. These were of two types, one conservative, the other practical. Both were to be ignored. Thus Sir Michael O'Dwyer complained in May that there seemed to be a danger that the reforms would be based on the expediency of satisfying politicians, and would disregard 'the views and needs of the solid masses'. But Meston, in a minute written in October 1917, explained: 'We must have a profound belief that the placid pathatic [sic] contentment of the masses is not the soil in which Indian nationhood will grow, and that in disturbing it we are working for India's ultimate good.' On the other hand, Meston, in this same minute, argued that it was impossible as yet to advance in the councils and made his suggestion for total self-government at a level below the provincial one. There was, he claimed, no half-way position between executive and popular control, for in any mixed system one side would have to give way when conflict arose: if it was to be the legislature then the concessions were a sham; if it was to be the government then home rule had already been attained. Meston opposed the various schemes which suggested partial devolution to the councils. Becoming converted to a line first put forward by W. S. Marris in his letter to Malcolm Seton at the India Office, Meston now asserted: 'An independent legislature and an irremoveable executive are utterly incompatible.' He thought it impossible to have (or in these schemes to avoid) an executive responsible to London and a legislature responsible to the electorate; it was equally impossible to have (or avoid) 'a distribution of power which enables the legislature to paralyse the executive, but never to remove it'.[108] To this logical and practical objection, Hill's and all such dualistic proposals had no answer.

Yet, as Meston had also insisted on an earlier occasion, it was impossible to stand still. The government had to respond to the changing political situation. After the August Declaration, the immediate danger of passive resistance passed—the proposal was not endorsed by the full Congress.[109] But Indian demands were unabated: the government had to go some way towards meeting them. Indeed the demands were increasing: all the time the government had to go further. Even Meston's scheme of local parliaments was to be a casualty—in its refusal to change the provincial councils it had too much of the appearance of standing still. The Declaration, therefore, found the Government of India ready to contemplate an increase in the powers of the legislative councils, an advance which they had condemned as premature and inappropriate. Chelmsford still insisted that they 'must not be oblivious of considerations of safety'.[110] But his recognition that 'the world has moved' and his implicit admission that the British proposals must remain within reaching distance of Indian demands, were enough to ensure that as time went on his position would also move and he would be prepared to recommend larger concessions. Meston argued, in a private letter to Chelmsford, 'a year ago, the enlargement and popularization of the Legislative Councils . . . seemed as much as we could hope to accomplish and as much as thinking India would expect'. But the position had greatly changed since then, both inside and outside India; and 'power without responsibility has been pushed into the region of the impossible'.[111] In September Chelmsford admitted that with the developments in the situation it was now possible that they would have to consider some transfer of power.[112]

The Declaration had laid down the direction of the advance. Chelmsford concluded (not altogether wrongly) that the use of the term 'responsible government' was an endorsement of the consideration put forward by Chamberlain: the Declaration had ruled out 'power without responsibility'. The Government of India's reaction was to reopen the question with the local governments. They circulated various reforms schemes—the proposals of Curtis, Gokhale, the Nineteen Members, the Congress and League, and other suggestions by Jinnah and the Aga Khan. Sir Claude Hill's note (slightly altered and redated 7 September) was also sent out for comment, although it had not been discussed in the Viceroy's Council. Hill added to his note an assessment of the August Declaration: he had claimed that the government in their despatch of November 1916 had 'definitely abandoned the position that legislative Councils are not to develop into Parliamentary institutions'; the Declaration, he now added, had made a final decision on this issue, and thus all proposals for reform had to suggest machinery suitable, or capable of being developed, for a parliamentary system.[113]

The long-delayed reply to the despatch of 1916 bore out this interpretation of the Declaration. At the end of September, the report of a second special India Office committee, under Sir William Duke, had complained of the failure of the existing constitution to provide for responsibility or administrative experience in the legislatures, and had recommended by a majority that, while as yet no form of responsibility of the executive to the legislature should be applied, the provincial councils should be allowed 'a definite measure of influence, leading up to eventual control' over portions of the budget and over such subjects as roads, minor irrigation, public health, local self-government, elementary education and excise.[114] The India Office despatch of 19 October 1917, replying to that of the Government of India almost a year before, in the main approved of the advances proposed in local self-government and the public services, but rejected the suggestions for the legislative councils: the scheme of 1916 gave 'weapons of opposition and offence' but no responsibility in matters of finance and administration. The Secretary of State asked how political training was to be achieved without such responsibility, and stated that one of the principles of the Declaration was that progress must take place 'by the progressive development of self-governing institutions'.[115]

Chelmsford was later to claim privately that Montagu had entered the reforms discussions 'at a moment when the policy was more or less cut and dried: it only wanted to be developed in detail'.[116] It is easy to see how he came to this conclusion: the central feature of the reforms was the acceptance of the idea of dualism. From Chelmsford's viewpoint this must have seemed to have come at the end of the line of development which had begun when his Council first tried to relate their proposals to the goal of self-government; which had been greatly extended by Chamberlain's endorsement of the objections to power without responsibility and through the rapid changes in the political situation; and which had only culminated and been confirmed in the Declaration of 1917 and the Secretary of State's despatch. In fact of course no decision had been taken before Montagu's arrival in India; but the main criteria for that decision had been established, the main objections had been canvassed, and the main alternatives presented.

Chapter 4. First Steps

ON 10 November 1917 Montagu arrived in Bombay. After spending some weeks in Delhi, he and the Viceroy began a series of formal hearings of local opinion in Calcutta, Madras and Bengal. These were followed by consultations with the local governments and the Government of India in Delhi early in the new year.[1] In the Indian press the Declaration had been received generally favourably, if without enthusiasm.[2] The Secretary of State's visit itself was intended and arranged as a public relations gesture.[3] Montagu suggested, and Chelmsford agreed, that they should receive deputations formally in public and in some cases follow this with private discussions *in camera.* The desire for full consultation was stressed in the government's communique calling for deputations.[4] Chelmsford sent a circular to heads of provinces urging that 'It is all-important that the interests of every class . . . should be represented'—local governments were to point out the need for action to any important group that was not alive to the needs of the situation.[5] The Home Department also stressed that local governments, while keeping numbers to a manageable size, should take a liberal view in allowing representations.[6] Montagu was at first distressed by the brevity and formality of the meetings with deputations, and even suspected that the Government of India were trying to hurry him out of the country. But, unlike the Secretary of State, the Government of India had realized that the interviews must be dealt with quickly: as it was, Montagu as well as Chelmsford 'almost danced for joy' when the meetings were finally over, and Montagu was later to try to resist Chelmsford's repeated urgings that he should not set a time limit for his departure but should stay until their work was finished.[7]

Opinion in England also had to be cared for, and Montagu wished to associate representatives of conservative and liberal opinion with his mission. Thus, he was accompanied by Lord Donoughmore and Charles Roberts, M.P., in addition to Duke and Seton of the India Office, and, at Chelmsford's suggestion, Bhupendranath Basu, newly appointed to the Secretary of State's Council.[8] In a different way, Chelmsford too sought to take care of important opinion in Britain—he wrote to Curzon, Chamberlain and Lord Selborne, warning that dyarchy was inevitable but, to Curzon, predicting that changes would not be too far reaching.[9]

The idea of an extensive report was, according to Chelmsford, his own. He had, he claimed, 'sketched in broad outline' to W. S. Marris, the draftsman, his idea of 'what shape the Report should take', before Montagu arrived: Chelmsford wanted something weighty to support their proposals.[10] The Montagu-Chelmsford Report, therefore, devoted the first of two parts to a critical survey of earlier constitutional developments; here the central and repeated theme was the inadequacy of the Morley-Minto reforms.[11] The conclusion, shorn of the diplomatic language of the Report, was foreshadowed in Chelmsford's letter to Curzon in November 1917: 'The truth is,' Chelmsford wrote, 'the millstone of the Morley-Minto reforms is round our necks. If it were in the region of practical politics to abandon the present line of advance, I doubt whether there would be a single individual who would say no.'[12] Montagu and Chelmsford had considered possibilities of 'wiping out' the Morley–Minto reforms and 'making a new start', but they felt that they had no alternative, for practical and political reasons, but to follow the path already set out.[13] The grounds for the Report's rejection of the Morley-Minto reforms were strongly influenced by what might be called the United Provinces' attitude —at several points Marris's drafting reflected or quoted Meston's minute of October 1917, which analysed the political situation and the reasons for and the line of advance in terms similar to those of the Report. Indeed in one key passage the Report echoed Meston's minute without acknowledging it—the Report stated, almost in Meston's words, 'We believe profoundly that . . . the placid, pathetic contentment of the masses is not the soil on which . . . Indian nationhood will grow, and that in deliberately disturbing it, we are working for her highest good'.[14]

Chamberlain's letters and the August Declaration convinced Chelmsford that some sort of dualism would be needed in the provinces.[15] The method by which this was to be achieved was also substantially formulated, in spite of the impression given by Montagu's *Indian Diary*, by the India Office committee set up by Montagu under Sir William Duke before the Secretary of State left England. Duke's report was notable as we have seen, for the important suggestion that some subjects—sanitation, local communications, local self-government, health, elementary education, and excise—might be transferred to the control of legislatures with small elected majorities, and that the legislatures should vote the provincial budgets subject to powers for restoring or maintaining expenditure for reserved subjects.[16] All the schemes seriously considered in India were variants of this idea. By the time he was ready to start discussions in Delhi in November Montagu had decided that the elected majorities would have to be substantial and suggested that the future modifications to the reserved and transferred lists should be effected by 'enabling bills' in the Government of India, subject to seven-yearly statutory enquiries.[17]

Various means of partially transferring responsibility were canvassed. Two variants of one—suggesting divisional or sub-provincial councils dealing with transferred subjects, and advocated chiefly by Lionel Curtis and the United Provinces under Meston—were discussed and ruled out in the Report, as politically inadequate and confusing controversial geographical adjustments with constitutional upheaval.[18] The other possibilities were to transfer powers either to a separate body at the provincial level— a lower house, or an assembly beside the existing councils—or to a modified single legislature which would also retain advisory functions in relation to reserved subjects. The Report favoured the latter: the legislature as a whole was to vote on the transferred subjects and on the budget, subject to the government's restorative powers for reserved allotments, but legislation for reserved subjects, if the government were to certify it as essential to law and order or the proper discharge of its duty, was to be dealt with by an advisory grand committee drawn from the legislature but retaining a bare majority for the government.[19] The legislative councils were also to be made more representative by the establishment of direct election on the basis of territorial constituencies, except possibly (and reluctantly) for Muslims and Sikhs where they were in a minority. The details of the franchise as well as of the transferred list were to be referred to separate committees of enquiry.[20] In all provinces (the Report recommended) government was to be conducted by an Executive Council of one service and one Indian member, and by a Minister or Ministers appointed from the legislature—it was to be government in two halves, one for reserved and one for transferred subjects, but (echoing

Hill's minute of June 1917) the halves were to associate and deliberate as a whole, only the voting being separate according to subject. The whole government was to decide on the budget, the governor adjudicating in any difference of opinion.[21] Originally Montagu had been prepared to delay the transfer of executive powers to ministers until the third legislative council after the reforms (after six years) when the presumption would have been that all subjects would have been transferred in the provinces unless cause was shown why some should be reserved. Meston and others had preferred the immediate transfer of a more limited number (as originally suggested by Duke's committee), and the Viceroy's Council, divided on this issue, had preferred to leave the question until local governments and public opinion had shown their preferences: in the end it was decided to give less sooner.[22]

This dualism in the provincial governments was the distinctive feature of the reforms: there are several points worthy of emphasis. It is right to stress that the idea of dualism was not new, but that it was a logical outcome of Chelmsford's questions plus the India Office addition. Progressively larger and larger concessions were proposed as the next step even after Montagu's arrival in India, but from 1916 the line of advance had been seen consistently (if at first imperfectly) as the development of responsible institutions. Moreover if this had not been the case, it is doubtful if the August Declaration would have been interpreted as it was by the reformers —Chelmsford, the Government of India, Duke, Meston, Montagu. On the other hand, it is also true that the August Declaration needed to be translated into action, and that the interpretation at this time was itself important. Later, officials and observers professed to interpret the Declaration in ways which excluded dyarchy or any transfer of responsibility; the promise of the Declaration was preserved because Montagu and Chelmsford chose not to interpret it in this negative way.

It has been generally assumed that the engineer of the dualist interpretation was Montagu; but it is probable that this idea is false. There were two factors influencing Montagu and Chelmsford: the historical consideration of Chamberlain's and the Round Table's tentative steps towards dyarchy; and the logical consideration that the progressive realization of responsible government could be achieved only by partial transfers of power. But, if we look more closely at the form of the transfer we may see that it corresponds closely to Chelmsford's definition of 'responsible government'; namely, government in which Indians should be able to say, and be known to have said, 'yes' or 'no' on specific policies, and not government in which formal responsibility of ministers to the legislature obtained—for the Indian ministers, though drawn from legislature, were at first to be guaranteed their appointments for the life of each council (their salaries were to be a reserved subject).[23] The Government of India were very early convinced that dyarchy could not be avoided. They endorsed the idea in a circular letter to the local governments on 11 December 1917—they put forward various methods of obtaining some dualism and sought advice not on the principle but on the scheme which produced fewest problems.[24] Montagu's *Indian Diary*, if read carelessly, might give the impression that he was compaigning for the acceptance of dyarchy, not his preferred means of achieving it. In fact there was no argument among the reformers about dyarchy itself: Montagu was its advocate but had no need to be its defender. As for his way of achieving it, the *Diary* records that in December 1917 Montagu found Chelmsford 'a much more eager convert'. than he was himself: 'I am doubtful about it,' Montagu noted, 'because some people really feel they are not ready for any responsibility.'[25]

The concomitant of progressive transfer of power was progressive devolution to the provinces. This subject too was hardly a new one, and two main rival schemes for financial devolution were in existence before Montagu and Chelmsford began their investigations. Both of these sought to do away with heads of revenue which were divided between the central and the provincial governments, in order that the budgets at each level could be quite independent. The scheme formulated by W. S. Meyer and H. F. Howard envisaged a complicated system of transfers of formerly divided heads, with fixed proportions of income tax and revenue payable to the central government, and subsequent provincial adjustments. Its rival, devised by J. B. Brunyate, proposed that all divided revenue should become provincial, though collected at standard rates fixed by the Government of India, and that fixed cash contributions should be made to the central government. The problem with any scheme was that very different patterns of expenditure and sources of revenue (notably the permanent settlement in Bengal and Bihar) were found in different provinces, so that any standardized system worked to the disadvantage of one province or another. Chelmsford had asked Montagu to consider, before he arrived in India, how this difficulty could be overcome, and also what corresponding relaxations would be possible in the Secretary of State's control over the Government of India. In January 1918 the finance question was placed before a sub-committee of Duke, Meston and Meyer; the Report adopted a modified version of the Brunyate scheme.[26]

On the wider issues of financial supervision the Government of India had in effect adopted the general principles of a note prepared by Sir L. Abrahams after discussions in the India Office— these amounted to allowing the provinces a certain limited increase in financial independence.[27] Again, on the broad question of legislative and administrative control, the Government of India had begun investigations among their departments on the possibility for a general relaxation (following conclusions in the Viceroy's Council that this was desirable)—the government circulated an office memorandum on 12 November 1917, the day after Montagu's consultations first began in Delhi.[28] Chelmsford favoured the retention of all the *statutory* powers of intervention enjoyed by the central government, with relaxations to be introduced by convention; Montagu wanted statutory changes to limit the central authority. The Report adopted Chelmsford's view: Montagu had decided he was ill-equipped to argue the question with lawyers like Chelmsford and Lowndes, and it was agreed that Lowndes should draft the relevant paragraph (212) in the Report.[29] Thus, for devolution as for dyarchy, the reforms discussions in India led to results within principles discussed earlier, and in accordance with the preferences of the Government of India.

The agreement in general on the provincial measures did not extend to the question of the Government of India and the Imperial Legislative Council. In December 1917 the Viceroy's Council refused to accept a paragraph introduced by Montagu, Duke and Seton into the Home Department's circular on reforms. The government claimed that their objection was to committing themselves before they had considered Montagu's proposed changes; but the disagreement soon proved to be more substantial: the Government of India considered that no extensive changes were needed in the central government at this stage. Montagu persuaded them that they must agree to some revision. The Report envisaged, therefore, that the Legislative Council would be replaced by a Legislative Assembly of 100 members with a large, preferably directly-elected majority, and a Council of State with a membership of 21 elected members, 4 nominated non-officials and not more than 25 nominated officials, excluding the Governor-General as President. Both chambers were to have full legislative powers, disputes to be resolved by joint sessions, except that the government would retain the power to reserve bills or amendments for decision in the Council of State in matters certified as essential to the interests of peace and order or good government. The budget was not to be voted, but, as in the provinces (though in this case with more limited functions), standing committees were to be associated with some government departments. Chelmsford and his Council had fought Montagu at every stage. They were eager that the imperial legislature should be made more representative, but unwilling for it to have wider powers. Gradually they conceded the bicameral principle, with an elected majority in the Assembly; Montagu agreed not to insist on an elected majority in the upper house, and it was decided that official and non-official members should be equal in number. As late as 20 February, however, Chelmsford was still trying to persuade Montagu not to include the central changes as an essential part of their proposals, and not until 6 March was the scheme of the Report accepted by the Government of India.[30]

On 15 March Montagu tried to reopen the question with an onslaught on compulsory voting by officials, and a proposal that the reserve powers of the Government of India should be vested, not in the official *bloc* of the Council of State, but in restorative powers for the Viceroy alone. Chelmsford had already allowed officials to vote on occasions as they pleased, and proposed to extend this in practice after the reforms to cover all but essential matters. But neither the Viceroy nor his Council would countenance the complete abolition of official voting. Montagu's '*adlati*' refused to support him on this issue, which developed into a 'great row' with Chelmsford, and the Secretary of State withdrew. The Montagu-Chelmsford Report recommended the proposal suggested by the Viceroy.[31] Thus, although they had had to agree to changes at the centre, the Government of India had not been forced to abandon any principle. The Report stated as general

criteria that the earlier steps towards responsible government
should be in the provinces, and that the Government of India
must remain wholly responsible to Parliament, with its authority
in essential matters indisputable.[32] These principles—the same as
those set out by Claude Hill in 1916—would not have seemed out
of place in the Government of India's despatch in November
of that year.

The assessment of the relative contributions of Montagu and
Chelmsford to the reforms has been prejudiced by the publication
of Montagu's *Indian Diary*. In several respects this is an unsatisfactory source. Its subject is the preparation and writing of the
Report: it omits the role of Chelmsford in beginning discussions on
the goal or in urging reforms (although at one point, recording a
discussion with a journalist who attributed all to the Secretary of
State, Montagu stressed Chelmsford's early contributions).[33] It
also makes no attempt to deal with the crucial decisions of the
period before Montagu's arrival in India. Moreover, not only is
the *Diary* the impressions of one man; it is also more than usually
distorted by circumstances: Montagu was writing or dictating
hurriedly at the end of long tiring days, often in bad health, with a
fever particularly bad in the evenings, and his opinions were
deliberately immediate and not considered. Thus the impression
given by the *Diary* is often intemperate and sometimes contradictory—for example Montagu strongly condemned Chelmsford's
formality with deputations on one day, and on another recorded
his tactful handling of Annie Besant.[34] Finally the *Diary* is concerned chiefly with recording Montagu's impressions and proposals: it mentions Chelmsford's disagreements, but rarely gives
a positive indication of the Viceroy's position.

Montagu praised Chelmsford for keeping the peace between
them: the rarity of their quarrels he attributed entirely to Chelmsford's personality, patience, self-control and receptiveness.
Chelmsford too found the degree of accord rather than the few
disagreements remarkable.[35] At the same time and on other occasions, Montagu criticized Chelmsford's lack of constructiveness:
soon after his arrival in India, Montagu complained that Chelmsford never expressed an opinion without consulting his Council.[36]
When, a month later, he made this criticism to Chelmsford himself, the Viceroy replied that he was not, like Montagu, independent:
he had colleagues and he was right to try to carry them with him

if he could.[37] Chelmsford interpreted his role later, in a letter to
Chamberlain: '. . . I had the responsibility of keeping the peace
and bringing the jarring elements together. Though the Report
is his [Montagu's] and mine, its proposals are, I may say, practically the accepted proposals of my colleagues and his.'[38] There is
no indication of this in the *Diary*, other than Montagu's final tribute. The original opposition and final agreement of Chelmsford's
colleagues are recorded without any indication of attempts by the
Viceroy to secure unanimity. Indeed, Montagu had some criticisms of Chelmsford's handling of his Council—on two occasions
he felt Chelmsford had been unhelpful through his failure to prepare the members by giving them full details: he had not made it
clear to them that in his first scheme Montagu intended the presumption to be that all subjects would be transferred in the provinces after the end of the third council unless the government
could show cause for reservation; and he did not inform them of
Montagu's designs on the Government of India and his idea for a
Council of State. It is difficult not to assume that these omissions
were a deliberate tactic, especially as Montagu admitted that the
Viceroy had out-manoeuvred him on the first of these occasions,
and also earlier by becoming a firm advocate of the revised provincial scheme about which Montagu had come to have some
doubts.[39] On one occasion Montagu complained that he had to
spend his time lobbying Chelmsford's colleagues, 'a task he ought
to do himself'. It is fair to suggest that Montagu was lobbying for
his own scheme, which would have been Chelmsford's 'task' if
he had approved. (Montagu made this complaint at a time when
Chelmsford had expressed his opposition to several features of
Montagu's proposals.)[40]

While the draft Report was being revised by Montagu, Chelmsford, Duke, Lowndes, Roberts and Marris, the Viceroy set himself up as a judge, making few positive suggestions but adjudicating
between the often warring elements of Secretary of State and draftsman.[41] This summed up Chelmsford's role—from the first Montagu had complained, with reference to the formulation of proposals,
'It is I that have got to do this thing . . .'.[42] It was thus valid and
understandable for Montagu to criticize Chelmsford's lack of
imagination in regard to details and expedients. Of course this
was partly a question of personality and aptitude. But Chelmsford could not have acted both as protagonist for particular schemes

and as adjudicator; and it was by choosing or pretending to be 'impartial'—which meant working as the representative of a government, not as an individual—that Chelmsford made sure of getting the reforms he wanted.

A comparison between the Home Department circular of 11 December 1917 and the Montagu-Chelmsford Report reveals a large degree of parity between the two. This is no measure of relative influence because of course Montagu was consulted on the circular. What the circular does represent is the level of advance which the Government of India were prepared formally to recommend; and its parity with the Report is in this sense significant. Nothing came of many of Montagu's ideas. We have seen that on no issue of importance did the Report go beyond not just what Chelmsford was, but what the Government of India were prepared to concede. Noteworthy also is Montagu's reaction when the consultations were concluded—before he was reconciled by the satisfaction of being involved in drafting what is a most persuasive and elegantly expressed Report. He complained (my emphasis): 'I have *come to an agreement with the Government of India* which nobody accepts. . . . where I fear that my own proposals may have been spoiled is in my desperate endeavour to find compromises at every stage.'[43]

This is not to deny that Montagu's pressure moved the government further than they might otherwise have gone: rather it is to point out that the Government of India effectively set the limits for the Report's proposals. This was in part the product of Chelmsford's interpretation of his role, his standpoint as a 'constitutional' governor. Its future importance was that it provided weighty endorsement for the Montagu-Chelmsford scheme, endorsement that was to prove invaluable for combating an intractable opposition among the local governors. The significance of Chelmsford's role, preempting criticism, may be judged from a remark of Lord Stamfordham: 'Even some . . . who are favourable to it [the Report] rather deprecate the Viceroy's having associated himself . . ., and wish he had remained with his Government, as it were, outside, with an open mind and as a friendly critic'. Thus there were two roles: that of Montagu, with his flair for hitting upon expedients to carry out agreed changes, and that of Chelmsford, with his more 'prosaic' ability to keep the peace and secure agreement.[44]

The picture given by the *Indian Diary* is thus misleading: Montagu did not wage war when he was in India, making a series of successful forays against the collective enemy—Chelmsford, the Government of India especially Meyer, the local governors, Marris, Vincent. Rather he put forward expedients for achieving agreed ends, which were scrutinized by the 'experts', led by Chelmsford, and approved or rejected. In positive details, in fertility of mind, Montagu's achievement was very great. In determining the extent of the advance, even in principle for the central arrangements over which Montagu forced major concessions, Chelmsford and his colleagues had matters much their own way. This is not to minimize either contribution: it is to describe them.

Montagu's first moves on returning to London, were to secure the support of the Council of India, and (on 29 May) to ask the Cabinet to agree to the immediate publication of the Montagu-Chelmsford Report. For the time the Cabinet were too occupied with war matters.[45] The Government of India, too, considered the Report. Their despatch of 1918 recorded that the proposals, although the responsibility of the Report's signatories, had been 'framed after prolonged discussion' with the Viceroy's Council—there were, they admitted, no doubt detailed recommendations on which some of them had divergent views, but they wished to convey 'cordial support to the general policy' of the Report.[46] Montagu was disappointed with this despatch, but Chelmsford explained that his problem had been to get a consensus between Vincent and Nair—Vincent, in Chelmsford's view, had been difficult because he felt slighted by the rejection of a chapter he had drafted for the Report, because he was strained and overworked, and because he was asked to agree to a cordial despatch just after the Delhi War Conference 'at which he had behaved foolishly' and knew it.[47]

Montagu, about the same time, began to have his own troubles with Lord Curzon who considered the Report 'a confused document' ('only the manner of the grand Mogul', commented Montagu), and who, though agreeing generally to its publication, suggested in May that some of it might first have to be omitted.[48] In Cabinet, he opposed allowing Montagu and Chelmsford to defend their proposals in public. Montagu replied that, as they were both 'responsible up to the neck', he declined to stay in office unless he could conduct a vigorous defence on his own account (while stressing that the Cabinet had not accepted the recommendations). The Cabinet were impressed by the endorsements from Montagu's and Chelmsford's Councils and from Chamberlain, and agreed to publish the Report in full without committing themselves to actual proposals.[49]

This incident set the pattern for the future progress of the reforms scheme. Chamberlain had tried to warn the Cabinet that, if they were to agree to publication without making a statement on principles, they might be forced to go further than they wished;[50] but throughout the following months the Cabinet repeatedly took procedural decisions without first deciding on their policy. Montagu would ask for some move—appointment of the committees called for in the Report to consider questions of franchise and the subjects to be transferred, appointment of the committee on the India Office, preparation of a draft Bill—or he would oppose some measure, especially several attempts to have the Report itself referred to a parliamentary joint committee. In the resultant lobbying Chamberlain was the key figure, and Curzon was outmanoeuvred: though he began by refusing to agree to any steps until he had made up his mind on the Report, time and again Curzon would consent to something on certain conditions (a compromise with Montagu arranged by Chamberlain) only to find that he was soon asked to waive the conditions, on the argument that he was already committed to another step by his previous acquiescence. 'My strongest objection,' he wrote to Montagu, 'arises from the feeling that . . . the Cabinet collectively and I myself in particular are continually being squeezed into fresh positions which will probably end by fatally compromising our independence', thus committing them to measures 'of which some of us at bottom disapprove'.[51] What had happened already, in the preoccupations of the war, over the Declaration itself, was being repeated over the acceptance of the Report.

Indeed, particularly in the face of the apparently united front of Secretary of State and Government of India, the Declaration was the chief of those inadvertent decisions which committed the Cabinet to further stages: Chamberlain had pointed out, of the Report, that although a revolution it was one already carried out in August 1917. Critics were thus made to seem guilty of revisionism, of opposition to a policy which, as Curzon himself had to admit in the Lords,[52] had already been decided by the Cabinet and accepted by Parliament. Chelmsford commented to Montagu that people acclaimed the Declaration because they were 'too stupid or too lazy' to work out what it meant, and then, when some one tried to apply it, they objected—he used to say 'that this was the attitude of the I.C.S. towards Reform'.[53] It was an attitude which could not survive: every step taken by the Cabinet, every committee appointed, every day without a hostile decision by government or Parliament, made it more probable that there would be reforms substantially like those recommended in the Report.

Thus, on the one hand, the policy which was emerging in London accorded with the Government of India's programme— Chamberlain in particular spoke their language in his advocacy to Curzon and the Cabinet. And, on the other hand, the interpretation of the August Declaration that was being insisted upon was the one they had accepted and endorsed. Of course, in detail, they could only be spectators. Their support helped persuade the War Cabinet to act, but they could have little influence on the forms of legislation to be proposed—except, it is true, indirectly through Meston and Marris who had been seconded to help in the India Office.[54]

The initiative returned to India with the appointment of the reforms committees. The Secretary of State had proposed one committee under Lord Southborough to consider questions of franchise and division of subjects. Chelmsford urged separate personnel and reports, in the interests of efficiency, with joint meetings to be arranged if necessary. Montagu agreed, but decided (against Chelmsford's advice) to retain Southborough as a common chairman for the two committees. In the event Southborough made himself responsible mainly for the franchise committee, and R. Feetham, the Deputy Chairman, dealt with the subjects committee. The proposed terms of reference—broadly to devise schemes bearing in mind the recommendations of the Report—were not disputed by the Government of India, except for one substantive point: Montagu had suggested empowering the franchise committee to plan for direct election where possible, except for considering special provisions for representing 'illiterate classes'; Chelmsford pointed out that prejudging the issue of communal representation by this narrow provision would be resented in India, and Montagu widened the authority accordingly. A further change made it clear that there could be no going back on dyarchy: Montagu had first suggested requiring the subjects committee to take into consideration the principles and the illustrative list given in the Report (paragraphs 212–13 and 238–40, and Appendix II); but in the final version this formula was strengthened and the committee were obliged to take into consideration the illustrative list and to be 'guided by' the principles (of a division of subjects).[55]

Southborough's committees were to work through a round of provincial hearings and discussions, and the Government of India took on the role of general overseer. They had asked the provinces to prepare schemes, and urged on them the need for haste: as they explained, in a telegram to several local governments in mid-October, they were having 'great difficulty in preparing a programme . . . owing to [the] unpreparedness of some provinces in spite of the fact, that they were asked more than 3 months ago to prepare the requisite material and they must impress on the local Government the necessity of expediting this work to the utmost possible extent'. Chelmsford informed Lord Southborough that he was unwilling to press too hard lest the local governments should give inadequate attention to complex problems; but at the same time he explained privately to Willingdon that it was imperative to carry through the reforms and that even temporary setbacks would jeopardize support: despite provincial difficulties, therefore, the effort *must* be made.[56] Chelmsford was also concerned to preserve the principles of the Report. Southborough consulted him over an attempt to circumvent dyarchy, when Sir B. Robertson, Chief Commissioner of the Central Provinces, wrote: 'I have frankly declared for a preliminary period of training with no divided heads'. Chelmsford replied that this was, as Southborough thought, outside the committee's terms of reference, and that Robertson should be told so 'politely but firmly'.[57] Similarly Chelmsford sharply informed Lord Pentland and the Madras Government that he 'would be obliged' if they would 'immediately' prepare a scheme for the division of subjects, even though (as would be noted in Southborough's report) they disapproved of dyarchy.[58]

Another role for the India government was to counter opposition. In India there was little they could do. There, public reactions to the Report were almost uniformly unenthusiastic. The Viceroy sent home an early summary of newspaper verdicts: some were disappointed, some reserved judgment, some condemned outright, but only the *Times of India*, the *Civil and Military Gazette*, the Rangoon *Gazette*, and two United Provinces papers (the *Pioneer* and the *Indian Daily Telegraph*) applauded the scheme.[59] Individual Indian commentators generally deplored the arrangements for the Government of India as insufficiently progressive; but recognized 'moderates' such as Banerjea, Sastri, Sapru and Wacha otherwise gave their support. Only Patel and Ayyangar opposed an Imperial Legislative Council resolution calling the Report a definite advance, although there were some abstentions including Sarma, and Jinnah, Malaviya and Khaparde had also opposed the motion in debate.[60] Tilak's initial reaction was that the proposals were cheese-paring and entirely unacceptable; Gandhi, on the other hand, admitted that he preferred the scheme 'as a framework' to that put forward by the Congress and League.[61] At their special session in Bombay in 1918, the Congress declared the Report's scheme unacceptable unless it were amended to allow full responsibility in the provinces and partial responsibility in the central government; this conclusion was endorsed at the Delhi session later in the year, and thus rejection of the final scheme in 1919 was inevitable—as was the breach with the 'moderates', now combined under their own banner, that of the all-India Moderates' Conference (later the National Liberal Federation). Annie Besant was the only prominent leader of the 'advanced' wing to defect from the Congress on this issue. With her Home Rule League reconstituted for the purpose, she was to conduct a vigorous campaign during 1920 against Gandhi and the Congress and in favour of the reforms, which she then hailed as a 'death-blow' to the autocracy.[62] Both moderates and extremists, however, agreed that the Government of India arrangements should be made more liberal. Montagu's reaction, in October 1918, was to begin to wonder what would be acceptable to both the moderates and Chelmsford.[63] He did not propose to raise the matter at this stage—it would have been bad tactics to have suggested any further advance before the fate of the reforms scheme was more assured—but to Chelmsford this suggestion must have seemed like an early warning that his and the Secretary of State's paths were likely to diverge as discussions progressed.

In England, however, the India Government's support of the reforms was helpful in the face of the Report's mixed reception. The press was sharply divided: the *Daily Telegraph*, the *Morning Post*, the *Spectator* and the *Saturday Review* attacked the Report, but it was applauded by *The Times*, the *Manchester Guardian*, the *Daily News*, the *Daily Chronicle*, the *Daily Express*, *New Statesman*, *India* and *Nation*. Montagu professed himself disappointed at the *Daily Telegraph* over which he had taken 'some trouble'; but he claimed he had 'got the *Times* quite easily', and had also convinced J. L. Garvin of the *Observer*. He also interviewed Sir V. Chirol who was writing for *The Times* and favoured Curtis's 'two governments' plan. The people with key influence in London were probably Austen Chamberlain, Philip Kerr and Lord Curzon. Chamberlain proved himself 'a tower of strength' on Montagu's side. Kerr, unlike many Round Table members, was a convert to the Report, and thus brought to bear his very considerable influence on the Prime Minister in favour of the scheme—when he resigned in 1921, Kerr was told by Montagu that he did not know how his Indian work, in so far as it impinged on Downing Street, could continue to prosper: Kerr had given such helpful advice and assistance. Curzon, as we have seen, was an enigma; Montagu wrote: he 'amuses me, interests me, irritates me'.[64] Montagu suspected that Curzon had been influenced by the main opponent of the scheme, the former Governor of Bombay, Lord Sydenham, who, backed by the *Morning Post*, presided over a campaign centred on the Anglo-British Association but reaching even to India. Pamphlets hostile to the reforms were issued by the Association; Sydenham sent circulars to firms and Chambers of Commerce warning that trade would be harmed. He gave Curzon the benefit of his views: 'The certain results of this scheme will be the end of all British authority in the civil govt. of India within a few years'. Montagu sought to counter such activities by meeting groups (including Sydenham's) and by setting up a propaganda committee in the India Office. Lord Donoughmore, who had been with Montagu in India, had early had a 'very satisfactory' meeting with selected members of the Conservative Party. As early as August, moreover, Montagu decided that Sydenham's group was becoming more and more isolated. At the same time he concluded —correctly as we have seen—that Curzon, in spite of his opposition to dyarchy and parliamentary concessions in the provinces,

would be 'driven by the general attitude in the country to adherence in the main'.[65] Also in January 1919, partly in order to
embarrass and neutralize conservative opposition among peers,
Montagu had Sinha raised to the Lords as Under-Secretary of
State for India.[66]

The reactions of the local governors in India seemed likely
to create greater difficulties. Chelmsford had tried to carry them
with him on the reforms, at first by keeping them informed, and
then, at Montagu's suggestion, by involving them in the reforms
discussions in Delhi in January 1918.[67] But opposition to dyarchy
had early become apparent. In October 1917 local government
replies had made it clear that, except in Bengal, dyarchy would be
rejected, and that thinking was, on the whole, very conservative—
elected majorities, limited budgetary control, and standing committees were about the limits of the advance suggested for the
councils. In January 1918 the governments, faced with the
Government of India's advocacy of the dualist principle (in their
circular of 11 November 1917), openly argued against dyarchy,
although some—the Governments of Madras (with Pentland dissenting), Bihar and Orissa, and the United Provinces—favoured
forms of sub-provincial transfers of power. Bombay, rejecting all
dyarchies, put forward a scheme of their own whereby the legislature would gain budgetary control and the right, except for
reserved subjects, to introduce legislation without the governor's
consent, while executive authority remained undivided.[68] At the
1918 governors' conference a compromise was arranged, suggested
by Meston, whereby dyarchy would be started earlier in some
provinces than in others and a power of recalling transferred subjects would be safeguarded. The division of opinion had been
immediately apparent and, although Chelmsford had made what
Montagu called a 'short and very admirable speech' and Montagu
had rounded on Vincent (who had sided with the dissenters), no
agreement had seemed possible, even when the local governors
went into session amongst themselves under the chairmanship
of Pentland as the senior governor. Chelmsford had then suggested that he and Montagu should chair a further meeting, as
Pentland was 'impossible', and under their influence Meston's
compromise had been accepted. Montagu thought none of the
governors believed in it.[69] Willingdon described it as uneasy and
unworkable—and to prove this he very soon repudiated it and

returned to his former position.[70] In the early formative stages, Chelmsford had suggested, when Willingdon, Meston and Robertson were engaging in preliminary confabulations on the reforms, that he wanted the best minds at work on the problem and not agreement for the sake of it;[71] but as the Montagu-Chelmsford scheme became finalized he had become more eager that there should be general acceptance at least of the principles on which it was based.

After the Report was published, Ronaldshay agreed heartily with nearly all the recommendations; Willingdon was irreconcilable to what he called Montagu's 'rotten "dyarchy" idea'; Harcourt Butler thought it unworkable; Craddock made it clear that he thought it went beyond what was necessary (although he conceded that if it had a conciliatory effect on all but the most extreme Indians it would have been a 'most brilliant piece of statesmanship').[72] Chelmsford's reply to the criticisms, as expressed to Willingdon in July 1918, was that he defied anyone to give 'progressive realization of responsible government' except by dyarchy, and that any transitional scheme was open to criticism: but the critics should suggest an alternative which was not equally objectionable.[73] Before the end of 1918, however, Chelmsford continued to try to circumvent the opposition by arguments and discussions. Claude Hill spent two nights in Bombay arguing with Willingdon who later told Chelmsford that he would not try to stop his scheme if it proved the only liberal advance possible; but Willingdon declined to abandon his own government's plan for unitary government, which relying as it did on Indian cooperation and the governor's veto was suitable to his abilities. Hill concluded that the soundest thinker in Bombay was Rahimtoola who dissented from the local scheme on the grounds that it did not fulfil the August Declaration. Willingdon's successor, Sir George Lloyd, discussed the issue with Meston, at Chelmsford's special request, but decided that, although he did not favour the Bombay scheme, he was not happy about dyarchy either.[74] As persuasion had not been successful, Chelmsford presented the governors, at their conference in January 1919, with the challenge he had first suggested to Willingdon and which Lloyd had also put forward as a good tactic to adopt: the Viceroy asked the dissenters to formulate their own scheme, no doubt hoping that this would reveal the disagreements among them and at the same time show them the difficulties.[75] O'Dwyer, Butler, Craddock, Beatson-Bell and Robertson agreed on a proposal whereby Indians would be associated with but not responsible for government. Willingdon, now in Madras, continued to support his own proposal. Ronaldshay and Gait had approved the Montagu-Chelmsford scheme. Lloyd had been absent, dealing with a serious mill-strike in Bombay. The breach with all but three governors was now complete, and the Viceroy concentrated his efforts on trying to counter the effect of this in London.

His response was to refer to the Declaration of 1917. He admitted that the governors' opposition was formidable but insisted that it should be made quite clear to the British government that they would have to decide whether or not they intended to implement their announced policy: if they did, then the Montagu-Chelmsford scheme was the only possibility—the five governors' proposals, like all schemes of unitary government, made no provision for the gradual transfer of responsibility. Moreover, in Chelmsford's view the proposals would not work: the 'best chance' was to have 'a frank dualism'. Finally, however, Chelmsford admitted that the first need was to have something soon—he would have accepted an unsound scheme rather than have nothing.[76] He had tried to persuade Lloyd to argue on his behalf, that he could not see how the five governors' scheme complied with 'the principle of August 20th'; but Lloyd had preferred to concentrate his advocacy on the one point that further delay must be avoided.[77] Chelmsford quoted Lloyd's view for the benefit of the home government.

Montagu was once more alarmed and more conciliatory. He agreed that the five governors' scheme was unsound, but suggested that it might be possible to counter both Indian and official opposition to dyarchy by liberal concessions—for Indians presumably over the Government of India, and for the governors by one of two alternative proposals in the provinces: the executive councils could be half official and half non-official and appointed by the governor (not the Crown), or the government could consist of the governor and ministers only, with the reserved subjects administered by the governor with the help of official advisers who would not be members of the government.[78] Chelmsford disagreed: it was necessary to emphasize the division of subjects so that Indian responsibility might clearly be seen, and to emphasize separation so that friction might be minimized.[79] Other disagreements were also appearing. Montagu had been unhappy at some of the suggestions in the 1919 despatch which gave the Government of India's detailed views on the reforms; Chelmsford had insisted he was trying to protect the principles of the Report, particularly in his adoption of the idea of maintaining a separate purse for transferred subjects (which the Report had not favoured), in his disapproval of the transfer of higher education, and in his strong opposition to any further concessions at this stage in the Government of India.[80] The governors' dissent had made it imperative, of course, that the government should remain united, and the despatch had pleased all Chelmsford's Councillors except Sankaran Nair (who thought it too conservative).

On 14 May Montagu gained Cabinet approval for introducing his reforms bill, which he had drawn up with a Cabinet committee comprising Sinha, Milner, Fisher and Chamberlain.[81] The bill met with little opposition in Parliament and was quickly referred to a joint committee.[82] It was at this stage that the effect of the governors' dissent was likely to be most dangerous, and the chances of a rift between Montagu and Chelmsford were also increased. In addition to their different responses to the governors and their growing divergence on the issues stressed in the despatch of 1919, they were also at odds over some of the recommendations of Lord Crewe's committee on the India Office, particularly the proposed abolition of the Secretary of State's Council. Under the influence of W. S. Marris, Chelmsford's government repudiated any formal relaxation of the Secretary of State's supervision—arguing that constitutionally this must imply either a transfer of the control from Parliament to the Indian legislature (which was unacceptable) or an increase in the already formidably autocratic character of the Government of India (which was undesirable).[83]

Nonetheless, in spite of these differences, the bulk of the proposals could be accurately represented as being what the Government of India wanted. It is no exaggeration to say that without this support weighing against increasing opposition from both public and government in both India and Britain, the reforms would never have been carried. In itself this is perhaps of no great significance, for the same would apply to the contributions of people like Montagu and Chamberlain; but for the understanding of the Government of India it is of great importance: the fact that (as they knew perfectly well) they could have jeopardized the reforms if they wished, but did not do so, and the fact that they did not allow their disagreement on details to be confused with rejection in principle, argue that the new constitution was basically what they did want.

In 1918 the government's sub-committee on reforms had been replaced by Meston, appointed as a special officer to coordinate the work on the reforms—to prepare the Government of India's case and provide close and informal liaison with the Southborough committees and the local governments.[84] In continuation of this role, and on the excuse of bringing his special expertise to bear, Meston joined the consultations in London. As he told the Lords, 'the Viceroy . . . and his advisers deputed me to this country to plead the cause of Indian reforms, as they see it . . .'.[85] At a time when their influence would have been expected to be minimal, the India Government had succeeded in bypassing the Secretary of State and introducing their own representative as a separate influence.

Meston has provided, in a series of remarkable letters to Chelmsford, a detailed account of his manoeuvres, his co-operation and disagreements with Montagu, and his success in swaying policy. Meston became a leading member of the committee on reforms set up in the India Office, and was the first witness before the Parliamentary Joint Committee.[86] The Government of India wanted him to secure several objectives. They wanted the Crewe proposals for the India Office to be changed so that the Council of India and the Secretary of State's statutory powers over the Government of India would be retained—Chelmsford was prepared to see a convention evolve whereby the Secretary of State would not interfere with the will of the legislature in matters not essential to peace and good government. Secondly, the government wanted British authority unimpaired at the centre: they were unwilling to have more than two Indian members of the Executive Council, or any dyarchy, or any voting of the budget, and they insisted on a positive legislative power through ordinances if the Council of State were to be a full revising chamber. Thirdly, they wanted the details of franchise and functions to be left to rules to be drawn up by them, not included in the Act. Finally, they wanted dyarchy in the provinces, but worked in such a way that efficiency would not be impaired in essentials and the separation of the two halves would be obvious: they wanted a separate purse for transferred subjects and were unwilling for the budget to be voted especially for reserved subjects; they wanted to give the local governor power to appoint the president of the legislature and to make sure he was experienced in parliamentary procedure; they also wished to reserve the subjects of higher education and the development of industries.[87]

There were several principles behind these preferences. In the first two areas, the Government of India were insisting that the Secretary of State's (and also the Government of India's) statutory authority had to be maintained as long as full sovereignty and responsibility had not passed from Parliament to the Indian electorate; and that the Government of India's powers had to be unimpaired to reassure British interests and preserve British supremacy during the transitional period—the transfer of budgetary control, for example, would have given the Indian majorities in the imperial legislatures effective power to shape policy, whereas the further concession on the Council of State, although it meant that British supremacy had to be vested in what the government considered the less satisfactory instrument of the ordinance, did not alter in the last resort the distribution of power. In the third element, the omission of detailed rules in the reform Bill, the government again demonstrated their belief that arrangements within general principles should remain the responsibility of the authorities in India, and should not be pronounced upon by Parliament. Finally, in the provinces, the government wanted friction between the two halves of the executive and the two roles of the legislature to be at a minimum—they were unwilling to make concessions over the budget and the separate purse because they wished to avoid the prospect of disagreements over transferred and reserved allocations, and the hypocrisy and bitterness if the government were forced to employ restorative powers for essential but unpopular supplies. The objections to the transfer of higher education and industries had different motives—the government were ready to transfer primary education (where the possible advances would tend towards making education free and compulsory, changes best introduced by Indians), but were not pleased to relinquish their paternalistic control over the universities and over industrial expansion, areas in which local and communal loyalties were thought likely to prove obstacles and in

which an era of improvement was promised by the advent of two
major commissions of enquiry (the Sadler on Calcutta University,
and the Indian Industries') instituted under Chelmsford.
Montagu opposed the Government of India on most of these
points: he wished to do away with the need for the Secretary of
State's sanction on non-essential matters, to have a third Indian
member in the central executive, to have both imperial and provincial budgets voted by the legislatures, and to have a joint purse
and the transfer of higher education in the provinces.[88]

The joint committee rounded off its discussions by voting on a
series of resolutions set out by Lord Selborne. Meston was not
supposed to know of these but in fact had discussed them with
Selborne in advance. The resolutions supported the Government
of India on most points—the Secretary of State's responsibility
was to remain unimpaired, the Governor General was to have a
power of ordinance, the Bill was to include only the total strength
and official ratio (and no details of franchises) for the legislative
assemblies, there were to be separate purses by agreement, and
the provincial legislatures were to have only advisory powers on
reserved legislation. Montagu tried to reach a *concordat* with
Selborne whereby he agreed to most of the propositions but sought
support for changes in the Secretary of State's responsibility, and,
in the central government, for the voting of the budget, three
Indian members and parliamentary under-secretaries (which
Chelmsford disapproved of but did not oppose as a vital point).
Meston found himself having 'a horribly strenuous time' between
Montagu and Selborne—Montagu trying to persuade him to
abandon his advocacy of the Government of India case and work on
Selborne's resolutions to see how they could be applied in prac-
tice.[89]

The joint committee began its consideration of the resolutions *in
camera*, and Montagu had much his own way. On the second day,
however, Meston was shown the committee's conclusions on
financial arrangements and sent in a strong message saying they
were meaningless and impractical. He was promptly invited to
attend future sessions. Meston's objections may be assumed to
have been to that combination of the joint and divided purse
schemes in the provinces, as recommended by the Joint Committee Report when discussing Part one, clause 1 of the Bill—for
Meston had criticized the provincial arrangements, to Selborne, as

a surrender not a compromise; and E. Hilton Young, an officer who accompanied and helped Meston, reported that they had carried almost everything on financial arrangements for the division between the *centre* and the provinces, defeating the idea of a standard scale of provincial contributions and the idea that there should be a guarantee that no province should pay more in any one year than its original contribution.[90] For Meston, however, the incident's significance was clearly in the future: later he was able to report, in general, that he had recovered much ground that he had hardly hoped to see again. He had been accepted as a regular member of the joint committee, and was called upon to repeat the Government of India's views, without hostile cross-examination, whenever they differed from Montagu's.

The most serious difference of opinion, as Meston had predicted, occurred over Montagu's insistence on changes in the Report's proposals for the Government of India. In the committee session, Montagu suggested doing away with the Secretary of State's sanction when there was accord between government and legislature, introducing certain subjects where the Governor-General would accept the will of the legislature, and allowing the legislature to vote the budget. Lord Midleton attacked these proposals as 'irresponsible', and the committee adjourned for luncheon after a heated discussion. That afternoon Meston attended a conference between Midleton and Montagu. Midleton pointed out the dangers of a divided joint committee report and Montagu proved conciliatory. He abandoned his position on dyarchy in the central legislature, modified his demand for budgetary control and agreed that the changes in the Secretary of State's role should be included in the committee's report but not the Bill.[91]

The report of the joint committee was therefore not too unpalatable to the Government of India. They lost out on the third Indian member for the central executive—which Meston thought the only disastrous decision—and on the transfer of higher education. But they had their way over leaving the detailed rules out of the Act, and in retaining the statutory responsibility of the Secretary of State—indeed on Meston's advice it was provided that any relaxation of the powers should be subject to the prior approval of both houses of Parliament. In the Government of India there was to be no dyarchy, no parliamentary under-secretaries and only limited legislative control over the budget—military, political and

certain other subjects were not to be voted upon. In a number of
points—the selection of experienced presidents for the legislatures, the power of positive ordinance, and the rejection of
Montagu's idea for a quinquennial review of functions (as opposed
to a ten year consideration of the reforms as a whole)—the Government of India's view was upheld. In other respects, where their
preferences were not complied with, attempts were made to meet
their objections: thus provincial budgets were to be voted, but
the government was to have 'real' powers to enforce supplies for
the reserved subjects; there was to be a joint purse initially but
the government was to be able to allocate a definite proportion of
revenue for each of the two halves of the government should friction
develop.[92] In these provincial arrangements, of course, Montagu
too had little reason for dissatisfaction, but most of his designs for
the Government of India, as developed in 1919, were either defeated or rendered harmless.

Meston, finally, drafted the Joint Committee report, after
Montagu had angrily rejected Selborne's version; and, now ele-
vated to the Lords, was sent by Montagu to lobby parliamentarians
while the Bill had its third reading.[93] The reforms were thus, at
last, approved—probably earlier, thanks to Montagu and Chamberlain, than once seemed likely, and nearer, due largely to Meston,
to what the Government of India had wanted.[94] Chelmsford's
role, however, had been forgotten. Sir George Lowndes wrote to
him: 'What you have initiated, and have worked for during more
than three and a half years, . . . will be for all time a great land-
mark of courageous leadership. . . . For the moment Mr. Montagu
rather fills the stage at home, but the honour is yours, and we all
know it here'. Chelmsford replied that he was touched—this was
'the only recognition' he had received, and, although the main
thing was that the reforms were through, it seemed that they must
'congratulate themselves'. Chelmsford's role and also his dedication and commitment had been underestimated. Yet Stanley
Reed recalled that 'Chelmsford was *fou* with the report; he could
think of little else the moment current business was put aside'.
Chelmsford's irony in reply to Lowndes was both an echo
of that enthusiasm and a foretaste of the disappointments to
come.[95]

W. S. Marris was now appointed Commissioner of a new Reforms Office in the Government of India, to replace Meston and

supervise the introduction of the reforms.[96] The Bill had left details to be decided in India in two main matters of the electorates and the constitution of the executive councils. There was some opposition, on grounds of expense and lack of work, to the idea of having equal numbers of Europeans and Indians on the executive councils (in addition of course to the Indian ministers) if it meant, as Chelmsford suggested, that the provinces must decide to have a council of four (two European officials and two Indian non-officials) or possibly three (one European official and one Indian and one European non-official) or, for the smaller provinces, two (European and Indian, possibly both officials). In Madras Willingdon argued for two European officials and one Indian, the Europeans to leaven the inexperience already introduced by the Indian ministers: 'The nearer I get to it,' he explained, 'the more, *honestly*, I feel that we must not go too fast.'[97] The provinces did not agree on what should be done. Bombay argued against four councillors but was uncertain what would be better. In Bengal Ronaldshay and all three of his Councillors favoured retaining the existing arrangement of two officials and one Indian non-official. Maclagan in the Panjab wanted one official European and one official Indian (because a suitable official Indian was available), whereas Sir Frank Sly in the United Provinces preferred (also on grounds of availability) an official European and a non-official Indian. Chelmsford explained that several of these suggestions were precluded by the joint committee's recommendations, and Madras, Bengal and Bombay then expressed their preference for three councillors, one official European and two non-officials, European and Indian; but Montagu ruled this out as well, interpreting the joint committee's recommendations as requiring either two or four members. He also objected to the Panjab idea for an official Indian member. Chelmsford stressed to the local governors that sufficiency of the European element was a 'vital point' and must be allowed to outweigh considerations of extravagance. Madras, Bengal and finally Bombay agreed to ask for four councillors; the remainder were to have two. Parity between European officials and Indian non-officials was to be maintained throughout.[98] A curious situation had thus arisen out of the division of the functions of government. Part of the government had been transferred to Indian control, but for the remainder, subjects in which Indians had not hitherto had effective influence, it was argued that Indian non-official involvement should not be allowed to fall below the level which had previously obtained in an *undivided* government. This arrangement represented a real advance in Indian influence over the reserved subjects. Electoral arrangements had to be made at both imperial and provincial levels. The Reforms Office prepared a scheme for an Imperial Legislative Assembly of 100 members, elected by general, landlord, Muslim, European and Indian commerce constituencies. They referred the scheme to an advisory committee which gave approval subject to slight modifications increasing the membership to 103. The Government of India later decided to allow an extra seat to the Central Provinces. Electorates for the Imperial Assembly varied in size—under 20,000 in Assam but more than 180,000 in Bengal.[99] The Council of State, it was decided, should also be formed by direct election, except for Executive Councillors (entitled to sit in both chambers, though to be voting members only in one), and for a certain number of nominated non-officials. The Reforms Office again suggested a scheme with general and Muslim seats according to the proportions of the Lucknow pact, and with electorates of about 2000 in major provinces or less in minor. Again the advisory committee substantially approved the proposals, the government resisting suggestions for the representation of Indian commerce and of non-Brahmins, but abandoning the idea of any limit on the size of the electorate provided that the electors were persons with administrative experience or professional eminence, or representatives of industry, commerce and landed interests—the electorate totalled about 3000 in the United Provinces, but only about 1,000 in the Central Provinces.[100]

Provincial arrangements were largely decided at the heads of provinces' conference in January 1920 and involved an electorate ranging in size from rather under $1\frac{1}{2}$ million in the United Provinces to about 140,000 in the Central Provinces—the provincial councils in Madras and Bengal were elected by about one million voters, and in Bombay and the Panjab by about 500,000. In all cases these figures represented substantial increases not only in terms of the actual electors in the former system of indirect election, but also in terms of the constituencies which had elected the electors.[101] The only significant step after the provincial conference was the campaign waged by Willingdon against non-Brahmin representation in Madras. Willingdon was strongly

opposed to communal representation, which he thought would increase bitterness, and argued that it could not be justified for non-
Brahmins when they were in a majority of eight to one in the
Madras electorate. But the government under Pentland had agreed
in principle, and both Southborough and the Government of
India had endorsed this agreement, so that some concessions had to
be made: Willingdon offered to reserve half the general seats for
non-Brahmins, in addition to the nineteen nominated places, all
for non-Brahmins (five Indian Christians, eight zamindars, and
six members of depressed classes), and the thirteen Muslim seats.
He put this suggestion to a conference of Brahmin and non-
Brahmin leaders, and, when it was rejected by the latter, gained
agreement that Meston should arbitrate in the dispute. Under
Meston's award non-Brahmins received 28 (or less than half the
65 seats); in the elections, however, as if to vindicate Willingdon's
view, non-Brahmins won 50 seats, and all three ministers were
therefore non-Brahmins—Willingdon had to bring two Brahmins
into his Executive Council in order to make use of their abilities.[102]

The great debate in this period continued to be between the
Government of India and the Secretary of State. One question
at issue was the joint committee's idea of appointing for the
legislatures, in the first instance, presidents who had had Parliamentary experience. Montagu at first accepted the India Government's suggestion that this should apply only in the three Presiden-
cies, but, after Harcourt Butler had warned of the bad effect such a
distinction would have in the United Provinces, the Secretary of
State urged the appointment of British presidents whenever possible. In the Government of India, Hailey thought this 'very impractical', and Marris stressed that not only would it be extravagant
(legislatures would sit for only six months) but also such presidents,
by their ignorance of the vernaculars, would militate against
improvements in rural representation in the new councils. Significantly S. P. O'Donnell, in the Home Department, declined to
discuss this question with the advisory committee, on the ground
that it would favour presidents from Britain and argue that trans-
lators could be employed in the rare cases of vernacular speeches.
Clearly, behind the objections was some idea that imported presidents would unduly enhance the status, and perhaps too effectively
champion the interests, of the new assemblies. Indeed Marris was

convinced that Montagu was 'bent on using ... unobtrusive devices ... to bring the provincial executive governments in reserved subjects and also the executive Government of India as rapidly and decisively as possible under the control of their respective legislatures.'

Thus Marris returned also to 'the old battle ... now fought twice over, once with Mr. Feetham, and once over the Crewe Committee's report'—resisting Montagu's attempts to include in the Rules under the new Act a provision which precluded his interference whenever executive and legislature were in agreement. As Meston had claimed before (without convincing Montagu), there was a world of difference between 'divestment of power, and mere delegation'. Marris again insisted that where legislatures were not to have control but only influence (over the Government of India and reserved subjects in the provinces) Parliamentary supervision had to be retained—and this by requiring previous sanction for the introduction of bills and not by subsequent veto. Yet, he observed, such sanction was required by law in certain circumstances in the provinces (and presumably would be required only in these cases), while for the central government there was no legal provision so that all that was needed, if Montagu wanted to do away with previous sanction, was for him to *refrain* from making executive orders requiring it. Marris concluded that, by wanting the Rules specifically to forbid such sanction, Montagu really sought to make the criterion for non-interference to be agreement between government and legislature, with the implication that he would *not give* his sanction when disagreement made it necessary to apply to him. This, said Marris, would give the Indians the power to decide whether or not the Secretary of State would be involved, which was an 'insidious means of displacing Parliament in favour of the Indian legislature'. The Government of India put this view strongly, trying to impress Montagu with constitutional considerations, and eventually won the day. (Marris similarly opposed Montagu's advocacy of standing committees: not only would they benefit the legislature to the disadvantage of the executive, but the tendency would be for them to assert control over the departments and thus subvert ministerial responsibility—they had no place in a parliamentary system. Originally, however, the India Government had made practical not constitutional objections (Marris dissenting) and as a result the joint committee had provided certain safeguards; so that now Chelmsford declined to fight the issue again and told Marris he was 'unduly apprehensive'.) The Government of India, then, had continued their rearguard actions against Montagu, reserving their strength for the relatively few matters they considered essential; and had continued also on the whole to succeed. After all it was not as if the two sides disagreed on fundamentals: Montagu's proposals were intended to meet Indian opinion and did not arise out of a more liberal goal, nor indeed any desire to do away with the ultimate British control on which the Government of India insisted; while equally in that government, for all its conservatism, Marris admitted privately (what had not yet been said in public) that '. . . it is desired to promote the Indian [Imperial] legislature eventually to Dominion status . . .'.[103]

Thus the Montagu-Chelmsford reforms were introduced.[104] Elections were held; Assemblies opened. Indian legislators took part in government not only as advisers but for the first time as decision-makers. But the Indian National Congress decided to boycott the elections. Moderates such as Sastri and Banerjea in the National Liberal League, and a sufficient number of other Indians, decided to co-operate with the reforms and some of them entered the Assemblies. The reforms had offered partnership. India's oldest political organization had declined the offer. It had been taken up by splinter groups. The reform policy had foundered on the rocks of politics.

But, whether it foundered or not, it had had a deep impact on government policy. The central feature of this account of the evolution of the reforms has been the involvement of the Government of India: in the 1916 initiative, the Montagu Declaration, the 1918 Report, the Act of 1919, and the subsequent rules. The government had set out a programme, and accepted the extensions which were made by Chamberlain and then Montagu. They were involved in Montagu and Chelmsford's deliberations, and thus it was effectively their agreed policy which was protected and furthered in London by Montagu and Chamberlain. The outcome was either what they had wanted, or what they were prepared to accept: it was not something forced on them from outside against their better judgment. Thus the government were convinced about the direction and purpose of the constitutional changes. This is not to say to whom the reforms should be attributed—such has not been the intention of this account. It is to say that the evidence does not support the view of the Government of India as an agent not an actor in constitutional matters. It is also to provide a starting-point from which we can go on to ask what impact their involvement and conviction had on political policy in general.

Part Two

POLITICS

I THE EVOLUTION OF POLICIES

Chapter 5. Tactical Non-interference

THE situation in India was changing. British policy had been undergoing a long process of adjustment to political India. A recent commentary has shown how, in the nineteenth century under Lytton and Dufferin, different policies emerged from a debate on the proper attitude to the English-educated, and revealed, in the effective exclusion of Indians from higher administration, the ascendency of the goal of permanent autocracy. This tendency was also strong enough to prevail against the personal opposition of Ripon.[1] Lord Curzon went ahead to partition Bengal in defiance of local sentiment, arguing that it was useless to try to persuade people, who would be convinced only by a *fait accompli*. He has been accused of owing more to efficiency than to vision; but he too had a kind of vision, dangerous to Indian advance, in his belief in the Englishman's sacred duty to maintain the Indian Empire. He was the supreme exponent of 'good' rather than self-government, and suppressed Indian opinion efficiently, more by ignoring it than by incarcerating its leaders.[2] After Curzon, this position became more vulnerable, and willingness to conciliate politicians increased in rough proportion with their vehemence and popular support. Lord Minto, Curzon's successor, recognized that the Indian National Congress could not be ignored, at the same time as he prepared to deal with 'revolutionary' crime. It was no longer possible for the scorn, with which Lytton and Curzon had regarded educated Indians, to find a place in public policy—even in the Indian Civil Service, the voice of change had to be heard.[3] But Minto still believed that the Congress represented a section which would never play a large part in government.[4] During the 1914–1918 war, however, the need for adjustment suddenly became more acute.

There were many reasons for the acceleration in the rate of change. Democratic ideals were abroad; Japan, an Asian nation, and Ireland, a British colony, had asserted themselves against imperial powers; in India, among other factors, wartime loyalty

and hardships seemed to justify hopes of political concessions—
rumour reported, accurately, that these were already being discussed by the government. As hardship grew more severe, Indian
expectations multiplied.[5] Moreover, by 1916, nationalist politics
had entered a critical phase. In the United Provinces there were
stirrings among Muslims (*ulama* and younger politicians who
shared some of their attitudes) such as were to lead to the formation of the *jamiat ul ulama-i-Hind* and the capture of the Central
Khilafat Committee.[6] In the country in general and the Congress,
influence and standing were being won by 'extremists', politicians
who advocated more militant nationalism, short of violent revolution, under such leaders as the Hindu revivalist, B. G. Tilak, and
the Irish Theosophist, Annie Besant. Tilak, in particular, had
spent a lifetime gathering support, and few literate families in
Maharastra can have escaped his influence.[7] With the war, economic
distress and burgeoning political interest, the time had come to
reap the benefits of this long campaign. Congress members, on the
whole, under moderate leadership, had merely informed the government once a year of their opinions as educated Indians; the new
agitators tried to create a climate of opinion among people at large,
and to use this support to bargain with the government. As the
Congress at first was slow to change, Tilak and Besant formed
Home Rule Leagues, and, for the first time, Indian opinion confronted the government as a permanently organized and active
opposition. The Leagues introduced a simple demand, borrowed
from Ireland, and, using this slogan in their name and in newspapers and lecture tours, sought, in Besant's phrase, to 'awaken
the masses'. Impatience with Congress politeness and petitions
had already led to terrorism,[8] for which the government could have
only one answer; now impatience was being channelled, more or
less within constitutional limits, into a new and ultimately more
dangerous activism.[9]

The older nationalism could not remain unaffected. At Lucknow
in 1916, as part of a new emphasis on broad representation and
unity, the Congress entered a brief but fateful alliance with the
Muslim League, itself already transformed by young men from
the United Provinces. In successive stages Congress organization
was strengthened and made permanent at both local and national
levels, using the Home Rule approach and sometimes the local
branches of the Leagues. Those who favoured less forceful

methods gradually left, and the Congress found, at the moment when it seemed to wish to develop as a national alternative to the British system, that it could not avoid turning into a disciplined political party. Indian nationalism acquired, if not always new people, then new perspectives and methods; the Congress came to provide, at the same time, a militant accompaniment to debates and a positive alternative to violence. Gandhi, already appealing to the masses by his championing of the grievances of the ryots in Champaran and Kaira and the mill-workers of Ahmedabad, was both the chief beneficiary and an agent of this change.[10]

It has been recognized that this development in Indian politics was answered by a corresponding change in government policies. What has not been understood is that the British had always had two replies to political activity—conciliation and repression—and that these had always coexisted. In one sense perhaps repression could be seen as furthering autocracy, and conciliation as a necessary corollary of constitutional reform. But the dichotomy cannot characterize a whole administration. Chelmsford's government might promise self-rule, but they too used repression, and were at times impressed by Curzon's style of convincing by *fait accompli* not persuasion. This should not be taken to mean either that the promise was false, or that repression was the sum of the policy towards agitation. It is equally wrong to see a smooth retreat from executive restrictions,[11] or to suppose that a policy of non-interference supplanted another of repression at any given time, say in 1920.[12] Government attitudes must be distinguished in terms of different kinds of political activity.[13]

They chose between repression and conciliation, according to circumstances. In theory under Chelmsford they distinguished carefully between constitutional politics and 'anarchism', and, in practice, very moderate or very extreme agitation posed no problems: on the one hand, positive concessions to Indian demands were being discussed at the highest levels, and, on the other hand, to the problem of what was called 'sedition', the government were considering a most Curzon-like reply. In dealing with the control of agitation, Chelmsford's practice was to allow local governments the same independence and give them the same support as he himself had been guaranteed by Chamberlain.[14] But in May 1916 he pointed out to Willingdon in Bombay that they had nothing to fear from constitutional agitation reasonably carried on, meaning to suggest, as he explained in July, that they should be on their guard 'against excess of zeal in the repression of public opinion'[15]— a principle similar to that laid down in 1918 by Edwin Montagu when he wrote to Chelmsford that dangerous or unconstitutional agitation should be firmly put down, but 'properly conducted political warfare however objectionable' should be left alone.[16] There was no questioning of this; government policy was clear, at least to the government. The problem was one of definition. It was not new; rather it was inherent in any double-edged political policy, or indeed in the bureaucracy's coexistence with constitutional reform. Thus W. S. Marris, Officiating Secretary in the Home Department, had written in 1913, after the attempt to assassinate Lord Hardinge, that it was incumbent on the Government of India and the local governments to consider the connection between 'anarchical' crime and the 'political circumstances of the country' and to unearth and suppress existing conspiracies. It was thought clear that the outrages prevalent in Bengal were not 'the last flicker of expiring anarchy in one Province': the conspiracies were 'a living force in India'. The government's attitude had hardened at that time, and local governments were instructed to take 'continuous and systematic action . . . to enforce moderation in speech and writing, and to check the expression of views and criticisms which may conceal, but thinly, incitements to resistance of the authority of Government'. Hardinge's government argued, through Marris:

Though the inspiration of anarchist outrages may stand outside all direct connection with ordinary political agitation, it is the excesses of the latter which prepare the ground for the inculcation of anarchical doctrines and create an environment in which such doctrines find adherents. It follows as a consequence that any too indulgent toleration of such excesses may be the direct or indirect cause of morbid growths especially among young and impressionable minds which lead in the end to atrocious crimes such as that perpetrated on the occasion of the State Entry into Delhi.[17]

Definitions were indeed becoming confused, and thus, in 1913, the answer to terrorism was the curious idea of 'enforcing moderation': the effect was to narrow the acceptable limits of agitation.

Chelmsford, on the other hand, emphasized another area of ambiguity. He went so far as to argue that it was 'impossible on paper to draw a distinction between the Self-Government which we advocate . . ., and Home Rule, as advocated by Mrs. Besant and Tilak . . .'; his colleague, Claude Hill, also questioned that it was 'perfectly possible to draw' 'the line between true constitutional advocacy of reform and extravagant demands couched in language which excites to unconstitutional opposition'.

Faced with terrorism, Hardinge's government were content to conclude that there was no effective difference between violence and 'extravagant demands'. But by Chelmsford's time politics were becoming ever more complex. The government, accustomed to the occasional debates of the Congress, had to meet a new situation with the Home Rule Leagues, at a time when Gandhi and the Congress had not yet been fully converted to Home Rule and its methods.[18] The results were alarming as early as 1917. Meston told the Government of India at that time that there was spreading in the countryside 'a vague notion that in some unknown way the British raj is going wrong or is going under, and *swaraj* is coming to put all things right'. This, Meston held, together with the 'power of challenge and obstruction' introduced in 1909 by the Morley–Minto reforms, had discredited Curzon's policy of doing 'what was right for India whether India altogether liked it or not'. As a result, according to Meston, Chelmsford was trying to govern, as had his immediate predecessors, by 'bargaining and negotiation', 'a steady yielding to assaults' which always left 'some bitterness behind on both sides'.[19] The Home Rule Leagues created a new category of argument, protest and agitation which were neither pure politics, in the old Congress sense, nor revolution. Indian leaders claimed the Home Rule demand was not seditious. At least one court agreed. In 1916 a Poona magistrate had required Tilak to deposit sureties of good behaviour; Tilak had appealed, and, to the local government's surprise, had been upheld in the High Court on the ground that his speeches, taken as a whole, were not calculated to create disaffection.[20] Now the central government had to decide as well. How was the demand for Home Rule to be categorized? Should the Leagues be suppressed, as sedition-mongers, or conciliated, as organs of constitutional politics?

A debate began, centred on Annie Besant. Local governors differed in their approach, some like Meston and Lord Carmichael in Bengal meeting with her; others like Willingdon, Robertson, Pentland and O'Dwyer wishing her outlawed along with the

Home Rule demand. There was division on the issue also in the Government of India, with Sir Reginald Craddock, the conservative Home Member, advocating strong measures, which Chelmsford would not accept, though he tried to conceal the differences by insisting on the need for provincial discretion. Under pressure from Craddock and the governors, the Government of India issued a circular in March 1917 to clarify their position: it called for 'firm discouragement' of the Home Rule campaign but not of 'constitutional advocacy of reform'.[21] This was very ambiguous, but did not give the provinces the unlimited discretion which most of them wanted. Under further pressure from Willingdon, the government issued unequivocal instructions forbidding a general ban on Home Rule and allowing action only against activity intended to promote disorder and disaffection.[22] They wished to avoid any action which 'might even suggest' that they were trying to 'stifle fair criticism or legitimate movements'.[23]

This clear assertion of principle was not matched in practice. Bombay were allowed to extern Besant in June 1916; and Chelmsford warned Chamberlain: 'I hate all this suppression but India is in too inflammable a state to admit of lighted sparks about.'[24] The Government of India supported Madras in June 1917 when, on their own authority, they interned Besant and two associates: the local government justified their action in terms of the March circular, but their motive was transparent, to end Besant's activities and the influence of her newspaper, *New India*. The danger here, as Meston pointed out, was that Indians would interpret this to mean that government was 'hostile to any real constitutional advance'.[25] Besant had expressed explicit fears that it was 'practically proposed to strangle by violence . . . political educative propaganda'.[26]

In September 1917 the Government of India changed their minds, and ordered a defiant Pentland to release Besant. They had been influenced by pressure from Montagu, and by discussions with M. A. Jinnah, then a member of the Imperial Legislative Council—Jinnah's attitude to Besant convinced them that many politicians 'would be glad to see her disappear',[27] and the release was an attempt to help her do so. But, as Chelmsford insisted and Montagu confirmed, the Government of India had made their own decision. Circumstances had changed their minds—at last Montagu had announced the goal of self-government and his intention to visit India for reforms discussions. The internment of Besant had caused widespread demonstrations of public sympathy; thus her release was an 'almost inevitable concomitant'[28] of Montagu's visit, intended to create a favourable atmosphere for discussions. To refuse the release, Chelmsford explained to Montagu, was to run 'grave risk of jeopardising the success of your visit and the possibility of setting the lines of political advance. We should, in fact, have stultified our whole policy.'[29] Thus the release was not only a tactic, 'for the purpose of allaying the political agitation';[30] it was also an 'inevitable concomitant' of the goal of self-government, without which that 'whole policy' would be 'stultified'. The proposal to allow Indians to participate in government implied and required a more liberal attitude to Indian agitation and demands.

From this decision—which was in effect no more than the conclusion that Home Rule should henceforth come within the category of constitutional agitation, not to be suppressed—there developed a consistent policy which may be called 'tactical non-interference'. It implied further limitation of provincial discretion—governments were now required to assess the wider repercussions of their actions (of which the centre was to be the judge), and warned that the India Government would press 'very strongly' for the submission to an independent tribunal of any restrictions not removed.[31] Conciliation meant central needs had to prevail over local. Shortly after Besant's release Chelmsford forced an indignant O'Dwyer to retract and apologize for a speech which ran counter to his policy by criticizing Home Rule and politicians. The incident created a situation 'quite as bad as the Ilbert Bill',[32] and convinced Europeans that Chelmsford was a dangerous radical. But, as Chelmsford was to explain in 1918, his 'only policy' was 'to endeavour to enlist' the co-operation of the educated classes, at present 'almost to a man against the government'.[33]

Accordingly, the Government of India approached Besant in a new spirit. After her release she tried to persuade the government to release Muhammad Ali, one of two brothers interned, during the war with Turkey, as pan-Islamic conspirators. This possibility was already being explored. At the end of August Vincent had argued that the brothers could not be interned indefinitely and that the present, with (as he believed) Muslim feeling less bitter and pan-Islamism in decline, might be a good moment to release

them, in return for guarantees of good conduct (as with Besant).
Meston opposed this, and argued that the Alis had been interned
for treasonable activities not excessive political zeal. His view,
though consistent with the government's new approach, was
unsupported by any evidence, and indicative of the special concern
felt over Muslim leaders because their community was supposedly
disaffected and 'martial'. Nevertheless an approach was made to
the internees asking whether, if released, they would undertake
not to assist the King's enemies, and to refrain from unconstitutional methods. They replied that they accepted 'above all else
God's commandments', and would give the undertaking subject
to the 'fullest political liberty'—at the same time the censor intercepted a telegram from Muhammad claiming as a religious liberty
the right to side with Turkey in the war. The government decided
such an undertaking was no undertaking at all. A file was compiled
on the Alis' activities, and reinforced the decision that it was impossible to bargain with them.[34] Thus was made the crucial mistake of appearing to treat Muslim leaders more severely than
Hindu.

Nonetheless, the government were ready to discuss the matter
with Besant. Vincent and Du Boulay met her at Simla while the
Viceroy was away on tour. She was not satisfied with their answers,
and asked to see Chelmsford. The Viceroy's Private Secretary
made several attempts to arrange a meeting, but Besant was
unable to co-ordinate her movements with the Viceroy's tour.
Chelmsford hoped he could use the interview to encourage Besant
to 'take a more temperate view' of what was possible 'as an immediate step in the direction of political advance'. His policy met
with the strongest objections. Sir Charles Cleveland of the Central
Intelligence Department, armed from his files with a formidable
indictment of Besant and the Theosophical Society, pronounced
the lady a thoroughly unsuitable person to be received by members
of the government. She was, he concluded, 'a charlatan in religion'
and an enemy of British dominion. Chelmsford replied that the meeting was 'not a question of doing honour to Mrs. Besant'; rather it
was a 'question of expediency'. Similarly, when Willingdon
expressed his disquiet, calling Besant a dangerous intriguer who
should not be recognized as a political leader, Chelmsford replied
at first that the protest puzzled him, and later added that, while he
agreed with much that Willingdon said about Besant, he did not

see that an unsuccessful mission would enhance her reputation.[35]
In the following months, the new policy was consolidated by
apparent success. In Madras they bewailed the loss of prestige; in
Bengal they made dire predictions of future disaster; but the
Government of India professed themselves well pleased with the
present calm.[36] Chelmsford seemed to go further than his Council
—whereas they admitted (in response to London) that Besant's
release left serious unrest in India between Hindus, Muslims and
Europeans, Chelmsford (absent in camp) stressed that, in spite of
some European discontent, he had 'no reasons to be dissatisfied'.[37]
Indeed he thought that events had proved the policy 'wise' and
'absolutely justified'. Besant was touring India. The Viceroy
believed it 'would be asking too much of human nature, especially
her nature, to expect her to refrain'—limelight was 'necessary to
her existence'. But she was counselling moderation.[38] The government continued to watch her with a wary (or in Cleveland's case, a
jaundiced) eye. Thus, in April and May 1918, she was criticized
for an intemperate response, in *New India* and a public speech in
Calcutta, to the exclusion of Tilak's deputation from England.
But, in response to the Home Department's query, Chelmsford
was content to wait, without writing to warn Besant, and later she
redeemed herself by advocating recruiting.[39]

Thus tactical non-interference was confirmed. In June 1918,
Montagu drew Chelmsford's attention to the publicity being
given to a provocative letter written to President Wilson by Sir
Subramania Aiyar, a former High Court judge who had espoused
Home Rule. The letter was being widely distributed in the United
States; it complained of Besant's internment and informed the
President:

you and the other leaders have been kept in ignorance of the full
measure of misrule and oppression in India. Officials of an alien nation,
speaking a foreign tongue, force their will upon us; they grant themselves
exorbitant salaries and large allowances; they refuse us education; they
sap us of our wealth; they impose crushing taxation without our consent; they cast thousands of our people into prisons for uttering patriotic
sentiments—prisons so filthy that often the inmates die from loathsome
diseases.

When this letter first came to the Home Department's attention,
in January 1918, the general view, supported by Cleveland, was
against prosecuting but in favour of issuing a formal warning.

However the Viceroy and Secretary of State had known of the letter at the time of the reforms discussions in Madras, and Montagu in particular had 'trounced' Subramania then. Chelmsford told Du Boulay of this, and the Home Secretary agreed to abandon the idea of further action. Subsequently, after increasing publicity, Subramania was informed privately of the government's displeasure and the reason he had not been prosecuted, and his attention was drawn to the rules governing political activity by government pensioners. Later Montagu's reprimand was reported in the press, and Subramania announced that he could meet 'no more glorious fate . . . than to be the object of official tyranny'. Some of Chelmsford's Council then favoured reprisals, but Chelmsford did not and the dissenters did not press their view. Cleveland remarked only that the offence was common property while the government's response was not.[40]

In June therefore Montagu was returning to an old issue: he was alarmed at pressure being exerted in Britain to have Subramania's K.C.S.I. withdrawn. Chelmsford replied reporting what had been done, and declining to act publicly. Montagu accepted this and, rather mixing his metaphors, wrote to urge Pentland not to waste his heavy artillery on second fiddles. 'We want to walk warily', Chelmsford explained; 'no-one who had experience of the results of interning Mrs. Besant last year wants to repeat the mistake'. (He did not intend to make a martyr out of this 'silly old man'.) For the first time Chelmsford had admitted that the internment of Besant, however justified in law, had been wrongheaded.[41]

This lesson, now admitted to have been learnt over Besant, was thus applied to other leaders of her persuasion. In April 1918 Madras wanted to extern Tilak and Bipin Chandra Pal: the centre objected because such action might have jeopardized the War Conference which they were holding in Delhi. Madras, bowing before the inevitable, withdrew their suggestion, discovered moderation in the speeches of their unwelcome visitors, and remembered that they too were about to appeal at their provincial conference for an end to political strife.[42] In August the same local government suggested that official pensioners might be prohibited from participating in agitations directed against the government or 'liable to cause embarrassment to them'; and Meston, in support, wondered only if the proposal went far enough—he believed a pensioner should be permitted to 'hold any opinion he pleases' provided (it seems) he did nothing about it. The Government of India, however, rejected the proposal. Nor did they welcome a Bombay scheme for increasing magistrates' powers over public meetings: such measures were not worth the ill-feeling they would create.[43] Under the new scheme of things, co-operation with or loyalty to the British was not to be coerced; and central government now decided tactics.

But, also in August, Bombay were permitted to place Tilak under an order forbidding him to speak in public. In giving a speech on war recruitment, Tilak had remarked, or so the government were informed, that Indians were 'treated like slaves' (why should they 'come forward to protect India?'); that the bureaucrats wanted 'mercenaries so their power will remain inviolate'; that the Indian army, mainly Muslims and non-Indians, was ready to shoot down Hindus 'without compunction'; that no army could be raised 'if the educated classes . . . are not made to feel that India is their own country'. Vincent's reaction had been: 'This speech . . . is about the "limit". But I suppose Tilak's prosecution would do more harm politically than this speech can do.'[44] The Bombay Government, however, had argued that the need for recruitment, which such speeches were supposed to discourage, outweighed the risk of agitation if Tilak should defy a ban and have to be arrested. The central government had allowed themselves to be persuaded; and Bombay had minimized the risk by allowing Tilak, who was about to leave for England, to speak before the Congress session in spite of the orders against him.[45] Thus non-interference did not carry all before it. At first there were instances of the repression of figures who seem similar to Besant, but to whom the tactical policy was not immediately applied.

Gandhi is the most famous of these. It was probable that the policy would be applied to Gandhi. His credit started higher than Besant's, and his methods were not dissimilar. But on 9 August 1919, during the agitation against the Rowlatt Bill, the Government of India allowed the Panjab Government to exclude Gandhi from the province.

Several factors seemed to have convinced the government that action could not be avoided. Firstly, there had taken place in Delhi on 30 March a *hartal* which had ended in violence. The Delhi authorities wanted to extern Gandhi who proposed to visit, but Vincent pointed out that this would have meant the dangerous step of having to arrest and prosecute him in the city. On the other hand this might well occur if he *were* allowed to visit. As a better alternative, Meston, Lowndes and Vincent agreed that Gandhi should be ordered to return to and remain in Bombay Presidency. Secondly, by publishing his *satyagraha* leaflets without a licence, Gandhi purported to be defying the law. On 8 April, the Government of India agreed with Bombay that, when the law was being openly defied for political advantage, it was better to prosecute, and Vincent authorized them to move under the press acts. Later at a conference in Delhi with Chelmsford, Vincent and Lowndes, on 11 April, Lloyd argued that they could not 'abandon all the functions of Government'. Chelmsford agreed that they must be wary but 'perfectly firm'. In the event it was found that Gandhi could not be prosecuted; but the principle of his arrest had already been agreed before the Panjab request to extern him.

Thirdly, the Panjab was admittedly a special case. Chelmsford had been uneasy at the fervour of the recruiting campaign under O'Dwyer;[46] the aftermath of this, added to the problems of the return of disbanded soldiers and the Muslim grievances over the Turkish peace terms, were seen to have contributed to a serious situation, and the Viceroy thought it 'of the first importance' to avoid the spread of unrest and to allow the local governments full discretion in measures to restore order. Finally, the central government believed that they were applying their agreed policy. O'Dwyer had wanted Gandhi deported to Burma, and Vincent had demurred on the usual grounds: 'it would cause a conflagration and would alienate the sympathy of many who do not at present approve of Mr. Gandhi's conduct'. Similarly, on 8 April, Chelmsford had personally instructed the Home Department to formulate a definite plan of action to deal with possible developments in passive resistance, so that local actions might be co-ordinated, and to instruct local governments to issue if necessary simply-worded manifestos explaining the Rowlatt Bill, sympathizing with rational opposition, pointing out the moral of the Delhi incident, calling for co-operation, and warning that the government would deal rigorously with movements which endangered the peace. Gandhi's leaflets might be met, Chelmsford thought, by confiscating his printing press. A copy of these instructions was sent to Bombay.[47] Chelmsford later defended Gandhi's exclusion, explaining to Montagu: 'the temper of the

Delhi mob was very sullen; Gandhi's avowed object was to induce men to break the law, and it had been made clear that he could not control the excitement he aroused; therefore his arrest in Delhi would have been inevitable and would have led to even worse riots'. This may have been subsequent rationalization. However, it demonstrates that the government, even in the action against Gandhi, were still considering priorities. The wider implications of non-interference were not forgotten, even though Gandhi's exclusion was approved. The actual decision was taken by Vincent, in consultation with Meston and Lowndes, as Chelmsford was away on tour.

Also in accordance with their usual policy, the government had issued meticulous instructions on the manner in which the exclusion was to be carried out. Following the lines of a note by Vincent,[48] local governments were advised that Gandhi was to be treated with 'every possible consideration', and that force was not to be used unless he disobeyed the order. He was to be informed that 'the Government would be willing to consider the position later should he give [an] explicit undertaking to refrain from inaugurating a campaign to break the law'. In the instructions issued to the Governor-General's Agent in Rajputana, in case Gandhi were turned back there, the government added that if Gandhi disobeyed the authorities 'should not arrest him, but merely use such means as may be necessary . . . , treating him with all consideration'. It is almost certain that the central government intended this in the Panjab. They even seem to have thought that this was what happened—even in confidential reports they do not refer to the action as an arrest, although it is difficult to see what else it could have been. Gandhi was 'sent' or 'escorted' back to Bombay. He himself had given reason for hope that an arrest would not be necessary: he had written instructions to *satyagrahis* that 'All police orders are to be implicitly obeyed'. The government at that stage did intend to arrest Gandhi, but only under ordinary law, after his return to Bombay.[49] The exclusion was a vast miscalculation; but not thought of as a contradiction of existing policy.

Thus, even within acts of repression, one finds signs that the tactical doctrine was becoming established. Even executive measures now had a surgical appearance. Thus, too, in April 1919, when the Bombay authorities were permitted to deport the journalist, B. G. Horniman, the move was planned carefully in advance and carried out swiftly and secretly. Willingdon had earlier urged deportation; and Chelmsford had then advised the local government to choose their moment well, to have a ship ready, and to allow no time for farewell speeches. When Sir George Lloyd replaced Willingdon in Bombay, before the deportation, he announced to Meston that 'he was not disposed to begin his career by conferring unnecessary martyrdom';[50] later, however, he visited Chelmsford to urge wholesale deportations, including Jinnah, Gandhi, Mrs. Naidu, and Jamnadas Dwarkadas. The Home Department asked Bombay to consider the possibility that such deportations would cause more trouble, and, though they would have agreed in part if necessary, they refused to act against Jinnah, and ruled that Gandhi should not be deported unless something further happened to make this unavoidable. Lloyd had to be satisfied with deporting Horniman. The Home Department busied themselves with having a ship in readiness; Lloyd chose a moment 'when popular excitement was temporarily allayed'; and, in accordance with Chelmsford's original instructions, Horniman was sent off quietly on a waiting steamer. There were no demonstrations. It is possible that Gandhi's forbearance (chastened as he was by the Panjab disasters) may have had something to do with the calm, as claimed in the *Pioneer*. But at least the Bombay Government were able to report that the atmosphere of the Presidency had 'improved out of all knowledge'.[51] Tactics had not ruled out such repression, but had restricted it and changed its style. It was now measured and discreet. A similar approach was adopted when the Ali brothers announced that they considered themselves no longer bound by their internment orders (which they were already defying). The central government ordered that they be imprisoned, and issued detailed instructions regarding the suddenness and discretion with which this was to be done. They used executive powers, but expressly to avoid publicity.[52]

The later handling of Gandhi also was more circumspect. The immediate response to the outcry at his exclusion from the Panjab was to abandon all thought of arresting him. He was being helpful in limiting the violence in Ahmedabad, and Chelmsford and Lloyd were agreed that 'Interned he would be a rallying cry to the disaffected; out he may prove of great assistance . . .'.[53]

As before, commitment to the policy was not uniform: Gandhi

was reported to have advised members of the Sabarmati Ashram not to identify to the police 'those whom they are weaning from crime', namely some rioters guilty of incendiarism during the disturbances. Cleveland insisted that this was a criminal offence and Gandhi was liable to prosecution. But Marris noted: 'I think the right line is probably to refuse to make a martyr of Gandhi but to fine his followers'. Gandhi was interviewed by the District Magistrate of Ahmedabad, but otherwise the matter was dropped.[54] In May 1919, Lloyd wrote to Montagu his view that Gandhi was 'really pretty wicked' and would eventually have to be arrested and deported; but when he saw Gandhi he told him that the government would take no action. At this, Lloyd reported, Gandhi

smiled and said, 'I wish to goodness Sir you would arrest me'. I said, 'No Mr. Gandhi, this is a luxury I reserve entirely for those who surround you and who [sic] you mislead. If they break the law they will be dealt with and you will be left until it suits me'. He pointed out frankly how unpopular that would make him with his friends and I could only add how much I regretted inconveniencing him in this way, but suggested that he should try some foreign missionary work for a bit.[55]

In early June Lloyd thought Gandhi was losing ground daily; but when Gandhi announced his intention to resume his campaign on 1 July, Lloyd expected serious trouble—he had tried quiet methods, he told Montagu, and he would now have to 'stamp out the evil once and for all'. He had lost faith in talking to Gandhi: 'argument with a lunatic is a pastime that is generally unprofitable—', he noted to Chamberlain, 'and insanity of his kind is particularly difficult to deal with.'[56]

The centre were not so easily discouraged, but certainly tactics were again in question. At first there had been only a distant danger of campaigns to refuse revenue payments, and, in spite of a plea from the Panjab, Marris had thought any risk of this must be taken.[57] But in June Gandhi was again thought to be intending actively to break the law, and was even threatening to publish a letter of Muhammad Ali's, which government had proscribed and which Gandhi himself had called 'inflammatory'. Marris advised 'I do not think we ought to risk, and I think we ought to have the support of all reasonable people in resisting any attempt to revive the *Satyagraha* movement in the form of any breach of the law.'

Instead they could declare the movement an illegal association. Vincent was unhappy about this. Like Lloyd he thought Gandhi was losing influence, and believed Gandhi might act in the hope of gaining support. 'We should as far as possible,' he wrote, 'give him no opportunity of attaining his object.' To Vincent—and here he differed from Lloyd—the necessity of action against Gandhi was something to be afraid of, to be avoided if possible, to be undertaken only if the government's hands were forced, and then by prosecution not internment so as to minimize public sympathy. He suggested that Gandhi should be interviewed by the Bombay Inspector-General of Police, to find out what he proposed and to warn of consequences of a breach of the law.[58]

The Panjab Government now also urged action, and asked for a legal opinion on the possibility of proclaiming the promotors of a *hartal* an illegal association. The experts thought it was possible; but Lowndes argued that it might be in Lahore, where a *hartal* could lead to a breach of the peace, but not elsewhere in India. Vincent and Chelmsford accepted that a declaration (under part II of Act XIV of 1908) might be made on this point for Lahore alone, with Vincent adding (and getting agreement from Maclagan by telephone) that this would be used only in a 'case of real necessity'. The central government continued to place most of their hope in a diminution of Gandhi's influence, though they agreed that he should not be encouraged 'in his attitude of a self-constituted redresser of wrongs'.[59]

Gandhi then avowed his intention of breaking the law by leaving Bombay, and the centre, realising that he would have to be stopped, again accepted that this might mean prosecution even though, as Vincent predicted, it would 'cause trouble and possibly disorder'.[60] But Vincent still greatly preferred that Gandhi should be kept in Bombay by any means other than prosecution, and the government put forward his earlier suggestion that Gandhi should be interviewed in Bombay and told that, despite his claims, there was no guarantee that civil disobedience would be any less disastrous in July than it had been in April, and moreover that the eve of the conclusion of hostilities with Afghanistan was 'a most unsuitable occasion on which to risk . . . internal disorder'. This remarkable appeal was duly delivered. It seems to demonstrate a considerable understanding of Gandhi's thinking; and it was successful. Gandhi expressed his willingness to suspend civil disobedience until any date, not too far distant, which the government might prescribe. He also promised to give notice of its resumption and to limit it to himself and his coadjutors. He declared that he did not propose to enter the Panjab for the present. The bargain had proved even more remarkable than the appeal.[61] Montagu had suggested to Lloyd that when Gandhi found he could not force the government's hand, 'without committing himself to the sort of action that is all against his principles, he should be an easier problem to tackle'. For the moment there seemed some grounds for this optimism. Lloyd agreed that Gandhi had been glad of the excuse to abandon his campaign for a time; he persuaded Chelmsford to allow Gandhi to announce that the suspension had been at government request.[62]

The obvious next step was to see if the restrictions on Gandhi could be removed. Lloyd and Montagu both suggested this in July. But the Government of India had enquired of the local governments whether they thought it necessary to retain their ban on Gandhi: they envisaged retaining the restriction only for the Panjab, where Gandhi promised not to go, thus avoiding the risk of having to arrest him. But Delhi, Bihar and Orissa, the Central and the United Provinces, Bengal and Madras all expressed their preference for having Gandhi confined to Bombay. At the end of July Montagu told Chelmsford that he 'presumed . . . the order prohibiting Gandhi from entering Delhi or the Punjab . . . will be suspended in view of the undertaking he has given to Lloyd'.[63] Chelmsford denied this; and Montagu repeated the suggestion on 12 August. Vincent noted: 'I am not myself at all sure Gandhi's presence now would cause a breach of the peace but we are bound to give weight to the opinions of local Governments'. But the Viceroy replied independently again resisting Montagu, followed by the Home Department, who wished to combat Montagu's idea that Gandhi's presence always had a tranquillizing effect. At the end of August, however, Chelmsford advised the Secretary of State that restrictions on Gandhi would soon be lifted. M. M. Shafi proposed that local governments should be asked about removing the restrictions on the eve of the arrival of Lord Hunter, chairman of the committee which was to inquire into the 1919 disturbances. This was agreed in Council on 5 September. A later report attributed this decision to the fact that in September 'the political situation . . . reverted to normal'.[64] By and large the provinces concurred, although Madras and Bengal continued to express doubts, Delhi pleaded for delay, and the Panjab wanted to wait and to prevent Congress from being held in a disturbed area (Amritsar). There was some sympathy for the Panjab's view in the Home Department, but Marris disagreed, and Vincent noted: 'I think we should definitely decide to remove the restrictions . . . in the middle of October unless something unforeseen happens'. The government ordered the restrictions to be lifted on 15 October; in Bombay Presidency they had already been removed. At the last moment Bombay reported that Gandhi had made an objectionable speech and proposed to visit the Panjab; but in the Home Department it was remarked that the latter was to be expected, and, with regard to the former, 'there is no intention of putting any further restriction on Gandhi at present'.[65]

The impression which emerges is of a policy unfolding. Now Gandhi, with even more cause than Besant in 1917, was not to be interfered with unless absolutely necessary. His campaign, like that of the Home Rulers, was dangerous and in a doubtful category somewhere between politics and revolution, because it too attempted to secure mass participation and a permanent opposition. At times Gandhi seemed to put himself beyond the law—and therefore apparently to end any debate about how he should be treated. Yet even then the government found room to manoeuvre, for the old certainties about how properly to deal with different categories of agitation had dissolved, and in their place tactical non-interference was becoming ever more firmly established.

Even more telling in this respect is the subsequent fate of the Ali brothers. They were released on the eve of the Amritsar Congress. The question had been shelved since the failure of the initiative in 1917, except during March and April 1918, a period of anxiety about Muhammad's health. In August 1919 it was decided not to release the brothers until after the announcement of the peace terms with Turkey and some further period to assess Muslim reactions. But this decision was evidently not final. In October the question arose of allowing the Alis to visit their mother who was ill. In the end this was not permitted as the mother's condition improved; but before this Vincent had observed that it would be a bad grievance if she were to die while her sons were barred from visiting, and the Home Department Secretary, C. W. Gwynne, suggested that a decision should await the outcome of discussions then being held about a royal act of clemency—the implication being that the timing of the release was still an open question. On 15 December Vincent proposed, with Hill and Lowndes concurring, and Barnes cordially agreeing, that it would be unwise to exclude the Alis from this amnesty, on the grounds that (as Vincent wired to Chelmsford on tour) it was 'desirable to placate Muhammedan feeling which would be irritated by the exclusion' compared with indulgence shown to other political prisoners.[66] This brought the policy towards Muslims into line with the approach now being generally adopted; that approach had been under fire but clearly was far from on the defensive.

There are two reasons why the tactical approach had not become established more quickly. In the first place, though the Government of India were formulating a consistent policy, they were continually under pressure to revert to an earlier approach. Even the India Office, in November 1918, wondered if they should prosecute the Home Rulers for the design of mock postage stamps issued for publicity and fund raising. This may seem trivial: yet it was symptomatic of the challenge Home Rulers presented, as opposition with funds and publicity, almost an alternative to the *raj*. The Home Department declined to act, on the ground that prohibition would only advertise the stamps, which had not been very successful.[67] They took a similar view early in 1918 when Madras prohibited the flying of the Home Rule flag; and they would not allow the Bihar and Orissa authorities to follow suit: Vincent thought the prohibition 'unwise' and likely to 'cause more trouble than the flag'.[68]

This provincial opposition was the most difficult. Some of the governors, notably Meston, approved of the tactic of non-interference. But others did not. In particular, Willingdon, as Governor of Bombay and later of Madras, repeatedly showed his lack of sympathy with 'softness'—he wanted the Government of India to 'stiffen up' and stand no nonsense. He believed in the efficacy of a 'straight talk' such as he had given the Home Rulers at the Bombay War Conference; he recognized that this was 'exactly the opposite' of what Chelmsford seemed to want. He did not share the Viceroy's hope that extremists, if left alone, would discredit themselves; and, although he sometimes admitted that there were risks in acting against prominent politicians, he felt sure that these should be braved. When Tilak announced that it would not matter to him if Turks or Germans took over from the British, the only answer, according to Willingdon, was to 'put a stopper' on to him. In 1919, similarly, Willingdon vowed he would either 'shoot or deport' Muhammad and Shaukat Ali. His opposition was to increase as time went on.[69]

Under Pentland, the Madras Government's disapproval had already resulted in obstruction. In November 1918 *New India* printed a passage heralding the fall of three pre-war autocracies, Russian, German and Austrian, and asking if the fourth, British India, was to remain 'to the amazement of, and a menace to a world set free'. The Madras Advocate-General considered these sentiments made *New India* liable to forfeit its security under the Press Act. The India Government asked what Madras proposed to do, and were asked in turn what they wanted done. The Home Department replied that they could reasonably expect to know the local views on that, and Madras answered that their 'view of the mischievous character' of Besant's influence was 'unaltered', but that they did not propose to act as they understood that 'issues affecting the whole of India' were raised. This was an explicit reference to the terms of Besant's release, and amounted to a refusal to govern: they believed there was a danger, but out of pique declined to act or to take responsibility for not acting. The Home Department did not want Besant penalized; but the Madras behaviour was objectionable, because without local co-operation sensible decisions were impossible. Chelmsford noted on the file: '. . . Madras won't play, and we must wait for a new Governor'.[70]

Later, in 1919, however (as we have seen with Gandhi) the strongest objections came from the Panjab. In October, in response to a query from Montagu, the Home Department asked that all restrictions on Tilak should be removed. The Panjab Government declined. The Home Department took the view that their reason, the danger of Tilak's presence provoking disturbances, was 'double-edged', and W. S. Marris, the joint Secretary, sent a demi-official letter setting out the other side of the case. Maclagan, the Governor of the Panjab, then launched a fierce attack on central policy. He argued that the Panjab had problems enough without Tilak. He saw the Home Department pressure as another in a series of 'extraordinary difficulties' in which (he implied) the Government of India had placed him. He had wanted the continuance of the Seditious Meetings Act, the exclusion of Gandhi until after the forthcoming Congress session at Amritsar, the postponement of Lajpat Rai's departure from the United States—and all these had been refused. Now, in Tilak's case, he was being asked 'to let loose in the Province the most dangerous agitator of all', one who 'specialized . . . in the reduction to the level of everyday life . . . of [the] high sounding phrases used by other politicians'.

The Home Department were taken aback and suggested that Montagu should be told that they could hardly go against Maclagan's wishes. Chelmsford took the question in Council, and the Department's view was upheld, subject to reconsideration after the forthcoming Amritsar Congress or if the Secretary of State returned to the subject. Their decision was influenced by the fact that Tilak was in England, and not known to be returning for the Congress. The Panjab were informed—with Vincent objecting to the language of their protest—and an explanation was also sent to the India Office. Chelmsford wrote privately to Maclagan calling his government's letter 'unfortunate and ungracious', and the Governor apologized. To Vincent Maclagan explained that he had thought the Home Department were acting under pressure from London and his protests had thus been directed chiefly at the Secretary of State. It was true (as Vincent admitted in a marginal note to Maclagan's letter) that there had been pressure from Montagu; but, from the first, the Home Department itself had declined to accept the Panjab view, and the Council decision had been concerned mainly with the impropriety of dictating a policy (on a relatively minor matter) in the teeth of local objections.

The question was not left there. W. M. Hailey, then Finance Member, was in Delhi, and was asked to talk to Maclagan. Next day it was discovered that Tilak *was* planning to return to India, and thus his exclusion was no longer academic, but likely to cause ill-feeling or disturbances. Montagu again pressed for an end to the restriction; and in the Home Department Gwynne noted that the Congress were more likely to get out of hand if Tilak were excluded than if he were present, and that it would be better for government 'to beat an orderly retreat now'. Vincent saw Maclagan personally, early in December, and persuaded him to give way. He had displayed the Panjab civilian's orthodox nervousness and desire to keep his own preserve free from the contamination of outside forces.[71] The Government of India refused to accept this: they had been thwarted, but only briefly. Such exclusion would have been contrary to precedent, as when Tilak was allowed to address Congress in 1918, or when, in November 1917, exclusion orders were not enforced to allow him to visit Delhi with a Home Rule deputation on reforms.[72] The centre were committed to an approach quite the opposite of provincial insularity. And yet every act of opposition to their policy slowed down the spread of tactical conciliation to wider arenas.

The second major impediment was more fundamental. In June 1919, in response to complaints and reflections from Colonel Beadon in Delhi, prompted by the recent unrest, W. S. Marris wrote a long note setting out the government's dilemma. The problem, he stated, was the same in essentials as that which presented itself when Besant was interned, or when Gandhi began *satyagraha*: 'Is agitation conducted in the name of constitutional liberty which is likely to lead to disorder to be permitted up to the point at which disorder actually occurs; and if not, can we do anything to stop it beyond what we do now?'—or, more graphically, 'Since we cannot rule by machine guns can we acquiesce in a campaign which must from time to time bring the machine guns on the scene?' The problem, he thought, was that the present weapons (the Press Act, the Seditious Meetings Act, and others in the armoury of repression) were 'all rather a denial of our own principles', used 'intermittently and reluctantly', and 'too big and clumsy to deal with nine tenths of the actual mischief'. The reforms (being a half-way measure) were bound to result in agitation, but would make control harder than ever. The Secretary of State should be told, Marris went on, that 'the unrestrained freedom of misrepresentation is a menace to our State', and Parliament should be asked if it were 'prepared to see the administration weakened and brought to a standstill'.[73] Obviously, for Marris, the contradictions between democracy and autocracy were not yet resolved, so far as they affected the policy towards agitation.

Thus stated, it is clear that the policy of tactical non-interference had a major disadvantage, that it did not, in itself, make a contribution to solving the basic difficulty, already aired in the disagreements of 1917, of 'drawing the line' between constitutional and unconstitutional action. At what point (if any), Marris was asking, as had his predecessors, did the dangers apprehended from activities which were themselves permissible in terms of the democratic goal, justify the use of measures which were 'all rather a denial' of that goal, of the government's 'own principles', in order to preserve control. While non-interference was conceived of as tactical and repression was not abandoned, this problem inevitably remained.

But the decision over Besant in 1917 had marked a turning-point after which the theoretical difficulty gradually retreated. Marris, in 1919, demonstrated that, although the debate continued, one side of it was increasingly disarmed. He did not for a moment suggest that the way to prevent the administration's being 'weakened or brought to a standstill' should be strong measures. On the contrary he insisted: 'I certainly do not advocate repression'; he could make no concrete suggestions except for discussions and better propaganda. Only on these points, too, did Vincent take him up, and the wider implications of the note seem to have been shelved. The difficulty Marris noted was not removed; it was merely forgotten.

The force which obscured it was the force of precedent. The Besant policy became established because it was thought successful. It was extended because the alternative (as with Gandhi) was thought to have failed. And as new figures and styles of politics came within its orbit—as did Tilak, then Gandhi and then the Ali brothers—it became the *established* way in which these leaders were treated. Thus when we talk of the policy unfolding as time went on, what we are seeing is the inertia of the administration being shifted by experience—from supporting repression where 'necessary', to supporting non-interference where possible. Thus the reform policy, which had led to the shift in 1917, was affecting the official approach to politics.

Chapter 6. Repression

REPRESSION, the other aspect of government policy, was not so much the opposite as the accompaniment of non-interference. In theory it was applied to lawlessness and violence, not politics. But by 1916 the government in India had armed itself with strong powers to deal with what it called political crime.[1] The principle was well established that the executive must be able to circumvent the ordinary judicial process in order to deal promptly with sedition. Minto's and Hardinge's governments had had little difficulty in establishing a procedure to be adopted towards political action involving violence. They were helped by two main axioms: first that the problem was special, serious and widespread; second that it was related to other extreme political activities.

The Bengal Government, in particular, supported the view that only executive powers could cope with terrorism. It is true that during Lord Carmichael's term as Governor, they opposed deportation, and unsuccessfully sought moderate Bengali support for anti-terrorist measures; yet even then the local government had consistently called for new powers, and by the end of the war had so far rewritten history as to forget Carmichael's reluctance altogether. Indeed this was not (as has been suggested) a liberal governor standing out against a central government bent on draconian measures. The picture was more complicated. Certainly Reginald Craddock, the Home Member, had argued, as he would later over Annie Besant, that there was no 'via media' between repression and 'futile conciliation'—but he was referring to those politicians (admittedly numerous) whose constitutionalism he held to be insincere. Accordingly he could blame the Bengal upheavals ultimately on the permanent settlement, which made for weak administration and created a discontented middling class—an explanation which suggests no positive solution for terrorism short of what was impossible, a complete transformation of Bengali society—and yet in practice, even in the minute in which he put forward this view, he did advocate positive measures as well as or instead of repressive ones. Thus, at times, we find the Government of India urging positive reforms on a local government which wanted to rely on repressive legislation. Carmichael's dispute with Craddock was chiefly over the importance of trying to carry moderates with them; and where the Government of India were unhappy with Carmichael was over the lack of vigour with which the agreed repression was being practised. In the debate under Carmichael the argument, from P. C. Lyon and Sir Syed Shams-ul Huda in the Bengal Government, was that substantive reforms should precede not that they should replace the taking of repressive powers: opposition in principle to such enactments should not be deduced from doubts or slowness over exercise of the powers.

As Bengal saw it, the Government of India had forced them, in January 1910 (after Morley had brought pressure to bear against deportations), to proceed against revolutionaries under ordinary law, and the results, in the Howrah Gang Case, when 40 out of 46 defendants were acquitted, had discredited this procedure. (The view was not shared by the Government of India who considered the case badly handled.) As a result, Bengal began in 1911 to advocate special legislation to give them additional executive powers. The central government repeatedly suspended judgement on the need for legislation, and in 1913 suggested that a constructive policy also was required. An inquiry into Bengal district administration ensued. Not until December 1913, in the latest of a series of conferences between local and central officials (in this case the Bengal Inspector-General of Police and Sir Charles Cleveland), did the centre agree that conspiracy trials were unlikely to succeed, and that it was desirable to pass legislation to allow orders of compulsory residence and surveillance. Even then the Government of India worried about the controversial nature of such a law, and advised the Secretary of State that instead they should use Regulation III of 1818. Lord Crewe demurred, and recommended that Bengal should pass the surveillance law. The Bengal Passport Bill, drafted in 1914 to meet the case, was dropped eventually as it pleased no-one; but in 1915 the Defence of India Act gave the powers which Bengal had wanted.

In 1913 Hughes-Butler, the officiating Director of Criminal Intelligence, had urged vigorous application of Regulation III, but William Marris in the Home Department recommended instead a 'special temporary Act' empowering a commission of one executive and one judicial officer and one non-official to require security from or surveillance over members of 'dangerous revolutionary asso-

ciations'. Craddock had suggested the commission to review
Bengal administration and also an ordinance to set up machinery
on the Marris lines (omitting the non-official). But, among
Craddock's colleagues, Ali Imam had opposed both his suggestions;
Butler, though prepared for an Act (not an ordinance), thought
administration should first be improved; and Wilson, accepting an
Act, threatened to resign if Regulation III were used except for
'extraordinary political offences'. The Viceroy, Hardinge, believing
it most important to bridle the press and not yet proven that an
ordinance was unavoidable, also had stressed the need for positive
measures. Thus it was the Bengal view, that a new law was
needed, which had come to be accepted in 1915; and the seed of
that acceptance, as well as of postwar repressive legislation, can be
seen in Home Department notes of 1913. The 1915 Act was not so
much the result of Craddock's seizing an opportunity, as the
outcome of a long debate in which Bengal had led the way. Bengal
proposed, moreover, to reopen the question of legislation when the
Act expired after the war—in 1917 when Vincent, as Home Member,
called for an amendment to allow review of cases by independent
tribunal, Ronaldshay (Carmichael's successor) opposed the idea
partly because such a concession would be one way 'to make some
distinction between war-time and post-war conditions' when a
permanent measure was introduced.[2]

The problem in Bengal was certainly serious. Lord Hardinge
described the province as 'seething with sedition'. Armed rob-
beries (or dacoities) and assassinations of police and informers
were, by his account, 'almost of daily occurrence', and 'it was
practically impossible to secure a conviction by the ordinary
process of law'.[3] This rather overstated the position; nonetheless
there was a bad situation which had deteriorated under Hardinge.
Austen Chamberlain believed that both the Viceroy and the local
Governor had neglected the problem;[4] Chelmsford had to dissuade
the Secretary of State from intervening, and himself set about a
vigorous investigation. Shortly after taking up office he went to
Calcutta, read the files on the subject, and had a long interview
with the Governor. He asked Carmichael to give him a comprehensive report on the action his government had taken, and their
proposals for remedial measures and the postwar replacement of
the Defence of India Act. Carmichael replied that they would
investigate the result of the use of wartime powers to see in what

form they should be retained. This response evoked no great enthusiasm in Lord Chelmsford—Carmichael had written, he said, perhaps 'the sort of note which Lord Carmichael would write.' Indeed Chelmsford later called the Bengal Government 'invertebrate', marked by 'floppiness'.[5] There was general dissatisfaction at the 'period of virtual "laissez-faire"' under Carmichael; and Sir Beauchamp Duff had even recommended the Governor's recall. As a result and under pressure from London, Chelmsford's government tried to spur Bengal into action, advocating full use of the Defence of India Act. Earlier, Hill, 'with unexpected & welcome help from the excellent Lowndes', had been trying to combat the 'HD view' that, in spite of a worsening situation in Bengal, no remedies should be devised until there was a change of personnel in the 'hopelessly bad' Bengal Government.[6]

The pressure under Chelmsford did not mean unlimited local discretion. In May 1916, after the murder of a police officer, the eighteenth in eight years, Bengal tried to persuade the Home Department to allow even wider powers, especially the use of Regulation III of 1818 at local discretion to imprison 'suspects'; in August they also asked to be allowed to prosecute for the possession of (not only for circulating) seditious literature. The Government of India refused the former request, and, in agreeing to the latter, urged 'the greatest discretion' in sanctioning prosecutions and provided that the new rule should apply only to those documents whose dissemination would be dangerous 'under existing war conditions'. As it was, this proposal, which had earlier been refused by Hardinge, was opposed by Nair and Lowndes; and even by Craddock was advocated subject to the proviso that possession must be 'conscious' and with 'intention to circulate'.[7] In general, therefore, the centre believed the Defence of India Act provided quite sufficient powers; what they wanted was more effort from Bengal.

The Government of India themselves, meanwhile, pursued some immediate remedies; in particular they sought an arrangement with the French, whose territory, Chandanagar, was alleged to be an 'anarchist centre' and refuge. Agreement was difficult, but eventually, in 1918, the London authorities concluded a *projet d'accord* whereby the French agreed that British Indian 'seditionists' would be immediately expelled and French subjects placed under surveillance.[8]

Chelmsford too placed some emphasis on positive remedies. He reported in September 1916 that his government were 'not unmindful' of the need to tackle 'the root-cause of the evil'. He interviewed several of the Bengal officials. His conversations convinced him that educational reform lay at the heart of the remedy. It was believed that 'anarchical' crime, largely committed by *bhadralok* Hindus, was partly the expression of frustration at the lack of opportunities for those with a liberal education; and Chelmsford hoped, as had his predecessors, for advances in technical education and some channelling of talent away from law and government service and into commerce and industry. Chelmsford was also strongly in favour of a proposal to transfer the Presidency College away from the heady political atmosphere of Calcutta;[9] and, urging that education was 'at the bottom' of most of the Bengal problems, he favoured and supported the general review of Bengal secondary and university education undertaken by the Sadler Committee.[10] The situation needed this thorough investigation: the Director of Public Instruction, Bengal, had stated in his annual report for 1915–16:

The present condition of secondary schools is undoubtedly prejudicing the development of the Presidency and is by no means a negligible feature in the existing state of general disturbance. . . . [I]t is in the high schools, with their underpaid and discontented teachers, their crowded, dark and ill-ventilated rooms, and their soul-destroying process of unceasing cram, that the seeds of discontent and fanaticism are sown.[11]

In reply to the Government of India's call for suggestions for substantive reforms, the Bengal Government had endorsed the ideas of the commission on Bengal district administration, which had recommended a reduction in the size of administrative charges, and also local self-government, industrial development and educational reform. The local government had decided to advance the first and last of these, in spite of wartime financial stringency, as matters of urgency.[12]

It was obvious that Bengal administration needed overhauling. The Government of India had suggested that organization would have to be strengthened, and in January 1917 the Secretary of State urged that East Bengal districts and police station areas should be split up, as recommended in the District Administration Committee report. Dacca, Midnapur and Mymensingh districts were divided during 1918;[13] and several police station areas had also been made smaller.[14] Some police were also being armed, and squads were formed to protect Special Branch officers investigating 'conspiracies' and thus in danger of assassination.[15] Several improvements were made in police pay and special allowances. Numbers were also increased; and a new class of 'writer' constables, with a higher pay scale, was introduced to attract better recruits. In 1918, however, average police earnings in Bengal were still below those of local durwans, coolies and mill-operatives, and below those of the police in Madras and Bombay. In 1920 Bengal police were understaffed, by one thousand out of a nominal 19,000; and, in spite of recruiting drives and annual pay rises, wastage was continuing at an increasing rate.[16] But the Bengal Government maintained that the problems of the police were separate from the question of 'revolutionary' crime—this was handled by the Special Branch and not by the force in general. The intelligence staff had been enormously increased by both temporary and permanent appointments, and their deployment had been improved in the districts. In 1916 Bengal intelligence staff comprised 11 inspectors, 15 sub-inspectors and 37 constables. In 1917, after two increases, the permanent establishment was 20 inspectors, 51 sub-inspectors, 43 head constables, 351 constables and 36 confidential clerks—representing a total increase of 438. The Calcutta Special Branch was also strengthened by more than half.[17] About the same time as these changes, the number of outrages in Bengal decreased. There were 64 in 1915–16, but only ten between January 1917 and February 1918.[18] This period, however, coincided also with the more vigorous application of the Defence of India Act. The cause of the improvement was therefore not certain.

The question of permanent legislation had not been lost sight of. Following Chelmsford's inconclusive exchanges with Carmichael in April 1916, the Home Department asked Bengal what would be needed after the war; and in July the local government replied strongly urging special powers.[19] In a despatch in October, the Secretary of State also, while urging freer use of repressive powers, hinted that this would be difficult after the war and suggested the continuance of some of the Defence of India provisions. He pressed for an early decision.[20] Thus the Home Department came to be considering the whole problem of 'revolutionary' crime, including the possibility of introducing measures of 'a more stringent and far reaching character'.[21]

Craddock envisaged special tribunals to punish anarchists, an idea opposed by Barnes (who called it a sort of Star Chamber) and Du Boulay, who preferred preventive measures. The Legislative Department, in a note drawn up by Muddiman and Lowndes, recommended quasi-judicial commissions to deal with suspects— Lowndes, as he later explained, believed that those about to be punished should have the benefit of the ordinary law of evidence; but he was prepared to go further with preventive measures, such as restrictions imposed on suspects. This view was supported by Meyer, Hill, Barnes, and later, with some modifications, Vincent. There were differences of opinion, therefore, but (with the single exception of Sankaran Nair who thought constructive steps sufficient) the Members agreed that executive powers, tempered with some judicial element, should be available to tackle anarchism.[22]

The subject of a replacement for the Defence of India Act was thus under active consideration as early as 1916. Chelmsford had stressed that no time should be lost and 'the matter thoroughly thrashed out before the occasion arises'[23]—though he believed strongly that actual legislation should await the end of the war. But there had been delays—the Bengal Government and then Vincent as the new Home Member had needed time to study the question—[24] and as yet no firm decision had been taken. Moreover, a further problem had arisen. The wartime measures, by deliberate policy, had been applied not only to Bengal terrorists but also to a wide and ill-defined area of political activity. The result had been severe criticism from Indians, both privately and in the press. Accordingly the Bengal proposals of July 1916 had sought to modify the wartime provisions, in the hope of making them more acceptable without sacrificing essential features. The local government proposed that the application of executive powers should be subject to the prior scrutiny of advisory committees, that there should be no provision for rapid trial by Commission and that the new Act should have a life of only three years.[25] Even more important, in 1917 Lord Ronaldshay, the Governor, suggested that the whole question should be referred to a semi-judicial commission of enquiry. He thought it necessary to convince public opinion in India and Britain that extraordinary powers were needed, and, as

it was not thought possible to publish the evidence of the conspiracies, either because it was itself objectionable or because it
was based on testimony secured by promises of secrecy, a commission sitting mainly *in camera* was the obvious answer.

The Bengal Government suggested an inquiry officially on 21
June 1917, and the Government of India endorsed the idea on 16
August. But Ronaldshay had noted it in his diary as early as 26
May and included it in a letter (later lost at sea) to Chamberlain on
27 June.[26] The centre were evidently not thinking of an inquiry in
December 1916 when they appointed an officer on special duty to
summarize information on record in the C.I.D.;[27] and in February
1917 they opposed a resolution by M. B. Dadabhoy calling for a
committee on Indian anarchism. Evidently, then, the inquiry was
Ronaldshay's invention. But, equally, the idea found supporters.
Dadabhoy's resolution had been admitted in order to give an
opportunity to convince Indians that anarchy existed and to test
the mood of the legislature. Claude Hill, supported by Nair and
Lowndes, had advocated such publicity, and, though William
Meyer had been opposed, Craddock had agreed. On this occasion
nothing was done, presumably because of a lack of non-official
interest—the resolution was negatived after only one speech, that
of the mover.[28] Ronaldshay's ideas suggested another way of
gaining the same object, and it may be assumed that those
Members who had supported one form of publicity would also
support the other. As a Home Department demi-official later
remarked, of possible postwar proposals, 'we realise that they will
be exposed to violent opposition and criticism from those who will
not accept the Government of India's statements of the extent of
the conspiracies and the need for special powers to deal with
them'.[29]

The Government of India proposed to the Secretary of State a
committee headed by an eminent English judge, with one English
and one Indian judge from the Indian High Courts, one Indian
non-official and one British official with executive experience. But
the government were also ready to decide what was needed. At a
conference held in Calcutta in December 1917, to concert official
positions, Lowndes, Vincent, and officers from Bengal, Bombay and
the Panjab, agreed on necessary lines of legislation: they envisaged
special courts, modifications in the laws of procedure and possibly
evidence, and something like the Defence of India rules.[30] The

inquiry committee was thus not intended to help a decision; it was purely a public relations gesture.

For this reason the committee's personnel and procedure had to command public confidence, while its decision, favourable to government, was ensured by having it base its deliberations largely on 'documentary evidence already available', that is, on official sources. Indeed elaborate depositions and selections of correspondence were prepared; Ronaldshay rightly had no doubts that he could convince the inquiry of 'the existence of a widespread and dangerous conspiracy'.[31] The committee was appointed at the end of 1917 under the Scottish judge, S. A. T. Rowlatt. Montagu had found it difficult to recruit a chairman in Britain, and the India Government had hoped for a more famous name. But otherwise they had no reason to be dissatisfied. The committee studied the statements placed before them by the governments of Bengal, Madras, Bihar and Orissa, Bombay, the Central and United Provinces, the Panjab, and Burma, and by the Government of India. They also heard verbal statements from officials except in the case of Madras, and in the Panjab and Bengal they 'invited and secured the attendance' of individuals and deputations representing 'various non-official points of view'. The result was the Rowlatt Report, which vindicated government policy and favoured the continuance of wartime powers, as the government wished. Official and judicial evidence had carried most weight; and the procedure was by no means above suspicion.

But the Report is a dextrous document. In the India Office, Holderness hoped that it might 'open the eyes of many Indians to the mischief wh. political movements of the kind incited by Tilak bring about'. There, as elsewhere, the Report was held to carry 'a great authority by reason of the eminent men who have drawn it up'. The Government of India were well satisfied.[32]

The Rowlatt Report had examined those crimes, mainly dacoities and murders, which the committee characterized as 'revolutionary'—crimes known to be a result of conspiracy, involving groups and advance planning; crimes carried out for political motives and by *bhadralok* youths; crimes shown to be interconnected, as revealed in confessions, the movement of loot and the sharing of weapons and information (notably on bomb manufacture); and finally crimes arising out of these other types, in particular the murder of police, prosecutors and witnesses in

conspiracy trials, and the theft of arms to be used in dacoities and
murders. The Report traced the crimes to revolutionary societies
which had grown out of Barinda Kumar Ghosh's *Anusilan Samiti*,
especially the Dacca branch which had been directly implicated
in the Barisal conspiracy case of 1913. These societies were claimed
to be working 'very largely in concert', attempting to subvert
students, and espousing 'revolutionary' aims.[33]
The Report's own evidence was perhaps not totally convincing
in these regards. The impression given was of deliberate campaigns
of terrorism—one letter, discovered in 1916, boasted in the name of
the 'Finance Secretary of the Bengal Branch of the Independent
Kingdom of India' that 'adequate punishment' was being inflicted
on police officers; this 'Independent Kingdom' also professed to
regard robbery as something in the nature of tax-collection.
Such reasoning was reflected in other documents. But the 'revolutionary' societies (as the Report admitted) were not altogether of
one mind—there was even one instance of a pamphlet disapproving of violence and dacoities.[34] The Report also made no
attempt to gain an historical perspective on the long-standing
incidence of violent crime as a characteristic of Bengali unrest. Nor
did it make a general survey of the alleged subversion of students,
and, although it cited one or two schools as notorious, it was
content to show intention rather than prove success in this policy.
Moreover the rules and ceremonies of the Dacca *samiti* displayed
religious as much as political fanaticism; the Report did not
differentiate between the two.[35] And, while documents were found
exhorting members to secrecy, the societies often seemed ama-
teurish, the adherents proving remarkably indiscreet, keeping
incriminating documents and even lists of members. On the other
hand, judgments in the various conspiracy trials did bear out the
Report's picture,[36] and the authorities had uncovered and destroyed
three main conspiracies whose instigators had planned uprisings
and arms shipments and made contact with the Germans. One
conspiracy centred on Bengal had ended with a gun battle and the
death of the leader of the Jugantar party of Calcutta, a group
already responsible for a resurgence of crime in that area.[37]
Having identified the problem and established how serious it
was, the Report went on to advocate the remedy already decided
upon by the government. A token interest was shown in positive
and administrative remedies, but there was no assessment of

possible ways of avoiding executive powers. The courts were pronounced inadequate, partly because of the danger of intimidation
of witnesses, the reliance on confessions and other evidence not
admissable in law, and the difficulty of attributing blame to
individual members of a gang, but also because of shortcomings in
the judicial system. It was claimed that there had been 210 outrages
since 1906, and evidence of the complicity of 1088 persons, but
only 84 convictions in 39 attempts at prosecution. Thus the
Rowlatt Committee argued that the 'forces of law and order
working through the ordinary channels were beaten'. No attempt
was made to correlate this with figures for crime in general. There
were, for example, 28 outrages in Bengal in 1915, but 18,841
'serious crimes' in the Dacca police range alone. There, all crime
was increasing—along with civil unrest, for the Dacca battalion
was called out 65 times between April 1912 and July 1918. And,
as B. N. Sarma was to tell the Imperial Legislative Council, the
prosecution rate for 'revolutionaries' did not compare unfavourably with that for other serious crimes. In ten trials involving 192 persons, 63 were convicted and 82 bound over: this was
33 per cent success compared with nine (1912) or eleven (1915) per
cent for murder. The Rowlatt Report itself admitted that the
number of confessions had increased as war measures 'broke the
morale' of the revolutionaries.[38]

The Committee also conceded that there was only a very small
number of 'conspirators': they concentrated on the nature not the
extent of the problem. Taking up an odd stance for a quasi-
judicial body, they quoted (apparently with approval) the Panjab
Government's argument that 'it is most undesirable at the present
time to allow trials of any of these revolutionaries ... to be pro-
tracted by the ingenuity of Counsel and drawn out to inordinate
length by the committal and appeal procedure ...'. Sir Verney
Lovett later explained that the main point for him on the committee
had been whether or not the government was going to protect its
servants and subjects; and clearly 'revolutionaries' were being
seen as a special case, not amenable to ordinary control, demanding
special measures.[39]

The the Rowlatt Committee recommended some changes in the
law of evidence, but concentrated on a method of continuing the
extra-judicial wartime powers. Following the lead of the Bengal
Government, they sought to hedge the powers about with safe-

guards. They proposed that the measures should be introduced in any area only by express notification of the Governor-General in Council and then in three stages according to the seriousness of the situation—the first stage would allow expeditious trials; the second would permit the demand for security or the application of certain orders and restrictions, all such actions being subject to prior investigation by an independent authority; and the third would permit arrests and searches without warrants and detentions for up to one month pending an order, again subject to investigation (though not necessarily beforehand) and also to scrutiny of the conditions of detention, by independent committees. These powers were to be available throughout the country—it was thought impolitic and unwise to confine the provisions to Bengal. They were to be applied only when needed. The Committee had recommended special emergency powers, applicable if necessary to a tiny minority, who, because their activities were believed to be dangerous and uncontrollable, were not to be given the ordinary benefits of the law.[40]

The Government of India duly received the Rowlatt Report and published a censored version. They had decided to introduce legislation as soon as possible, and in the exact form of the Committee's proposals. They were concerned not to waste the good effect they anticipated from the publication of the Report.[41] As time went on, moreover, their desire for haste became greater. Vithalbhai Patel, sharing the general puzzlement at this, was later to claim that they were making one of the 'blunders which a Government not responsible to the people is likely to commit in moments of excitement'.[42] But haste was deliberate. By 1919 the government were worried at the imminence of the signing of the peace treaty, which they expected to occur at any moment. They did not wish to be accused of using wartime measures unfairly. It is also probable that there was some truth in Sastri's suggestion in the imperial legislature that the government were trying to reassure English opinion and so facilitate the acceptance of the reforms scheme. Certainly the government believed that the 'revolutionary movement' would be 'far more likely to impair the chances of political progress . . . than anything else'. Austen Chamberlain also stressed the link between reforms and continued executive powers—he believed 'The more democratic the Government becomes the more fatal disorder is likely to be'.[43]

The government were also over-sanguine about the reaction to their proposals. In September, G. S. Khaparde had tried to postpone consideration of the Rowlatt Report by passing a hostile resolution in the imperial legislature. The government argued that a unanimous report by such distinguished men could not be ignored, and all but two of the non-official members agreed with them. Sastri, Banerjea, Shafi and Sapru declared Khaparde's resolution inopportune; Sapru added that he had read the Report asking if it read like fact or fiction, and had decided it read like fact. Even Jinnah opposed the resolution, although, unlike the others, he made it clear that he would also oppose the Report's proposals when the proper time came. The government regarded the outcome of this debate, as noted by officials in the India Office, 'as indicating that legislation on the lines proposed would not be unfavourably received'.[44] This optimism was encouraged in February 1919 by the defeat in the Bengal Legislative Council of another hostile resolution.[45] Chelmsford's assessment of his own Council was that opposition had 'slackened off'. He called his opponents the 'Malaviya faction', and thought that, although the government were having a strenuous time, they were 'on solid ground'. In March he considered the position 'healthy'.[46] His government were thus hurrying to pass the Rowlatt Bill while the good humour lasted.

The same arguments applied of course to agitation outside the Legislative Council. Gandhi and the Congress had declared their opposition to the continuance of repressive executive powers. Gandhi had pleaded and cajoled, and threatened to invoke the weapon of passive resistance. This was the first time he had suggested using his methods nationally, and the government underestimated the threat. Chelmsford was pleased to find that Sastri and Banerjea had spoken out against Gandhi's campaign. He interviewed Gandhi himself and found him a little shaken by the government's sympathy with his objections to the Bill and by smaller amounts of support than he had expected among legislators. But Gandhi, decided Chelmsford, had 'passive resistance on the brain' and was now committed to his campaign. Chelmsford concluded that the government would have to call Gandhi's bluff; he expressed himself 'quite happy' defending his position, and judged that Gandhi had not chosen his ground well for a 'thoroughgoing passive resistance movement'. Montagu was wrong to presume that they were in for 'a period of great agitation'.[47]

But, if opposition in and outside the legislature was underestimated, it was nonetheless recognized that delay would increase
and not diminish the difficulties. Vincent told the legislators, 'the
more the Government yields in this matter, the greater force
would the agitation obtain'. He was probably right. Most of the
Council members who were attempting to delay the Bill admitted
that they believed, as Vithalbhai Patel put it, that 'the only way to
improve this Bill is to entirely drop it'. A delay would have raised
hopes. Patel said that, with postponement, 'the Government might
see the unwisdom of passing this measure at any time'; and Rai
Bahadur B. D. Shukul went so far as to admit that it was expected
with the agitation, 'that the Government would . . . drop the Bill
altogether'.[48] This hope was perhaps well-founded. The minor
permanent proposals of the Rowlatt Report were embodied in a
second Bill, which was eventually abandoned after the government
had given in to a demand for republication.[49] Moreover, as was
never very far from anyone's mind, a delay on the main Rowlatt
Bill might well have meant that it would have had to be introduced
before the new reformed Legislative Assembly, where it would
have had the double disadvantage, as far as the government were
concerned, of souring the atmosphere and of being in danger of
defeat. Before the war such difficulty had been experienced in
trying to pass a similar bill through the Bengal Legislative Council
that the attempt had been abandoned, and the measure left to the
Government of India.[50]

The government therefore had good reasons for haste. It is less
easy to see why they were so determined to go ahead in the face of
Indian objections. They were beginning to enunciate the principle,
later to grow in importance, of giving effect to the wishes of the
legislature. In 1920, over the Dacca University Bill, they explained
to the Secretary of State that 'it would be impolitic in a case of this
kind to use our official majority on the eve of the introduction of
reforms to override non-official opinion freely and strongly
expressed'.[51] Moreover, the introduction of the Rowlatt Bill—a
decision to 'override non-official opinion'—followed a new concern
to *limit* the application of executive powers. In March 1918 a
general order was issued instructing local governments to work the
Defence of India Act with discretion—it was not to be used
indiscriminately, nor 'merely because the accused person happens
to be a suspected revolutionary or because the crime is believed to

be in pursuance of a revolutionary conspiracy'. The ordinary law was to be used where possible and the special powers evoked 'only when clear necessity . . . can be established'. Hitherto the government had 'invariably accepted' any local request to apply the Act; they now served notice that they would do so no longer. The change was to reverse the tendency to 'supersede the ordinary criminal courts in respect of the ordinary crime of the country'— a tendency which was unattributed but which dated, as we have seen, from 1913. Now repression was to be limited to those crimes which were both dangerous and not amenable to judicial control.[52]

Of course, as we have seen, leaders and publicists with no direct link (nor in some cases even sympathy) with terrorism or violence had fallen foul of the Defence of India Act; and the Government of India were also recognizing the ill-feeling about this. Later, after the armistice, they were to become even more wary about using the powers 'in normal conditions'. Early in 1919 local governments had been instructed to consider lifting such restrictions; and in August, when Vincent discovered that a ban on public speaking by Asaf Ali was still in force in Delhi, though supposed to have been removed in June, he commented: 'We have said a good deal about not using D. of I. rules (save as a war measure . . .). I do not think it can be said, conditions in Delhi are abnormal now.' Later that year, C. W. Gwynne of the Home Department noted, with Marris agreeing 'generally', that repeal of such legislation as Regulation III of 1818 was 'ultimately inevitable', given the 'trend of public opinion', its distrust of non-judicial punishment, and its strong feeling that the very existence of repressive legislation tended 'to create occasions on which its adoption may become desirable'. Thus the government would find it 'more and more necessary to depend solely on the courts'.[53] Vincent's strict attitude over Asaf Ali accorded with the policy of non-interference; Gwynne identified a trend which this policy encouraged.

Moreover, if the Rowlatt Bill seems to run counter to the tendencies of Chelmsford's administration, it certainly did not conform with Edwin Montagu's ideas for Indian government. He made every conceivable protest, except the only effective one of refusing his sanction. He found much that was 'repugnant' in the Rowlatt proposals—they 'made a radical think hard'. He asked, without success, for the Bills to be accompanied by a concession, the abandonment of Regulation III of 1818. He wrote that he loathed the retention of wartime measures and dreaded the perpetuation of that sort of police government which, he claimed, had given Sir Michael O'Dwyer a 'cheap' success in the Panjab. He predicted that the government would not be able to use the Rowlatt powers in the conditions of the future.[54] In the face of this pressure, in defiance of Indian opposition, in apparent contradiction of their own predilections, the Government of India pressed on with the main Rowlatt Bill.

There were several reasons for their persistence. The first was a belief that the measures were unavoidable. Vincent told the legislature that the Rowlatt Bill was an infringement of normal rights, but one that could not be avoided. Lowndes professed a great dislike of such legislation, and claimed he would have opposed it, had it not been necessary. Chelmsford wrote that no-one regretted the step more than he; but, he argued, it could not be postponed. He told the Legislative Council that the government could not contemplate 'the sudden release from restraint and control of the forces of anarchy'; they could not shut their eyes to the 'existence in India of definitely revolutionary organizations'. He agreed with the Rowlatt Report that the forces of law were beaten; he did not believe India would be untouched by the 'reaction against all authority' that was abroad; he did believe that the government had to defend their 'friends in India from the criminal few'.[55] One idea occurred again and again. Chelmsford thought the government would be failing in their duty if they did not act. Vincent claimed, 'we are responsible for the public peace in this country, and it is out duty to take such measures as may be necessary to secure that'. At the end of the Rowlatt debates, he declared, 'The conscience of the Government . . . is clear. We are acting from a deep-rooted conviction that we are right'.[56] After the passage of the Act, when Patel petitioned Chelmsford to withhold consent or reserve the Bill for the King's assent, Lowndes agreed that either was a possible course but went on: 'I am not prepared to advise that it should be adopted as I believe that His Excellency has throughout accepted the necessity of the Act . . ., and it has from the first been recognized that we could only pass it in the teeth of the Indian Members'.[57]

Chelmsford's was a government in which due respect was given to 'expert' opinion. Home Department officials might lay down, on grounds of policy, the line to be taken with 'agitators'; but 'revolutionaries' were thought to fall within the competence chiefly of the C.I.D.—Sir Charles Cleveland, whose advice was almost never liberal, was thus the leading expert.[58] Moreover, if there were any danger of the conviction faltering, the Bengal Government were ready to give encouragement. They argued:

We have unfortunately the best reasons for going on with whatever checks have been imposed by the measures taken under the Defence Act. Men are still abroad who were known to be leaders in the revolutionary movement; they are still . . . endeavouring to foment trouble, and simply because sedition has been checked for the moment, we should not be justified in assuming that it does not exist.
. . . this revolutionary movement in Bengal was not the product of the war. It was accentuated by the war, but there is no *a priori* reason why, because . . . the war is over, we should discard measures which we have found so useful.[59]

The Government of India thought the new Bill was the least objectionable way of meeting the need. Regulation III of 1818 was more repressive, and to use the Defence of India Act in peacetime was to break a pledge. It was undesirable, too, to proceed by ordinance. The government thought it their duty to face the legislature—it enabled them to consult public opinion (which they proceeded to ignore), and was altogether 'more open and honest'.

The government thinking was thus a strange mixture of high-mindedness and muddle. The Bengal authorities were perhaps more single-minded, with their steadfast reluctance to consider the basic question of whether or not wartime measures could be justified in peace merely by their being useful. But the Government of India, although they claimed to have seen this dilemma, did not carry through their reasoning. They could not break a pledge not to use the Defence of India Act after the end of the war; but they could re-introduce the Act in a slightly different form. They could not proceed by ordinance, but they could ignore the advice of the non-official legislators and carry the Bill by official majority. The difference, the effect of their 'openness', was little more than to publicize their measures and antagonize the legislators.

They argued, of course, that the will of the legislature could not prevail in an essential measure. Lowndes told the Council, in the Rowlatt debate, that 'no reasonable Government' could give way before a threat of agitation; they were responsible for policy and

could not surrender their own judgment.[60] Montagu, too, accepted
this argument, and the thinking which had led up to it. He had
agreed that the Rowlatt Report had 'focussed attention' on the
urgency of the terrorist problem; he was 'firmly convinced' that
extra powers were needed to fill a gap in the government's armour.
Thus he accepted publication of the Bills; he defended the main
measure in Parliament with the extraordinary claim that it was
'the most liberal Act of its kind ever produced'. Indeed, when the
government in their haste introduced the Bills without sanction,
causing something of a flurry in the India Office, it was admitted
that the Secretary of State was unlikely to have disallowed them,
and Montagu, after sending a mild telegram asking for information,
later gave his approval, over the objections of Basu and Sinha. He
acquiesced in measures he disliked because he was reluctant to
interfere, but also because he had been convinced that the measures
were necessary—the Indian legal system was so bad that these
dangerous expedients could not be avoided. He too accepted the
view of the Rowlatt Committee that the ordinary forces of law had
been beaten.[61]

It may be seen that this conviction of the necessity for the Bill
had two main props. The first was the experience with the Defence
of India Act, and the second was the existence of the Rowlatt
Report. First, the belief that repressive powers had been successful,
strengthened the case for making them permanent. Chelmsford
had warned the legislature in September 1916 that it was impossible
to 'tolerate the indefinite continuance of dangerous activities', and
in Calcutta in December he concluded that the government had
been able 'seriously to check' the progress of the 'revolutionary'
movements by depriving conspirators of liberty.[62] In October 1917,
S. R. Hignell of the Home Department noted in a demi-official
letter: 'a situation which was getting out of hand before the war
had been controlled with a very considerable amount of success . . .
by the use of the Defence of India Act and Regulation III of 1818.'
And, the next year, in February, during discussions about papers
to be placed before the Rowlatt Committee, the Home Department criticized the Bengal deposition for ignoring the period of
'laissez-faire' (as they saw it) under Carmichael. Hignell then
suggested that this 'dirty (and now almost worn-out) linen' should
not be washed before the Committee; but, after a discussion
between Chelmsford, Vincent and Rowlatt, it was decided that a

statement on this period would be of value:[63] we may assume that
its purpose was, by way of contrast, to highlight the good effect of
firm applications of repressive powers. The containment of the
problem was presented as being due to imprisonment without trial
when trial was thought impossible; the government were not going
to abandon this weapon. Chamberlain had actively advocated its
use; the Bengal Government argued that at the least it would have
to be continued in some form to avoid the dangerous situation of
the sudden release of the detenus on the expiry of the Defence of
India Act, six months after the peace.[64] The effect, as early as
December 1917, was commitment not only to special powers but
to powers substantially similar to those in the Defence of India Act.

This commitment was not weakened by subsequent events or
changing attitudes, however, largely because of Rowlatt's findings.
In a sense the British were trapped by the Report. Chelmsford
claimed that it gave him 'no choice but to act'; his government told
London that it left 'no option as to the introduction of legislation'.[65] Certainly such advice, from a unanimous committee, left
little room for manoeuvre. Some members of Parliament had
shown an interest—a question in the Commons as early as October
1918 raised the matter of the action to be taken; some 'severe
criticism' had already been heard over the delay in making copies
of the Rowlatt Report available in England, a 'blunder' which had
exercised the India Office where it was thought to call for a 'very
sharp censure'.[66] Even more important, the Report had reinforced,
in a quite spurious way, the government's conviction that it was
necessary to perpetuate the repressive powers. The Home Department explained in August 1918 that the recommendations involved
'legislation which it would have been difficult to justify to the
public and to the Legislative Council unless it had been supported
by the real authority' of the Committee. But the Committee had
based their recommendation on the evidence supplied by the
government, and their remedy merely endorsed earlier government
thinking. As far as the Government of India were concerned,
neither the evidence nor the proposals should have gained authority
from this process.[67] Both evidence and proposals did so. The effect
of the Rowlatt Report was to forestall any official questioning of
the need for special powers.

The Report's myopia was also the government's. We have seen
how the committee failed to deal with the perspective of Bengal's

record against crime in general, and how, on their own evidence, we may question their findings on the movement's dangers and the chances of control by the courts. The reluctance to reconsider basic assumptions was not new. Ever since the Government of India had finally been converted to new legislation, in 1914, the basic assumptions had not been re-examined. In 1916 P. C. Lyon had suggested an announcement, before any repressive legislation, on self-government, indianization of the higher public services and devolution of power upon democratic Indian institutions (namely, enlarged provincial legislatures with 'more interest in the control of the finances'); and in the event of course the British more or less followed this timetable in 1919. (Lyon later remarked on the similarity of his ideas and what he took to be Montagu's.)[68] Indeed; for the question in 1919 was the need for legislation, not the use of repression, and under Chelmsford, just as under Carmichael, reluctance about the second did not prevent advocacy of the first.

We have seen that for Bengal the Defence of India Act had merely delayed a permanent enactment; in their view the end of the war would not 'materially alter the circumstances'. But the Home Department as well, as early as their letter of 6 May 1916, when they asked Bengal what (if any) special powers would be needed after the war, had not seriously put at issue the fundamental question, whether any special powers would be needed.[69] Thus contrary indications were ignored. In May 1916 the Bengal Government had argued, briefly, that the Defence of India Act had *not* been effective; on the other hand Vincent had quoted a letter from a conspirator claiming that 'Some of our best men were lost . . . we had to drop the idea of an immediate rising' (though 'local organizations' were allegedly intact). In October 1918 Ronaldshay reported that his government had had gratifying success in their endeavours to prosecute the 'revolutionaries' in the courts—from January to August there had been 34 prosecutions, 28 of them successful.[70] These differences and this highly significant development, like the contributions of the improvements in and the strengthening of the Bengal police, seem not to have entered official calculations in 1919—though repression had been ruled out for a whole category of political activists and was, by Government of India orders, to be applied more selectively even to 'revolutionaries'. The Rowlatt Report had already given its verdict. It had made the response of increasing the executive powers a habit, which existed independently of any readiness to use the powers once they had been obtained.

There was one more major reason why the government persisted with the Rowlatt Bill, and that was the view, also favoured by the Rowlatt Committee, and encouraged for that matter by the elite character of the terrorist movements, that 'revolutionaries' were a special case. In the Rowlatt debates, Sastri had argued that the government seemed to be saying 'these are wicked people, it does not matter how they are dealt with'.[71] This was perilously near the truth. The Rowlatt Committee favoured extraordinary means partly because they would be applied only to a minority; the Government of India would never have considered such powers for general application, but argued that they could not avoid special powers for special circumstances.

The influence of this idea can be seen in the concessions made on the Rowlatt Bill. Of course these were partly in the hope of reconciling opinion. The Act was made temporary, to remain in force for only three years, because discussion with the moderates had shown that this might be useful. Just as the Rowlatt Report had softened its proposals by calling them 'preventive', Chelmsford announced that he had every hope that 'when the three years . . . have passed away, it will be found that the crime . . . has passed away also'. The government planned minor concessions in committee because these too would 'facilitate matters'; and by the end of the debate of 14 March 1919, quite apart from changes in committee, they had accepted a large number of amendments designed to protect the accused. There were several provisions to ensure the proper cross-examination of witnesses by the defence, and some to limit the discretion of the local governments. Death sentences were not to be passed unless the judges were unanimous; there was to be a lessening in the effect of the continuance of restrictions originally imposed under the Defence of India Act.[70] And when these concessions did not reconcile opinion the government were puzzled—as Vincent complained to the legislature, they had not been unreasonable.[72] But, though Ronaldshay considered that even earlier Home Department emendations to the Bill were a dangerous and unnecessary weakening,[73] the government had been concerned, as the Select Committee put it, not to destroy the efficacy of the procedure.[74] They opposed any arrogation of executive functions to the judiciary; they refused to concede anything not compatible with the needs as they saw them. The main purpose of the concessions had not been conciliatory, but to define the government's intentions more clearly.

This had been Vincent's line when commenting on earlier drafts of the Bill. He proposed one alteration 'to make the Bill apply to the particular offences . . . only when they are connected with any movement to promote sedition or disaffection'. He supported another amendment with the arguments that 'this legislation is to be restricted to what may really be called seditious movements and that we are not re-enacting the provisions of the Defence of India Act, though we retain some of the powers . . . for use in certain circumstances'.[75] Similarly, the main Bill's short title was altered from the 'Criminal Law (Emergency Powers) Bill, to the 'Anarchical and Revolutionary Crimes Bill'. The long title and some clauses were amended similarly, and to the preamble were added the words, 'for the purpose of dealing with anarchical and revolutionary movements'. In one clause the words 'prejudicial to public safety' (defining an offence) were replaced by 'connected with any anarchical or revolutionary movement'.[76] The abortive second Bill, the Indian Criminal Law (Amendment) Bill, also gave a definition of sedition, which, though fairly wide, specified what the government had in mind; they were concerned with the instigation of the use of criminal force against the government or public servants. The particular case of the Bengali terrorist was obviously intended here. All these changes were intended to allay fears that the special powers would be used to suppress legitimate political activities.[77]

The government clearly believed opposition was based on misapprehensions. They distributed, through Deputy Commissioners, District Publicity Boards, schools and colleges, hundreds of thousands of copies of translations, pamphlets and posters to explain the real character of the Act.[78] Thus the amendments chiefly had the effect of restricting the application of the powers to those crimes which the government thought had to be dealt with in this way; and it was this conviction which encouraged the belief that the better the Act was known the more opposition would be disarmed. Moreover, Sastri and Jinnah in debate had claimed that the main Bill was repugnant to Western justice; and Vincent, in reply, had admitted that this had 'moved all of us and prompted a careful reconsideration of the facts'—he had made it clear that only the 'practical point of view' had sustained the government in their resolve. But he had countered the idea that the measures were repugnant to justice by the contention that the powers would become available only under very special circumstances, and that even then they would apply only to certain people.[79] This in no way contradicted the members' argument, but evidently it had made the government happier about it. The concessions, clarifying the purposes of the Bill, thus had the effect of wedding the government to a procedure they found distasteful.

The 'special case' idea was indeed the guiding principle of the Bill, the only point to much of its machinery. More than anything else, it reconciles the apparent contradiction in government attitudes which the Rowlatt Bills represent. Lowndes told the legislature that the government's policy was one of 'wait and see', but that they intended to arm themselves in case of need.[80] The powers were what the government said they were—for emergencies, held in reserve, to be applied only to political activity which in official eyes had crossed the dividing line and become political crime, and indeed only to that in special circumstances and in its most serious forms. The repressive powers were not, in theory, any part of the general policy towards political agitation, but were the ultimate deterrent.

Ironically they were never used, so great was the outcry, but it is wrong to think (as some have done) that this proves the Act unnecessary; rather the government relied on earlier powers of repression. Certainly it proved to be not worth the trouble it caused: the first Rowlatt Bill, the only repressive measure enacted under Chelmsford, was the occasion of serious disturbances, met with official reprisals of exceptional ferocity. And, though in its final form it was temporary, qualified, and altogether weaker than its wartime predecessor, this is not to say that Indian opposition was misguided. We have seen why the government persisted; neither of the two main grounds was encouraging for Indian politicians. The point was that official arguments carried no conviction. The Bills were widely thought to be intended (as one newspaper put it) 'to suppress in future all national agitation and political activities'. Of course rumour and misrepresentation added to the suspicion, but the crucial matter was loss of confidence; as the paper explained: 'it is useless for our rulers to try to convince us . . . that the measure will be applied only against revolutionaries and after full consideration. Indians who have recently had a taste of the Defence of India Act, can place no reliance in this matter on the words of a man like Lord Chelmsford.'[81] Thus, not only was the habitual response of the government discredited by former repression of politicians, but, by its persistence, it also signified that the new approach marked by Besant's release was not thorough-going or reliable. In the second place, the 'special case' argument had a more shadowy side than that presented by the government. Crime detection and prosecution figures were bad for many crimes in India and especially in Bengal; anarchist offences were a small proportion of the total. Yet these few anarchist crimes needed special powers—it was because they were directed at the constitution, at British power. Many Indians evidently concluded from this that the British were determined to hold on to that power, whatever their constitutional pronouncements.

The government did try to make repression more palatable to the politicians. In the first place, they sought to use minimum powers and to treat prisoners as leniently as possible. In the second place they used committees of enquiry, as with the Rowlatt Committee. Thus several committees were set up to vindicate the application of repressive powers or to reassure the public on the lot of prisoners. (Later, in a similar way, the Hunter Committee investigated the use of executive powers during the 1919 disturbances, and a legislative committee was allowed to review the use of repressive powers over the press.)

As part of the first element in this conciliation within repression, the Government of India received monthly reports on State prisoners from district magistrates. The Home Department officials would dearly have liked to have dispensed with some of the routine aspects of this supervision, but Vincent ruled that these had to continue. Indeed, he ordered a register to be kept and checked at intervals 'in order that we may be certain that the requirements of the law are fulfilled'. There was only one complaint of maltreatment in 1917—a prisoner at Dacca was threatened by a warder, and, although the magistrate suggested that the prisoner was known to be difficult, the warder was transferred. In May 1918 the central government issued instructions, following a question in the legislature, that local governments were 'to ensure that in every case of serious illness, special attention, medical and other, is given to the detenu concerned and that should death in any case supervene, full enquiries are made as quickly as possible'—the government's investigation had revealed that no deaths or breakdowns in health could be attributed to internments, but that some deaths had not been made the subject of an enquiry.[82] Some prisoners tried to use hunger strikes as a means of protesting against their confinement—such strikes (at Alipur and Midnapur) were dealt with by transferring prisoners to other jails or by forcible feeding. The government instructed that forcible feeding was to be resorted to before the hunger striker was too weak—it was 'the duty of the Medical Officer-in-charge by every possible means to preserve life', the means including feeding tubes and necessary force.[83] Prison deaths were too much of a political embarrassment; the treatment of prisoners had to be above suspicion.

At Midnapur a hunger strike also resulted in measures to reduce the number of prisoners, to give them better cells, more exercise time, writing materials and more books. Later in 1918 these changes were extended in revised prison rules which divided all 'political' prisoners—those detained by executive powers—into two classes, dangerous and not, and allowed privileges to the latter while retaining strict control for the former.[84] It was also decided that the non-dangerous prisoners should not be kept in gaol. The Bengal Government proposed and the Government of India agreed that these prisoners should be detained in isolated but healthy places where attempts could be made at their education and reformation. In late 1919 it was agreed that a camp should be established in Upper Burma, complete with school rooms, playing fields and a guard of Gurkha and Sikh military police. The recurring cost was to be more than a quarter of a million rupees a year. Later, finding they had fewer prisoners than expected, the Bengal Government decided on a smaller camp in Bengal.[85]

Checks on and improvements in the conditions of prisoners were one way of representing the government as lenient. Amnesties were another. In March 1917, the Viceroy wrote to Lord Carmichael of his hope that, if there were no recrudescence of crime, they would be able to announce 'a very general measure of amnesty' after the war. In August 1917 Montagu suggested that it would be politic to announce an amnesty as a prelude to the reforms discussions. The Government of India thought an amnesty 'obviously desirable . . . if . . . compatible with the public safety'. The local governments opposed any general amnesty and generally favoured the distinction, which (as we have seen) was suggested by the United Provinces, between those restricted for 'extravagance of speech' and those penalised for 'conspiracy to murder or to incite to rebellion or for trafficking with [the] King's enemies'. There were not many detenus within the first category—and most local governments were prepared to lift such restrictions. In Madras, when they had lost out over Annie Besant, the government agreed to release one other political agitator. In the Panjab, however, any relaxation continued to be opposed.[86] In November 1918, after the armistice, the Government of India suggested to the local governments that they reconsider the cases of Muslims detained for pro-Turkish activities: they should consider only whether the release would be prejudicial to safety, and should not maintain restrictions for mere political convenience. There was some opposition to this proposal in Bengal, Coorg and the United Provinces, but by January 1919 most governments had agreed to release Muslim prisoners, even including those involved in the 'silk letters' conspiracy. The Secretary of State objected to the release of Maulana Mahmud Hasan and his followers, interned on Malta for their part in this conspiracy; Montagu held that the release would be 'gratuitous encouragement' to the agitation over the Turkish peace terms, but withdrew his objection when the Government of India replied that in their opinion 'any pro-Turkish agitation is more likely to draw strength from the Maulana's detention than from his release'.[87]

In 1919, when the reforms proposals were finalized, Montagu suggested a wider amnesty. The Government of India agreed that the amnesty 'should be as wide as [is] consistent with public safety'. It was announced in a proclamation of 23 December 1919. The Government of India urged the local governments to release (and, according to their interpretation of the proclamation, to pardon) all 'political' prisoners except those convicted of murder or other serious crimes of violence. The Government of Bengal had argued earlier that this proviso should be made explicit in the terms of the proclamation lest popular expectations should be raised too high. The Government of India had supported this view, but Montagu refused, arguing that such a proviso might have allowed the release of conspirators while detaining their 'dupes'. Ronaldshay, the Governor of Bengal, found this reasoning 'unexpectedly stupid'. Montagu's main reasons, later to be better expressed, were firstly that arrests without trial were 'tolerable only if releases are sought whenever they can possibly be justified' and secondly that, under the terms of the proclamation, the local governments could already refuse any release on the grounds of public safety. Montagu's idea was that the government should interpret the amnesty widely and then act promptly against anyone who subsequently 'misbehaved': he later criticized Chelmsford for not proceeding in this way with Shaukat Ali. The Bengal authorities, on the other hand, believed that, if certain categories were not specifically excluded, each continued detention would have to be defended and would create disappointment undermining the good effect of the amnesty. They were already following Montagu's ideal of 'releases . . . whenever . . . justified'—nine hundred detenus had been released before the amnesty—and they did not see how they could release a sufficient number so as to appear to respond to the spirit of a general proclamation. Ronaldshay attended a meeting of the Viceroy's Council to discuss this dilemma; it was decided that it was necessary to offer to release, subject to assurances of good conduct, even the sixty detenus whose continued detention had been recommended by the local government.[88] By mid-1920 only eighteen remained under detention in Bengal. In the Panjab 1,682 out of 1,779 had been released. In January 1920, in the whole of India, only nine (out of 310) had remained subject to restrictions under the Defence of India Act and one (out of 132) under the Ingress Ordinance, although fifty-five were still confined under Regulation III of 1818.[89] In most provinces the 1919 amnesty had represented a sudden upsurge in a policy of progressive release. The Government of India's policy remained to release detenus as far as was thought safe—the intention was to mollify their use of executive powers. The amnesty, in the form insisted on by Montagu, had forced them to step up the releases and reconsider the question of safety in order still to achieve this aim.

Alongside these deliberate shows of moderation, came the same impulse in its second form, the committees for public reassurance. In March 1918, in reply to a proposal made by Surendranath Banerjea in the Imperial legislature, the Government of India outlined a three part plan. They announced their intention of setting up two types of advisory committee, one to consider the cases of existing detenus and the other to make recommendations on any future detentions; they also proposed to institute a system of non-official prison visitors to supplement the present arrangement with district magistrates.[90] The main object of these changes was to ensure that the public were not dependent entirely on official sources for information about detenus. The government had first suggested advisory committees in 1917; now the Bengal authorities had some objections, but, although the central government accepted more limited terms of reference for the Bengal committee, they insisted on their policy. Other local governments also were reluctant to reopen cases; the Government of India asked them to reconsider. Their scheme was eventually adopted in all provinces to which it applied.[91] The Beachcroft–Chandavarkar committee in Bengal and the Abdur Rauf–Lindsay committee in the Panjab later published findings which overwhelmingly approved the government's use of its executive powers.[92]

After these committees had started their work, a 'Civil Rights Committee' began campaigning about the conditions of detention in Bengal. In connection with this campaign Annie Besant approached the Government of India and accused the Bengal police of ill-treating and torturing political prisoners. Du Boulay noted on the file: 'There is a lot of rubbish here, but I am afraid we must treat it seriously—moreover it is urgent as it may form the basis of attacks in council.' Chelmsford had already assured Besant in an interview that he would see to the investigation of any complaints which she could make specific. Thus the central government asked officially for an investigation. The Bengal Government thought they should have referred Besant to them, but the centre insisted that where the liberty of the subject was restricted by executive action it was necessary 'to meet and refute complaints . . . not *prima facie* malicious'. The Bengal Government set up a committee, comprising C. J. Stevenson-Moore and Sir Benode Chandra Mitter, who reported that, of eleven specific allegations, two were admitted by the prisoners to be false, one was minor and unreliable, four were withdrawn, and four were found to be quite unfounded. A version of their report was published.[93]

Thus the government tried to mitigate against the worst repercussions of repression. But the government could be only as good as its officials. So much had to be left to local discretion. The central authority laid down general principles, but even when a crisis arose supervision was usually little more than a nominal check that general principles were being observed. In extreme cases a subsequent investigation could be mounted. In most cases the Government of India were powerless to intervene. This was true of the application of repressive powers, in cases of only local interest. It was also true of the control of disturbances. In 1917, for example, there were serious communal riots in Shahabad district, Bihar. Before the outbreak a local magistrate had arranged a *modus vivendi* in one village whereby the Muslims were to sacrifice a goat provided by the Hindus instead of a cow as usual in the Bakr Id. No higher official was aware of this agreement until after it had been violated and the village had become the starting-point of widespread disorders. During the riots, moreover, policy was decided almost entirely by the local commissioner, and, although the situation was not badly handled, the approach was influenced by the quite unproven assumption that there had been a widespread Hindu conspiracy. The Government of India were scarcely informed of the course of events, let alone given the means to judge the suitability of the measures taken locally. They were not able to act until after the event, when they received reports from an officer who had investigated the outbreak.[94]

This pattern of immediate local initiative and subsequent inquiry was both typical (as we shall see with the 1919 disturbances) and deliberate. Even when they had been informed, the government consistently refused to interfere in local arrangements, in what were basically questions of judgment in matters on which local officials could claim expertise: policies towards communal relations, riots, 'seditious' speeches, the press, Indian leaders—all political questions. Political policy was peculiarly lacking in supervision, for of all departments of local government this alone was not subject to financial control by involving capital expenditure and budgetary allowances. The Chelmsford government asserted themselves in several areas, including the use of repressive powers, by insisting on national interests which had to override local considerations. But the effect of this was necessarily limited; there remained large areas in which not infrequently there were discrepancies between policy at the centre and practice in the districts. It was this disability, as well as the Government of India's own failure to heed Indian opinion over the Rowlatt Bill, which was to discredit the repressive powers and undermine the central efforts at appeasement.

II POLICIES UNDER CHALLENGE

Chapter 7. Disturbances

IN dealing with riots and disturbances, which had to be repressed, there were three approaches open to the central government for the minimizing of subsequent political agitation. They could lay down general standards of conduct and try to ensure that local authorities abode by them; they could take steps to convince opinion that no unjustifiable measures had been taken; and they could recompense and punish where mistakes or abuses had occurred. In April 1919, with the serious disturbances in the Panjab, all three of these lines of defence broke down.

Many causes underlay these disturbances. These were extraordinary times. There was, for example, coincident with the riots, remarkable fraternization between Hindus and Muslims; but in general feelings were tense. Thus, in Delhi, where communal violence had occurred in the recent past, the Arya Samaj leader, Swami Sraddanand (or Munshi Ram), was allowed to preach in the Jama Masjid, and at the same meeting the Imam was accused of having eaten bacon with the British Deputy Commissioner, and was 'grossly assaulted' by a fellow Muslim. Hakim Ajmal Khan, the veteran leader, had to intervene in the melee and the meeting broke up in some disorder.[1] This memorable occasion was an outcrop suggesting deeper layers of grievance and unease.

The war's end had not brought the expected relief. Political demands had not been met in full. The Rowlatt Bill had increased apprehension, particularly because of the rumours surrounding it: that farmers would have to give government half their ploughing animals and half their produce, that brides and grooms would be inspected by British doctors, parents would be taxed a sum equal to that spent on any marriage and Rs.25 for every child born, and that no more than four men would be allowed to sit together or follow a funeral.[2] Thus was a law which transgressed the political leaders' borrowed liberal ideas translated into a mass grievance. The ground was fertile enough: a serious food shortage continued and prices in most commodities were rising sharply; between five and six million were dead as a result of the influenza epidemic, between 50 and 80 per cent of the population having been affected.

The disturbances began at Delhi on 30 March and spread elsewhere after the news of Gandhi's arrest. (The C.I.D. had predicted that the Delhi hartal would be a failure.)³ Riots were severe in Bombay city and Ahmedabad, but most serious and widespread in the Panjab. The general unrest was therefore not a complete explanation: there is no strong case for suggesting that problems were particularly severe in the Panjab. One million had died there of influenza, and epidemics of plague, cholera or malaria had struck annually since 1915. But the incidence of influenza in the province, though high, was lower than in the Central Provinces where there were no disorders, or than in Delhi and Bombay where the situation was more easily controlled. Rumours were prevalent in the Panjab, but official propaganda under Abdul Aziz, Joint Secretary of the local Publicity Committee, was also very active, giving a lead to other local governments. House-to-house surveys in 1916–17 had uncovered rates defaulters and increased the yield by 30 per cent in Lahore and 55 per cent in Amritsar; and yet, though this was doubtless the cause of some ill-feeling, the rioters were not apparently drawn from householders. And, finally, the political excitement of the war years had probably been felt less in the Panjab than in any other major province; in September 1917 Chelmsford described it as 'the really quiet Province in India'.⁴

The reason for the severity of the troubles in the Panjab was sought at the time, especially by the local government, in talk of a conspiracy. Lord Sinha advanced this suggestion in the Lords. At one time even Bolshevism was mentioned, though supposedly its 'spirit' rather than its agents had spread. But even at the time the Government of India saw 'no signs of central organisation', and, although there had clearly been *ad hoc* collusion in the cutting of telegraph wires and attacks on trains, subsequent enquiry bore out the Simla view. It is well-known that Charles Cleveland privately admitted that there was 'organized agitation' but 'no traces of organized conspiracy'. Later assessments detailed the undoubted anti-British character of the riots but no more: acts of sabotage were laboriously listed, evidence was collected even on reaction from the Ghadr party in America, but as proof of the conspiracy alleged by the Panjab, none of this carried conviction.[5]

A later explanation, put forward by Willingdon, Lloyd and Montagu, among others, was the nature of Panjab administration under Sir Michael O'Dwyer. It was claimed that the Lieutenant-Governor's zeal in army recruitment had created anxieties and hardship. Chelmsford too ascribed the disturbances partly to nervous excitement after the war, and he had earlier made anxious enquiries of O'Dwyer about the effects and the methods of his recruitment. In general it was felt also that O'Dwyer had practised 'strong government'—Chelmsford considered his policies 'repressive'—and that the explosion of feeling had occurred because the local government had kept, in Willingdon's phrase, the 'screw on too tight'. There was some justification for this description, and O'Dwyer himself admitted that he had not been in close relations with the political classes. But, it should be noted, the Muslim rural population, including some who had used force against army recruiters, were, in O'Dwyer's words, 'everywhere actively loyal', as were most of the Sikhs. Moreover, there was no evidence of disbanded soldiers among the rioters; the number of persons in the Panjab dealt with under executive powers before 31 January 1919 was less than one-eighth of the number so dealt with in Bengal and less than one-tenth of the all-India total; and on 1 April 1919 only 24 out of an original 145 were still restricted in the Panjab under the Defence of India Act, and seven out of 400 under the Ingress Ordinance. Only four people were excluded from the province in April, in spite of O'Dwyer's intention of isolating the Panjab from outside influences. In the use of the Press Act, too, Panjab interventions, though generally agreed to be more restrictive than elsewhere, were not in fact more *numerous*.[6]

For a more complete explanation of the disaster in the Panjab it is necessary to look closely at the measures taken to control the disturbances in different parts of India.[7] The least difficulty, of all areas where disturbances occurred as a result of the anti-Rowlatt protests, was experienced in the Northwest Frontier Province. There, as excitement rose, the Chief Commissioner, Sir George Roos-Keppel, confined all troops to the cantonment and told the police to keep as little in evidence as possible. He met a deputation from the Peshawar Union Committee, organizing the protest, and after discussion persuaded them to cancel further demonstrations. They later sent him a memorial appreciating his sympathetic handling of their protests.[8] The success of these methods was repeated elsewhere, among agitators less amenable and more politically experienced. In Bengal, Lord Ronaldshay remained in close contact with C. R. Das, B. Chakravarti and Surendranath Banerjea, met a number of Indian leaders at Government House and enlisted their cooperation in condemning violence, issued a proclamation in vernacular languages, addressed a deputation of Marwaris, and, except in one instance of shooting, later made the subject of a magistrate's enquiry, avoided 'provocative' action by the police or military.[9] In Bombay the Police Commissioner delayed the use of fire-arms in spite of violent attacks and interference with trams and shops, and then called on Gandhi himself to help quieten his supporters. Gandhi was permitted to hold an enormous meeting, and the city returned to normal without a shot having been fired.[10]

Moderation was also shown elsewhere, in more serious situations. In Viramgam, where local authority broke down and the city was given over to rioting, looting and arson, the situation was controlled by the arrival of a small force of sepoys, the imposition of a curfew and orders to open shops, but also by meetings with local leaders. In Ahmedabad there were even more serious riots— 51 government and a number of other buildings were burned, with damage estimated at Rs.14,24,000; 28 persons were killed. The District Magistrate imposed a night curfew, and in several incidents troops were ordered to fire; but leading *satyagrahis*, including finally Gandhi himself, were asked to assist the authorities, and on at least one occasion the magistrate ordered that arrested persons should be released in order to appease the crowd.[11] Even in Delhi the authorities had tried to take 'unobtrusive precautions' before the *hartal* of 30 March—extra police and troops were kept in readiness but out of sight. When rioting broke out, the authorities waited two hours before giving the order to fire on the crowd; and next day the Deputy Commissioner refrained from taking action against 'the turbulent' because, in his view, to do so would have 'brought on serious disturbances'. On 2 April all troops were withdrawn as they were thought to be adding to the excitement. Meetings were later allowed so that 'the crowds might be given something to do'. Then, when there were renewed troubles on the news of Gandhi's arrest, attempts were made to work through local leaders—the District Magistrate, the Deputy Commissioner and the Commissioner held a series of meetings asking for co-operation. Some of the leading Home Rulers were enrolled as special constables. Swami Sraddhanand, as the Delhi authorities admitted later, 'did really work with us and try to get the *hartal* stopped' on 15 and 16 April. Military patrols remained and there was some further shooting, but order was finally restored more by tact and persuasion than force. Vincent thought 'the police and troops behaved with great restraint and moderation'.[12]

In all these local measures there were certain common features, which accorded with the general approach favoured by the Government of India. Local authorities tended to allow peaceful demonstrations, to avoid provocation by the police and military, and to use as little force as necessary, holding off firing on crowds, shooting for as brief a period as possible, removing pickets and withdrawing troops immediately order was restored. Finally, and perhaps most important, they remained in contact with Indian leaders and called meetings to enlist their support. The picture in the Panjab, however, was very different. Demonstrations were banned, provocative orders and punishments instituted, and the Lieutenant-Governor prided himself on the fact that his government 'had no parley with extremists'. Indeed they arrested them. And the military were not kept out of sight and quickly withdrawn; they were put in charge. This occurred deliberately, quite apart from martial law: O'Dwyer later explained that it had been necessary 'to keep the troops *en evidence*' because of rumours of mutiny. He even made the extraordinary threat, to a meeting of Indians (government supporters) who urged troop withdrawals, that if disorders continued 'there might be some difficulty in restraining the British troops who were much excited by the news of brutal murders' of Europeans at Kasur and Amritsar.[13]

The details of the disturbances are well-enough known.[14] Meetings in Lahore had led to riots. In Amritsar local leaders, Kitchlew and Satyapal, who had earlier disobeyed orders banning them from public speaking, were arrested under the Defence of India Act, and, expecting repercussions, British infantry picketed railway crossings. A crowd were intercepted at the railway bridge by armed police; members of the local Bar persuaded them to return to the city. Later a larger crowd returned, stoned the picket and were fired upon. The crowd whose members had been aroused by the arrest of their leaders were enraged by the casualties among their number. They returned to the city, set fire to the Post Office and attacked the banks, killing in all five Europeans. The local Commissioner handed over to the military. The Panjab authorities reported 'a state of open rebellion' in the countryside between Amritsar and Lahore, and requested the imposition of martial law. In the Home Department, Du Boulay commented 'we should not hesitate to comply . . . in view of Lieutenant-Governor's statement that open rebellion exists and the situation is critical'. He telegraphed, for permission, to Chelmsford and Vincent, who were both absent from Simla.[15] Thus the Panjab request was granted, and military and civil authorities combined to enforce a harsh and in some cases vicious discipline upon the province.

Measures in Lahore, for example, were increasingly severe, out of proportion to the problem, and unfortunately not unique. Colonel Frank Johnson, the military commander, first introduced a curfew and forbad gatherings of more than ten people. He ordered *langars* (cooked food shops) to be closed, threatened to shut off water and electricity supplies, and warned owners of property that they would be likely to suffer severe reprisals if shots were fired at the police or bombs thrown in the vicinity of their holdings. Next day, on 16 April, Johnson ordered students at the Dayanand Anglo-Vedic College to report four times a day for a roll-call, demanded the immediate ending of the *hartal* on penalty of suffering any loss resulting from the forcible opening of businesses, forbad *lathis*, forbad walking more than two abreast, and threatened property owners with 'severe punishment' if damage occurred to proclamations and notices displayed on their property. On the 17th he threatened shop-owners with arrest and summary trial if they continued their *hartal*; he introduced more parades of students; he ordered the arrest of all male students and staff of Sanatan Dharm College in reprisal for the removal of a martial law notice. On the 21st he requisitioned from Indians pedal-drawn cycles and lights and electric fans for the use of the troops. Johnson was evidently prepared, although he had announced that loyal and law-abiding citizens had nothing to fear, to punish before he had established guilt and to hold the whole community to ransom for the good conduct of a minority. Under such control Lahore remained quiet; but the *hartal* dragged on. Johnson's

methods were more likely to create bitterness and defiance than
co-operation.

Order had also been restored in Amritsar. But the city had then
come under the control of General Dyer, who published a proclamation forbidding public meetings, and on 13 April (before the
imposition of martial law) fired without warning on a gathering in
the Jallianwala Bagh, inflicting very heavy casualties. He also
introduced an order requiring all Indians who wished to pass to
crawl the length of a street where a European woman missionary
had been assaulted. On the same spot some young offenders
against prison discipline were publicly whipped. Dyer's actions
were later supposed by some to have 'saved the Panjab'; in fact,
while they cowed the people of Amritsar, already under control
before the firing in the Bagh, they had a serious effect elsewhere
in the province. News of the firing, of martial law orders in Lahore
and Amritsar, and of other excesses, helped to inflame the situation. The measures were offensive in themselves; the offence was
compounded by the fact that they applied only to Indians. Disturbances continued to spread in the province. Telegraph wires
were cut, public buildings attacked, railway lines torn up. Damage
to property in Gujranwala (where the authorities had lost control
and been forced to use aeroplanes against the rioters) was estimated
at 24 lakhs of rupees; at Amritsar it was thought to have been
more than 60 lakhs. The Seditious Meetings Act and then martial
law were applied to the districts of Gujranwala, Gujrat and
Lyallpur; and repressive measures remained consistently in excess
of what was necessary—for example, Lyallpur came under martial
law on 21 April, by which time there had been no disturbances in
the whole province for three days, except for the cutting of telegraph wires.

Considering all the disturbances there had been least trouble
where consultations with the Indian leaders started before any
outbreak of violence and where soldiers were least in evidence.
Most trouble occurred after measures against Indian leaders and
after police or soldiers had fired on crowds. This is not necessarily a comment on the validity of the government's actions; it
is a comment on the order of events. Obviously in some cases
police and troops had to intervene, even to fire on crowds. In
Delhi, for example, it was necessary for the police to protect
shopkeepers and railway officials on 30 March when violent

attempts were made to enforce the *hartal* at the railway station. But such intervention was a two-edged sword, to be handled with care. To bring in troops was always in one sense a provocation, and in India might have tragic consequences, for the soldiers were usually outsiders and prone to misread the situation. Thus, during the Delhi riots, a procession shouting 'Mahatma Gandhi ki-jai' was halted by a detachment of Manipuris whose officer did not understand Hindustani and thought he was facing a hostile mob. He ordered his men to open their magazines and a shot went off accidently into the air. The procession became very excited, and an ugly confrontation was avoided only by the arrival of a local C.I.D. officer who explained what had happened and told the soldiers to allow the crowd to pass. Such errors were not of course always recovered in time, and the more arms there were available the more serious the consequences of any mistake were likely to be. Thus, it is possible that in Delhi the police were unwise to try to make arrests at the railway station, and, at the cost of more shooting, to drive the crowd further and further away. Patience, such as was shown at Bombay and later in Delhi as well, would have been less expensive in lives, and perhaps more effective. Each official reprisal not only created an immediate danger, but also further inflamed the general situation. Thus the India Government gave the main impulse when they agreed to Gandhi's arrest. The Panjab precipitated trouble in Amritsar by arresting Kitchlew and Satyapal—as was admitted in a Home Department telegram on 11 April.[16]

In Amritsar also was what is perhaps the best documented case in which firing unleashed worse violence. The order of events is confirmed by the official press communique, and by two reports, printed on 13 April in the *Civil and Military Gazette*. In the first report, a Mr. Jarman, the Amritsar Municipal Engineer, described how he was cycling into the city, with three European companions, when he met a crowd coming towards him. The crowd took no notice of the Europeans. Fifteen minutes later, however, Jarman heard a crowd rushing back shouting, 'They have killed two of us. Bring *lathis*.'—this crowd set fire to the Post Office, smashed the windows of Jarman's office, and went away (as was discovered later) to murder two Europeans at the National Bank. In the second report, in the same edition of the *Gazette*, one A. Ross of the Chartered Bank told how he too had encountered crowds passing through the city, without understanding what was happening, then had seen wounded being brought back, and then had heard the crowds returning shouting, 'Burn and loot the banks'. The interpretation suggested by these accounts was in fact adopted by a judicial committee set up to consider the operation of the martial law trials. B. K. Mullick gave as his view (on the Amritsar Leaders' Case) that 'the evidence seems . . . to show that the acts committed for the purpose of obtaining the repeal of the Rowlatt Act were all peaceful. . . . On the 10th April the arrest of Satyapal and Kitchlew was followed by firing at the overbridge. This appears to have so infuriated the mob that they proceeded to attack Europeans and European Institutions'. The other judge on the committee disputed with Mullick on a point of law, whether the defendants had been 'waging war'; he held that the actions of the mob had had to be considered 'as a determined attempt not only to take revenge for the firing but also to force the hands of the Government'. But even this judge, B. Chevis, did not contradict Mullick's view on the cause of the violence; he was prepared to concede that 'the immediate causes of the outbreak may have been the deportation of Satyapal and Kitchlew and the firing on the mob'.[17] In this instance at least the causal relationship between reprisals and violence is surely beyond question.

Obviously underlying grievances provided the climate for disturbances, and obviously some local differences in severity may be explained in local conditions—one might point to the political backwardness of Peshawar, the slowness of Bengal to accept Gandhi's leadership, the particularly deep feelings in Ahmedabad over Gandhi's arrest, a certain irritation among the more educated in Amritsar and Lahore over O'Dwyer's methods. It is possible too that the situation in Amritsar was worsened by the weakness of the Deputy Commissioner, Miles Irving; and there are even some signs of incapacity among the local police— after the disturbances three Indian officers were censured for failures of duty and in 1920 others were implicated in extortion, bribery and burglary.[18] Yet it is difficult, given the clear difference in Panjab methods and the unmistakable evidence about crowd reactions, not to conclude that the violence was largely due to government action: it is in this, not in grievances or political organization, that the province is clearly distinct. Chelmsford admitted, without openly criticizing O'Dwyer, that the problem

had been dealt with equally effectively in other provinces and
with less violence; he went on, 'If only people would realise that
the day has passed when you can keep India down by the sword'.[19]
The Government of India's role was limited, as the control of
riots was largely in local hands. They tried to help by issuing a
reassuring communique on the Rowlatt Act; the document produced was unfortunately pompous and not altogether reassuring in
tone. On 12 April censorship was imposed on inland telegrams to
prevent the transmission of news of the disturbances or of troop
movements. But for the most part the central authorities did little
beyond approving action taken at local discretion and promising
full support. Chelmsford explained that his policy was to support
each government 'as far as possible in measures it considered
suitable'.[20] His government, as we have seen, promptly acceded
to requests for extra powers; and, though he was in camp when
the outbreak began, all decisions were, as usual, a collective
responsibility: 'I have rightly or wrongly developed the system of
Council or in other words constitutional Government out here,'
he later explained to Montagu; during the Panjab disturbances,
he claimed, he had had 'with the solitary exception of Sir Sankaran
Nair's protest against the *continuance* of Martial Law . . . the whole-
hearted support' of his Council.[21] Willingdon concluded from
Madras that the Viceroy had 'stiffened up well' and was 'determined to put down the insurrection at all costs with a strong
hand'.[22]

But the collective decisions of the Government of India did not
involve restoring order 'at all costs'. H. D. Craik, the Home
Department's Deputy Secretary, promised the European Association that government would 'not hesitate to employ any action,
however drastic, to protect the lives of its law-abiding citizens';[23]
but Chelmsford set down for O'Dwyer two 'cardinal principles'
as conditions for his promised support for local actions. No
greater force or more severe methods were to be used than were
necessary to maintain law and order; and actions were to be such
as would leave behind as little bitterness as possible. In order to
achieve these ends, Chelmsford added, the civil authorities were
not to allow the military an absolutely free hand.[24] Martial law
was proclaimed only for a specified range of offences (those named
in section two of the Bengal State Offences Regulation 1804), and
the ordinary law and courts were to be retained for ordinary

offences. In all matters the army was ordered to co-operate with the civil authorities. On 18 April the Commander-in-Chief directed the local army commander in the Panjab, General Beynon, to 'act in close communication with and on the advice of [the] Lieutenant-Governor'. The military authorities had argued that it was impossible to place an army officer with executive powers under the local government, and the Government of India agreed with the general principle that the supremacy of the military authority (where it applied) must be maintained.[25]

There were later to be attempts to blame the whole catastrophe on this insistence by the Government of India upon the legal supremacy of the army. But there was no suggestion that the civil authority should be abrogated. On 16 April the Panjab Government had reported that they had issued orders making punishable acts not punishable by ordinary law, and granting punitive powers to selected military and civil officers. The powers were to be used with tact and commonsense and without 'irresponsible violence'— 'Force . . . should never exceed the immediate necessities of the case'. The Government of India had replied that under the martial law regulations only the General Officer Commanding had the power to issue such orders but they noted that he had been asked to co-operate with the local government, and suggested that he should be requested to ratify the instructions. The Panjab Government acted on this advice. O'Dwyer had written to Chelmsford on the 16th: 'We were terribly in the dark as to the non-statutory side of martial law and aren't yet quite clear'. In 1920 he wrote to *The Times* and the *Morning Post* claiming that the Government of India had denied the martial law administration the benefit of civil advice; in fact civil and military authorities, following the Government of India's instructions, had conferred daily in Lahore and were in close contact elsewhere, while several of the officers later censured for their conduct were not military but civil. Dyer's measures in Amritsar were instituted before the establishment of martial law.[26]

Chelmsford had given clear instructions ordering moderation; these instructions were indorsed by the local government. Yet they were not observed. The imposition of martial law was no excuse for this neglect; but confusion was one of the reasons that the excesses were allowed to continue. The Panjab Government, for example, requested that the punitive powers for certain officers

(ratified by the army command on 19 April) should be made
retrospective to 30 March. Some officers, they reported, had
already exercised such extended powers in spite of efforts to make
the position clear. The Home Department professed to be puzzled,
and informed the Panjab Government that they had understood
that ordinary courts were being used for ordinary offences, that
special tribunals were trying offences specified in the martial law
ordinances or added later, and that courts established by the
military were trying only those offences created under martial
law. Any other procedure was an irregularity. They asked for an
officer to be sent from the Panjab to discuss the matter with them.
At this point, on 4 May, the Government of India began to
realize, as had the Panjab Government, that it would be necessary
to pass an act of validation and indemnity to regularize these local
actions. Chelmsford was most concerned, for the moment,
therefore, not with legal correctness, but with ensuring that the
personnel of any summary tribunal was 'above reproach'. He was
not sure that some of the young officers would not 'see red'; but
he was also aware that summary procedure would be 'a most
effective weapon'. His government accordingly agreed to allow
selected *civil* officers to be appointed to summary courts for all
minor offences, provided that there were no sentences imposed
other than those permitted by the ordinary law.[27] Thus alarm at
the situation (as reported to them) and awareness of the needs of
hard-pressed administrators also limited the effectiveness of
central supervision.

There was one case in which the Government of India respected
local advice to the extent of refusing to reverse a policy they believed to be wrong. For the special tribunals, the military authorities had passed a general order excluding counsel from outside the
Panjab. There had been some 'agitators' among the applicants
and it was feared they would delay or inflame the trials. Complaints
were received by the Government of India— including some from
Surendranath Banerjea, Motilal Nehru, and a meeting of the
Calcutta Bar. The Commander-in-Chief telegraphed General
Beynon: 'Unless good reasons exist to the contrary the Commander-in-Chief considers refusal impolitic; but responsibility for
decision rests with you'.

There was a strong feeling at the centre—represented by Marris,
Maffey, Vincent and particularly Lowndes—that the policy was

unwise. O'Dwyer was later to claim that his government too had not favoured exclusion, provided the applicant's purpose might be assumed to be professional not political, but that Beynon had strongly objected to having to make such distinctions. It seems very unlikely that this is true. The Panjab Government wanted the exclusions (as O'Dwyer admitted) because they objected to the admission of C. R. Das, Hasan Imam, Baptista, Motilal Nehru and Juinati Asaf Ali. At the time they made a solid front with the military, O'Dwyer arguing that sufficient local counsel were available (and supplied by government if necessary) and that outside counsel were not ordinarily admitted to the Panjab High Court, to which he wished to make the tribunals conform as closely as possible. He maintained this position both by letter and on the telephone early in May, and the Home Department, having ascertained that the eleven or twelve prisoners then involved had thirty counsel between them, seemed to be about to let the matter rest. O'Dwyer's later version almost certainly refers to a period towards the end of May. Chelmsford intervened and suggested that the exclusions were responsible for much of the criticism of martial law (still being retained for military reasons connected with the mobilization in Afghanistan) and that it would be much easier if the prohibition were removed. At this point, not earlier, O'Dwyer agreed to recommend to Beynon that there should be a relaxation, Chelmsford having agreed that power could be kept to exclude particular individuals. Beynon, supported by Maclagan as incoming Governor, then argued that individual exclusions would be more objectionable than a general ban. Chelmsford took the question in Council. The Home Department had ascertained from the legal experts that they would be within their rights to order the local government to admit the counsel; but the Government of India decided not to interfere during the continuance of martial law. They showed their disapproval however, by calling the exclusions 'unwise' in an Order of Council. Vincent had strongly urged this, suggesting that they should say 'unwise and likely to create great difficulties' but Marris had pointed out that while they purported not to interfere, they were in fact applying great pressure and that therefore they should either revise the order themselves or express milder doubts. Accordingly the Viceroy's Private Secretary, it seems, deleted part of Vincent's formula. The Secretary of State showed more courage, and ordered postponements if necessary to allow outside counsel to appear; by this time martial law had ended and counsel were being allowed to attend.[28]

In most cases, however, the Government of India did try to intervene when they found Chelmsford's 'cardinal principles' were not being observed. In response to protests from Gandhi and C. F. Andrews about public whippings, for example, Chelmsford telegraphed to O'Dwyer on 23 April: 'I wish to point out . . . the very grave effect that these whippings are having on public opinion throughout India. I am ready to give you my support in every way, but I think it right that you should know that I consider this particular form of punishment should be avoided as far as possible and the least publicity given'.[29] 'Whippings' were inflicted 'on the buttocks with an ordinary cane' and were lawful under the Indian Penal Code; in Lahore some 66 persons received 832 stripes in private after sentence by a summary court, and about 190 persons were similarly punished in other parts of the province. A small minority of the sentences was carried out in public. Chelmsford's first reaction, hearing of the 'whippings', was to ask if it were true and, if true, legal. But Vincent laid stress on the undesirability of public punishment, and, though Chelmsford's telegram is capable of a wider interpretation, it was the bad publicity which was emphasized.[30] On 22 April the Commander-in-Chief had instructed General Beynon that 'public opinion in India was markedly opposed to corporal punishment' and that he would be glad if the authorities 'would dispense with punishments of this nature'. Chelmsford also refused a request for a public whipping at Kasur; he insisted that the flogging and the 'crawling' order at Amritsar offended 'against all the canons of wise punishment'.[31]

On 30 April, nevertheless, the Panjab asked for clarification on the interpretation of one of the martial law ordinances relating to the special commissions set up to try offenders against martial law. The local government asked if the authority given to pass 'any sentence authorized by law' allowed the commissions to pass any sentence authorized for the particular offence under trial, or to pass, for that offence, any sentence authorized for any offence. They were really asking if the Commissions could be allowed to pass lesser or additional sentences for the main offence of 'waging war against the King-Emperor', and they were particularly anxious

to extend the power to order whipping to cover any offence,
notably for arson, rioting or receiving stolen property. The Government of India interpreted their ordinance strictly, and refused to
allow any general application of whipping. Rather, early in May
Vincent had called for facts on deaths, whippings and other
measures, in order to publish them and counter rumours. The
reports proved so indefinite as to be unlikely to be believed if
published. Also, as they were unwilling to publicize the divergence
between them and the local government, the Government of India
urged O'Dwyer in May to announce that it would no longer be
necessary to resort to whipping and such methods. Failing in
this too, they continued to remind the Panjab of representations
they received on the subject; and later, in October, Vincent
pressed the local government for an inquiry into the whole question of public floggings, following a report on them by C. F.
Andrews in the *Independent* of 26 August. This inquiry was
eventually undertaken by the central government.[32]

Chelmsford had taken the opportunity, while objecting to the
whipping and the 'crawling' order in Amritsar, to repeat one of his
'cardinal principles'. This form of punishment, he explained to
O'Dwyer,

is not deterrent and is calculated to leave behind the maximum amount
of bitterness. It will be regarded as intended to aim at racial degradation. It is not imposed on the guilty, but on Indians as a race. A punishment of this sort will be remembered with rancour long after the stern
lessons of justice will have been forgotten. I hate to write and cavil at
what is being done at a time when we all owe you so much for your
prompt handling of the situation and I know how high feelings are
running among your European population. But we have to live with
Indians after all this is over, and we should do nothing which leaves
unnecessary bitterness behind. No province is self-contained and the
Panjab, important as it is, is only a portion of a much greater India, and
I feel confident that throughout India the racial animosity which exists
at present will be intensified a hundredfold when this story is told, and
cui bono?[33]

O'Dwyer, who pointed out that he was not responsible for actions
by the military (in this case General Dyer), had also been shocked
and asked that the order should be withdrawn.[34] In such cases,
of course, the damage had already been done.

Thus the excesses occurred. The Government of India were

hampered in any intervention both by declared policy and by circumstances. The practical difficulties of supervision were enormous. O'Dwyer, as he admitted to Chelmsford on 27 May, had been unable to give the Government of India a clear picture of the situation.[35] At times, because of interference with railways and telegraph, only wireless communication could be maintained between the governments and with different parts of the province. Chelmsford could presumably have left Simla and visited the disturbed areas in the Panjab—but this would have weakened or superseded the local government, and put the Viceroy out of touch with headquarters and thus with other parts of India.[36] And, even without special difficulties, it was, as Chelmsford recognized, 'always difficult to control the man on the spot'. O'Dwyer had recommended the Viceroy's 'cardinal principles' to the military authorities, but on his own admission, niceties were not always observed when everyone was 'working at high pressure'. The greatest problem of supervision was undoubtedly the gap between Simla and Lahore. There, O'Dwyer himself believed that martial law could not be operated 'without taking the kid gloves off': the Lieutenant-Governor set the tone for the province. He later claimed that, even in Lahore, Colonel Johnson did not always follow his advice: Johnson reduced and eased the student roll-calls, but 'moved slower than . . . suggested' over relaxing the curfew, opening the Badshahi mosque, and returning commandeered vehicles. But, as we have seen, there were daily conferences; one of O'Dwyer's contemporary reports states that Johnson 'generally submits his *orders* to us for approval' and 'I now and again have to do some pruning'. It seems that basically O'Dwyer approved of the methods being adopted, and the reservations which he remembered later were over details and timing. The attitude of mind current in his government is typified by their remark, justifying the 'salaaming' order, that a similar rule was enforced by the occupying powers on the Rhine; in the Home Department, Craik noted drily, 'I am doubtful whether it is good politics to refer' to that. Later, considering the case of a young civilian censured for misconduct, C. W. Gwynne remarked that the officer had 'acted in a manner which at the time and under the *regime* then obtaining was calculated to please those in authority: in other words he followed the example of those above him'.[37]

On the other hand, when O'Dwyer did wish to intervene (or

was instructed to do so), he too faced difficulties. Thus he prevented General Dyer from imposing an enormous fine of Amritsar
on the basis of claims for damages, but was not able to stop the
General's 'crawling' order. Indeed, Miles Irving, Amritsar's
Deputy Commissioner, reported that he had suggested to Dyer
that an order to remove shoes would be more in accordance with
Indian custom, but Dyer had adhered to 'crawling' on his own
responsibility. Similarly, he had added, to Dyer's proclamation
threatening to disperse by force of arms any gathering of more than
four men, 'the words "if necessary" in the draft which I was asked
to edit in legal language'; but subsequent events made it clear
that Dyer had taken no notice of this qualification. The situation
was thus doubly or triply difficult for the central government:
their problems with an unsympathetic Governor were compounded
by his and his subordinates' own problems of supervision. The
centre were able to deny O'Dwyer his wish to have martial law
proclaimed in Delhi—because the local authorities there were not
favourable to the idea. (The city was quiet and they could not find
any evidence to support O'Dwyer's claim that Delhi-based
emissaries were disturbing the Panjab.) But any matter internal
to the Panjab was much more difficult to control effectively from
the centre.[38]

Too much could be made of these difficulties of course. They
should not conceal the lamentable failures of determination and
initiative in the central government—for example over the exclusion of counsel or the lack of more active efforts to prevent
outlandish punishments. Wholly to excuse the centre would be
merely to adopt O'Dwyer's tactics: when, before the Hunter
committee on the disturbances, he tried to shelter behind tech-
nicalities. It is not enough to note that excesses were contrary to
Chelmsford's declared policy; one must also ask why the policy
failed, and admit the gross want of supervision and the almost
total unpreparedness for the administration of martial law. Not
until 18 June were systematic files opened on each of the trouble
spots.[39] On the other hand, it is right to mention the difficulties
and stress that the excesses were contrary to instructions. The
centre did try to see that their policy was followed, and the extent
of their efforts has tended to be underestimated. Indeed it appears
to have been deliberately concealed. In November, following the
dispute with Maclagan over the government's refusal to exclude

Tilak from the Panjab, Chelmsford wrote in indignation at the tone of Maclagan's protest:

When I remember my support of the Punjab Government during the past six months; when I see myself pilloried in every Indian paper because of my unwavering support; when I reflect that this support was given, as you know, often with reluctance, but that no word has ever been spoken by me either to the Secretary of State or publicly even suggesting reluctance, I feel that I have full right to complain . . .[40]

In short the record of the central government will not support the otherwise apparently natural assumption that the Panjab tragedy contradicts the political policy which we have seen evolving in response to constitutional changes.

The government had failed in their supervisory role. Now they could only try to minimize the after effects of the repressive local actions, and to vindicate as much as possible of the administration during the emergency. There were still some difficulties in their path.

One of the first needs was the removal of the conditions under which excesses had been possible. Chelmsford urged the withdrawal of martial law on 12 May, on the grounds that it was no longer needed and that the longer it remained the more difficult it would make the future situation. O'Dwyer opposed this, at least for Lahore, Amritsar and Gujranwala. (He had no objection for Gujrat and possibly Lyallpur.) After consultation with General Beynon, Colonel Johnson, Sir Edward Maclagan (about to take over as Lieutenant-Governor), J. P. Thomson (Panjab's Chief Secretary), and others, including the Officiating Agent for the Northwest Railway, O'Dwyer suggested that it was necessary to finish the trials under martial law, that the civil administration would become more difficult if it were withdrawn, and that the railway interest needed to be protected. It would be undesirable to have to restore martial law once it had been withdrawn; it was necessary to exclude some persons from the province; and martial laws had been reviewed and in a number of cases relaxed. Chelmsford disliked this stand, and claimed that he would have insisted on withdrawal if it had not been for the Afghan war. For the time being, therefore, his government accepted the local view, except for Sankaran Nair who resigned in protest over the delay. The government recommended the abrogation of martial law in

Gujrat and Lyallpur, and on 28 May it was announced that it had ended in Gujrat and would be withdrawn in Lyallpur as soon as the military force there had been increased (to satisfy Panjab objections). Martial law was abrogated everywhere on 9 June, except for railway lands. A further ordinance (No. VI of 1919) allowed trials to continue. The delays in the return to normal had not helped to restore confidence.[41]

The Act of validation and indemnity also aroused alarm. The government's draft Bill validated and prevented legal proceedings in respect of all sentences, punishments and other actions done in good faith and in the reasonable belief that they were necessary to maintain or restore order. Compensation was to be paid for property used under martial law. The Secretary of State suggested that it would be wiser to indemnify officials for actions and not to validate all sentences; but the government pointed out that without validation they would presumably have to release all those convicted summarily, and the Secretary of State concurred. In the Bill presented to the Imperial Legislative Council, however, the government circumvented their own objection by introducing a new clause validating all confinements under martial law, but no other actions—officers were merely indemnified against legal proceedings, unless they had acted unreasonably or not in good faith. The effect of this change was to make it clearer to the legislature that there was no question of prejudging the validity of actions or preventing proceedings against officers. The Home Department also asked for the preamble to be changed so that there was no suggestion that the legislators agreed that martial law had been necessary. To help the debate Sir William Vincent announced that all summary cases would be referred to two High Court judges for review, and two extra non-officials (one Indian and one European) would be added to the committee of enquiry which was about to consider the disturbances. Two-thirds of the non-official members of the Council supported the Indemnity Bill (six out of eighteen voted against it). Chelmsford attributed the result to the good work of the new Education Member, M. M. Shafi, and to the moderation of Vincent and the persuasiveness of Lowndes. But the passing of the Act, however necessary it may have been in legal terms (as the Judge Advocate-General had certified), did not help to reconcile the public to martial law administration, and added credibility to the argument that the government was trying to conceal grave abuses.[42]

It was the more important, therefore, to convince Indians that the prisoners held in gaol or already punished had been properly tried, and, where appropriate, were being treated leniently. The first martial law ordinance had provided for trial under Regulation III of 1804, whereby sentences only of death and forfeiture of property could be passed. The government removed this anomaly by further ordinances allowing a minimum sentence of transportation for life for waging war, and lesser sentences for other offences.[43] Severe penalties were needed, in Chelmsford's view, to prevent a recurrence of the disturbances; but reductions were readily considered as soon as the situation returned to normal.[44] The martial law commission had early recommended that the local government should bring some sentences down below the minimums permitted to the commissioners, and the government agreed. The judicial review, announced by Vincent during the Indemnity Bill debate, was to apply to all cases whether or not the offender applied for it, except where sentence had already been served. The Government of India had already decided to remit all sentences other than those for offences which were serious under ordinary law. Maclagan wanted to consider reducing sentences for such serious offences, and had already begun his own review; he suggested that he refer to the judicial enquiry any cases on which he felt doubt.[45] Maclagan's changes were designed to adjust sentences so that none was lighter than that which a Panjab magistrate would have imposed for a comparable offence, and in August the Governor considered that existing sentences represented the 'irreducible minimum' in terms of this principle. Vincent had exposed him to some gentle pressure, in a demi-official letter of 11 August, when the Home Department were resisting Montagu's suggestion for an amnesty to accompany the Indemnity Bill. Understanding that Maclagan was 'disposed to treat a great majority of offenders with great leniency, and indeed to remit sentences altogether in a great number of cases', the Home Member emphasized that 'in so far as you feel [it] possible to take this line, you will strengthen us in our rather difficult position *vis-à-vis* the Secretary of State'.[46] The extent of the reductions was, indeed, one of the reasons put forward against the amnesty in December 1919.[47] An overwhelming majority of

prisoners was released by the end of 1920: perhaps not quickly
enough.

The purpose of the judicial enquiry in the Panjab was not,
however, merely to provide machinery whereby leniency could
be shown to political prisoners. It was to demonstrate that the
special courts had functioned justly. At this stage good results
were still anticipated from publicity and investigation. Thus in May
the Panjab Government ended its secrecy by inviting visits and
reports from representatives of 'moderate' newspapers such as the
Bengalee and the *Times of India* and *Justice*. So too several
articles, some very favourable to government, were taken from the
Indian Mirror and made into a pamphlet for distribution in India
and abroad.[48] But just as better information tended to increase not
reduce public indignation, so the findings of the reviewing judges,
B. Chevis and B. K. Mullick, proved less than satisfactory for the
government's purpose. Of the twelve officials responsible for trying
summary cases, five were praised or found to have been generally
satisfactory in procedure and record; but the judges also criticized
the methods of three, representing 84 of the 550 cases reviewed.
The officials criticized were Major Shirley, the Provost Marshall,
Captain Doveton at Kasur, and B. N. Bosworth Smith. In the
case of the last, it was particularly unsatisfactory that he, who had
investigated the crimes, should also have conducted the trials—it
was perhaps not surprising that he recorded an unusually large
number of defendants who pleaded guilty. Moreover, one or both
of the reviewing judges considered that there was unsatisfactory
evidence or wrongful conviction for over one hundred defendants
in summary cases—and these were found under all the officers,
including those whose procedure was thought satisfactory. (Indeed
examination reveals, in spite of the judges' findings, that all the
records of the summary trials, with the exception of one officer
who dealt only with petty cases, were fairly scanty especially in
particulars relating to defence evidence.) In addition, when they
came to consider cases before martial law commissions, both
judges recommended five pardons, fourteen releases and two
reductions in sentence. Mullick suggested a further five pardons
and one release. These figures represented the failures of the
administration in a certain number of the trials. (The judges did
not deal with all cases, but only those referred to them by the India
Government or selected by the Panjab for a further opinion: for

commissions the judges dealt with 51 of 114 cases.) In spite of these results, the Panjab suggested, in February 1920, a press communique to convince people that the trials had been fair. They wanted to stress that the judges had approved the general procedure and endorsed the findings in all the most serious cases. Where they recommended releases, the government had complied —by this time all those convicted summarily had also been released.[49] A considerable number, however, remained in prison and some had been executed, so that any suspicion of irregularity in the trials was bound to increase public resentment.

The Government of India recognized that in non-judicial aspects also the administration and supervision of martial law had been defective. When martial law was applied to Peshawar in May 1919 because of the Afghan war, magistrates and not soldiers were employed in its administration, and Roos-Keppel, the Chief Commissioner, was made military governor in order to minimize dislocation.[50] This looks like a lesson learnt, though of course similar methods might not have prevented the Panjab excesses, many of which were committed by civil officers or before martial law applied. Thus, the main step, if government were not to be unprepared in future, was to tighten up on the control of personnel in emergencies—based as it was, in the case of martial law, on rules drawn up in 1804. Early in 1920, the government put an officer on special duty to devise a set of martial law instructions.

These were ready in April. The military were to be instructed to interfere as little as possible and to co-operate with the civil authorities, and to transfer charge as soon as order was restored. Martial law officers were to remember that Indians were British subjects; they were to conduct trials carefully and without awarding excessive sentences. Whipping was not to be ordered except where it was permitted under the ordinary law or for crimes of violence. Martial law orders were not to offend classes, individuals or religious feelings, and were not to involve racial discrimination. If military force were to be employed it was not to exceed the minimum necessary. The Government of India proposed to print these instructions—which were no more than a formal statement of their former policy and Chelmsford's 'cardinal principles'—and to distribute copies in confidence to all Divisional and Brigade Commanders and to district officers, for further distribution to subordinates should martial law be declared. Copies of the first

chapter of the manual, containing general principles, were also to
be issued to all police officers and magistrates; the contents were
to be made known to all commissioned military officers. These
matters were confidential in detail, but the government were able
to announce their existence publicly.[51]

The Government of India would have been inclined to leave
matters there as far as published reassurances went, and hope that
in time both disturbances and repression would be forgotten. In
this regard Chelmsford regarded the Afghan war as a 'godsend'—
it diverted public attention from internal matters. The government made sure that all news, except for military details, was
made public. Montagu, however, was not satisfied with silence
about the Panjab disturbances. He first asked for an enquiry early
in May 1919. He endorsed Bhupendranath Basu's plan for
restoring confidence; this included the pardon of all those convicted except in cases of crimes of violence, and a public commission of enquiry. Montagu announced to the House of Commons:
'You cannot have disturbances of this kind and of this magnitude
without an enquiry into the causes . . . and the measures taken'.[52]

At first, Marris suggested that an enquiry, if completed by
September, would strengthen the government's hand. But Vincent,
while conceding this, believed that such a swift outcome would be
impossible, questioned what the scope of the enquiry would be,
and feared a resurgence of bitterness as a result of publicity. The
government had earlier resisted a suggestion from Surendranath
Banerjea for an enquiry into the Delhi riots of 30 March. Chelmsford and Vincent had decided that it was out of the question until
the situation had settled down, but was to be considered then.
Vincent had written to Banerjea to ask for support, and Delhi had
conducted their own enquiry by means of a magistrate's inquest.
Thus Chelmsford replied to Montagu's first query: 'I have always
contemplated announcing an enquiry into these disturbances
when order has been restored and normal conditions prevail. I
have held my hand, however, because I do not wish to give the
appearance of discouragement to officers who are performing
onerous, distasteful and responsible duties.' Thus his government
had envisaged an enquiry, but did not wish to put the whole
administration publicly on trial, reawakening interest and publicizing grievances; they favoured departmental investigations:
they saw 'serious disadvantages attending the investigation of

matters about which feeling both European and Indian has been deeply stirred'. They had concluded that three incidents might have been unreasonable: the public floggings, the Jallianwala Bagh firing, and aerial bombing of crowds at Gujranwala. They conceded that there might have been others. But they informed the Secretary of State that they would 'certainly have preferred to be left to make such enquiries as were necessary . . . and to deal with any . . . officers whose conduct might be found to deserve either censure or punishment in the ordinary course'. They agreed that they were 'bound to see that . . . measures taken . . . are reasonable' and 'to enquire dispassionately into any cases where there appears to be any reason for thinking that . . . limits have been exceeded'. But they did not like the Secretary of State's way of achieving this end.[53] In short they wanted justice—if necessary retribution—but they feared publicity. They knew that, if given the material, Indian politicians now had the skill and the machinery to make capital out of the government's errors and excesses.

The government's objection was endorsed by Sir George Lloyd, who wrote to Montagu of his fear about the consequences of an enquiry. Harcourt Butler suggested similarly that an enquiry would enhance racial tension, and that acts of clemency would have a better effect. Montagu advised against being apprehensive at things 'being thrown into the melting pot again as a result of an Enquiry': he thought that the situation was becoming quieter, and that an enquiry was 'the only possible way to deal with the Punjab situation'. He wished to avoid a 'pompous indictment' of Chelmsford's administration, but insisted that it was necessary to dissipate 'monstrous allegations'. It seems clear that Montagu rather underestimated the seriousness of the events in the Panjab and hence the danger of ill-feeling as a result of 'monstrous' revelations. A private letter of Seton (instructive also for *his* attitudes) records that he found it 'very hard to forgive' Montagu for telling Lady O'Dwyer, 'oddly enough in Malaviya's words, that he didn't know why there was all this fuss about Lahore, where not even a pane of glass had been broken! The fact is that all these insects who were here about Reforms kept buzzing in his ear.' It is probable too that Montagu saw good tactical reasons for an enquiry: as Marris pointed out, Montagu's case for further constitutional reforms would be weaker if the disturbances were due to 'agitation and misrepresentation working on economic discontent and race prejudice' (as Marris seemed to believe) but stronger if they were the result 'of iron bureaucratic rule as typified by Sir Michael O'Dwyer' (as Montagu thought).[54]

Vincent saw Chelmsford on 2 June to urge the 'very strong reasons against an enquiry'. But Chelmsford replied that he thought it 'inevitable' and that it had already been promised by Montagu. Vincent accepted this, and thus, in view of Montagu's Commons announcement, the India Government proposed an enquiry to cover the Panjab, Delhi, Bombay and Bengal, and to investigate the disorders and measures taken to deal with them. They objected to including causes in the investigation, lest it allow politicians to attack the whole administration and thus 'leave a dangerous legacy of bad feeling'. For members they suggested a chairman from Britain, a high-ranking military officer, a senior civilian and an Indian; meetings would be in public unless the committee directed otherwise. Of the local governments which were addressed on this scheme, Bengal was strongly opposed to an enquiry and Bombay thought it would be open to the most serious objections. The Panjab Government agreed to an enquiry and were prepared to allow it to discuss causes; Delhi thought an enquiry 'inevitable' but added that it was unfortunate that it should be held at a time when the country might have settled down again.[55] In their reply to Montagu the India Government set out these objections, but agreed an enquiry was unavoidable, and modified their original proposals so as to include a second Indian member (to represent both Hindus and Muslims) and to allow investigation into the question of whether the disorders were organized, and if so why and by whom. Thus they included some consideration of causes without risking a general investigation of past administration—they had accepted the Panjab point of view, as they had realized that Montagu had mentioned 'causes' in his Commons statement. They also wished to minimize the risks by having the committee appointed by and reporting to the Government of India.[56] A Council resolution sponsored by Malaviya later called for the committee to be unconnected with the administration—leading to acrimonious debate in the legislature—and Vincent too had favoured a committee appointed by the Home Government. But the India Government argued that they were responsible for reasonable administration and should appoint the enquiry unless the Home Government had lost confidence in them (which they had not).[57]

A majority of Chelmsford's Council also agreed that they should not now conduct their own preliminary enquiry, on the grounds that it would be thought to anticipate or prejudice the main committee. Vincent, supported by the Army Department, had been in favour of an immediate departmental enquiry conducted by a High Court judge, a military officer and an Indian. He had stressed the immediate need to take action against some officers. Lowndes led the opposition to this, gaining Chelmsford's agreement, and Montagu also supported the majority view.[58] The Government of India had therefore not only accepted a public enquiry; they had also transferred to it exclusively the decision on the disturbances and the hopes for appeasing public opinion.

Some enquiries continued—for example the Judge Advocate-General (A. Caruana) was asked to inquire into the legality of summary courts set up by Beynon, after Syed Hasan Imam had questioned this in the *Independent* of 31 July. But for the most part such investigations were shelved or diverted. Thus Marris suggested, following a report in the *Amrita Bazar Patrika*, that they should inquire into the use of aeroplanes at Gujranwala. Vincent agreed and Hailey interviewed Captain Carberry, the officer involved, who also sent in a written report. But the purpose of this investigation was now to help the government defence—as was the case also with a wider suggestion of Marris (which Vincent refused) for a conference with Maclagan to review the 80 or so cases of firings, including that at Amritsar. The policy had been laid down as a matter of importance by Chelmsford, while supporting Lowndes against the preliminary enquiry:

The Army authorities should get statements from the various officers concerned so as to have a connected history to lay before the Commission. . . . The Punjab Government should in like manner put together their papers . . . and consider the witnesses who will be necessary to substantiate the officers' account. I believe in this way it will be possible to put before the Commission a convincing and full statement of the Government case, without resorting to a procedure which will undoubtedly be described as intending to 'blanket' the investigations . . .[59]

As well as trying to ensure the result, it was necessary to make sure that the Committee would be as useful as possible; the government favoured appointing a well-known English judge as chairman. None was available, and they were forced to accept the appointment of a little-known Scottish judge, Lord Hunter. Chelmsford expressed his disappointment at this decision. The government were also unable to avail themselves of the prestige of Sir Edward Gait, as he was personally unwilling to serve, and it was decided that it would be invidious for the head of one province to sit in judgment on the affairs of another. The government had decided that it might help the Committee if they agreed to suggestions in the Imperial Legislative Council, where Indian members led by Malaviya requested a third Indian member on the Committee and were prepared to accept an extra non-official European as well. The government asked Tej Bahadur Sapru to be the third Indian member, and when he declined appointed Jagat Narayan. The other Hindu member, Chimanlal Setalvad, had been among the counsel excluded from the Panjab under martial law; Narayan had been a critic of the Panjab Government in the past and had contributed to the Panjab Relief Fund. The local government had drawn these facts to the attention of the Government of India, but had not protested—on the contrary they thought the information might be useful later in showing the impartial constitution of the committee.[60]

Public acceptance of the Committee was nevertheless put at risk by a disagreement with the Congress. The All-India Congress Committee had appointed a sub-committee under Malaviya to attend to the question of the Panjab enquiry. This sub-committee demanded that the principal local leaders should be released from prison for the duration of the enquiry, in order that they might give evidence before the Hunter Committee and thus assure people that the investigation was to be full and impartial. The local government offered to provide facilities for any prisoners who wanted to testify—they would be released on bail for as long as necessary to allow them to give evidence and instruct counsel— but Malaviya refused to be satisfied with anything less than unconditional release on security. Accordingly the Congress decided to boycott the Hunter Committee, and instituted their own enquiry under Motilal Nehru. No prisoners gave evidence to the Hunter Committee, although some were represented by counsel. A few prisoners who had been released later offered to travel to

Bombay to testify; Lord Hunter declined their offer on the grounds that after six weeks in Lahore his committee had completed their hearings on the Panjab.[61]

In their report the Hunter Committee on the whole vindicated government policy, including the actions of local officers. They considered, for example, more than thirty-six instances of firing by troops, police or (on two occasions) from aeroplanes, and justified all but two.[62] But this favourable verdict was not very useful. Firstly the Indian members of the Committee had written a minority report. They questioned the existence of a rebellion and the need for martial law, but admitted that some persons were rightly tried for waging war, and did not contradict the majority's general approval of government policy; except in a few cases they dissented rather over the severity of the condemnation of particular excesses. Nevertheless the existence of a division on racial lines inevitably undermined the persuasiveness of the official enquiry as a whole. Secondly the Congress committee had reported strongly condemning the Panjab Government and the Government of India, and making (on the evidence of a different set of witnesses) accusations of excesses even greater than those revealed by the Hunter Committee. Finally, and most of all, the positive findings of the majority and minority reports of the official enquiry had been completely outweighed and obscured by the discovery and publication of the details of one incident, the massacre at Jallianwala Bagh in Amritsar.

General Dyer had arrived in Amritsar and taken control before the imposition of martial law. He decided on 12 April to issue a proclamation forbidding public meetings, and had this proclaimed in several parts of the city. On the afternoon of the 13th he was informed that a meeting was being held in the Jallianwala Bagh, an almost completely enclosed square. He marched to the square with troops and an armoured car, entered with the troops through a narrow alley, and immediately ordered the soldiers to open fire. More than 1,500 rounds were fired, directed at the thickest parts of the crowd as they tried to escape through the only other exit. Casualties were high—the number of deaths was later estimated officially at just under four hundred, and by the Hindu charitable organization, the Seva Samiti, at about 530—and the casualties would presumably have been higher if the entrance to the Bagh had not been too narrow for the armoured car. Dyer then left the scene without making any arrangements to attend to the wounded. The evidence before the Hunter Committee had made it clear that this shooting was completely unjustified. Dyer had at first claimed that his object 'was to disperse the crowd', but, under cross-examination, he admitted that probably he could have dispersed the crowd without firing and that he 'meant to punish those who had disobeyed the order and to give them a lesson'; he had thought he would 'make a wide impression through the Punjab'. He admitted that he would have used the armoured car if it had been possible, and that he stopped firing because ammunition was running low. It was revealed that the crowd had not been riotous— they were listening to a lecture—and that Dyer had not given them any warning or a chance to disperse. It was suggested that the proclamation forbidding meetings had been inadequately publicized and that many in the crowd were villagers who had come to Amritsar for a traditional festival.[63] It was this body of evidence which provided the main shock to opinion.[64] Dyer's action bore no resemblance to established practice or instructions. The Panjab Government was later to order that no unnecessary violence should be used under martial law. The Panjab Police Rules stated:

4. When an officer . . . determines to resort to the use of fire-arms, he shall, when the circumstances of the case admit of this being done, before giving the order to use such arms, give . . . to the crowd a special warning that if they do not disperse an order to fire upon them will be given, and that the Police will fire with buckshot or balled cartridges.

6. As a rule only very few files should be allowed to fire at first. Three or four shots . . . may suffice to disperse a large crowd; but the officer . . . must use his discretion . . .

8. No firing should be permitted a moment after the necessity for it has ceased to exist.

These rules, though not binding on a military officer, were presumably still in force until martial law had been declared.[65] The shooting at Jallianwala Bagh had been shown to be indefensible in motive and out of all proportion to what was necessary.

To the Hunter Committee O'Dwyer justified the firing, asserting (apart from the discreditable argument that it stopped the rebellion elsewhere) that Amritsar was in a state of 'tumult and revolt on 12th April'. But the Commissioner of Amritsar Division gave the lie to this: he reported, 'We lost control of Amritsar on 10th April and did not recover control of the city till 12th April'. Amritsar's quietness on the 12th is confirmed by a circular telegram sent out by the Home Department.[66] There was, therefore, no apparent need for further action next day, except to disperse an illegal gathering. According to the evidence of Captain F. C. C. Briggs, who had been attached to Dyer's staff, the General had been warned on the morning of the 13th that a meeting was to be held that afternoon. Dyer had made no attempt to prevent it and had not believed that the meeting would be held. Briggs also claimed that on the 12th Dyer had mentioned that he intended, once his proclamation had been well-circulated, 'to take strong measures'.[67] Dyer's own evidence bore this out: on hearing that the meeting was being held, he had made up his mind, he said, 'that if his order was defied he would shoot straight away'—he had made up his mind before he had assessed the needs of the situation.[68] In his official report on the incident, he stated that 'It was no longer a question of merely dispersing the crowd, but one of producing a sufficient moral effect, from a military point of view, not only on those present, but more especially throughout the Punjab. There could be no question of undue severity'.[69] This point is very important, for it disposes of the argument that the extreme position taken by Dyer before the Hunter Committee was a distortion introduced because an honest soldier was harried and out-manoeuvred by Hindu lawyers far too clever for him. On the evidence of his own report, written in August 1919, there can be no doubt that Dyer acted in the Bagh unnecessarily and for improper motives. [It is difficult not to interpret Dyer's own explanations of his purpose and his admitted intention of teaching the crowd a lesson, as revealing that the shooting at the Jallianwala Bagh was a deliberate and premeditated attempt to revenge the murdered Europeans of Amritsar.] It was the job of the soldier to keep order, not to instil terror nor to act as judge and executioner.

Sir George Lloyd concluded that the misfortune was that a 'thoroughly stupid' (though perhaps honest) soldier had had to deal with such a situation.[70] Certainly Dyer's conduct at Amritsar was not altogether out of character, in spite of his 'distinguished' record: in November 1916 Chelmsford had complained of a 'policy of adventure' pursued by Dyer in Sarhad in South-Eastern Persia; Dyer had been removed and in Chelmsford's view the position had improved.[71]

Before the Hunter Committee and the revelation of the details, the Amritsar shooting had not received the attention it warranted. The bombing at Gujranwala (which the Committee also criticized) had been objected to, as had some of the more bizarre punishments under martial law. There was no mention of the Jallianwala Bagh in the complaints of the moderates' conference at the end of April 1919; not one of many questions in the House of Commons mentioned the shooting before August. The All-India Congress Committee passed a resolution on 8 June, mentioning the Jallianwala Bagh first among many other incidents. Malaviya's version of the events had been reported by the C.I.D. in July, but the action was given no very special emphasis in a long list of possible points for criticism sent that month to the Panjab from the Home Department. Even opposition to a public enquiry does not seem to have been due to knowledge of the enormities likely to be uncovered: in June 1919, Marris noted, 'The Punjab Government is certainly not aware of the storm that is threatening to break over their heads, and I am not at all sure how far the Government of India are aware either'.[72] Not until the Imperial Legislative Council debate on the Indemnity Bill in September was the shooting singled out for attention, with fairly full accounts made public. But even then there was little attention paid in the India Office, or, it seems, the India Government.

The main reasons seem to have been lack of information and the talk of rebellion. In the first place, not only was the crucial point, Dyer's motive, not yet known, but there was confusion also over almost every detail of what had happened. The number of casualties was uncertain. As late as October Marris was unhappy about the general information—only vague estimates—sent to the India Office. But more detailed figures were available only in the district officers' reports; Chelmsford did not see these until 27 September. As far as the Jallianwala Bagh was concerned, the India Government first reported casualties of 200, and this was repeated in the London *Times* of 19 April. On the 17th the government had corrected their first report by adding that the casualties were deaths, and, by a coincidence, this second telegram seems to have been received in the India Office *before* the first, at 11.00

a.m. on the 17th rather than 10.00 p.m. Thus the India Office was not in possession of misleading information; and yet only the first message was communicated to the press. Full particulars were not given to London, however, until 28 May, and these were based on Dyer's estimates of one death for every six rounds fired. This was the calculation normal in France, but (as Marris hinted) it was questionable whether conditions in the Bagh were comparable with those in the trenches. A proclamation calling for names of those killed was made on 7 August, and on 3 September the Amritsar Deputy Commissioner sent in a list of 291 names— 211 residents of the city, 29 from nearby districts and 44 unknown.[73]

In addition to this confusion, there was a dispute about the wounded. It was first assumed that the wounded would be about three times the number dead (the proportion usual in war); but later it was thought that such a high ratio was unlikely with close range firing as occurred at the Jallianwala Bagh. The Seva Samiti verified only 192 wounded—and, although the number must have been higher, given a natural tendency to conceal participation in the Bagh meeting, the Government of India, in repeating the Samiti's figures, argued that it was at least possible for the number of wounded to be lower than the number killed. The number of deaths also remained under-estimated until September when Sir William Vincent suggested in the Imperial Legislative Council that there were probably about 301 (instead of Dyer's 200) and 334 in the Panjab as a whole.[74]

Of course, even 200 deaths represented a very large number, as great as that for fatalities from all the other incidents during the disorders, but the situation in the Panjab was being presented by the local government and others in terms of conspiracy and rebellion. Perhaps the scale of Indian natural disasters should also be remembered—quite apart from the influenza epidemic, for example, nearly 2,000 people died in a cyclone in Bengal in October 1919. But, most of all, it was belief in a rebellion which allowed these casualties to seem not out of all proportion, and perpetuated the misinterpretations of Dyer's actions. The shooting had been presented to the local government, and in turn to the Government of India and the Secretary of State, as a necessary action in a dangerous situation. The Commissioner at Amritsar considered that 'the blow . . . saved the central Punjab from

anarchy, loot & murder'. The Government of India had earlier
reported the shooting (on information from the Panjab) with the
explanations that 'At Amritsar there was defiance ... of a
proclamation forbidding public meetings, and it was necessary to
fire on the mob', and that 'Further particulars show that fifty
sepoys faced unlawful assembly of 5,000'. General Dyer gave a
brief verbal report to O'Dwyer during a fifteen minute interview
of 16 April. O'Dwyer had already approved the firing, in spite of
his first reaction of 'serious anxiety', because of pressure from
Beynon and in the midst of decisions on troubles elsewhere in the
province. No written reports were received in London until
October—Dyer had not made his, with the first mention of his
motives, until August. It was, even then, submitted to the Army
Department, not seen by the Viceroy. Montagu and others had
met O'Dwyer on his return to Britain, but had not received the
impression (according to Sir T. W. Holderness) that the force
employed by Dyer had been in excess of the necessities of the
situation. Indeed O'Dwyer had left the Panjab before seeing
Dyer's report. Accordingly the details of Dyer's evidence came
as a surprise.[75]

Montagu had a reply drafted for the House of Commons stating
that 'Until the evidence of Genl. Dyer reached this country last
week the S/S was without information as to what took place in the
Jallianwala Bagh'. He meant, as he explained later, that he did
not know the details as they emerged before the Hunter Committee. He had suggested that Dyer should be relieved of his
command, when telegraphing to the Viceroy early in June, but his
objections had focused on Dyer's 'crawling' order, which still had
his main attention, with other 'inexcusable' orders, as late as
September 1919.[76] The Government of India, too, had been in
ignorance. Chelmsford explained to Montagu that in April he had
known of the small number of Dyer's force, the fact that the proclamation had been disobeyed, and the possibility of Dyer's being
attacked if he hesitated. He knew no further details until he read
Dyer's evidence to the Hunter Committee.[77] In reply to Montagu's
call for Dyer's dismissal, Chelmsford had telegraphed of the
General's 'otherwise admirable handling' (that is apart from the
'crawling order') and had urged that to act against him would give
a handle 'to political sensation-mongers ... when things have
practically settled down'. Thus, at this time, in June 1919, he was

not considering the Jallianwala Bagh shooting. In July 1919 Chelmsford had noted, in general, that 'there is little more in our possession than scrappy telegrams with no connecting line of narrative'; and Cleveland had commented that 'What had happened that night of the 13th in the Suharwala [sic] Bagh is shrouded in mystery'. And the suggestions made at that time to the Panjab Government had mentioned only that the shooting might be thought 'unnecessary' and to have 'resulted in excessive loss of life', being 'unduly prolonged' and in 'an enclosed space without exits'—almost as if the fault were in the location rather than the judgment and intent of Dyer.[78] After the Hunter Report Chelmsford still argued that Dyer's evidence had been exaggerated, that Amritsar had been in a state of rebellion, and that Dyer had been right to consider that position; but nonetheless he now admitted that Dyer had been wrong to think of himself as responsible for the state of the province, and he no longer opposed Dyer's dismissal. His change of heart seems to have come during December, as full reports became available, for, whereas in November he thought that Dyer, though a bluff soldier, had well survived his ordeal before the inquiry committee, by 31 December he was no longer accepting any excuses: Craddock had suggested that Dyer had not realized there was no way out of the Bagh, or that his judgment had been impaired because the assault on the European missionary had been much worse than had been revealed, but Chelmsford was merely sceptical that there were any unknown facts about the assault.[79]

He explained to Montagu that he had not acted earlier because he had been waiting for the Committee to report. Such scruples typified his handling of the situation. Montagu suggested he should have made public his private objections to flogging and the 'crawling' order, and have announced his moves to forbid them. But the Viceroy had believed that, in such a serious situation, it was essential that subordinates should feel they had full support. Montagu had agreed that it was right to support the local authorities at the time, but suggested that this did not prevent expressing an opinion afterwards; Chelmsford had explained that, although he was not defending 'O'Dwyerism', his principle had been to assume his officials right until they were proved wrong. (The excuse was a trifle disingenuous. Normal procedure, as outlined by Chamberlain in 1916, was for officials thought responsible for offences, to be suspended pending an inquiry—their retention of positions of authority was recognized as likely to create dangerous feeling. The difference in the Panjab case was that normal procedure—an *internal* government inquiry—had been suspended.)[80] The government could have been quicker to investigate the details of the Jallianwala Bagh incident. But their neglect was to some extent matched by a delay in public awareness generally. The many casualties were of course bound to cause alarm and resentment, especially as very large estimates were being made— Gandhi quoted Swami Sraddanand's suggestion of 1,500 and Malaviya's of 971.[81] But [not until the details and motives were revealed to the Hunter Committee was the shooting shown to have been a massacre.] From this point the Government of India began to lose the capacity to limit the progressive alienation of Indian opinion. Bhupendranath Basu noted: 'just as another great act of conciliation was about to be inaugurated, the Punjab incident fell like a thunderbolt riving in twain the reuniting forces of the great war . . .'.[82] It was hard to see how to recover the situation.

The Government of India had been anxious to forestall the Congress report by earlier publication of the official committee's verdict. They did not succeed in this, but nevertheless were fairly satisfied that 'little interest' was being taken in the Congress accusations. They had been advised by the Panjab Government that the investigation had been 'frankly partial', evidence being in the hands of relatives of the accused. To Montagu, who suggested a further enquiry into these accusations, they stressed that the non-official investigation had been undertaken by parties already publicly committed to a condemnation of the Panjab administration, and that their report was patently biased and exaggerated— complainants could take action through the courts if they wished (although only two minor cases had been instituted). But the government nevertheless investigated all of the major Congress allegations against government officers, and made, for their own purposes, detailed refutations of the Congress evidence. This approach had been followed from the 'first fruits' of the Congress investigation, allegations by Satyapal of the torture of prisoners, as published in the *Bombay Chronicle* in February 1920. The Panjab Government suggested sidestepping the complaints with the excuse that they should have been made earlier; but Vincent, while accepting this for the moment, noted that they would 'be forced to make enquiries later'. He had regarded such accusations as matters 'of importance and urgency' and advocated early denials where possible.[83]

The criticisms from the Hunter Committee could not be dealt with so informally. It was necessary to issue a statement. The initial reaction of Chelmsford's Council was to accept the majority report almost without exception, and to admit the cogency of much of what the minority had said, agreeing with them particularly in disapproving of long prison sentences. In the government's view, Dyer, having acted beyond what could reasonably have been thought necessary and with inadequate humanity, should be compelled to retire—Chelmsford told Montagu: 'I cannot contemplate the retention of a man of his mentality and with his record'. The government agreed that Dyer's proclamation should have been published more widely, condemned his failure to give a warning beforehand or medical assistance afterwards, and found his continuation of the shooting after the crowd had begun to disperse to be indefensible and a misconception of his duty. But they did not propose to prosecute Dyer; they intended to remain neutral in the event of a private prosecution. The government also criticized O'Dwyer's approval of Dyer's act—they thought it would have been 'wiser' if he had found out the details first—but they intended to exonerate the Lieutenant-Governor from any other censure. For the other officers who had acted improperly, the government proposed to ask the Panjab Government to take appropriate action—certain conduct should be condemned and some officers censured. The Delhi and Bombay authorities should be commended. Regret should be expressed for the lives lost, and steps announced which would prevent any repetition of the mistakes or the misuse of power. In March 1920, J. L. Maffey, the Viceroy's Private Secretary, writing to Vincent, had supported a suggestion of Sastri that the lack of a government expression of sympathy for the loss of innocent lives was causing a continuation of bad feeling; Maffey had hoped that the right note could be struck in the Government of India resolution. The government also proposed to announce that compensation would be paid to victims and dependants suffering on account of the Jallianwala Bagh shooting.[84]

Montagu proposed that the British Cabinet also should make an announcement, and suggested that the Government of India resolution should begin with the Cabinet statement and go on to give the government's views. The government thought this an unusual procedure and argued that any omissions on their part would be construed as disagreement. It was eventually decided that the two governments should publish 'despatches' specially written for the purpose and based on the Government of India's proposed resolution and the Cabinet's statement. The Government of India wished to give their 'despatch' a date as near as possible to that of their real communication to the Secretary of State, if not of the Viceroy's telegram of 21 March, then of the draft resolution sent in the week of 10 April: they were anxious to counter charges that they had delayed unduly. Montagu did not agree—it would have publicized the delays which had occurred in London, and there had already been parliamentary questions on the publication of the Hunter report—and therefore the Indian 'despatch' was dated 3 May; the Secretary of State's 'reply' was dated 26 May, the date of its publication along with the Hunter report.[85]

In their 'despatch' the Government of India defended the exclusion of Gandhi, which had been criticized by the minority report of the Hunter Committee, and endorsed the favourable findings of both majority and minority on the action taken in Delhi, Ahmedabad, Viramgam and Bombay City. The minority had argued that there had been no rebellion in the Panjab, no conspiracy and no justification for martial law, but the majority believed that there had been a rebellion, that martial law had been justified, and that, although there was no evidence of a conspiracy, it was difficult and perhaps unsafe for the government at the time not to assume there was. The Government of India, with Shafi dissenting, accepted the majority view and pointed out that they had had no choice but to rely on the Panjab reports of a rebellion and a critical situation needing martial law—they quoted the local government's telegram in full. Both minority and majority, with different degrees of severity, condemned detentions without trial: the Government of India, while justifying more preventive detentions, admitted that long imprisonments, especially in nine cases singled out by the minority report, had been a serious error. On trials in general the majority had had favourable comments, while regretting that certain cases had not been tried in the ordinary courts and criticizing the exclusion of outside counsel.

The Government of India agreed with this view. The use of air-
craft on two or three occasions at Gujranwala had been criticized
by both reports, the minority adding that the pilot had not used
sufficient discretion: the Government of India were not prepared
to criticize the pilot but agreed that instructions had been inadequate—they proposed to issue better instructions. Thus far the
government's 'despatch' followed their original intention of endorsing the majority view. On the central matters, however, they
went further.

Both reports had had severe criticisms of certain martial law
orders: the majority condemned the 'crawling' order of Dyer and
the public flogging of certain offenders, the students' 'roll calls'
imposed by Colonel Johnson in Lahore, an order of General
Campbell requiring Indians to salaam on meeting Europeans,
and other 'fantastic' penalties; the minority added objections to
almost all of the Lahore orders, to the flogging of a marriage party,
and to actions by three officers, Colonel O'Brien, Bosworth Smith
and Jacob. The Government of India accepted almost all the
criticisms of both reports. They announced that steps would be
taken to avoid 'fantastic' penalties in future and that the officer
who ordered the flogging of the marriage party had already been
censured—in fact they asked the Panjab Government to reopen the
case and consider further measures. They admitted that some
(though not all) of the Lahore orders had gone too far—they agreed
with the minority particularly in condemning the confinement of
students and professors after the destruction of a martial law
notice on college property. It may be that the government's condemnation would have been total, given the needs of the situation,
if they had not earlier defended one of Colonel Johnson's measures
to the Secretary of State—the Home Department had justified
the order threatening imprisonment, fine and whipping for continued refusal to open shops, on the grounds that closure had been
an expression of resistance to the government and that anyway
the order had not been invoked.[86] As it was the government concluded in their 'despatch' that the administration of martial law
had been 'marred' in particular instances by a misuse of power, by
irregularities, and by 'injudicious and irresponsible acts', and they
announced their intention of issuing instructions which would
associate civil advisers formally with the military in future
emergencies; they also reported that they had asked the local

government to take action against the officers who had been criticized.

On the crucial matter of Dyer and Jallianwala Bagh, the majority had criticized the failure to give warning or stop firing as the crowd dispersed, and the fact that Dyer had decided on firing before he had arrived at the Bagh or been confronted with an emergency; they condemned his attempt to create a moral effect and denied that his action averted a rebellion. The minority added to these criticisms strong condemnations for Dyer's failure sufficiently to publish the proclamation forbidding meetings, his suggestion that he would have used machine guns, his firing until his ammunition was almost exhausted, his assumption that the crowd in the Bagh consisted of persons guilty of the earlier outrages, and his failure to attend to the wounded. The government agreed with both reports that warning should have been given, that the continuation of firing was indefensible, and that the firing was in excess of the needs of the occasion; they supported the minority view that the proclamation was insufficiently published and that the wounded should have been tended. They criticized O'Dwyer as in their draft resolution, and announced that Dyer was to be asked to resign. They ended their 'despatch' with a reminder that only 88 out of 1779 were still in prison as a result of the outbreak, with an expression of regret at the loss of life and a promise of compensation, and with the observation that the lesson of the disasters was that non-co-operation (currently being advocated again by Gandhi) was too dangerous a weapon.

The Secretary of State's 'reply' differed from the 'despatch' in the vehemence of its language. The Secretary of State recorded his tribute to the officers who had not been criticized, and stressed the British Government's 'obligation' to and 'fullest confidence' in Lord Chelmsford personally. Montagu justified martial law. But he admitted that its administration had been marred, not generally but also not uncommonly, by a spirit which promoted improper and inhumane punishments, humiliating to Indians and causing unwarranted inconvenience—as if the officers involved had been governing a hostile country. Dyer, in the view of the Secretary of State, had violated the British Government's principle of using the minimum necessary force, and thus had caused 'lamentable and unnecessary' loss of life. His 'crawling' order (here echoing Chelmsford) 'offended against every canon of civilised conduct'; at the Bagh his failure to give a warning had been 'inexcusable' and his failure to tend the wounded was an 'omission from his obvious duty'. He was 'not entitled to select for condign punishment an unarmed crowd which . . . had committed no act of violence, had made no attempt to oppose him by force, and many members of which must have been unaware that they were disobeying his commands'. Dyer's 'conception of his duty . . . was so fundamentally at variance with that which His Majesty's Government had a right to expect from and a duty to enforce upon officers . . ., that it is impossible to regard him as fitted to remain entrusted with the responsibilities which his rank and position impose on him'. The matter was being referred to the Army Council.

Thus the condemnations made by the majority of the Hunter Committee had been clearly endorsed by both the Government of India and the British Government: the Government of India sought to place some emphasis on the difficulties of the situation, but on the main points their position, if not their terminology, was close to that of the Secretary of State and not greatly removed from that of the minority report. (Indeed a later office summary of action taken against individuals in all cases quoted the minority report as the basis for censure.) Chelmsford professed himself perfectly satisfied with the procedure adopted. But he admitted: 'Of course . . . we shall not please anyone, but that is not our business. The European community will be offended at our judgment on Dyer, and the extremists wanted either my or O'Dwyer's head on a charger. . . . I think, however, that the ultimate verdict will be that we have been strictly judicial in our treatment of the matter.'[87] Montagu was also apprehensive about the results of the publication of the Hunter Report and the two 'despatches'; later he admitted that he might have made a mistake in ordering an enquiry. He had written to Lord Hunter in August 1919 that the government had nothing to fear from a searching enquiry and that the purpose was to restore public confidence. Later he wrote to Lloyd (who had always been apprehensive): 'until the enquiry opened, I had not the slightest conception that anything would be revealed which would cause us embarrassment. I thought the enquiry would justify everything that had been done, and the Government of India assured me that they had nothing to fear'.[88]

The English language newspapers responded predictably. All those which were English-owned, except the *Times of India*, gave varying degrees of support to General Dyer, 'the saviour of the Panjab'. All those which were Indian-owned, except for *New India*, the *Indian Daily Telegraph* and the *Indian Mirror*, considered the majority Hunter report to be whitewashing and called for more severe penalties for Dyer.[89] This racial division did not bode well for the usefulness of the government's 'despatches' in restoring confidence among English-educated and politically-minded Indians. Any chance of a good effect was lost, however, when the British Parliament debated the Hunter Report and the action taken against Dyer. There were[Members in both Houses who were prepared, as Meyer explained to Chelmsford, to praise Dyer for actions they would have condemned as 'Hunnishness' if they had been committed by a German general in Belgium. But Montagu, as he himself admitted, made the situation much worse by delivering a provocative speech in the Commons.] Maffey, who was in Britain on leave, called this speech 'utterly deplorable': it gave the impression only of 'nervousness, pallor and lack of judgment' so that Maffey could feel antipathy 'sweeping all over the House'. Montagu spoke heatedly, abandoning his prepared speech, and was rattled by hostile interjections; he tried to label Dyer's defenders as advocates of a doctrine of 'frightfulness' and he thoroughly 'ruffled' the Conservative Party. The Government carried the vote in the Commons, after rallying support, by 247 votes to 37; but in the Lords they were defeated 129 to 86, a result described by one contemporary as 'the most lamentable & discreditable vote of even that lamentable and discreditable House'. The sole issues, in Maffey's view, had become: 'Is it English to break a man who tried to do his duty?' and 'Is a British General to be downed at the bidding of a crooked Jew?'.[90] The *Morning Post* started a subscription for Dyer, who had been forcibly retired; the fund was eventually to reach £26,000. In India officials and military were formally barred from contributing to the fund: this was small reply to the damage already done to Indian opinion.[91]

A further factor compounding resentment was the action taken against the officers who had been criticized. The local government censured three of their European officers—one of these (Bosworth-Smith) was forced to retire early. (On the other hand one Indian police officer was reduced in rank and another reduced and retired as a result of their failure to try to deploy police under their command to prevent the murders of three Europeans in Amritsar.) The Panjab authorities had defended the actions of the Commissioner and Deputy Commissioner of Amritsar; the Government of India insisted that these officers (Kitchin and Irving) had improperly abdicated control to the military, and censured them for this. S. M. Jacob, A. J. O'Brien (of the 'salaaming' order at Gujran-wala), Penhearow (who had had a marriage party flogged), and Marsden (a junior officer responsible for flogging schoolboys at Kasur) were all either censured or criticized, and the Panjab Government were ordered to refrain from promoting them without reference to the India Government. O'Brien later left British service and in May 1920 was thought to be employed in a native state. The military authorities declined to censure Beynon, or the airforce officers responsible for bombings. But Campbell (of the 'salaaming' order) was informed of the Commander-in-Chief's regret and displeasure at his measures; the Commander-in-Chief declined to accept any excuse from Colonel Doveton, another inventor (at Kasur) of injudicious and irregular punishments. No action was taken against Colonel Johnson who had been similarly inventive at Lahore—he was a territorial officer and since demobilized.[92] Many of the censured officers resented their treatment, but the government would not compromise with them. Thus Bosworth Smith had wanted to avoid loss of pension by later retirement; supported by the Panjab (Vincent suspected Thomson, the Chief Secretary, of being responsible), he asked that the India Government should at least state that his retirement was not due to his conduct. They declined; and Chelmsford noted that they had been 'very materially impressed' in their decision by Smith's 'conduct during the Punjab rising'. Similarly, Marsden later requested an interview to explain himself, and was refused. C. W. Gwynne confessed to 'a very considerable sympathy' with him, but he was given no greater comfort than a guarantee that his record as a whole would be taken into account in considering his promotion, and the observation that the Government of India were 'particularly pleased to learn . . . that he was thanked by many persons, including Mr. Gandhi, for his considerate and courteous attitude'.[93]

Equally, while adhering to what they had done, the government declined to do more. In the face of continuing Indian demands, Montagu, although he had agreed in April 1919 that 'The use of force on a substantial scale . . . was no doubt the right course', and had suggested in his 'despatch' that censure would be an appropriate reaction to the excesses, now argued that 'more substantial punishments' would have been a better salve to Indian hurts. He was particularly alarmed at the prospect of future promotion for the censured officers. Lord Willingdon had suggested to him that the dismissal of some of the officers would have an enormous effect.[94]

Chelmsford pointed out that censure would permanently be taken into account in any promotion—one of the officers had already been passed over twice for positions for which he would otherwise have been a strong contender. The officers themselves felt the censure very strongly, and the Amritsar Commissioner had decided to retire as a result of government disapproval. Moreover, Bosworth Smith's forced retirement was equivalent to a fine (due to loss of pension) of Rs.12,000. The full Council, Chelmsford reported, had considered several factors in assessing the proper action. They felt that they had to make allowance for the difficult conditions and the previous good records of the officers. They had to act in accordance with their own resolution promising support and with the expressed opinion of His Majesty's Government that prevention not vindictive punishment should be their main object. They had to consider also the effect of harsh punishments on the rest of the service, and the pain and humiliation already caused by the public criticism by the Hunter Committee and the government. Finally they had to take into account the action against Dyer, the most serious offender by far—the Government of India had done the most they could by refusing to employ him, the Army Council in Britain had made this ban general and forced Dyer's retirement. The Government of India argued, therefore, that forcible retirement was the most severe punishment they could inflict on officers guilty of lesser offences. Chelmsford did not agree that dismissals were necessary or would be justified by the majority report. He strongly deprecated Montagu's suggestion that the expediency of influencing the non-co-operators should take precedence over the justness in the government's treatment of its officers.[95] Chelmsford had been, as he claimed, 'strictly judicial': but Indian opinion needed some

punitive show sufficiently harsh to ease the grievance—words
censuring officers may perhaps have been good justice, but they
were bad propaganda.

As Gwynne put it in 1921: 'Indian opinion has not fully realized
the very serious nature of the censure of the Govt. of India or
rather its effect upon individual officers not only on their minds
but also upon their future careers'. What had been done had not
been done with sufficient sense of drama. Much of it remained
locked up in the files. Thus, when there were rumours of the return
to office of J. P. Thomson, who was deeply implicated in the
public mind with the past excesses, Vincent promptly wrote to
Maclagan that he and his colleagues were 'rather exercised' at the
rumours and not sure that Thomson, though 'undoubtedly of
very great ability', was 'the right person for this office [Panjab
Chief Secretary] at the present juncture'. But the effect of this
exchange, like any influence on the promotion of censured officers,
was negative and could not be made public.[96]

Yet perhaps it is unlikely that any government action would
have sufficiently captured public imagination: with such distrust,
Dyer would have had to be hanged and half the Panjab service
dismissed—and European opinion would not have stood for that.
In January 1920 the Amritsar Congress had called for the im-
peachment of O'Dwyer and the recall of Chelmsford. In February
some newspapers had begun to assert that 'Montagu must go'.
The Indian demands were too high to be satisfied—and this was
true over a wide range of opinion: Chelmsford refused to attend
a conference with Bombay moderates late in 1920, arguing that it
was impossible to discuss the Panjab on the basis of the moderate
demands for the dismissal of or non-payment of pensions to the
censured Panjab officials, for modification of the Turkish treaty,
and for a promise of total self-government (except for foreign
relations and military affairs) after five years.[97]

Chelmsford could not see how to heal the hurt. His government
declined a wider amnesty, in spite of legislative resolutions in
February and March 1921, on the ground that there remained only
prisoners convicted of serious crimes and not under special regulations. Chelmsford refused to act further against Panjab officials
but proposed to compensate Indian sufferers more liberally. Sir
Valentine Chirol urged that the government should 'repudiate more
emphatically . . . the deplorable conclusions which Indian public

pinion has drawn, not altogether unreasonably, from many of the
things that happened in the Punjab and have happened since in
egard to them'. Chelmsford replied that they had already clearly
epudiated the doctrine of 'preventive massacre' and the practice
f 'punishment by humiliation'.[98]

In the central issues, then, the Government of India returned to
heir policy of keeping quiet and hoping the ill-feeling would pass.
But in some matters they did try to shift their position in reaction
o pressure of opinion. In May 1919, J. P. Thomson had suggested
hat the cost of military operations might be recovered by a levy
on districts under martial law. Marris had doubted that this ex-
reme measure would be expedient; Vincent had been '*prima facie*
against' it; Hailey had argued that it would be 'altogether beyond
he power' of the districts to pay. The Legal Department had been
dubious about legality, and the Commander-in-Chief had not
hought it desirable. With such a chorus, the Home Department
naturally turned down Thomson's idea—though (character-
stically) they agreed to try to justify a case in which such a levy
had already been imposed. Chelmsford had noted on the draft
etters: 'It is no use putting such a pecuniary fine on the guilty
districts as will cripple them for many years to come. This would
only breed discontent.' As time went on this suggestion was inter-
oreted more generously. Eventually the government abandoned
even the idea of recouping the cost of police actions, which had
oeen an established principle hitherto. At first they decided that
he levy of about Rs.18½ lakhs placed on Amritsar under the
Police Act should be met from provincial balances, provided the
municipality agreed to its repayment from direct taxation over
ive years. When the municipality refused, the Panjab Council
oroposed to pay nevertheless, and the India Government sought
he Secretary of State's sanction for this course. The local government also decided not to collect the cost of extra police from
Gujranwala, Amritsar and Lahore.[99]

Similarly a proclamation under the Police Act had announced
as early as April 1919 that compensation would be payable in the
Panjab—though there were complicated legal questions involved,
and it was decided that only moral and not legal responsibility
pertained to government in the case of Europeans murdered at
Amritsar. At first the local government had suggested a pension
of up to Rs.5·0 to be paid for Indians disabled or killed, where

families were more or less destitute. The centre had not agreed, arguing that the payments might then be construed as attempts to buy silence at a time when the disturbances were being investigated. But a total of Rs.12,000 was quietly distributed by the Government of India to the dependants of villagers killed at the Jallianwala Bagh, and, once the Hunter Committee had reported, a further Rs.15,000 was provided for dependants living in Amritsar.[100]

In March 1921, however, a resolution was moved by Jamnadas Dwarkadas declaring the 'firm resolve' of the Government of India to maintain that the British connection was 'based on the principle of equal partnership and perfect racial equality', regretting that the Panjab martial law administration had departed from this principle and deeply wounded 'the self-respect of the Indian population' and calling for 'adequate compensation', comparable with that awarded to European sufferers, for the families of those killed or wounded at the Bagh. A third clause demanding 'deterrent punishments' of the officers responsible was deleted without a division. The Home Member stated that the government regretted that martial law was 'marred by acts which were injudicious and improper', and gave assurances that the Panjab Government would be asked to deal generously in awarding compensation. The remainder of the resolution was carried unanimously. Further attention to the question of compensation was only just, as hitherto priority had been given to property over people, and to Europeans over Indians (even though some European claims had been refused). The figures show that Indians killed or wounded were regarded as partly culpable, whereas those who lost property were not. The Hunter findings had changed this; and, as a result of the Assembly resolution, the India Government ordered the Panjab to form a committee to carry out the legislature's policy. (Thus far Amritsar victims had received less than Rs.20,000 while the relatively few European sufferers had been given just under Rs.5 lakhs.)[101]

Finally, even in the matter of repressive legislation, a change was taking place. At first, Chelmsford, against his personal wishes (for he knew the decision would be misinterpreted), had accepted the advice of Maclagan and the moderates, Surendranath Banerjea and Sirdar Sundar Singh, and disallowed a debate on Panjab affairs in the Imperial Legislative Council. When Montagu suggested it might be best to repeal the Rowlatt Act, the India Government refused. But, since April 1920, the Home Department had been taking special note of any such 'resolution or request from any important body, or person'; as early as July 1919, Bengal had advised it was not worth the risk of using the Act, and in August the Government of India had agreed, with the proviso that the Act should be used in preference to more severe measures if this could be done safely. Montagu's view had been that the only satisfactory procedure was 'open prosecution and conviction in the Courts', and that repressive executive powers, however justified by committees, were only second best.[102] In January 1921 Chelmsford decided to move towards an acceptance of this view. He suggested a legislative committee to consider the repressive powers, including the Rowlatt and Press Acts.

It was in this atmosphere that the Panjab was finally debated in the legislature, on the Dwarkadas resolution. The government considered the general tone of the debate good. In March too the question of the continued detention of 86 martial law prisoners, raised in the Council of State (the new upper house), was dropped when Vincent undertook to do what he could in individual cases if clemency could be shown to be desirable. Stanley Reed, though sceptical himself, reported to Chelmsford that his Bombay friends thought the Panjab issue was now dead.[103]

It was not. The problem was that the shock had not only strengthened the resolve and added to the racial and religious estrangement of the politically minded; it had also affected classes which, although to some extent already influenced by popular agitation, had seldom felt very strongly about politics. To some extent the popular shock was such that the reaction was accepted into popular imagination and remained impervious to government appeasements. The re-writing of events is evidence enough of this mythologizing. Thus, there can be no doubt that Miss Sherwood was attacked and severely wounded at Amritsar; the judgment in the case against eight youths convicted of the assault recorded: 'The witnesses who are particularly good and . . . entirely unshaken in cross-examination prove'—and there follows a graphic account of how the lady was chased, seized, thrown down, struck with fists, caught by her hair, given five or six blows on the head with a shoe, and finally knocked to the ground and struck on the head with a lathi. Yet, in Bombay, the *Lokasangraha* of 13 September 1919 reported (according to the official translation): 'If Barrister Chowdhari did not tell a lie . . ., (and if he had . . . Government would have taken him to task), then we can say that the missionary lady . . . did not even receive a scratch. For these imaginary six wounds . . . six Indians were hanged . . .'.[104] One need not debate the guilt of these particular defendants to see that, in the race hatred stirred up by the British in the Panjab, truth was one of the victims.

At the time of the disturbances, a letter from Rai Sahib Bishamber Nath to the Viceroy demonstrated a new development, a strange combination of loyal phrases, conservative acceptance of British paternalism, and rigorous indignation at the Panjab atrocities: it was this side of Indian opinion also which had been alienated. Bishamber Nath wrote:

Your Excellency, you are great and God has made you great. The destiny of India . . . is entrusted to Your Excellency's charge. India, or at any rate a great majority of it, expects great benefits at your hands. Do not pray, great as you are, be led away from the right course by the attacks of those who do not appreciate the inner greatness of your heart and the good which is in it. It is the tree laden with fruit at which everybody throws a stone and it is a tree laden with fruit which bends itself to the ground notwithstanding efforts to the contrary. Do pray in your greatness show mercy to the poor and innocent teeming millions of India and so mend matters that it may soon tread on a prosperous and progressive path. My heart throbs at the critical state in which India is and the present situation has, in fact, affected my liver. . . . For the sake of all that is great and good, pray adopt a conciliatory policy.

Bishamber Nath correctly predicted in another letter: the Panjab repression 'will be an evil day to the peace-loving subjects of Government, and the Government also, with this thorn in their side, will not have a smooth and peaceful time of it'.[105] Neither in their supervision at the time, nor in their subsequent actions, had the Government of India been able to satisfy the Bishamber Naths of India.

The loss of confidence at this time was crucial because it was more general than ever before. It was fundamental because it demonstrated once again the necessary divergence between India and her foreign rulers—not so much in the horrors of Amritsar, as in the inability of the Government of India to repudiate them adequately (in Indian eyes) without abandoning the British administrators on whom the raj depended. The British were not the 'tree laden with fruit' and they could not bend themselves to the ground against their own efforts. The centre's attempts at appeasement, nevertheless, brought them closer to the Indian viewpoint—on the details of punishment and compensation, and in the major issues of rejecting first the excesses, then the attitude which made them possible, and finally the special powers on which they depended. Even in this unexpected area of government activity we can see signs of the impact of the reform policy; but as well we see points at which the ultimate incompatibility of bureaucracy and self-determination also is revealed.

Chapter 8. Against *Satyagraha*

THE war raised expectations and changed attitudes, and none more than those of many Muslims. After the war, Muslims became increasingly involved in politics, and politics with them. By 1920, no grievance was more potent or of more general importance than the supposed wrongs done to the Khilafat, as the Caliphate was known in India. The Government of India had anticipated the danger, but had been powerless to avoid it.

Throughout the war they had treated Muslims with particular concern. At sensitive moments, such as the revolt of the Sherif of Mecca or the announcement of a secret treaty proposing to cede Constantinople to Russia, the policy was to suppress alarming and inflammatory news, allowing it to 'trickle in' unannounced, but to give private explanations and reassurances; to put right or avoid grievances (as with the assistance given to *Haj* pilgrims), but to oppose agitation when it was thought dangerous, as with the so-called 'silk letters' conspiracy and other expressions of extreme pan-Islamism.[1] A similar mixture of caution, conciliation and toughness marked the handling of Muslim riots in Calcutta in 1918.[2] The Afghan War in 1919 was also handled with an eye for Muslim feelings—full publicity was given during the campaign, and afterwards Chelmsford insisted on a conciliatory attitude to the Amir in spite of the strongest objections from London and Lord Curzon in particular.[3] The critical issue, however, was the question of the Turkish peace terms. The Government of India made strenuous efforts to place the Muslim viewpoint before the British Government and the Peace Conference; they insisted that, for their purposes, the minimum concession was the retention by the Caliph, of Constantinople and of nominal suzerainty over Mecca. The government were not convinced on the merits of the case— the authenticity of the Turkish Sultan's claim to the Caliphate was at the least a matter of debate; and Chelmsford's private view, not remarkable in a man whose son had been killed in Mesopotamia, was that Turks deserved much the same treatment as Germans and Austrians. The fervour of the government's advocacy was a mark of the emotional impact which the Khilafat issue had had on

Indian Muslims after the war. In 1914 Hardinge had sought statements from the Nawab of Rampur and the Muslim League declaring their loyalty and appealing for Muslims to dissociate themselves from Turkey. As late as July 1919 a pamphlet by Maulana Faizul Karim, attested to by all the principal pirs and ulama of Sind, denied the Sultan's claim and supported the Sherif's revolt.[4] By 1920 Hardinge's policy would have been hopeless optimism, and the Maulana's pamphlet a betrayal of his community: the time for rationality was past and government policy reflected this. Even Shias now seemed tacitly to endorse the importance of the Caliph. Indian influence, however, on a matter of international politics, was inevitably small; and, even apart from this, there was no hope of the Government of India's views prevailing. The British Government had decided against any such concessions as early as 1916.[5] Lloyd George, Lord Curzon, Lord Hardinge, Austen Chamberlain, members of the India Office, even Edwin Montagu, all displayed degrees of hostility to Turkey and readiness to see it dismembered.[6] The Government of India, soon seeing the hopelessness, sought to prepare by warning that the peace terms were likely to be severe—this was stressed in private meetings and in the Viceroy's reply to a Muslim deputation in January 1920.[7] They also sought to publicize their own efforts. When harsh peace terms were offered in May 1920, Chelmsford issued a statement extending his 'encouragement and sympathy'. The Central Khilafat Committee, formed to direct the Muslim campaign, responded, in a letter signed by eighty-two Muslims and endorsed by Gandhi, by asking the Viceroy to make common cause with them, even to resign if necessary.[8] In the face of such aspirations, Chelmsford's stand was inadequate. Yet, by expressing sympathy he had come near to a public admission of a divergence between his policy and that of the Peace Conference.

Curiously, the strictly conservative and illiberal demand for the continuance of the Turkish Empire—the Khilafatist leader, Shaukat Ali, wanted it to stretch from Morocco to the Khanates of Central Asia[9]—was to become the centrepiece of a campaign for Indian self-government. The Khilafat issue combined with others to feed Gandhi's non-co-operation campaign of 1920–22, a major challenge in both extent and novelty. The special problem of Muslim unrest had resulted not so much in a distinct Muslim policy as in the general policy in extreme forms, either more conciliatory or more repressive: though the latter was dangerous for the government in the support it generated for such leaders as the Ali brothers, yet the strategies in theory accorded fully with tactical non-interference. But with Gandhi's campaign it was again possible to argue that this policy had failed—that Indians were not appeased, agitation not contained. The story of the government's measures against *satyagraha* is therefore one of a series of questionings of the established policy.

The first crisis came in March 1920 when Gandhi, who had joined the Khilafatists, called a *hartal*. From Bengal Ronaldshay had expressed alarm at meetings organized by Shaukat Ali and Maulana Abul Kalam Azad in co-operation with a group of Calcutta pan-Islamists. The meetings had passed resolutions which declared that Muslim loyalty was conditional upon favourable peace terms; and similar declarations were to be featured in the proposed *hartal*. Ronaldshay recommended that the government should make a public disavowal of this idea. The Home Department considered that the situation was worsening, and saw the question characteristically as a balance between the danger of unchecked agitation and that of action against individuals. In Council Vincent favoured the issuing of a government resolution warning that action would be taken against agitators. His colleagues were uneasy, but did not like to oppose the Home Member in his own field. The other local governments were consulted and did not favour the suggestion—Bombay, the Panjab, Bihar and the United Provinces strongly disapproved. Chelmsford decided not to accept Vincent's advice, and made no announcement. He explained to Montagu that he had thought a government statement would be 'unwise': government sympathy had put the Khilafatists 'somewhat in a quandary'; threats of repression would only give them cause for complaint. He agreed to allow Bengal to make a local announcement if necessary; but no such announcement was made, nor perhaps was possible in view of the silence at the centre. Government servants were warned that no exception would be made to the general prohibition of their participation in political demonstrations.[10]

The initial response to the Khilafat campaign, therefore, was to continue the cautious, tactical approach. Several factors helped this decision. The central feature of Chelmsford's approach had been to appease Muslim feelings, not to oppose them. The sensi-

tivity to Muslim insecurity during the war antedated the more
general shift in policy in 1917, so that the likelihood was that the
Muslim presence in the nationalist campaign would, if anything,
restrain the government further. Hindu–Muslim entente, three
years after Lucknow, was not itself an emergency, especially as it
was expected to be shortlived. In June 1920 there was a joint
meeting in Allahabad between the Central Khilafat Committee
and a Congress committee; but police reports suggested that both
this entente and support for non-co-operation were more apparent
than real, largely because of Hindu fears about Afghan aggression.[11] The government were aware that local religious upsets
continued, and that conservatives, with whom their communications were good, were often outraged at extravagances committed
in the name of unity. Ominously, at the Amritsar meeting of 1919
the Muslim League had decided that its aims should be 'to protect
and advance political, religious and other rights and interests of
Indian Musalmans'. The word 'religious' had been added at the
suggestion of Jinnah.[12]

There was also some truth in the argument put forward by
Gandhi himself, that his influence had helped to wean 'the party
of violence from its ways'.[13] In June the movement was believed
to have passed into the hands of fanatical Maulvis. But then at the
Allahabad joint meeting the Khilafat Conference appointed a
sub-committee to direct its campaign; and the effect of this Hindu
participation was to avert or delay some of the more flamboyant
Muslim proposals—Hindus had made it clear, for example, that
any advocacy of joining an Afghan invasion would result in active
Hindu opposition.[14]

Gandhi's non-violent approach also presented difficulties in law.
In May 1919, Vincent and Marris, after consulting the Legislative
Department, had suggested to the local governments that it should
be possible to prosecute *satyagrahis* as an unlawful association
under section 15 (1) of the Criminal Law Amendment Act (XIV)
of 1908—they had added the usual rider to the effect that this was a
'two-edged weapon' giving 'an easy opportunity to martyrdom'.[15]
But in June 1920 the government requested further legal opinion
on the feasibility of prosecuting Gandhi and Shaukat Ali under the
Indian Penal Code for their advocacy of non-co-operation. The
Home Department stressed that this was only in case it was
'considered necessary to take legal action later'. The legal opinion,

however, stated that prosecution would be doubtful and therefore unwise, probably at least until the third stage of Gandhi's campaign,[16] which would seek to encourage the resignation of Indian police and military. (It was thought possible that Shaukat Ali might be tackled earlier, as his speeches tended to use stronger language.)[17]

Gandhi postulated a symbolic divorce from the alien rulers. He envisaged the surrender of titles, suspension of legal practice, non-participation in government loans, withdrawal from government schools, abstention from the reformed councils, avoidance of official functions, refusal to join the army, and boycott of British goods. The positive side was stressed in attempts to form national schools and to provide arbitration in place of the courts.[18] The campaign required that Gandhi should gain control of the Congress, and fire the public imagination. To the government the prospects of this campaign seemed slight—and this too encouraged their non-interference. The surrender of titles was the easiest form of non-co-operation: by the end of May few titles had been relinquished.[19] Other stages would require more courage and greater sacrifice. Chelmsford believed the lure of office would prove too strong for a successful boycott of the councils, and he expected that Gandhi would not carry the Congress on this—they could not afford to abdicate and leave all political initiative to their rivals. Chelmsford calculated also that total withdrawal from government schools would present the Congress with the problem of educating eight million pupils, or the choice of leaving them without education.[20]

Thus he explained to Montagu that he was not gloomy about the prospects; he could not convince himself that non-co-operation was practical. All they had to do, he thought, was 'keep cool'. Chelmsford was not even convinced that Gandhi was seriously seeking political advantage: he quoted an explanation from Bombay, that Gandhi was merely out to cause trouble through 'pique and vanity'. Chelmsford conceived his main task as one of convincing people 'of the folly of the whole thing'; he knew he would 'never convince them by repressive measures'.[21] He avoided interference not because he hoped to convert the agitators, but because he knew persecution might create sympathy for their ideas. His view of Gandhi's campaign was such that in August 1920 he hoped that the point for action would not come.[22] He referred an uneasy Montagu to past experience. His government had earlier resisted a clamour, some of it from Montagu, for action against Subramania Aiyar. The inaction had succeeded: Sir Subramania had been forgotten within two months. Chelmsford admitted he was comparing small things with great, but insisted the principle was the same: Sir Subramania's case had taught him that they must exercise patience also with Gandhi.[23]

As before, the policy was also confirmed by apparent success. The Khilafat Day in March was observed generally by Hindu as well as Muslim shopkeepers, but there were no disturbances and government servants did not take part. In Bombay the Muslim community split when loyalists voted against the conditional loyalty resolution. A secret meeting was believed to have approved Gandhi's plan for progressive steps in *swadeshi* and non-co-operation; but signs were also reported of a reaction against violence and objections to the boycott of British goods.[24] A further week's *hartal* was called in April, but local governments reported either little interest or complete failure—though they stressed that there was much plotting and that speeches were still violent in tone.[25] Gandhi called another *hartal* for Sunday, 1 August; it was given impetus by the news of Tilak's death. Almost all shops closed in Maratha districts, in Madras, and in headquarter towns elsewhere; but most local governments stressed the lack of general observance or enthusiasm.[26] Thus every stage in Gandhi's mounting campaign was qualified, in government reports, by reservations and hints of failure. Non-interference seemed to be containing the threat.

Remarkably, the prevailing mood of the central government in mid-1920 was one of confidence and optimism. There was a tendency, from the lowest district officer to the Viceroy, to write reports which minimized the dangers: perhaps they had come to believe their own propaganda. They concluded that violent language might be defeating itself and that there was little evidence that non-co-operation would catch on. Several provinces had reported that agitation was spreading less quickly or was abating. In some places moderate councils were thought to be prevailing; in others speeches seemed less violent. In Nagpur Muslim leaders had declined to endorse *satyagraha*.[27] The government recognized that it was hard for moderates to abstain, particularly with elections near, but they hoped for the isolation of the protagonists of violence.[28] Chelmsford was impressed by the *Leader* of 14 May

1920, which admitted that the government had 'displayed an exceptional equanimity of temper at a time when no efforts have been spared to fan religious passion'.[29] In June the Home Department noted that the non-co-operators were becoming less extreme —the campaign was to be limited and voluntary; private servants and government employees were not to be coerced. The Home Department concluded that the Khilafat agitation did not seem to contain 'much real feeling' any more.[30] The Gandhian challenge was not being mounted sufficiently quickly to shock the government into a change of policy.

There remained, as also in the past, enough danger to ensure repression was kept in reserve. Police reports remained 'alarming', and the government knew that incendiary issues were before the public. Apart from the peace terms, the Hunter Committee Report on the 1919 disturbances prevented much improvement in the Indian temper—especially in view of the European reactions. Chelmsford pointed to parliamentary debates and a provocative stand by the European Association; he recorded without satisfaction a 'similar and particularly fatuous resolution' by the Bihar Planters.[31] The Home Department were aware that the mid-year calm could be a lull before the storm, that the agitators, rather than trying to sustain indefinitely a high pitch of excitement, could be biding their time—Shaukat Ali was alleged to have 'roundly abused' local leaders in Delhi for 'premature activities'.[32] It was also possible to interpret any retreat from extremism, indeed the whole of Gandhi's contribution, as a temporary ploy by fanatics, calculated to arrest the defection of the moderates and widen the base of the movement. There were signs that the extremists were trying to consolidate their position. Gandhi had been elected President of the Home Rule League, and it was recognized that it might be dangerous if he succeeded in converting the League to his programme. The Home Department watched such organizational developments with particular attention.[33] In one circumstance, when certain members of the Khilafat Committee appeared in Mussoorie where peace negotiations were in progress with the Afghans, a few people including the young Jawaharlal Nehru were arrested on the advice of the British negotiators supported by C.I.D. reports. Optimism was tempered by nervous surveillance.[34]

The government made ready to act should a new crisis develop.

Local governments were instructed to compile lists of principal agitators against whom action might be taken. Some minor figures were prosecuted. At a departmental conference on 24 June, Vincent, stating where the line was to be drawn between non-interference and prosecution, explained that the Home Department did not want to depart from the former policy 'except against individuals whose evident intention was to incite to violence or to tamper with the Army'. The conference recommended prosecutions in such cases, as well as counter-propaganda, and the deployment of C.I.D. officers to help local governments. This, a fair representation of the government view, was reported to local governments in a demi-official of 3 July.[35] It was not a shift from the position in April. The conference had been prompted by pressure from the Army Department whose officials had become 'greatly exercised' at attempts to disaffect soldiers or recruits. Both the Home Department and the C.I.D. were sceptical—understandably as the army could cite only one case of interference—and the exhortation to prosecute in such cases came from a wish to appease the army and not from alarm at the situation.[36] At the same time, moreover, the wider intention of the army, to reopen the question of policy towards agitation, provoked a fierce response from the Home Department and then from Chelmsford. The Chief of the General Staff, C. W. Jacobs, had written: 'What we require is that Government should act firmly and strongly against the movement'. Monro supported this, though in milder language. The Home Department retorted that their policy was still that decided and opposed by the army in April, 'a policy of abstaining as far as possible from interference, in order to avoid making martyrs of fanatical leaders or precipitating disorder'; nothing had happened to change their view, and 'it would be a mistake of the first magnitude in the present combinations of circumstances to launch a prosecution against Mr. Gandhi'. However, 'where an obvious and clear breach of the law is committed by individuals, overstepping the limits chalked out by the leaders, we are all for action'. In a later note the Home Department Secretary put this even more strongly: 'the General Staff Branch . . . were in our opinion pressing for a line of action which will encourage the Khilafat agitation and precipitate disorder'. The Army Department were far from happy, but Chelmsford noted sharply: 'While I am always prepared to listen to what the General

Staff may have to say on questions affecting the Army, it must be understood that notes impugning the settled policy of the Government are quite irregular'.[37] Thus although he was ready to agree to action against persons tampering with troops, the Viceroy abruptly ruled out of court any pressure for wider changes in policy. Similarly, when Montagu suggested that steps be taken against persons using seditious language, the Home Department were unwilling to comply.[38] To do so might have meant attacking people of importance, and they preferred to use even the ordinary law only against those minor figures for whom the notoriety of martyrdom was not sufficient to compensate for its discomfort.

Indeed this distinction is near the heart of the policy of non-interference. Later in 1920, for example, Harcourt Butler was to query the possible contradiction in a Home Department circular of 4 September, which called for 'non-interference' in paragraph 3 and for 'vigorous action' in paragraphs 5 and 6. McPherson, the Secretary, noted that the first related to 'leaders of the movement, responsible for the preaching of non-co-operation in its non-violent form', while the second referred to 'agitators preaching violence'.[39] This was the thinking behind the earlier demi-official of 3 July, arising out of Vincent's remarks to the departmental conference, and behind Chelmsford's refusal to listen to the army on one hand while conceding their point on the other. Non-interference was to be the policy against national leaders and those who advocated non-violence; repression was to be employed against minor figures and those who advocated violence. It is important to note that the degree of power and prominence of the leader and the nature of his speeches were two separate factors, and that, in practice, the former was the more important of the two.

As well as with the Army Department, there were several disputes with local governments in mid-1920. Madras wanted to extern the Khilafat leaders, notably Gandhi and Shaukat Ali. The central government repeatedly refused to allow this, noting that persecution was just what Gandhi was inviting, and insisting that there were all-India implications on which they must decide. It was obvious, they felt, that Gandhi would defy such a ban, and thereby force them to arrest him. In the case of Shaukat Ali, it was remarked in the Home Department (by C. W. Gwynne) that externment, apart from helping his cause, would seem like callousness so soon after the Viceroy's proclamation on the peace terms, and that, in general, it was necessary to continue with 'non-interference, if possible, and action under the ordinary law when necessary, and resort to special legislation only in the case of great emergency'.[40] At this time, also, the Panjab Government wanted to apply the Seditious Meetings Act to the Lahore area; the central government refused. The Panjab insisted that violent speeches were becoming worse and worse, and that the situation was dangerous—15,000 railway workers had gone on strike, and there was unrest among Muslims and Sikhs. In fact, violent agitation was confined to a small section, the communities were divided internally and there was only conjecture about political involvement in the railway strike. The central government could not understand why offenders had not been prosecuted under the ordinary law, but gave as their categorical opinion, 'that it is desirable to avoid the application of repressive measures to the present political situation, if this can possibly be helped, till it has been seen whether the non-co-operation movement . . . is going to obtain substantial support or prove a failure'. They had no wish to show their hand by a fresh notification under the Seditious Meetings Act. They forbad the taking of any action while Gandhi and Shaukat Ali were visiting Lahore. They wanted to be informed well in advance if the local government proposed to act under existing sanction after the leaders had left. Chelmsford still maintained that policy should not necessarily be concerted, that local governments should be allowed latitude; but he insisted also that all-India considerations must be allowed to influence local action. In this case, the government were 'most anxious to avoid precipitating disorder'; they wanted some weapons in reserve.[41]

The Government of Bombay also met with a refusal when they requested permission to use the Defence of India Act to take sharp action against Mullahs and others who were spreading false rumours in Sind; the Government of India ordered proceedings to be taken under the ordinary law if possible. On this occasion, however, the local Governor, Lloyd, agreed; he wrote to Austen Chamberlain: 'All my officials wanted me to prosecute right and left from the beginning, but I would not do so. . . . I determined to . . . be patient till I got a good opportunity'. Later a prominent religious leader, Pir Mahbub Shah, was prosecuted, despite his going on hunger strike, and then released in a gesture of 'benign contempt'.[42]

Also in mid-1920, some Muslims took their protest further and tried to emigrate from India. This, the *hijrat* movement, was perfectly legal, but there were clearly dangers in any large movement of people towards the Afghan frontier, with prospects of excitement at the starting-points in Sind, the Central Provinces and elsewhere, *en route* in the Panjab or Baluchistan, and at the final departure point, Peshawar. The government, therefore, tried to discourage the pilgrim-emigrants. In July a special train had been allowed to carry 750 from Sind to Peshawar. This provision was at first temporarily and then permanently removed following protests from the Panjab, Baluchistan and the Northwest Frontier Province—the desire to conciliate had to give way before the need of maintaining order. There were other limits too. Vincent and M. M. Shafi endorsed a private suggestion in May 1920 that a deputation from the frontier should visit the Hedjaz at government expense to report on conditions and thus reassure Indian Muslims. But this was vetoed in London. (On the other hand, Rs. 10 lakhs were budgeted for the assistance of Haj pilgrims.) In addition, the Foreign and Political Department advised the Chief Commissioner on details of handling—that only restricted numbers should be allowed to leave for Afghanistan, to give time for propaganda among the remainder; that postal censorship should be imposed to isolate the Northwest Frontier from the Panjab and thus contain the movement. Earlier the Department had urged prompt legal proceedings against the most violent agitators. One leader had already been interned and another excluded from the province; and the Chief Commissioner of the Frontier Province, Sir Hamilton Grant, was ready to deal 'relentlessly' with any outbreak of disorder. He combined this policy with one of explanation, making a speech himself in Peshawar, and sending a party of 'influential Khans and Maulvis' to one troubled district to 'persuade people of their folly'.[43]

Discouragement and local control kept the exodus within bounds. The Afghan welcome cooled; Gandhi's non-co-operation movement provided an alternative protest within India; and abruptly the *hijrat* collapsed. Chelmsford stressed that it had been best to trust to local officers to persuade people out of their folly, and that it had been important not to interfere with a largely religious movement, even when it was believed to be politically inspired. He authorized Grant to make a public appeal for funds

AGAINST *SATYAGRAHA* 231

to help emigrants who were returning to India—many of them had sold their lands and possessions and had nothing to return to.[44] The Viceroy had rebuked Grant for sending in inadequate reports,[45] but there had been no practical divergence in policy. The *hijrat* movement was treated with the familiar mixture of conciliation, propaganda and control.

The same principles had been confirmed for the non-co-operation campaign. The tactical approach seemed to have been accepted as a dictat and unhesitatingly applied. In July Chelmsford had set out the conditions under which he would abandon non-interference. His government would allow Gandhi 'full rope', he informed the Secretary of State, 'unless and until collision is precipitated by action of non-co-operators, or if it becomes clear that [the] movement is likely to prove an unexpected success'.[46] These conditions had not been met.

In the Home Department, C. W. Gwynne concluded that the non-co-operation movement was a failure, that Gandhi as a result was seeking martyrdom by becoming quite unreasonable in his speeches, but that it 'would be a great mistake to take any serious notice' while actual results remained as harmless as at present. His superiors, H. McPherson and William Vincent, agreed generally with these orthodoxies. Gwynne had remarked that 'The non-co-operation movement is almost dead, if not quite. The hartal of the 1st August was in reality a fiasco.' And Lowndes added, of Gandhi, that 'the man is desperate at the non-success of his policy' and that, left alone, 'the non-co-operation movement and with it his personal influence will die of inanition'. He suggested that they might state publicly their view that to take legal steps against Gandhi would be 'merely playing into his hands'. Chelmsford, when consulted, 'did not wish any action to be taken . . . at present'.[47]

But in October Chelmsford admitted that non-co-operation had caught on more than expected. While the government looked on, Gandhi had achieved a tremendous coup. He had originally adopted the Khilafat campaign and converted it to *satyagraha*. Then he fused the religious issue with a national and racial one by stressing the enormities of the British response to the Hunter Report. To many, especially young Hindus, some of whom had not been very active in politics but were now aroused, Gandhi seemed to present the only sane and positive response to these indignities.[48] Thus Gandhi tightened his hold on the Congress until it endorsed and identified itself with both the Muslim grievance and the Gandhian method. The government had predicted that this would not happen. The Special Calcutta Session was a personal triumph for Gandhi. Congress emerged committed to a first stage which conformed almost exactly with Gandhi's programme. The details of the campaign were controversial and there were differences of opinion. It had taken a long debate in full session before Gandhi was able to have his way; and earlier the Subjects Committee had argued for several hours and proved unable to reach a decision— it was divided three ways between Gandhi's supporters (such as Shaukat Ali, Yakub Hasan, and Chakravarti), his partial supporters (Malaviya, Das and Pal), and his opponents (Mrs. Besant, Jinnah and Jamnadas Dwarkadas). Moreover, in the government's view the result in full session had been achieved by a 'juggle'—that is, delegates had been able to vote only for *satyagraha* in some form (Gandhi's motion or the Das amendment excluding the Councils from the boycott), and about half had abstained.[49] However, with the decision passed, many of the doubters fell into line. By 26 September forty-five Council members or candidates had withdrawn, mainly, the government believed, out of loyalty to the Congress. C. R. Das and the Bengalis he had led in opposition to the boycott were among those who conformed.[50] It had been agreed informally at Calcutta that those who could not abide by the majority decision should leave the Congress. This is, therefore, the measure of Gandhi's victory, but also of the new political maturity of the Congress. With this the movement became more disciplined and dangerous. Gandhi, Motilal Nehru and Patel were appointed to frame instructions for the campaign. Gandhi's position was unassailable.

In October the victory was made permanent and institution-alized. The All-India Congress Committee considered and adopted instructions for *satyagraha*; they made some alterations in the draft, mainly to strengthen its effect. A further sub-committee, comprising Gandhi, Kelkar, Patel, and Rangaswami Aiyangar, proposed that Congress delegates (one for every lakh of population) should be returned on a district basis; that the All-India Congress Committee should be reconstituted and reduced to more business-like proportions (with one hundred members); and that the expression 'constitutional means' in the aims of the Congress, Article One of the Constitution, should be amended to read 'peaceful and legitimate means'. The Subjects Committee, which had provided such a forum for disagreement at Calcutta, was to be abolished; every town was to have its own committee to encourage the movement.[51]

These changes required ratification at the next Congress session, due in January at Nagpur. In the interim Gandhi sought to mobilize local Congress committees and Home Rule Leagues to enforce the Calcutta programme. The Central Khilafat Committee was in the vanguard of this attack. Some of the proposals adopted by the Congress dated from plans laid in the early days of Gandhi's membership of the Khilafat Committee in May 1920. In September this committee had urged local branches to greater activity in organizing rural propaganda, volunteers and attacks on schools.[52] Gandhi's campaign also ensured that there would be only moderates in the new Councils, a situation which Chelmsford deplored.[53] Gandhi tried to enforce the boycott of the elections as well. Montagu considered this the one area in which the Congress had chosen its ground wisely: the poll was bound to be small and Congress could claim the credit for it.[54] The campaign also began to have some success among students. After a visit by Gandhi and the Ali brothers, the students at the new Aligarh University demanded the renunciation of government grants. The Principal banned outsiders from addressing the students; and the Syndicate called on parents to control their sons. Two hundred parents wrote to disapprove of Gandhi's interference, and another seventy called their boys home.[55] Congress also tried to involve students and young men by adopting the Servants of India idea of Volunteers—Congress apparently intended them not for social work but as substitutes for the police. The government thought this development potentially dangerous, and asked local governments to consider whether they had the powers to deal with the Volunteers if they should begin to drill with arms.[56]

The government were not convinced that non-interference would have to be abandoned, but their uneasiness was increasing. In advance of Nagpur the Home Rule League had adopted some of the Congress proposals, taking the name Swarajya Sabha. Their aim was now to attain, by continuous propaganda, swaraj according to the people's wishes, and they had dropped the qualifications

'within the British Empire' and 'by constitutional means'. Sir
Frank Sly had inquired whether the peaceful advocacy of such
'swarajya' would be an offence—he proposed to prosecute those
who incited to violence and wondered if the government should not
make a policy announcement.[57] His suggestions may be considered
to have added to the ground swell in favour of a public statement
as first proposed by Lowndes and refused by Chelmsford in
August.

Anxieties crystallized when Gandhi made a 'bad speech' which
left him open to prosecution. He told a Lucknow audience of 40
to 50 thousand that Indians were slaves, the government was
devilish, and to co-operate was sinful. He declared, it was reported,
'If after the atrocities and injustice which have been done to the
Punjab any Indian can remain loyal to this Government, I would
say that he is not an Indian, he is not a man.' The time for the
sword was not yet, and hence many who did not abhor violence
had opted for non-co-operation; when the Muslims did decide to
draw the sword they would first warn the English to withdraw 'if
they want to save their lives'. 'I also say,' he went on, repeating the
words for which a Muslim leader had allegedly been arrested,
'that if the Government will not ask God's forgiveness before
India, if it will not ask our forgiveness, it will surely be annihilated.
It is the duty of every Hindu and every Muhammadan to destroy
this Government'. The Director of Central Intelligence decided
this was 'seditious'. Although 'violence is deprecated', 'the
frequent references to the sword is a form of innuendo that may
not be disregarded by the more fanatically minded'. In the Home
Department McPherson agreed.[58] The Viceroy considered that in
this speech and his manipulation of the Home Rule League and
the Congress, Gandhi had virtually abandoned any pretence of
aiming at self-government within the Empire. He concluded that
Gandhi was giving way to wilder counsels, either because he was
conscious of failure or because he was surrendering to his Muslim
colleagues. The question of arresting Gandhi was considered in
Executive Council on 19 October.

The objections were that an arrest would probably lead to
disorder, consolidate the extremists, weaken the moderates, and
jeopardize the elections. There might even be industrial trouble.
The arguments for prosecution were that inaction might lead to a
worse situation, and that moderates might be discouraged through

an absence of protection. Chelmsford remained convinced that repression would not do, and there was no change in policy. (Lloyd had reported him 'quite resolute on the matter' before the Lucknow speech.[59]) The Viceroy was committed to non-interference not only in general but also in its application to the *satyagraha* campaign. He was not ready to admit failure or error. He rehearsed all the arguments against any arrest, and emphasized particularly that his policy enjoyed moderate support, which repression would squander, and that interference was the last weapon—there would be nothing should it fail. The government, he noted, had kept their tempers 'despite the greatest provocation', and should continue to do so unless 'actually driven into repressive action'. The time to act might come after the elections when moderate opinion might be persuaded to acquiesce—he hoped he could secure the partnership of the new Councils. Chelmsford believed time was on their side. He told Montagu: 'Each day of patience, each day nearer the establishment of the new Councils, is a day gained'. All local governments except Burma agreed with the decision not to prosecute.[60] Rupert Gwynne continued a campaign in Parliament to have Gandhi arrested; Montagu promised not to interfere, but he reported each renewed attack. Chelmsford's defence was simple: so far his policy had maintained order.[61]

Thus non-interference was reaffirmed. But at the same time the increased alarm showed itself in some tougher measures. The Panjab Government was permitted, at the end of October, to proclaim the districts of Lahore, Amritsar and Sheikhpura under the Seditious Meetings Act. At first religious meetings and meetings in the municipalities of Lahore and Amritsar were excluded from the restriction, but early in November these exemptions were cancelled and the Act was applied to the whole province. These steps were directed mainly against the Sikhs. Before the Lucknow speech, the Home Department had been content to direct district officers to discuss political matters with leaders, take no action that would alienate sympathy, reason with extremists, and encourage any reasonable politicians. Now, instead, the Seditious Meetings Act was back in force.[62] At the same time local governments in general were reminded to act against anyone who preached violence. The Home Department even suggested that the Bengal Government might consider prosecuting Abul Kalam Azad, following C.I.D. reports of violence in his speeches.[63] There were sixteen such prosecutions by 23 November, always with sobering effect.[64]

Once again the government were able to point to encouraging signs. Gandhi was now advocating that the procreation of children should be given up throughout India—reinforcing Chelmsford's belief that Gandhian 'folly' could be left to destroy itself.[65] Gandhi's success with students had not earned him much goodwill among parents, and the Home Department hoped his 'meddling' would do much to discredit his campaign. They also took heart from suspicions among some Muslims at the way in which their colleges and not those of the Hindus were being singled out for Gandhi's attention.[66] Non-co-operation was still supposed not to be making much progress. Even in the elections there were already 182 candidates for 55 seats. In Bengal and the Central Provinces there were signs of disagreements and possible splits among the extremists; in Bombay Jinnah and nineteen others had resigned from the Home Rule League as a result of its constitutional changes —they objected that only 61 of 6,000 members had been present.[67]

But Gandhi showed no sign of disappearing, and in early November the government began to consider action on several fronts. They wondered if they should institute prosecutions for all definite breaches of the law—there were doubts about the wisdom over a long period of the tactical use of penal laws: to some it seemed cynical and ill-advised to prosecute only when expedient not whenever the law was broken; and others agreed with Willingdon who declared that Gandhi and Muhammad Ali had been allowed to say 'such scandalous things' that he could not think they could say anything worse that would justify prosecution in future.[68] The government decided that a distinction must continue to be made between prosecution of local leaders for violent or seditious speeches, and prosecution of non-co-operators on the ground that the movement as a whole was illegal. The latter course was deprecated, and, although in theory national leaders might have been prosecuted for their speeches, no such prosecutions were made. The government were also considering action against persons who sent objectionable telegraph or postal messages, and the withholding of government advertisements from papers which advocated *satyagraha*.[69] The latter course was consistent in style with a suggestion of Harcourt Butler's, passed on at Chelmsford's instance to local governments at the end of August, whereby titleholders who had resigned their titles 'should not be molested, but also . . . should not be received by any official';[70] but when such a boycott was originally suggested for newspapers by the Board of Industries and Munitions there were some objections in the Home Department. Vincent favoured it, however, and on 16 November, with Chelmsford's approval, a blacklist of selected newspapers was recommended to local governments—the list included *Amrita Bazar Patrika*, *Bombay Chronicle*, *Young India*, *Hindu* of Madras, and *Searchlight* of Patna.[71] Such measures were not designed to counter disorders or acts of non-co-operation; they were intended to hinder the 'real danger', as Chelmsford described it, from the 'constant vilification of the Government'.[72]

Finally, the government decided to issue a resolution explaining their policy of non-interference and appealing for a strong effort to stop further propaganda among students and the masses.[73] With this public announcement, the policy of non-interference would seem to have received the accolade. But such proclamations always implied the threat of reprisals if the aims were not achieved; and this resolution of November 1920, in many ways the most confident and explicit assertion of Chelmsford's method, represented in other ways a hardening in attitudes as a result of anxiety. Clearly it derived from the suggestions of Lowndes in August and Sly in October, suggestions which had been expressive of concern. In July Chelmsford had hoped there would be no need for action. In October he admitted that action might be taken after the elections. Thus the resolution offered the public an unspoken choice between helping the policy of non-interference and facing the consequences of that policy's failure. The resolution was an attempt to support non-interference; but it was possible that it would become the first salvo in a campaign to secure moderate support for the suppression of *satyagraha*.

For the remainder of 1920 the government continued to interpret the situation in terms which suggested that non-interference was still effective. Government accounts remained largely optimistic. From Aligarh Gandhi had moved on to Amritsar and Lahore. He was reported as having created a temporary excitement among students. Islamia College, Lahore, had to be closed, although 350 students were said to have signed a protest against non-co-operation. The Anjuman-Himayat-ul-Islam, the controlling body of the College, voted overwhelmingly to remain affiliated to Panjab

University. Dr. Kitchlew took possession of some of the buildings, but was ordered to leave. By mid-November the college had re-opened, and by December it was reported back to normal. Some modifications in the constitution of the Governing Body were planned. At the Dayanand Anglo-Vedic College, Lahore, only three students out of more than a thousand were said to have withdrawn; but Khalsa College, Amritsar, also had to be closed. Its managing committee decided to ask for withdrawal of government control in the management of local schools, and the local government was prepared to grant this measure. Gandhi had gone to Allahabad where he addressed some two thousand students, thirty or forty of whom, it seems, signed their adherence to non-co-operation.[74]

At Aligarh, the Trustees had voted against non-co-operation, and in response Muhammad Ali with about one hundred students occupied the college grounds. The College Secretary called upon him to leave, and next day appealed for help to the District Magistrate and the police. After this show of force, Muhammad Ali was persuaded to withdraw peacefully. He addressed the students and told them to leave. The University Act was brought into force, with the Raja of Mahmudabad as Chancellor, and in December the University opened. A National College had been started in Aligarh, but (according to the government) at the end of November, with two bungalows and 100 students, it had achieved one lecture.[75] Muhammad Ali went on to Banaras, where classes continued as usual—there was no disruption reported even when Gandhi added his weight.[76] Calcutta had provided more fertile ground. Trouble had occurred in the Madrassa, and the Arabic Department had been closed *sine die*. But the government wrote to the parents, denying any wish to force their sons to attend, and asking for their wishes in the matter. The majority of students returned. The Madrassa re-opened, although attendance in the Arabic Department remained below normal. A National Madrassa was ostensibly offering tuition in the Zacharia Mosque—in December, the government believed, no tuition was being given.[77]

Elsewhere little serious trouble was reported. About sixty students went on strike in the Islamia College, Peshawar; half a dozen left Pachiyappa's College in Madras. In Bombay a national college was opened at Ahmedabad with some seventy students; there were some renunciations of the government connection, and scattered withdrawals of staff and students—the most significant being two assistant professors and thirty-three students from Gujarat College.[78] In Delhi there was minor trouble at the Anglo-Arabic School, and the Principal of Ramjas College resigned, declaring himself for non-co-operation.[79] The government's information suggested, therefore, that the campaign had resulted in minor dislocation, but that few students had been willing, in the *Leader*'s phrase, to follow Gandhi 'into the wilderness'.[80] The temporary success bore out Chelmsford's belief, shared by Montagu, that education was not a very likely arena for lasting non-co-operation.[81]

The elections were more seriously interrupted, but in few cases totally. There had been very few seats—none for the Government of India—with no candidates, though a number had only one. In all provinces except the Central Provinces a majority of seats was contested.[82] In Bengal, for example, there were 327 candidates for 113 seats in the Provincial Council, with no contest in nineteen out of ninety-four constituencies, and no seat without a candidate. In neighbouring Bihar and Orissa, 184 candidates sought 68 seats, two seats having no candidates.[83] In contested seats, polling varied. It was poor in some parts of Bengal and Madras, in the latter case being hampered by floods. In Bombay the poll was only 10–15 per cent; in Lucknow, on the other hand, it was 60 per cent, and in some urban areas in Madras it was higher still. In the Panjab an average number voted, but prosecutions were necessary over intimidation of voters and a near riot in Lahore.[84] About a dozen 'men of straw'—candidates whose obvious unsuitability was intended to discredit the elections—were returned in the Central Provinces, Bengal and Delhi (where intimidation was alleged to have ruined the election). Another five such candidates were returned to the Imperial Legislative Assembly. But the government had expected low polls, with a newly and greatly widened franchise; and in general they thought reasonably good Councils had been returned.[85]

In November Chelmsford had concluded that, with schools, lawyers, elections, and surrender of titles, they were 'winning all down the line'.[86] He was able to continue in this belief to the end of the year. In late December there was a lull in agitation. The non-co-operators were preparing for the Nagpur Congress. Chelmsford refused a suggestion that he should issue a conciliatory statement.

He did not believe this would have a good effect on the extremists, who would only find objections in the most innocent words.[87] Gandhi had embarked on a fund-raising tour as a prelude to Nagpur. Large numbers attended his meetings, but with mixed results. In Arrah his visit stimulated army recruiting. Bengal reported that Gandhi was venerated, but his programme regarded with the tolerance extended to children's games. The Home Department did not know whether enough subscriptions had been raised even to pay for the tour.[88]

The main issues before the Nagpur Congress were the proposal to change the aims of Congress, and the conduct and progress of *satyagraha*. The 22,000 delegates were divided between those who opposed any change in the aims, and those who wished to revolutionize them and openly seek a republic. Gandhi stood between, and secured a compromise, carrying his own resolution by a huge majority. He explained that the new aim of Congress, '*swaraj*', could be with or without the British connection as circumstances required. The Subjects Committee was divided on how to secure *swaraj*; but unity was preserved there through the resolution of C. R. Das: non-violent non-co-operation was to be put into effect as the Congress or the All-India Congress Committee decided. In the meantime parents were to try to withdraw children under sixteen and establish national schools; students were to devote themselves to *satyagraha* if their consciences so demanded; trustees, managers and teachers were to help to nationalize their schools. Lawyers were to make greater efforts to suspend practice, and merchants were gradually to boycott foreign trade. Village and provincial organizations were to further the campaign, and a band of national workers was to raise funds.[89] As with the Calcutta programme, these plans had been foreshadowed by the Central Khilafat Committee which had sent out leaflets ordering the establishment of Khilafat Committees in every district, reporting weekly to the central office through provincial branches, and also the use of volunteer corps for propaganda and fund collection.[90] The position of Das was a notable success for Gandhi. Das had reportedly gone to Nagpur to oppose educational non-co-operation; he was apparently won over after being waited on by Gandhi, Muhammad Ali, Kitchlew, Bipin Chandra Pal and others. Muhammad Ali had allayed his suspicions of pan-Islamism and the Afghans, by promising that Indian Muslims would be the first to fight if the Amir invaded. After the Congress session Das decided to give up legal practice and devote himself to *satyagraha*, and on his return to Bengal the majority of students left their classes. All opposition had been nullified by Nagpur; there was no prospect of a split in any direction. At a secret meeting on 28 December Gandhi and the Ali brothers had stood together and strongly opposed violence; in Congress their united front satisfied the sceptics, such as Hasrat Mohani and Swami Sraddhanand, for the time at least. The nationalists were ready for another period of intensive agitation. The pre-Congress lull had ended.[91]

The Home Department, however, decided that the adherence to Gandhi's programme was little more than a saving of face. The Council elections were no longer an issue: Congress had declared the representatives unrepresentative and called on them to resign, but this was little more than a matter of form. The boycott of schools and the withdrawal from the courts had not had permanent success in the past; they seemed no less impractical now. The government concluded that, whatever the appearance at Nagpur, the Congress leaders had realized the futility of their campaign. The government expected future agitation on a new front. They predicted that the main attention would turn to propaganda among the masses, particularly tenantry and labour.[92]

The government thought the rural situation worst in the United Provinces. In early January agrarian unrest broke out near Rai Bareli. Villagers destroyed the taluqdars' personal crops, and on two occasions, at a total cost of nine lives, the police opened fire when faced by large mobs. Non-co-operators were allegedly involved. But the villagers had genuine grievances, which the Commissioners of Lucknow and Fyzabad were ordered to investigate. The local government admitted that the Oudh Tenancy Act needed amendment, and hoping to secure concessions from the taluqdars, they appointed a special officer to undertake the revision. By 24 February the trouble had subsided. A number of agitators had been arrested.[93] The province was next disturbed by a strike in the railway workshops. There were attempts to stop a mail train, but the police kept the situation under control. The strike continued into late February, although at that time nearly all the running and office staff had returned to work.[94] Economic reasons also caused restiveness among schoolmasters, patwaris, and chaukidars.[95]

In Bengal, non-co-operators were believed to be instrumental in a strike of taxi-drivers. There were reportedly no economic grievances; the objections were to government control. Elaborate preparations were discerned, and the strikers refused to discuss matters with the authorities. The intention, the Bengal Government reported, was to paralyse Calcutta during the visit by the Duke of Connaught. The situation was serious owing to intimidation by upcountry Sikhs and Muslims. On 21 January, the local government considered there was strong evidence that the strike was out of control. Orders were issued suspending the licences of those who continued to strike, and the Government of India were asked to approve the deportation of non-Bengalis under the Defence of India Rules. The Government of India refused to agree to wholesale deportations, and objected to the use of a wartime measure long after the war. But they authorized the use of the Act, if absolutely necessary, to deport a limited number of up-country drivers to their homes. The cancellation of licences had some effect, and the strike was over on 24 January.[96] It was followed two days later by a strike of tramway employees. This was still not settled in late February. Anglo-Indian drivers were being given police protection; one shooting incident had been followed by a magisterial enquiry.[97]

Over the same period, at Muzaffarpur in Bihar, there was a serious outbreak of *hat* looting. It was believed to be committed or inspired by sympathizers with the non-co-operation movement. Local zamindars were encouraged to organize peons to protect the shopkeepers from terrorization, and the Commissioner was asked to prosecute where possible. Planters were warned of the need for restraint. This outbreak was short-lived.[98] In January there had also occurred in Bihar an incident in which a cooly was struck by a European for stealing sugar-cane. He claimed to be seriously hurt, although the hospital could find nothing wrong with him; his fellow-workers became excited and attacked the Superintending Engineer and two other Europeans. Twenty-five armed police were called in, and work was suspended. The government laboriously reported this trivial occurrence to the Secretary of State—demonstrating perhaps an excessive sensitivity to rural and industrial unrest.[99]

Elsewhere the government found other alarming omens. In the Central Provinces the bulk of the people in towns and larger villages was found to be familiar with the idea of non-co-operation. In the Panjab a propagandist committee had been formed under Lajpat Rai, and was spreading its ideas among the rural classes. The peasantry was already discontented; one officer identified the problems as the compulsory disbanding of soldiers and their reluctant return to their villages, the corruption of officials, and promises made or imagined during the war. The central government thought the situation potentially serious. Any problem in the Panjab was also complicated by the unrest among the Sikhs. The Sikh League had adopted non-co-operation, and a movement to contest control of the temples had been gaining momentum.[100]

In Madras there had been a long mill strike, in which the men would not abate their demands, and the management would not recognize the union. Also, in Malabar, a campaign for tenancy reform was causing concern.[101] In Bombay some districts predicted difficulty in collecting land revenue—although it was thought possible that this was no more than the usual attempt to secure remissions for a partial crop failure.[102] Two other signs were not encouraging. A large anti-cow-killing conference had been held at Kanwal in the Panjab, and the temperance movement was spreading in Bihar and Orissa. Both of these held the prospect of disorder. In February, the Bhagalpur Division in Bihar was disturbed by intimidation and picketing of liquor shops; in March similar trouble erupted in the Central Provinces—it began with attacks on liquor shops in Nagpur leading to more than thirty arrests, and ended with six deaths after angry mobs had rescued the prisoners and stoned the police.[103]

It was tempting to attribute all the unrest to non-co-operators. Some nationalist leaders encouraged this tendency. The Central Khilafat Committee sought to adapt the movement to its more active role: in the name of the president, Chotani, it issued a manifesto on the need for executive organization in the Congress and the Muslim League, advocating standing committees to control finance, national education, national industries, and propaganda.[104] In Bengal, B. Chakravarti, C. R. Das, Abul Kalam Azad and two others issued a village organization scheme pending further action by the Provincial Congress. It included the establishment of primary schools, village banks and arbitration courts, the boycott of foreign goods, and attempts to reduce the area of jute cultivation and prevent the consumption of liquor.[105] The inten-

tion was to carry the Gandhian programme to the villages. Later
the Bengal Government reported that Gandhi's influence was
spreading among the illiterate classes: rumours were being circulated crediting Gandhi with the fall in the price of cloth and ghee.[106]
In February, in an address in Lucknow, Shaukat Ali called for non-
violence and courage in obedience to Gandhi and spoke of the
awakening of the 'thirty crores', linking 'Hindus, Sikhs and Parsis'
(presumably he meant Muslims too), but also calling on 'Kisans,
labourers and aristocrats': in other words he saw the common
cause and leadership as socially as well as communally cohesive.
For kisans he also mapped out a programme: 'stop payment of
revenue when Mahatmaji issues his commands'. Earlier and more
directly, Shaukat Ali had welcomed the rural unrest in the United
Provinces as proof that non-co-operation would ultimately
succeed.[107] His brother, Muhammad, had warned students that
India would gain *swaraj*, if not with their support, then with the
help of agriculturists. A politician from Bhagalpur visited the
coalfields and announced the formation of non-co-operation and
labour associations.[108] The government were apprehensive about
the rural disturbances, and expected attempts to engineer industrial troubles for political purposes. The time was ripe for a
further hardening in the government attitude.

For most of January the original Gandhian programme did
seem to have fallen into abeyance, over most of the country, in
favour of the new attempts to widen the movement's popular
support. Panchayats in the Panjab, arbitration courts and Seva
Samitis in the United Provinces, plans to boycott the visit of the
Duke of Connaught, scattered withdrawals of students, a few more
national schools, a ban on overseas trading by the Umbrella Trades
Association: outside Bengal, these were the sum of a quiet month
for the official *satyagraha* campaign.[109] But the Home Department
had been wrong in predicting that Gandhi's programme had
failed and the main attention would turn to politicizing the masses.
The problem was probably that Shaukat Ali's vision of social unity
could not be achieved. True, *ulama* such as Abdul Bari seem to
have had success in mobilizing less educated Muslims, just as
Arya Samaj missionaries could arouse banias or Hindu peasants
on the question of the cow. But mobilization on secular, political
grounds was more difficult. In the United Provinces the kisan
sabhas formed between 1920 and 1921 seem to have been primarily

bodies of tenants with grievances against landlords or, especially, the agents of absentee landlords, the city banias and mahajans. A perceptive C.I.D. agent travelling near Allahabad in January 1921 reported that 'Zamindars look to Government to save them from tenants; but curiously kisans also look to Government to save them from landlords.' He found that 'the currency which Mr. Gandhi's name has acquired even in the remotest villages is astounding' but that the 'reverence . . . is undoubtedly partly due to the belief that he has great influence with the Government'. He found also that the agriculturists knew of swaraj but that they could not explain it—when told that it was the 'sarkar's own *hukm* that the Government . . . be handed over to Indians as quickly as possible' they were filled with 'genuine consternation' and would 'quote instances of mismanagement under Indian officials'. Gandhi, indeed, was thought of as anti-zamindar and not anti-government. 'The extent of the genuine distress' was 'very great', and made worse by population pressure. Landlords were widely believed—in some cases justly, whatever the law might say—to be avoiding rising prices by oppressing their tenants; and, interestingly, there seems to have been little or no activity where landlords were small local men. These factors minimized the usefulness of kisan sabhas as a weapon of nationalist politics.[110] On the whole peasants were not easy to control, and understood little about the inadequacies of reformed councils or the evils of a distant government; they were greatly interested in whether the rabi crop would fail as the kharif had done: their primary grievance (like that of the millworkers in Bombay) was not against the British but against a class of people to whom the politicians, apart from Gandhi, often enough bore close resemblance. There was not yet sufficient community of interest nor sufficiently advanced political education for the 'aristocrats' to feel safe in awakening those thirty crores, or for peasants and labourers to sacrifice their immediate economic interests to *swaraj*. By February Gandhi's original campaign, based mainly on the educated classes, had been resumed.

The commercial element had gained impetus with a fall in the exchange rate of the rupee—by 19 February it was only 1s. 3¾d. Many Indian traders, alleging an assurance from Montagu or the government that the exchange rate would be stabilized at 2s. 0d., declined to honour their overseas orders. Most of the important Piece-goods Associations passed resolutions against the payment of drafts at less than 2s. od. exchange. By mid-February, the exchange banks had proved unable to collect between £6 and £8 million sterling in bills, and uncleared stocks to a value of Rs. 16 crores had built up in Bombay. This was certainly a boycott of foreign trade; but, as the government pointed out, the majority of dealers was 'probably using [the] political motive as [an] excuse for evading serious loss . . .'. It was nearly the end of March before the importers decided to meet their bills—and then the Congress Working Committee promptly sought means to deflect the decision.[111]

Attention was focused more closely on the royal visit and again on education. The Duke of Connaught was in India to inaugurate the reformed Councils. The non-co-operators did not achieve a total boycott, but did produce a marked lack of enthusiasm in Bengal and Delhi. In Madras a rival meeting was held. Only in Bombay was the Duke greeted by cheerful and cheering crowds.[112] Chelmsford explained why the response was disconcerting:

. . . in recent years the attitude of India towards Great Britain has altered and we now have to face the hostility of an unscrupulous party which does not hesitate to employ every device however discreditable extending even to an attempt to belittle the importance of the Duke's visit.[113]

Lady Blanche Lloyd writing to Chamberlain captured the curious psychological effect which the situation had upon the British in India: '. . . it sometimes gives me the queerest feeling,' she wrote 'to think that here we are, living among, entertaining, and trying to do our best for, a crowd of people who mostly hate us all the time, not personally, perhaps, but for what we represent.' Gandhi himself wrote to reassure the Duke of Connaught that the demonstration was not against him personally, but against the system he had come to uphold: 'We are not at war with individual Englishmen . . .', Gandhi wrote, 'We do desire to destroy the system that has emasculated our country . . .'. This explanation was ominous. Gandhi went on, 'Non-co-operationists . . . must not be deceived by the Reforms that tinker with the problem of India's distress and humiliation'.[114] Gradualism then was not enough; and the Duke, about to open new, partially responsible assemblies, was rejected not personally but for what he represented. What he represented was reforms and the King-Emperor

The reaction to the visit was new and serious: there had been an attempt, partly successful, to achieve not only popular rejection of aspects of British policy, but also symbolic repudiation of the British connection.

Bengal alone had not been relatively free of educational disturbances during January. The Bengali students had been excited since C. R. Das made his grand gesture dedicating himself to *satyagraha*. Towards the end of the month there were extensive strikes among students in Calcutta, mainly in privately-managed colleges. The Madrassa was not affected. Large numbers of students collected in College Square and prevented candidates from attending law examinations. In Dacca the College and Madrassa remained open, but the situation throughout the province was grave and worsening steadily. Early in February the atmosphere was calmer, with schools, law colleges and university classes undisturbed; but all other colleges had been closed mainly to enable parents to remove their sons from the influence of the non-cooperators. A visit from Gandhi gave the strike impetus once more. The Education Department considered that the colleges should not be re-opened until students could attend without possibility of interference. A magistrates' order against obstructing students had apparently helped in Dacca, where the Government College was still open, but a similar notice had had no effect in Mymensingh. The probable result of re-opening in disaffected areas would be, in the Department's view, police intervention and street fighting.[115]

Gradually the resurgence spread to other provinces. In Burma more than half the students were on strike at the beginning of February; in Assam two colleges and a few schools were affected. In Madras five hundred students resolved to withdraw; in Bihar and Orissa there was a sudden strike in one college and attempts to intimidate students in others.[116] In Bombay seven hundred students declared themselves for non-co-operation, inspired by the example of Bengal. In early February only fifty or sixty had withdrawn, but the movement was encouraged by a Students' Convention under the leadership of Patel. By 21 February, 633 students had left; nine Anglo-vernacular schools, representing 2,771 pupils, had renounced government grants; Gujarat College had lost five professors; and thirty-eight teachers had left various other schools.[117] In the Central Provinces, at Nagpur, there were

250 students in national schools; by mid-February between 50 and 84 per cent of High School pupils were attending school, but numbers were declining.[118]

In the Panjab the campaign had been revived under Lajpat Rai. A virtually complete strike had taken place in the Dayanand Anglo-Vedic College when the Managing Committee refused to invite Lajpat Rai to address the students. The excitement was caught in other colleges in Lahore, and four in all were closed. The Government and Islamia Colleges were unaffected at first, but later their students voted for non-co-operation, began to disturb lectures, and put pressure on the staff to resign. In Amritsar a large majority at Khalsa College voted to leave and preach non-violent war in the countryside, and a number did quit the College after a meeting held by Dr. Kitchlew. The non-co-operators also held a well-attended Students' Conference at Gujranwala.[119]

The combination of this activity with the indications of industrial and rural unrest was sufficient to force the government's hand. And yet, such was the commitment to non-interference, optimism still prevailed sufficiently to save the main part of the policy. The government decided that the student unrest was mainly an ebullition to impress the Duke of Connaught, and was unlikely to be long-lived. Chelmsford predicted on 14 February:

> The students are seeing for themselves the damage they are suffering from this course and are gradually coming back. Gandhi's advice to them to take to the spinning wheel is not likely to encourage them. I am confident we shall win through, but we must have patience.

A little later he was buoyantly forecasting clearer skies and a better atmosphere, while admitting that the next two or three months (much of which would be in the hands of the new Viceroy) would test his optimism.[120] And again this optimism seemed justified by events. By mid-February the situation had eased, although on the 21st two Panjab colleges were still closed. By the end of the month most colleges had opened, and early in March local governments were reporting satisfactory or improving conditions.[121]

Nonetheless the situation was changing: it was true that each upsurge in Gandhi's campaign was relatively short-lived, but each was also more severe than the last. The government thought the non-co-operators were trying to force the pace, and that students were being recruited as propagandists among the masses.[122] There

was an inevitable reassessment of policy, with two results—
renewed efforts at appeasement, and a further stiffening of attitude.
Already, at the end of January, the government had re-opened
their campaign for a modification of the Turkish peace terms—the
Home Department again placed 'most strongly on record' the
contention that substantial concessions on the Khilafat could be
refused only on peril of very grave consequences for India. In
mid-February the Viceroy was most anxious that an Indian
Muslim delegation should be received and given some concessions
in the peace negotiations.[123] In January 1920 he had instructed the
Home Department to give 'all possible assistance' to Muslim
deputations including Dr. Ansari, Fazlul Haq and Saifuddin
Kitchlew; now in 1921 the government were also offering to pay
fares and expenses for a deputation comprising the Aga Khan,
Hasan Imam, Chotani (President of the Muslim League), and, at
Gandhi's suggestion, Ansari—the idea seems to have been originally Stanley Reed's.[124] About the same time Chelmsford received a
Bengali deputation and assured it: 'we have espoused your cause
and fought it in a way which ... I think would satisfy every
individual'. He concluded, 'I must again express my great sympathy with you and my determination to the last moment to press
every point we can in favour of your representation'.[125] Earlier
Chelmsford had urged that the Duke of Connaught might make a
conciliatory statement on the Khilafat question.[126] A second line of
appeasement was to emphasize the role of the new legislatures, in
the hope of establishing the reality of the reforms and consolidating
moderate opinion. The government had decided to make this
point by accepting resolutions that were moved in the legislature;
and they also suggested that the Duke of Connaught, in opening
the Imperial Legislative Assembly, should make specific reference
to this decision. They suggested that he stress that under the 1919
Act the government was to be influenced by the legislature 'to an
extent incomparably greater than ... in the past', and that
Chelmsford's government would give the 'fullest possible effect'
to this principle. The statement was delivered, after some verbal
changes, substantially in the form drafted by the Home Department.[127]

But appeasement was not enough. In January, the government,
apprehensive at rural and industrial unrest, had decided to address
local governments on the new situation. They were responding to

the supposed new direction of the campaign. While awaiting local
government replies, and as the situation developed, they settled on a
five-point plan. They would watch the attempts to disaffect rural
and labouring classes, introduce special legislation whenever
required, employ counter-propaganda, vigorously prosecute non-
co-operators who were guilty of inciting to violence or making
seditious speeches, and finally enforce general respect for the law,
for example in the case of clearly unlawful assemblies.[128] The first
three points were unremarkable, and the government had stressed
explicitly that they did not intend any great policy change. But the
last two provisions, with their stronger emphasis on the law and
prosecutions, represented another distinct hardening in attitude;
they continued the change which had been evident during the
previous year and, in November, implicit in the government's
resolution explaining their policy.

In late January, in Karachi, Abdul Rahman, the editor of the
local Khilafat paper, was sentenced to one year's rigorous imprisonment on a charge of sedition.[129] As with the central government's decision, this isolated action came rather in advance of the
events which were to stimulate the fuller use of stern measures.
During February these became more frequent. In the United
Provinces, public meetings were prohibited under the Indian
Penal Code in seven districts of Oudh, and several prominent local
leaders were arrested. Later a further eight persons were tried and
imprisoned for interfering with candidates for an examination at
the Sanskrit College, Banaras. A column of arms was marched
through Sultanpur and Fyzabad districts, and was reported to
have had a good effect. In March the Government of India agreed
to the application of the Seditious Meetings Act to four districts
for up to one year, after further disturbances in Rai Bareli.[130]

Meetings had been prohibited in most districts in the Panjab,
and in February the Secretary of the Provincial Congress Committee was confined to Lahore under the Code of Criminal
Procedure. In Madras the Calicut District Magistrate prohibited
Khilafat meetings and arrested Yakub Hasan and three others.
The Chairman of the Calicut Municipality resigned in protest. A
hartal was held in Madras to protest at these imprisonments, but
the police dispersed the crowd without great difficulty. In the
Legislative Council there was no division on a resolution against
the action, as the debate strongly supported the District Magis-

trate.[131] In the Northwest Frontier Province in March, when the local Khilafat Committee was widening its activities, the Deputy Commissioner of Bakka Kel was permitted to ban Khilafat meetings, with the intention, if defied, of arresting the leaders under the Frontier Crimes Regulations.[132] In the Central Provinces, the Vice-President of the Nagpur Municipality, Dr. M. R. Cholkar, was arrested under the Indian Penal Code. There was a large protest meeting and a general *hartal* in Nagpur, followed by some looting of liquor shops. Meetings were prohibited for a month, and there was no further trouble. The Deputy Commissioner interviewed the leading non-co-operators and warned them that the government was determined to maintain order.[133] A vigorous campaign against offenders in Bihar and Orissa was stigmatized by the *Independent* of Allahabad as a 'tide of repression'.[134]

The government were directing pressure largely at preventing public meetings and propaganda by means of the ordinary law. They reported that the provincial governments were encouraging the local authorities in more uniform and co-ordinated steps to counteract the non-co-operation movement. They believed that loud protests from the extremists indicated that the policy was hampering their activities.[135] The stronger measures did involve the risk of a final confrontation with the non-co-operators. In Delhi, for example, the Seditious Meetings Act had been in force since April 1920, after violent speeches at a Workers' Conference and an assault in the Jama Masjid over the Imam's retention of the title of Shams-ul-Ulama—the Home Department, while asking for non-interference to be continued, had suggested prosecutions but the Chief Commissioner, explaining that even if charges could be laid success would be doubtful, had asked for the application of the Act. Now, in February 1921, Chelmsford admitted that, because the Act was in force, Gandhi would have to be arrested if he showed 'deliberate and provocative defiance' on a visit to Delhi.[136] And such risks would be greater, the more widespread sterner measures became—the government were rather at the mercy of their local officials in such circumstances. But this was an increased rather than a new danger, for the government had always recognized that there might come a time when to do nothing would be wrong. As M. M. Shafi had explained in November to Willingdon: the 'policy of sitting tight and doing nothing is right *now*'.[137]

Similarly, when Gandhi proposed to go on to Lahore and

Amritsar—also places where the Seditious Meetings Act was in force—the Panjab Government proposed to instruct their officers to authorize one meeting in each place provided co-operators (if any) were also permitted to speak; on the other hand the officers were not to disperse unauthorized meetings by force, and were to prosecute organizers and provincial participants (but not Gandhi) —and only these after careful consideration. The Home Department were uneasy at this. S. P. O'Donnell suggested at first that it might be wise to tackle only organizers. Vincent, while criticizing the proposed restrictions on the number of meetings, suggested that any refusal to arrest Gandhi, if he were to break the law, would be a dangerous admission of weakness. Hailey, to the point, added that if the Panjab did not want to enforce the Meetings Act they should withdraw it. Chelmsford's view, as reported by Vincent on the file, was that Gandhi should be prosecuted if he broke the law and that illegal meetings should be dispersed by police though without firing except in self-defence and if unavoidable. It is a fair guess, justified by comparing Vincent's own minute on the subject, that the Viceroy had accepted the logic of the Home Member's argument but that the caveat about firing was his own addition. As usual he took the question in Council, and the government decided that as they had reluctantly agreed to the application of the Seditious Meetings Act they must now insist that it be properly enforced. They ordered that sanction should be given for meetings, on conditions as liberal as possible, with no insistence on co-operators speaking, but that, if an illegal meeting should be held, it was to be dispersed and the speakers, including Gandhi, prosecuted.[138] The government agreed with Vincent that they must not be exposed as not supporting the law, but equally, with him, they did not wish to provoke trouble.

The policy was in essentials the one confirmed in April 1920. We have looked throughout of course only at the policy towards figures of more than district status. Otherwise, central instructions would not have had such immediate impact: we need not doubt that each district officer had his own ideas about how to deal with agitators; and he seems often enough to have disapproved of the centre's style. Feelings and methods may be nicely gauged from this account by the superintendent at Meerut, who had

challenged these fellows, so-called volunteers, to come out. They won't
... and ... the reason is simply that they have been informed that they

will not be allowed to fill their tummies in jail at Govt. expense . . . but that they will be beaten, quite legally of course, "unlawful assembly", "dispersal by force", etc. etc. In many places arrests have been excessive but in most of these they have not been dealing so much with the Eastender as with the failed B.A. and it may be difficult to beat the nephew of a Minister! Anyhow here we have arrested noone except a speechifier and the city is calm. . . . We can raise far vaster numbers of volunteers than the enemy and we can, if we stick to it, hand India over to the best people after 10 years and clear out. If the big wigs get the wind up, emasculate us again as men have been emasculated for the last 2 years and generally show the white feather, we officials are clearing out in droves.

But as we have seen the centre's non-interference had never implied abdication of executive interference in politics, only abstention from a frontal attack on Gandhi's movement. In the last resort, if provoked, the government would uphold the law, although only with great reluctance if Gandhi were involved. Where possible, as with the ambiguities of 'sedition' in speeches, they invoked double standards, finding themselves more outraged and readier to prosecute for the extravagances of minor than of major figures. Thus neither the ever-present parochial idiosyncrasies nor the centre's call in 1921 for harsher local tactics should be taken as a reversal of their method or any intention of prohibiting non-co-operation. There was no real willingness to consider new departures in policy. When J. L. Maffey suggested to Chelmsford a novel scheme whereby the government would no longer extend to non-co-operators such facilities as the railways and postal or telegraphic services, Vincent doubted that such official 'non-co-operation' would be possible, Barnes was sure it was illegal, impractical and undignified, and Chelmsford echoed that he had always concluded that it 'would be both illegal and impracticable'. In another context, about the same time, he re-iterated the central precept of his thinking. The real danger, he maintained, lay in the extremists on either side—British ones who always saw 'in the big stick a remedy for every evil', and Indian ones who wanted nothing better than for the government 'to use the big stick'.[139] For several years Chelmsford had occupied the middle position, consistently and to his own satisfaction. The *satyagraha* campaign had not shaken his confidence in this approach.

This fact is remarkable, not only in terms of the challenge presented by Gandhi, who, though not fully successful, remained undefeated, but also in terms of the fierce opposition which Chelmsford's policy aroused at high levels. Those, like Lord Willingdon, who had opposed it from the first, were now confirmed in their opinion. Willingdon thought non-interference merely a failure of courage; he scorned it as the method of 'Hush. Hush'. Once, after an uneventful visit from Gandhi and Shaukat Ali, he admitted to doubts; but generally he became more and more incensed every time that 'd——d fellow Gandhi' came into his jurisdiction and he was not allowed to intervene. He wanted to act, and argued that they were allowing the non-co-operators to organize—the agitation would not be killed by 'a policy of drift'; 'masterly inactivity' was no way to govern. Some of his views were seen by Sir F. W. Duke and Lord Lytton, and cannot have increased confidence at the India Office.[140]

Of the other provincial heads, Lloyd, at a moment when he had lost all confidence in Chelmsford, wrote to Montagu complaining that Simla was hopelessly out of touch—'where it is firm it fails to be sympathetic, where it attempts to be sympathetic it succeeds only in being weak'. He believed that the release of Shaukat Ali had been a mistake—Montagu did not agree but admitted that he thought Shaukat should have been 'put back again immediately he opened his mouth'. Lloyd's idea was 'to pay out rope and hit the agitator hard', while still showing sympathy for nationalist hopes. After seeing Chelmsford in October 1920, Lloyd was again prepared to endorse the Viceroy's policy. He confided in Chamberlain that the repressive courses would have to be followed right through riots and bloodshed once it was begun, whereas Chelmsford's tactics, although they might do much damage, might succeed. At the end of 1920, however, Lloyd was convinced that Gandhi's movement had failed and that the government should destroy what remained of his influence. In the new year Lloyd wrote to Montagu that they could not 'go on drifting vaguely'; they must either make terms with Gandhi or repress his movement. At the end of February he was happier again; but he was never fully committed to Chelmsford's approach.[141]

The non-co-operation campaign convinced most of the other governors that the policy was misguided. Ronaldshay was reticent about giving his opinion, but he was clearly uneasy. He believed the non-co-operation campaign could end only in violence and that this was the aim of its leaders. He remarked that many people—later he mentioned particularly the 'loyal Muhammadans' —were 'puzzled at the length to which the extremists are permitted to go'. He made a speech at Krishnagar against the Khilafat and *satyagraha* movements, and believed that the favourable response from local leaders showed that 'there are two points of view from which to look at a policy of inaction'. He thought the government must make it clear that certain things, such as tampering with the army and the police, would not be tolerated. He was worried, in August 1920, that the central government had not 'publicly defined' their attitude, with the result that no-one knew where they stood and no uniformity of action was possible between local governments. Montagu, to whom these fears had been expressed, suggested that the Government of India might have had 'special difficulties' in making their attitude clear. No-one, he insisted, would stand in the way of any action against Gandhi once it was seen as really wise; but provinces had to be a little diffident in pressing strongly for action against someone whose activities had an all-India aspect.[142] Ronaldshay hinted at his uneasiness to Chelmsford, and, when pressed for definite suggestions, tentatively put forward, in March 1921, an idea that Gandhi might be prosecuted if he persisted in his campaign after a personal appeal offering concessions.[143]

Craddock's government strongly criticized the Government of India's policy in an official despatch at the end of 1920. Chelmsford replied sharply that, while he welcomed private comment, 'there must be no official criticism' when policy had been laid down distinctly; he hoped that there would be no 'recurrence of any such thing'. Craddock had urged earlier that conciliation was not understood in India and would have 'no permanent effect'. 'To the extremist,' he argued, 'the British Government is an enemy'; conciliation was interpreted as showing that surrender was near; the only policy was to give 'moderate and sensible men' a chance to come to the fore.[144] This view echoed that of the Chief Commissioner of Coorg, H. V. Cobb, who had sent the Home Department a strong minute in 1919; it had struck him that 'Our policy of late years . . . has been to neglect our well-wishers and treat them as a negligible quantity; but at the same time to go out of our way to try and placate or conciliate our enemies. It is a policy . . .

which has not met with marked success. . . . I cannot recall the name of any really prominent extremist who has been won over by it to our side. On the other hand, many staunch Indian friends have complained to me that loyalty is not a policy that pays.'[145] Such opposition, reading a different lesson from the upheavals of 1919, was thus not new; but by the end of 1920, it had become fairly general. Sir Frank Sly joined the chorus; Harcourt Butler was still recording his hostility many years later.[146]

It is important to understand what this attitude represented. There were three continuing elements: that conciliation discouraged loyalists and moderates, that it would not win over the extremists, and that it both allowed them the opportunity and encouraged them to preach unrest. It is not hard, therefore, to see why this criticism did not carry the weight which might have been expected. The Government of India had rejected all of these arguments. They did not place great faith in 'moderates', and anyway the most prominent of these publicly opposed the repression of extremists;[147] they no longer expected to win over the extremists—their policy was to buy time not favour—but they believed it was repression not conciliation that would assist the nationalist cause.

It would have been more serious if the Secretary of State had joined the dissenters, as at one time seemed possible. Montagu was in two minds about the policy. In July 1920 he came under pressure, with questions in Parliament, to act against Gandhi. He continued to fear the consequences of action more than the dangers of inaction—the nightmare of a Gandhi on hunger strike in prison was enough to convince him. But the campaign was more successful than he expected, and he too became worried at the need to encourage the moderates. He also made nervous enquiries about reports that the government had not prevented Gandhi from drilling recruits. 'Your policy . . . is a simple one,' he told Chelmsford, 'and we hope that in the end it will prove a wise one.'[148] There was no resounding confidence in that assurance. In November Montagu's defence of the policy was drafted, in a letter to Ronaldshay, as 'I think . . . the policy is a sound one'; Montagu corrected it by hand to read, 'I think . . . the policy is an intelligible one'. This was a fair account of his position. It was, he admitted, 'a gamble'—but at least it was a gamble with two throws; immediate intervention was a gamble with only one. He fell back on his policy of leaving such matters for decision by the men responsible in India. He wrote to Willingdon, sentiments repeated also to Chelmsford:

non-co-operation appears to be getting more dangerous, but I must leave it to people in India to decide how to deal with it. I never thought it would die of inanition. What I do think is that perhaps, and I speak with great diffidence, it is so impracticable and so disadvantageous that people will get sick of it.[149]

Three factors, therefore, encouraged the government to continue their old policy. Firstly, their handling of the situation was never openly challenged by the Secretary of State. Secondly, their own judgment and interpretation of wider issues required them to discount the basis of the local governments' criticism. Thirdly, as we have seen, their generally optimistic attitude to Gandhi's campaign remained unruffled by events: their alarm was answered by progressive hardening in their measures, and was never great enough to move them on the main principle of non-interference. There was also a final and decisive factor. Changing the policy required an act of courage: as Chelmsford insisted, repression of Gandhi would have been a final and irrevocable gamble which would have had to be carried through to the end. Without the pressure of unavoidable circumstances, the government were unwilling to take this step, and it was for this reason, it seems, that they allowed themselves to be encouraged by each successive lull in the non-co-operation campaign. But what was perhaps equally important was that this final factor also discounted the criticism: the Secretary of State was daunted by it; and even the local governments, for all their private grumbling, shared the same reluctance when forced to make official recommendations. When their replies were received (to the Home Department enquiry) in March 1921, only Burma was prepared to advocate that non-interference should be abandoned.[150] Other local governments, of course, now had to convince Indian colleagues, and perhaps to persuade Indian legislators.

Thus the last questioning under Chelmsford resulted in an endorsement of his policy. He had been vindicated also in a complementary direction. As he had hoped, he had gained the acquiescence of the legislative assemblies before embarking on stronger measures. Several local governments had received votes in support of their policies, and in the Imperial Legislative Assembly a resolution to ban repressive measures had been rejected. The feeling of the Assembly had been against any weakening of the local governments' position. A resolution had been passed approving the government's policy, while recommending the avoidance of any action under exceptional legislation. In March, the Home Department urged local governments to institute prosecutions more freely for incitement to violence, and against speeches 'calculated to produce feelings likely to lead to violence in the near future'.[151] This was the toughest position taken under Chelmsford. But its victims were to remain relatively minor figures only. Measures against Gandhi were specifically reserved to the central government as issues of national importance. The two main lessons learnt in dealing with Annie Besant—the dangers of interference and the need for central supervision—had not been forgotten.

Even Lionel Curtis, that 'high priest of Empire', had taken the authoritarian view. Writing to Chamberlain, he pronounced: 'There will be no rest in India as long as it is said "Unless you obey, the Govt. of India may get very angry." . . . There will be peace in India when there is a Viceroy who says "I *will* be obeyed".'[152] Curtis, with many others, failed to understand the situation. Truly the danger was from 'extremists on either side'. The official 'extremists' would have attacked Gandhi; against them Chelmsford and his government held out, occupying the middle ground. But Gandhi was already under attack. He too had had to hold out—against those, mainly younger Congressmen who thought him too cautious in his goals and also, even at Nagpur, against the challenge of a group led by Hasrat Mohani who wanted Congress to abandon non-violence.[153] There was a sense in which, compared with these extremists, Gandhi also occupied the middle ground. From the official viewpoint, Gandhi's agitation, like Mrs. Besant's, was ambiguous, half-way between legal protest and revolution. Gandhi too was half-rebel, half-loyalist. It was in June 1920, as his campaign gathered way and he planned to defy authority and undermine the law, that he wrote to Chelmsford calling himself 'a devoted well-wisher of the British Empire'.[154] The Government of India tried to be equally dextrous.

CONCLUSION

Chapter 9. Coherence

THREE lines of approach may be distinguished in the political policy of Lord Chelmsford's government. The first was a positive policy of response to Indian opinion, seeking to influence it and, as far as possible, to meet or forestall its demands. The second was a neutral policy which sought to counter agitation by tactical non-interference. The third policy was negative—the repression of agitation. In general the first two were applied to peaceful and constitutional movements; the last was directed against violent or 'revolutionary' outbreaks.

Positive reforms, including the changes in the constitution, were pursued both in response to Indian protest and in recognition of genuine needs. In a few cases, notably measures for the welfare of soldiers, the government sought to reward Indian services during the war. Montagu and Chelmsford were also attempting to find answers to larger questions than the solution of immediate problems or the avoidance of pending agitation: Chelmsford began his viceroyalty by asking what was the 'goal' of British presence in India; he ended it in the belief that he and Montagu had ensured that the goal would be to transfer power to responsible Indian legislatures.

The new constitution suffered a severe blow when it was boycotted by the Congress. It has been suggested, of course, that on the contrary the reformers had wanted the disintegration of Indian political movements, and that by separating 'moderates' in the Councils from 'extremists' in Congress they had achieved their aim. This goes too far. The government took measures to conciliate 'extreme' interests during the reforms discussions: as in 1917, when a furore arose over a letter written by Lionel Curtis, and officials were forbidden to take Round Table membership. The step was intended mainly to avoid compromising Meston (involved by Curtis) through a political storm just as he was about to represent India at the Imperial Conference; the Home Department explained that the letter had given rise to 'definite charges . . . that government servants in this country [for example, Meston] are combining with Mr. Curtis, and the "Round

Table" to give prominence to political views which are unpalatable to advanced Indian sentiment . . .'. As with the release of Besant, the government acted to neutralize even those fears and charges which they thought unfounded.[1]

The reforms themselves were also a response to educated Indians' demands and aspirations. Chelmsford explained that he had considered it necessary to see that the changes gave satisfaction, and 'probably wiser to give a little too much than too little'. He made a comparison between the Irish priesthood and the Indian intellectuals, both a small minority with influence out of proportion to their members. The Irish priests had become estranged from the British; Chelmsford wanted the Indians to be treated better—the Montagu-Chelmsford Report was saying to them, he believed, 'Come along and help us. We will guide you. . . . There are many difficulties in your path and you will realise them as you begin to face responsibility'.[2] Austen Chamberlain too had argued that the British had to show their good intentions to the nationalists: only by leading the movement for reform could they control it. Montagu had argued that any scheme must command public support in India.[3] The *Indian Diary* is contradictory on this point: Montagu was often despondent at the prospects of persuading the Government of India to accept anything which would be popular with the 'advanced' politicians, and he was aware that expectations were running very high; but he had some promises of support, and, by the time the proposals were finalized, had concluded that the Congress would accept them with a rider insisting on certain amendments.[4]

In short, the reforms were directed at loyalists of course, but also at all those Indians who believed in the advance to self-government. It is true that most local governments did not share the reformers' aims, and some used the reforms for local ends, such as too wholeheartedly encouraging loyalists at the expense of others—thus provinces could sabotage the centre's programmes. It is true also that the official response, when it was obvious that the moderates would be outvoted in the Congress, was to hope that they would combine in a separate organization. From this period comes most of the evidence which has been used to suggest that the reforms were directed solely at the moderates. Lord Willingdon went so far as to welcome a breach within the nationalist ranks. He wrote to Montagu that his difficulty was to per-

suade the moderates to act as politicians: 'They have got Tilak
& Mrs. B. & Co. committed to an entire non-possumus as regards yr. scheme. I want the moderates to keep them there & to
bring out their own policy & in a sense to "go to the country on
it". But all these Indians love a compromise & I am desperately
afraid that in order to save a row they may come to some compromise with Tilak & Co.'.[5] Willingdon had conversations with
moderates, and soon became optimistic at the prospects for a
moderate party. Moderates had held a separate congress in
Bombay; and Willingdon felt certain that there would be an
immense effect from this banding together in opposition to the
'frothing demogogues'. The extremists, he believed, were already
chastened.[6]

Montagu at this time also expressed the hope that 'moderates'
would break away from the Congress if they were defeated on the
reforms issue. Rather overstating his point, as was his custom,
he avowed to Ronaldshay that his 'whole aim in life' was 'to work
with the moderates and to regard the extremists as the opposition'. With Willingdon, he hoped for a 'Government party,
Indian, courageous and strong', in the new councils.[7] Chelmsford
hoped, more modestly, that there would be in the Assemblies
some members who would support government policies on their
merits. His government had organized propaganda to accompany
the publication of the Report. The first edition and newspapers
which featured it were sold out almost at once; Rushbrook
Williams prepared a pamphlet; Stanley Reed and K. C. Roy
surreptitiously circulated articles in support of the proposals.
This publicity was not directed at 'extremists'. Chelmsford too
had been influenced by their reaction to the Report—this had
convinced him that opposition was their *raison d'être* and that
they could not be expected to give it up.[8]

But these reactions after the Report was published must be
distinguished from the motives of Montagu and Chelmsford in
deciding on their proposals. Montagu claimed that he had 'never
expected to have extremists' with him over the reforms; he discovered this only when they had proved to be against him.[9] Indeed,
far from never expecting extremist support, Montagu remained
optimistic longer than most. He even suggested that Chelmsford
meet with extremist politicians in an attempt to avoid a hostile
decision by the Congress. Chelmsford refused on the grounds that

the bitterness of these people could not be allayed: their opposition would have to be accepted.[10] Chelmsford was appealing to realism, not to doctrine—for him, as for Montagu, the rejection of the 'extremists' was a reaction to their rejection of the reforms.

Moreover, if directing efforts solely at moderates was a new move, it was also an incomplete one. Firstly, the Government of India did not share Willingdon's enthusiasm for actively promoting a moderate party. This was a unilateral move on Willingdon's part—even Sir Stanley Reed told him he was backing the wrong horse. Thus Chelmsford refused not only to cajole extremists, but also to meet and encourage moderates. He believed this would discredit them. He did no more than interview members of the Imperial Legislative Council; be believed a 'constitutional' party was possible, but, unlike Willingdon and Montagu, did not think it wise to try to create it. Moderates were valuable only in so far as they seemed independent of the government. In the same way, when Montagu suggested supporting the reforms through a government newspaper, provincial durbars, and what amounted to a campaign by local officers, Chelmsford explained that he was satisfied with progress, and deprecated measures in which the hand of government was too obvious. He evidently took a pessimistic view of the government's standing. And his reservations about moderates were made considering the viewpoint of those hostile to British rule, of the committed not the uncommitted, of extremists not moderates. Of course it was precisely this consideration which in the event made the new Assemblies unsatisfactory—Chelmsford gained members who would not oppose him on principle, but, because of the extremist boycott, these members were no longer felt to be quite independent and their support was thereby less valuable.[11]

Secondly, even Montagu soon bemoaned the moderates' 'lack of drive or energy'. George Lloyd, finding that moderates would not repeat in public what they had said in private, concluded that as a force in Indian politics they were practically useless. Reginald Craddock pointed out that the moderates were subject to social persecution and newspaper abuse if they supported the government. In Madras, where he had sought a non-communal moderate alliance, even Willingdon became disillusioned. The extremists, he recognized, had a simple demand, 'Home Rule now', and a press at their command; the moderates lacked leadership and organization, and a positive purpose—they did not 'do anything'.[12]

Thus there had been some flirtation with the idea of a moderate party. But it had come only when extremist opposition was inevitable; moreover no-one believed for long that a moderate alternative was reliable or promising. The Government of India (like the Indian people) were looking more and more towards the extremists: it was already clear that they were the voice of the future. It had been clear to many when the reforms were being written; thus they had not been conceived primarily as a sop to government supporters, an attempt to divide them from their fellow nationalists. Subsequent events—the extremist boycott, the moderate acceptance, the government reaction—were an obscuring of the government's intentions, not their natural outcome.

Two factors have compounded this confusion. The first is semantic. Of course the reforms were intended to encourage co-operation with the British, and in this sense were aimed at encouraging 'moderates' (those prepared to co-operate) and discouraging 'extremists' (those who refused). But this precise distinction between different politicians was itself a product of the debate on the Montagu-Chelmsford reforms. Hitherto the government had applied the labels more loosely. Only after the reforms was it obvious that 'extremists' were those who disapproved of the proposals and turned them down, and 'moderates' those who disapproved but agreed to accept the scheme as a sizeable step forward. The difference was not in the changes each group wanted, but in whether they would accept the reforms if the changes were not made.[13] Thus it must be understood that Montagu and Chelmsford did not direct their reforms at *the* moderates. They were not seeking to bolster up one group of people at the expense of another; they were trying to encourage one type of attitude wherever it might be found. And, in the pre-Gandhian situation, this type of attitude, a willingness to share the government with the British, included a wide political spectrum, from politicians (like Malaviya) regarded as extremist in the old sense, to some conservative and much honoured representative of an aristocratic family. Thus the reforms were aimed at all; but some people excluded themselves—namely the new type of extremist, the non-co-operator, who emerged and was identified through his rejection of the proposals after they had been made.

In the second place, it is true that the reforms were not expected to give complete satisfaction, especially to extremists (in the old sense of the word). Montagu and Chelmsford had had to consider many factors in deciding how much could be conceded. Chelmsford was influenced by the calculation that the Congress were asking for much more than they expected. It was also necessary to convince European opinion in India—in passing any India bill in Parliament, this opinion, as Chamberlain pointed out to Chelmsford, carried disproportionate weight. Chelmsford introduced this argument when Montagu wanted to extend the reforms to the structure of the central government; he had argued, 'We have to convince people at home and Europeans out here' that the central authority was indisputable 'in fact'.[14] But to say that different interests had to be balanced in this way, and that 'extremists' were not going to achieve everything they wanted, is quite different from saying that the government disregarded extremists' views, or that they expected dissatisfaction to take the form of a boycott. It was not obvious in 1917, or even before the end of 1918, that there would be politicians who would reject the proposals out of hand. To anyone versed in parliamentary procedure, it seemed that the government had made a large concession which, if skilfully exploited, could lead in a short time to a complete transfer of legislative power. Administrators alarmed at this prospect, and perhaps a little surprised at their own daring, at first did not imagine that Indian politicians could mistake or afford to decline the opportunity.[15] Indeed the boycott, when it came, owed more to other events—the Rowlatt Bill; the Panjab atrocities; the rise of Gandhi, the Ali brothers and others with little hope of benefit from legislative opportunities[16]—than to precise criticisms of the reforms: the proposals were so new when they were rejected by the Congress that few had had the opportunity to study them in detail.

Chelmsford had argued that the whole of the educated classes had to be considered. Changes were necessary, he held, because Indians had to be allowed to take responsibility and make mistakes; the alternative was to leave them discontented until everyone went 'over the precipice together'. He had also stood up against what was being described as a 'white rebellion'. After the reforms proposals were published, he wrote to the heads of provinces stressing that a general protest would be most improper and would strain racial relations—the heads were to discuss the situation privately and without publicity with prominent members of the various services, in order to reassure them.[17] Thus the reforms were not intended to divide the nationalists, but, between the two opposing interests of politicians and bureaucrats, they were unlikely wholly to commend themselves to the more advanced Indian leaders. The government hoped they would be accepted nevertheless; at this point they miscalculated. We have seen why.

And yet it may be that what had happened was more fundamental than this account suggests. As Chelmsford saw, the situation in India was changing rapidly and Indian demands were growing all the time. Montagu and Chelmsford had proposed reforms which led deliberately towards self-government within the Empire. But neither of them looked further ahead than that. Both of them envisaged at least some vestigial British presence in India. The Commonwealth itself was still in process of evolution, and many people in Britain were less clear than the Dominion governments about the degree of independence now enjoyed in the former colonies. Montagu and Chelmsford had looked forward as far perhaps as Dominion status for India, but they had not foreseen that this was going to require the complete handing over to Indians of all things Indian—including the princely states—and the complete withdrawal of British sovereignty and suzerainty as well as of day-to-day control.

Certainly a process of assimilating the princes had begun. Their relations with the British were being standardized—a necessary step towards any change in status. They were also asked to form their own Council for regular and formal conference with the government—this, in a sense, was an attempt to relate them to the British Indian constitution. And Chelmsford had told them: 'your States also must move with the times'—demands for freedom from restraint would not be confined to British India, and princes too would need to create not a beautiful façade but a building men could work. But in none of these measures is there much evidence of serious thinking about the princes. The Montagu-Chelmsford Report promised that they had no cause for anxiety, and by 1920 probably no-one had worked out what

Indian self-government would mean to them.[18] The reforms, limited by ideas of continuing British presence, offered little to concentrate princely minds on a future need to come to terms with new rulers. Rather, because princely relations were a reserved subject, transferred where possible to the centre, there was a tendency in the reforms to isolate the princes from contact with Indian self-government.

Ambiguous conclusions may be drawn also from the reformers' stated preference, later strengthened by the Joint Committee, for a conservative counterweight in the legislatures for the educated urban classes. On the one hand, this might be a legitimate desire to widen political involvement in preparation for devolving power; but, on the other hand, it may be that the local discretion over rules and franchise was used to shift the balance towards rural or conservative interests the more readily because of bureaucratic resistance to liberal reform.[19] Such provincial intransigence would show up the partial and hence fragile commitment to reform, of the British taken as a whole—the more so in that then as now the wide divergences within the ruling elite were not always recognized. The key—for both princes and franchise—is clearly the continued belief in a permanent British role in India, based on the certainty that the sub-continent was not one nation and the idea that one section of the divided communities neither could nor should rule the whole. In this sense, the basis of the reforms, emphasizing provincial devolution and responsibility, was a comment on Indian disunity.

Thus, it is open to debate how far the reforms marked a substantive change in British attitudes. In Assam an Indian was placed in charge of police, judiciary and prisons;[20] but in Bombay Lloyd refused to give the Law and Order portfolio to an Indian— his excuse was Indian inexperience, and yet one of the councillors considered for the post was a new member and presumably less experienced than the then senior councillor, Sir I. Rahimtoola. Lord Sinha was appointed the first Governor of Bihar and Orissa under the reforms; but Lloyd, in spite of Chelmsford's categorical advice, was reluctant to see Rahimtoola appointed Vice-President of his Council (and hence Acting Governor when necessary)— and the Secretary of State shared some of Lloyd's doubts.[21] Later criticisms of the reforms included cases of lack of co-operation between the two halves of the government or between civil servants and Indian ministers. Clearly there was a deep residue of habits of racial superiority.[22] Nothing of course, as we have seen, convinced the Congress of this fact more than the actions, evidence and subsequent treatment of General Dyer.

Indeed, there were Indians now in the Congress who were seeing much further ahead than Montagu and Chelmsford, not systematically but emotionally. Their aim was *swaraj*; their demand was beginning to be complete independence. In the event the Commonwealth changed, independent status was explicitly recognized, so that Indians were eventually to be satisfied with something which did not look so very different in kind from what they had wanted before 1918. But there had been a change. There had developed an urge not only for the substance but also for the form of self-government. It was the product of impatience with and alienation from the British and their 'satanic' rule.[23] And perhaps no reforms could have satisfied this drive. It might be argued, for example, that Chelmsford's government's success in limiting changes at the Government of India level precipitated the Congress boycott. Almost certainly this was not the case. Objections that the reforms were inadequate hardened into rejection because of external factors, notably the aftermath of the Panjab disturbances. Yet, in addition, underestimates of the reforms were general. Perhaps Montagu and Chelmsford, directing themselves specifically to a goal, invited Indians to assess precisely what the British meant by self-government; and this of course revealed that the rulers and the ruled meant different things. Here is one reason why the reservations in the reforms were so galling and received so much more attention than the concessions. The British guarded some areas of the constitution. Reforms implied concessions within a system, when 'extremists' wanted the system to end.

This does not explain, however, why the leaders decided against disrupting the constitution from within, as they could have done. For example, in Bengal, in the only instance of real friction in the brief post-reforms period under Chelmsford, the new legislature was, according to Ronaldshay, 'seized with a fit of mad irresponsibility' expressed chiefly by reducing the police grant to 23 lakhs. Ronaldshay calculated that he would have to restore the grant by extraordinary powers or reduce numbers in an already short-handed force. This shows of course that British supremacy—and

British judgment of what was responsible conduct—stood undisturbed in the last resort, and on these grounds, as well as for the suspicion of the continuance of old attitudes, the Congress abstention would be understandable. And yet, as it happened, the dispute in Bengal was resolved not by executive action but by a skilfully stage-managed debate in which the practical consequences of the budget changes were brought home to the legislature, which in due course and by an overwhelming majority approved supplementary grants to save the situation: the conclusion here must be that Ronaldshay was showing extreme reluctance to go against the will of the new assembly,[24] and presumably, therefore, that the 'extremists' might have used the reforms, as Motilal Nehru was later to try to do, to manoeuvre the effective power away from the government. It was the political situation as a whole which decided the Congress against this course: the questions remain whether the pressure would have been more effective inside than it was outside the assemblies, but also whether the consolidation of Congress power through the attempts at controlled mass agitation was not a necessary stage of political evolution, and indeed whether quite apart from individual politicians the nationalist cause itself could have survived a period of co-operation at this time, in the prevailing atmosphere of suspicion, grievance and mistrust.

To stress the limitations and unpopularity of the reforms is not to deny they were deeply significant. It became fashionable to deride them; but what strikes one, in comparison with British attitudes prevailing in 1916 or even with Indian expectations as in Sinha's Congress address of 1915, is how extensive they were. In 1918 one writer proposed to end the Indian problem by promising a plebiscite after fifty years, to decide on British withdrawal—or, if 'sedition' continued in the interim, after a maximum of a hundred years.[25] The Montagu-Chelmsford reforms, though they did not decide the timetable, in effect set British and Indians together on a path which was to lead to complete provincial transfer in a little more than fifteen years and final withdrawal in less than thirty. In this sense their immediate practicality and the revealed short-comings were irrelevant—indeed were expected of a transitional arrangement.[26]

The statement of a goal and the first steps pushed the British firmly in the direction of the future, even though the goal was limited and the first steps hesitant, even though neither had commended themselves to the more demanding of the Indian nationalists. In another sense from the one Chelmsford intended, the reforms mapped out the way to go. The test of the commitment was not long in coming. One need not look as far as the debates about Dominion status in the time of Irwin. Even in 1922 Lloyd George told the House of Commons that 'in no circumstances' would Britain 'relinquish her responsibility', that 'it remains to be seen' whether a Western system of government was 'suitable for India', and that whatever the Indians' success 'as parliamentarians or as administrators' he could 'see no period when they can dispense with the guidance and the assistance of the small nucleus of the British Civil Service of British officials in India'. This accorded with the Montagu-Chelmsford view in substance if not emphasis, but it caused a sensation in India; and, when Lord Reading asked for assurances that the intention was not to renege on the pledge of 1917 or the promises of indianization, these assurances were forthcoming. Vincent, who was furious about the speech, addressed the legislature in terms which were described by Cecil Kaye, then Director of Central Intelligence, as follows: 'I have seldom been more impressed. . . . Its undercurrent—not in any way expressed in words—is that European Government in India is doomed, and that the not remote future must see its elimination—complete, or at any rate, almost complete. I am sure he is right . . .'.[27]

Indeed, as one civilian put it, 'if one drops the camouflage, the scheme . . . is not compatible with the continued existence of the I.C.S. on its old lines'; or, as Du Boulay wrote, 'These changes undoubtedly mean that the end of the great Indian services is on the horizon . . .' (for *gentlemen* would not serve under the new conditions). Meston, drawing up arrangements for the services, on the India Office reforms committee in 1918, had provided that some allowance might be made privately for members who, through 'colour prejudice', could not work under Indian ministers; but there was to be no *general* option of serving or not. The norm was to be that Europeans should adjust or leave. Meston had written in 1912 that '. . . it seems indisputable that dominion must be maintained so long as we are able to maintain it', but he had favoured a goal of colonial self-government, and in 1917 had argued, not necessarily contradicting himself, that they need not fear the passing of sovereignty. In 1912 William Marris had proposed admitting that 'if the day of colonial self-government ever comes for India she and not the Empire will then decide' whether or not she would remain a member.[28]

The 1909 reforms may be broadly characterized as a sop to Indian opinion; those in 1935, on the positive level, as an attempt to resolve practical difficulties. Those of 1919 were both of these things, but also centrally concerned with abstract constitution-making: the reformers tried to think about what sort of India they wanted to create—in particular a 'common citizenry'—and though the practical and political considerations made an alloy of this idealism, the mix was headier on this than perhaps on any other occasion. Thus the goal was made explicit, and to repudiate it became not only impolitic but dishonourable. Further concessions were inevitable; and, once self-government were attained, it was obvious that British suzerainty would last only as long as it was needed (as officials believed) and Indians wanted it.

2

The same idealism and the resultant political logic meant, as this book has sought to show, that the reforms decision inevitably spilled over into other spheres. It introduced changes both quantitative and qualitative. In executive councils, legislatures, electorates and local boards many more Indians were to be associated with government. They were bound to influence policies and change attitudes. Moreover, in these reforms, some Indians were to be not just associated but involved in government—they were being asked to administer and not just to advise the administrators. In all spheres this was to make even their advice more persuasive.

A range of policies in the political arena was affected. In dealing with agitation before September 1917, the government had accepted that once an illegality had been established to local satisfaction punishment would follow. They had defended against provincial attacks their principle of allowing constitutional agitation; but they had been uncertain about how their policy should apply to the Home Rule Leagues, and had acquiesced in contradictory local approaches. After the August Declaration, however, they realized that the main need was for calm. They believed this could be secured only by conciliatory methods. They began to accept that the normal reason for acting against agitators should be considerations of tactics and expediency. They saw, and insisted that local governments consider, the possible repercussions of provincial decisions. They argued that calm depended on avoiding the repression of those popular agitators who were known nationally.

In response to a new form of agitation the government had extended the principle of non-interference with political movements to cover popular agitation, rejecting the use of repression as an automatic reaction in this sphere; at the same time they conceived the idea of using this principle as a political tactic. Faced with a national movement, a national policy had evolved. This, a refurbishment of a traditional approach, remained Chelmsford's and Vincent's habitual method for coping with such agitation. The lesson learnt in 1917 with Annie Besant, repeated with horrible emphasis with Gandhi in 1919, was applied for the remainder of the viceroyalty; it encouraged the government to be tenacious in advocating the same approach in 1920 and 1921; it was left as a legacy for Lord Reading.

It is important to note that the two elements in the approach—expediency and principle—had become distinct. The same principle was in theory applied to local figures as to national, but in practice the interpretation varied. In April 1919, for example, K. N. Roy, editor of the Lahore *Tribune*, a 'strictly moderate' newspaper, was arrested on a charge of sedition; in June he was sentenced to two years' rigorous imprisonment. The Government of India agreed that the sentence had been severe, and, after the Panjab had refused to reduce it, they themselves shortened it to three months. But, in reply to Montagu's query, they stressed that Roy had been attacking government at a time of grave unrest, and having an effect on Panjabi readers which he would not have had on Bengalis accustomed to 'journalistic vehemence'. Montagu accepted this rather extraordinary justification, but wondered if it would not be wise, for reasons of policy, to make a distinction in treatment between political and criminal prisoners. The Government of India disagreed, refusing to believe 'the organisers and preachers of violence' 'less criminal than their misguided dupes', or to see how to distinguish between direct enticement and 'inflammatory speech leading to crime'. Montagu's reasoning seems to have been that political miscreants were likely to be more receptive to re-education. But, if this is debatable, the government's response was quite unsound: it is not true that to speak or write violently is the same as to plan or carry out a violent crime, and it is, if anything, more difficult in practice to distinguish between political actions according to probable results, than between political crime and 'criminal' crime. The government were on stronger ground when they argued that prisoners should be distinguished according to their crimes not their motives; but their arguments were really an attempt to assimilate the local action against Roy to their own scheme of things. Once a province had acted publicly, the centre found themselves (unless they were prepared for public disagreements) in the position of leading from behind, rather like Shah Alam bestowing an imperial title on General Lake. And yet, even in this case, their arguments are explicable only with reference to the policy of non-interference: the theoretical line had to be drawn between ordinary politics and politics likely to lead to crime, not between political and criminal motives, for the government firmly believed they must suppress crime not politics, and thus persuaded themselves that the politics to be suppressed were criminal in the same way as theft or murder.[29] It is to miss the point about the Government of India, to think of it primarily as a political animal, scheming about how to thwart Indian ambitions, and not as a bureaucratic organ, concerned for the application of rules.

But, as we have seen, political considerations were important, and thus, though the principle had to be flexible in practice, the tactic was not. It was never acceptable to brand Gandhi a criminal without choosing a suitable moment. For lesser figures, such as K. N. Roy, the moment was less important. The result was that the lines of government policy were blurred in the public eye. The inevitable outcome was a suspicion that the intention was to suppress politics, even though the pretence was of suppressing crime. The confusion of violence with the political activity which was thought to lead to it, resulted in the discrediting of repressive measures which some Indians had otherwise been willing to accept. The Rowlatt Act was one casualty of this hardening of attitude. The Press Act was another. More than this, the confusion undermined the positive effect which non-interference might have been expected to have. It also clarified the nature of that policy. It showed it to be a central policy, in one way independent of the

principle on which it was based. The vital feature of the approach
was the emphasis on expediency. Non-interference, although it
related to a principle, was strictly tactical.

Thus non-interference could also be seen always as interference
held in abeyance. It was recognized that prosecution would be
unavoidable or even desirable in certain circumstances. It is
fair to say that by the end of 1920 the policy was intended to
manoeuvre Gandhi into a position in which it would be safe to
arrest him. This is not to say that when Gandhi's arrest came in
1922 it was precisely at the moment Chelmsford would have
chosen. It has been described as a coup for Reading,[30] but it may
have been more the result of a fortuitous balance of forces influencing him. Lloyd had advocated strong measures in December 1921
but apparently allowed himself to be dissuaded. Vincent had
favoured an arrest then, and perhaps Chelmsford would have
agreed, in that Gandhi had openly repeated an offence for which
the Ali brothers had been imprisoned. But Reading's Council,
with its three Indian members, had overruled the Home Member,
apparently agreeing with Cecil Kaye, Director of Criminal Intelligence, that the arrest should be postponed until, if still necessary, it could be carried out 'with the support of the moderate
element'. In 1922, however, Lloyd and Willingdon visited Simla
and threatened to resign if Gandhi remained at large; thus,
according to Lloyd, they persuaded Reading to go against the
advice of his colleagues, notably Tej Bahadur Sapru. Whatever
the truth of this, it is clear that for such a decision the forces of
influence—British and Indian, central and provincial, the government and the 'moderate element' of the legislature—were those
forces which the constitutional reforms had created, and which
had already given rise to the policy of non-interference under
Chelmsford. He wrote to Reading that he was 'so glad . . . the
arrest, trial & sentence of our mutual friend Gandhi should have
passed off so quietly. It shows, I think, that you chose the psychological moment.' Chelmsford was right to believe that the moment
was of the essence—as it had come to be after the lesson of Annie
Besant in 1917.[31]

It might be thought that tactical non-interference, whose
advocates at their most optimistic hoped that agitation would
disappear if ignored, bore a family resemblance to Curzon's
policy of officially disregarding the Congress while allowing

some measure of appeasement. To maintain this would be to miss the point. Curzon believed his autocracy to be permanent and saw no reason to come to terms with Indian politicians; thus he refrained from attending to their aspirations. Chelmsford refrained from repression—because he envisaged transfer of powers and saw every reason for conciliation.

There is strong evidence, therefore, that it was the situation which produced the response, that the reform policy engendered the tactics towards agitation. Reading's first assessment was to deny Chelmsford's optimism, believing rather that agitation was really about swaraj and among the masses (hence dangerous), and concluding 'it is impossible to permit defiance of Government authority to continue. ... I know that in the next months it would be better to avoid opportunities for conflict, but nevertheless I cannot see Government authority persistently and openly flouted by incitements direct or indirect to violence.' It was in this mood that the Alis were arrested. But gradually Reading came to sound more like his predecessor: 'I may be optimistic about this but the impression is gradually being produced on my mind that Gandhi has passed the high-water mark of his popularity.'[32] Though of course Reading's view may have been objectively true, and more so perhaps than Chelmsford's optimism, what is significant is the change in tone, and hence priorities— away from bureaucratic support for 'Government authority' (automatic responses or rules), towards tactics which varied according to political considerations such as Gandhi's popularity. Thus it is possible to conjecture that here we are seeing the situation asserting itself.

Certainly Chelmsford's persistence, as we have seen, was not the result of enthusiastic support. There were a few voices favouring the policy. Percival Landon, whom the Prime Minister had asked to write to him on his tours in the East, was doubtful whether they should draw tight the noose, even if Gandhi ran his head into it. Ben Spoor, Labour Member of Parliament, reported to Montagu that nobody in India thought it would be wise to touch Gandhi.[33] But the rarity of unqualified support demonstrates the novelty of the government's approach; it may indicate that non-interference was not the wisest course. It is possible that Montagu and Lloyd, or even Ronaldshay and Willingdon, were right to have doubts, and that the task would have been easier if Gandhi had been stopped sooner or outlawed from the first. It is an open question whether Chelmsford's government, by using repression, could have retarded Indian political advance. It can only be established that they did not try to do so. Rather their policy became passivity tempered with legal action, even with regard to popular agitation, and a deliberate attempt to meet public opinion and further political progress.

Moreover, if the aim of British rule was the peaceful devolution of administration to Indians, then what is certain is that tactical non-interference, like the non-violent nature of Gandhi's opposition, made a large contribution to this end. It is probable that, had repression gained the ascendancy, had no lesson been learnt from Annie Besant, had Gandhi been imprisoned before his leadership was secure, then the Indian response might also have been different, and Chelmsford's legacy might have been a growing commitment to autocracy in the face of nationalist violence. Motilal Nehru told the Amritsar Congress in December 1919: 'violence cannot avail us. That is the special weapon of the West and we cannot hope to win freedom by armed force. But even if we could do so it would be a barren victory, a victory which would degrade and coarsen us . . .'.[34] The brutal reprisals in the Panjab had offered Motilal his stance of moral superiority; but, paradoxically, it had been partly the nature of his enemy—not least Chelmsford's government—which made it appropriate for such men as he to be the leaders of their countrymen.

3

The non-co-operation campaign forced the government to place added reliance and emphasis upon prosecution of minor figures, as an accompaniment to the continuation of non-interference at the centre. But it would be wrong to think that the advocates of conciliation were in any sense in retreat or disarray by the end of Chelmsford's viceroyalty. On the contrary non-interference was applied to or confirmed for wider and wider categories of activity as time went on.

Industrial unrest was growing, and there was a prospect of political involvement. But the government blamed strikes mainly on the disparity between price and wage increases, suspicions about profiteering and the capitalists' profits, the shortage of labour (accentuated by the influenza epidemic), and the reluctance of employers, especially in the Bombay mills, to grant concessions until strikes had occurred. Strikes were not yet accepted as a permanent public concern, but they were seen to be no longer a private matter Chelmsford's government evolved an attitude, very similar to his general policy towards agitation. They worked out rules restricting the use of troops in strikes, but encouraged diplomatic involvement by the local authorities as long as it was not obvious or compromising. Chelmsford's slogan was 'caution and watchfulness'.[35]

In the sphere of 'revolutionary' crime, too, conciliation gained ground, partly of course as a result of the end of the war, but also influenced by the new emphasis in policy. In 1919 restrictions were removed from the Ali brothers, accused of seditious conspiracy. In 1920 very large numbers of political prisoners—all who had not been convicted for crimes of violence—were released under amnesty. In March of that year, also, Vincent promised the legislature that the government would not use Regulation III of 1818 unless forced—an undertaking which moved towards that which had been called impossible when suggested by Montagu a year before.[36] Similarly the government abandoned the second Rowlatt Bill, with its permanent changes in the law. The Legislative Department claimed they had heeded 'official and unofficial opinions received'. But virtually all the official opinion, European and Indian, had favoured the Bill, as did a significant minority of the non-official opinion. Objections came almost exclusively from those non-officials who were politically active—from Bar Associations, District and Municipal Boards, and members of Legislative Councils—the very people who had been ignored in the passage of the first Rowlatt Bill. Only Robertson and the Chief Commissioner of Assam, Sir N. D. Beatson Bell, had expressed doubts about the wisdom of going ahead with the second Bill. The Government of India clearly shared these doubts. They may have been influenced also by Gandhi's offer to suspend civil disobedience if the Bill were abandoned.[37]

Most important, the introduction of the reforms in late 1920 was marked by confirmations of the conciliatory policy. To some extent these were inevitable reflections of the greater participation of Indians in the central government. But Chelmsford was also making concessions in a deliberate attempt to show that the 'extremist' boycott had been misguided. He wanted to prove that even in the much criticized arrangements for the Government of

ndia, the Indian representatives had an effective role. The first
eal test came in January 1921 when the government, despite the
dissent of the Commander-in-Chief, decided that they must agree
o reductions in the army budget if they were to be able to pass the
stimates in the reformed legislature. The only way of reducing the
llocation, it was decided, was to reduce army strength in India.
Chelmsford argued that, although the reduction would have to be
orced on the military authorities, he had to have something to
offer the new legislature. He was prepared to contemplate a
eduction in the number and proportion of British personnel in the
rmy. The Secretary of State protested; the King himself expressed
is concern. Chelmsford warned that if his policy were thwarted,
members of his government might claim the privilege of stating in
he legislature that they were voting under orders—if that happened they would never pass the budget, and Chelmsford would
have to use the extraordinary powers. Legislative members might
hen absent themselves from the Assembly or even join the
extremists'. The Secretary of State nevertheless insisted on
eferring the question to a sub-committee of the Committee of
mperial Defence in London. No decision was reached during
Chelmsford's viceroyalty, but later the reductions were refused—
even though Reading had adopted them, arguing that they were
not as large as was thought, and Chelmsford had continued to
support them in London.

At first sight, therefore, if the army case be taken as a measure of
British sincerity in their aims, as hoped for by Chelmsford, then it
eems that London was still ultimately dictating priorities,
undermining the reforms. But the lesson of India's participation
in international conclaves, her bargain over cotton duties and her
unilateral ban on indentured emigration, was otherwise: escalation
n the goal—from participation, to indianization, to independence—
was as natural for the army as for the constitution. In October 1920
he Esher Committee, appointed to consider army reorganization,
had recommended closer links with the Imperial Army, and,
contrary to Chelmsford's policy, a weakening in Government of
India supervision. The Imperial legislature reacted with a hostile
esolution on 17 February 1921 and a committee on 5 March; on
28 March in a series of resolutions it sought to establish the
principles that the army should be controlled in India, increasingly
ed by Indian and India-trained officers, and used for Indian

purposes or, if in imperial defence, then on terms of parity with Dominion armies. Though not immediately reflected in the army budget, nor indeed accepted by the India Government, such aims as these were already perceptible in one area, that of Indian commissions, where we have seen an important step forward. In 1921 the Commander-in-Chief, Lord Rawlinson, appointed the Shea Committee; this (at his prompting) advised complete indianization in 30 years. Even this was opposed in London. And yet, as Philip Mason has written, 'the British did busily dig their own grave, making a stumbling start with Parliamentary institutions and even more significantly with the introduction of Indian officers to the Indian army'. Painfully slow though progress was— far too slow for the pace of subsequent constitutional change— its direction, marked by policy in India, was unmistakable; and what the India Government had learnt, even in such a sensitive area, their masters in London would have to accept in the end.[3]

A principle of concern for the new legislature was followed, with more immediate results, in other spheres. On 24 February 1921 the government accepted a resolution of B. S. Kamat directing them to take steps, as far as practicable, 'to ensure that no action . . be taken on reports of commissions or committees . . . until an opportunity has been given . . . to the Indian legislature to express its opinion thereon'.[39] This statement reflected a wider intention of consulting the legislature. Similarly, in February 1921, to the Calcutta Club, an audience of Indians and Europeans, Chelmsford suggested—and (as we have seen) repeated his remarks to Montagu—that the reformed councils would be included in taking any measures necessary against extremists.[40] The logic of this was that methods not approved by the Assembly could no longer be adopted and that in general executive powers, unless reaffirmed by the legislature, were suspect.

This attitude was reflected in the government's policy toward the press, a policy which had been gradually changing. In March 1917 Chelmsford gave an 'uncompromising' reply to a deputation seeking abolition of the Press Act of 1910, but in August he suggested a liberalization of the Act after the war. In September 1918 the government refused a Legislative Council resolution for an enquiry and in October an unofficial suggestion from Montagu that they completely substitute judicial for executive controls Chelmsford did not favour amendment until after the verdict in

Besant's appeal to the Privy Council. By mid-1919, Charles
Cleveland was backing the Panjab Government in a campaign,
especially against the United Provinces, and most of all the
Independent of Allahabad, to see that 'every province' vigorously
attacked 'its seditious press'—and, though Vincent was generally
sceptical, the Home Department did make some gestures towards
recommending this. In December 1919 Montagu suggested a total
amnesty for the press; the Government of India disagreed, and
varying numbers were freed of control in different provinces. In
January 1920 the Secretary of State officially asked the government
to consider transferring to the courts the power of forfeiture
(though not imposition) of security. Judging from the comparative
rarity of forfeitures and the way the demand for security was used
as a weapon to prevent small concerns from operating, it was this
demand, not the forfeiture which was most effective in controlling
the tone of the press. Thus, in July, the Government of India
strongly advocated Montagu's idea to the local governments, as a
partial answer to Indian demands. The 'new political conditions of
the country', they asserted, 'justify a further relaxation of existing
restrictions.' The replies, received in December, mostly agreed.
But then Chelmsford telegraphed Montagu that his present idea
was to have Vincent move in the Legislative Assembly for the
appointment of a committee to investigate the press law and suggest
modifications. He was also, he claimed, prepared to allow an
enquiry into the whole range of repressive legislation including the
Rowlatt Act.[41]

The government moved for the repressive laws committee on 22
February 1921, rather less than a year after they had rejected a
similar resolution by Vithalbhai Patel. They gave undertakings
showing they intended a mainly non-official enquiry covering the
whole question of repressive laws and free to recommend the
abolition of the Press and other Acts. A committee under Tej
Bahadur Sapru, the Law Member, was appointed on 10th March,
and given the Secretary of State's despatch and a collection of
'seditious speeches' to consider. Lord Reading was later to remark
(of Regulation III of 1818, but with obvious implication for the
lesser powers) that he 'never expected that the Committee which
was appointed in Lord Chelmsford's time would do otherwise than
recommend . . . repeal.'[42]

Chelmsford had been concerned to avoid changing the law so

late in his term of office. Thus to bind his successor would not, he
believed, be good policy—if Reading wished to abandon the
powers, then he should do so and gain the good will. Chelmsford
was refusing to prejudice his successor's position; he was not
merely trying to delay or avoid the decision. By appointing the
committee his government had shown that they were prepared to
face the possibility of abandoning the Press Act. There would still
be control, but the simple and direct influence over the press
represented by securities and their forfeiture was unlikely to be
endorsed by any legislative committee. In May 1921, before the
committee first sat, Sapru and Vincent, the two official members,
were briefed and an order in council stipulated that the repeal
of the Press Act could be accepted; thus Reading's government
accepted the report 'in entirety' when it recommended the abandonment of virtually all repressive powers. In March 1922 the Press
Act, the Rowlatt Act and 22 other laws were repealed. This was the
logical outcome of moves under Chelmsford.[43]

    That first decision seems at first sight little short of amazing.
In terms of the principle in which the Government of India
professed to believe, there was perhaps nothing incompatible
between a possible abandonment of executive powers (supposedly
applied only to political criminals) and the prevailing situation, of
constitutional upheaval coupled with growing agitation. But, in
terms of government practice, it appears extraordinary that such
inauspicious times should have seen any relaxation or change of
heart. Why should this have occurred? It was not directly due to
the force of public opinion, which had been resisted for years;
it was not even due primarily to pressure from Montagu. In the
first place, the decision seems to have been taken in principle some
time between July and December 1920 when Montagu was calling
for a more limited change. In the second place, when the time came
to repeal the laws, Montagu showed signs of caution: he worried
about protection for the princes; he could not help feeling, he
informed Reading, that 'the substitution of legal process for
executive action . . . must be gradual' and the 'silly antics of the
non-co-operationists' were delaying the progress in that as in other
matters; and he expressed concern with regard to the powers of
deportation and internment formerly provided under Regulation
III of 1818, 'as to the difficulties of replacing them should an
emergency render it necessary to do so . . .'. And indeed, when in

August 1923 during the Alipore conspiracy case the Bengal
Government again called for a repressive law, they argued that 'the
position that the ordinary law is not sufficient . . . has never been
departed from'; and, though the Government of India did not
accept this, they did admit that in principle executive powers
would always be needed when a certain stage of revolutionary
conspiracy was reached.[44] No, the reasons for the change, under
Chelmsford, were those announced in the Calcutta Club speech,
the same that led to budget reductions in the army vote: the
reforms had been introduced, the Congress had boycotted them,
and Chelmsford had then resolved on a tactic of giving the new
assemblies as much weight as possible, to undermine the boycott
and to make the new constitution secure.

The move for the repressive laws committee was accompanied
by a debate on the Panjab disturbances, and followed the declaration made by the Duke of Connaught promising an 'incomparably
greater' involvement of the legislature in the formulation of policy.
Vincent, while defending the Press Act, admitted that generally it
was believed to be 'administered high-handedly' and to be 'unduly
wide' in scope. S. P. O'Donnell, Secretary to the government,
promised that future policy would be 'very largely influenced and
guided by non-official Indian opinion', and admitted that, as
members generally disapproved of wide executive powers, the
retention of such powers would be 'inconsistent with the spirit of
the new era' and with the government's desire to meet legitimate
Indian demands. Eardley Norton, a non-official European member
of the Assembly, responding to these remarks, said that he hoped
that in future the government would take the Assembly into their
confidence and not stand 'upon remote pillars in inaccessible
altitudes'. The appointment of the press committee was, he said, a
'happy augury of those more intimate relations which will exist
between the two sides of this House'.[45] Chelmsford and his
government hoped that Indians, both inside and outside the
Assembly, would draw the same conclusion.

As late as April 1920 Chelmsford had claimed that on matters of
law and order the only policy could be the 'indisputable supremacy
of the British raj'.[46] Less than a year later, in an attempt to work
the reforms and give prestige to the Assembly, he was apparently
willing to surrender one of the main weapons of that supremacy.
Repressive laws were the fruit of autocracy, tempered in the past

only in quiet times or when thought ineffective. On this occasion, however, their relaxation was being considered because they were 'inconsistent with the spirit of the new era', because the autocracy itself was being transformed. Chelmsford left the credit for abolition to Lord Reading; but for his government he wanted the credit of consulting the new Assembly in a responsible and constructive manner. He was not primarily interested in repressive laws or agitators; he was committed to the constitutional experiment. The effect of this concern, however, was that in the arena of politics the method of conciliation was firmly entrenched. The policy of tactical non-interference was supreme.

In March 1921, Chelmsford recorded his appreciation of his legislature. It has, he wrote to Harcourt Butler, 'fulfilled my highest hopes; ... it has shown a sense of balance and responsibility which could scarcely be surpassed. "Well begun is half done" and in leaving I feel happy that the great adventure, notwithstanding all the threatening storm clouds ..., has started under the fairest auspices.'[47] What Chelmsford's government had sought to show was that the reforms made very great concessions in what was envisaged as normal procedure, and that astute legislators could have made it difficult for abnormal procedures to be used. One observer considered that no Indian understood what had been conceded and that 'any Dominion which got the powers that India now has would have won everything it wanted in five years'.[48] In the Government of India deliberate policy encouraged adherence to the will of the legislature; and Chelmsford's constitutional methods ensured that his three Indian colleagues would have an impact upon policy. The same approach continued under Reading. Even with central finances, where the government had once resisted Indian participation as proposed by Montagu, the legislative committee set up under the reforms consisted of one official chairman and ten non-officials—'something of a rash venture', in Hailey's view, but also something to force responsibility in legislators faced with criticisms 'which otherwise officials would have to take'.[49]

4

Chelmsford's personal role in all the problems of government with which we have been concerned, is obscured by his insistence on consultation and 'constitutional' governorship. A special tribute was paid to him by Lord Sinha, both publicly and privately—on the latter occasion talking of India's *'rank ingratitude'*. Meston hoped history would be just to Chelmsford for his leadership of a great campaign. Bhupendranath Basu believed Chelmsford had 'saved the situation'; to Annie Besant he was the Viceroy who would stand out as having pursued a 'deliberate line of action, which has opened India's way to Freedom'.[50] Yet his personal unpopularity was striking. Calcutta was reported to have given him 'a very fair reception' on his last visit; but in Bombay Lloyd could not get farewell addresses for him from any Indian body, not even the municipality. He had reported to Chamberlain late in 1920 that he thought Chelmsford would feel only 'genuine relief' upon his departure in April.[51]

The Rowlatt Bill and the alienation of Gandhi had over-shadowed the successes—and perhaps rightly so, for these failures were crucial. Chelmsford saw the need to be political. But, faced with a tradition of secret government and a burden of accidents and atrocities, he did not have the sort of ability which would have been able to recover this ground. In his speech to the Calcutta Club in February 1921, he noted that he and his government were being called 'satanic'—'I am glad to think I still have a sense of humour,' he remarked. 'I have had many epithets applied to myself in my time, but the epithet of "Satanic" has broken entirely new ground.' Few rulers can have suffered such a campaign of vituperation as was undergone by Chelmsford at the end of his term. In 1921, Willingdon wrote—an epitaph for the viceroyalty—'The mere fact of Chelmsford's departure has done good.'[52]

This view cannot be left unqualified. Firstly, the fault was in Chelmsford's manner and not in lack of sympathy. His Calcutta Club speech stated the difficulty:

No man who takes up the post of Viceroy can have any but one desire: To magnify India in the Councils of the Empire; to espouse the cause of Indians within the Empire; to champion the aspirations of Indians so far as in him lies. But a Viceroy . . . must choose his own methods. The flamboyant speech, however much it may tickle the ear at the time, seldom if ever really achieves results. More can be done by quiet, un-ostentatious pressure: by arguments pruned of every epithet. I would say then: Trust your Viceroy and leave him to choose his own methods of working. He cannot be other than your champion.[53]

The Viceroy he spoke of was Reading; but the details referred to himself. Perhaps the achievements of Chelmsford's 'quiet pressure' are in retrospect impressive; but 'flamboyant speeches' might have popularized his policies and lessened the disasters. It is quite possible he was thinking of Hardinge when he expressed his distrust of ostentatious methods—a similar tone creeps into his references to his predecessor.[54] But he must have reflected on what an asset Hardinge's personal popularity would have been to him.

Secondly, one of the factors contributing to Chelmsford's unpopularity was undoubtedly the peculiar relationship with the India Office. Added to the stigma of the Mesopotamia Commission, was general suspicion or abuse of the Government of India. Perhaps Montagu's enthusiasm for new projects obscured what had already been done. Holderness, in a note seeking to correct the errors of the government, suggested in 1917 that minor decisions should be taken departmentally and that Council members should be kept informed. He showed that the Government of India were underrated even at the India Office.[55] Chelmsford in turn showed that he was not pleased to be instructed in practices he had already put into operation. In time there developed a feeling that the India Office was not really giving proper support. Craddock complained to Chelmsford that Montagu interviewed Indians who visited London, heard their grievances, and then promised to look into them—assuming that his officers were in the wrong.[56] Chelmsford's certainty of Montagu's support in 1918 was gradually replaced by cynicism at Montagu's 'extraordinary' sensitivity to questions in the Commons.[57] The Secretary of State was not thought altogether reliable. The Government of India had decided to send Meston to represent them before the Select Committee on constitutional reforms. Meston reported that Montagu's attack on the Panjab administration had become the general line for those who wished to cause trouble.[58] Later Montagu failed to prevent unfavourable peace terms for Turkey. In 1920 there was a disagreement over Chelmsford's conciliatory policy towards the Afghans— J. L. Maffey claimed that Montagu had been terrorized by Curzon. Roos Keppel (who favoured a strong policy) told him that Curzon was 'amazed at the invincible ignorance and optimism of the Government of India'; Maffey retorted, 'The Government of India are amazed at the invincible self-satisfaction and arrogance of Curzon'.[59] There were rumours that Montagu was unpopular in the House and with the Prime Minister—his reforms had not pacified India as he had promised; his fighting speech on the

Panjab disturbances had antagonized the Commons and put into jeopardy the vote supporting the condemnation of General Dyer. The Government of India's confidence had been eroded. In addition, there were attacks from all sides following the constitutional reforms and the Hunter Committee—most of these rebounded on the central government. The government's credit in India, as Maffey pointed out, was deeply affected by the credit given in England. There was not much being given—and Montagu did not seem to be providing the outspoken support that was needed to redress the balance.

Montagu was still popular with Indian politicians—and this too did not help Chelmsford. There had been some opposition to Montagu's visit in 1917 on the grounds that the presence in India of the Secretary of State would undermine the position and prestige of the Viceroy. The fears may have had some justification. Certainly Montagu received credit for most that was thought good, and Chelmsford blame for most that was not. He told his legislature in September 1918 that there were two schools of thought on the constitutional reforms—one thought the Secretary of State was the villain and the Viceroy his unhappy victim, signing against his better judgment; the other (the Indian politicians) thought that 'a sympathetic Secretary of State' had been 'enmeshed in the net of the cold hard bureaucracy'.[60] Neither view was flattering to Chelmsford. In a sense each denigration compounded all the others: the government's unpopularity with politicians influenced the assessment by the local governments, and their distrust—with its hints of disagreements—added in turn to the suspicions of the politicians. The difficulties with the India Office, the hostility real and rumoured, were the most potent element in this cycle. The reputation of Chelmsford and his government was not likely to survive the belief that there was a more liberal attitude and consequently disapproval in London.

Chelmsford's unpopularity but also his achievements are therefore traceable to his methods of government, which reflected both the strengths and the shortcomings of his personality. Inevitably his insistence on consultation and joint responsibility was misread as subservience. Paternalists like Lord Willingdon could not understand the method—Willingdon's verdict was that Chelmsford 'would never use his personal authority'.[61] In 1918 that other autocrat, Lord Curzon, wrote implying that the Foreign

Department dictated Chelmsford's policy on Persia. Chelmsford replied sharply: 'This is not so. I am not so presumptuous as to think I can rule India without the advice of my Department . . ., but equally on broad questions of policy my Departments do not run me.' He claimed, however, to be indifferent to imputations of weakness. Montagu once advised him to let himself go. 'Your instincts are right,' he wrote; 'your judgment is sound; let your colleagues know more fully what you want; let them feel your leadership.' Lord Chelmsford replied:

The policy of the attainment of the goal was my policy; . . . the policy of inviting you out was my policy, and I think you will own that I had only to lift my little finger and I could have obtained dissent from the majority of the proposals to which you and I with certainly the bulk of my colleagues have given agreement. I cite these things not to obtain credit, for they will remain locked up in our correspondence, but to show my deliberate method. I believe I can carry my colleagues with me, but if I can, it is not by the obtrusion of my own fiat, but by patience and command of temper.[62]

The contemporary verdict remained, and has marked the vice-royalty as a failure. Yet it is worthwhile to look again at its achievements. It had helped in the successful conclusion of a great war; it had fostered a new international and imperial status for India; it had investigated the possibility for changes in education and for state involvement in industry; it had tried to remedy the disability of economic exploitation and racial discrimination; it had devised a policy for dealing with a new type of agitation; it had refrained from beginning a conflagration by suppressing the Khilafat and non-co-operation movements; it had controlled the Hijrat; it had begun to loosen the strait-jacket of executive powers, but had reduced the threat of 'revolutionary' conspiracy; most of all it had initiated, fought for, worked out, defended and finally seen the introduction of epoch-making constitutional reforms. It had done all this while staff and money were in short supply; while energies were diverted by unprecedented difficulties with nationalist agitation; while both the Government of India and the Viceroy were supposed to be less than usually distinguished by ability or imagination. The reputation and the achievement contradict one another.

It is not difficult to see how this happened. The Jallianwala Bagh infected all, and did so at a time when rising prices, epidemics, Muslim grievances and social insecurity—all matters outside the government's control and some of them world-wide problems—magnified and distorted the public reaction. Chelmsford, for all his personal charm, was not ready with informal speeches and imaginative gestures to restore confidence. His greatest coup—the reforms, the deliberate relating of government policy to the goal of a future transfer of power—was at first attributed solely to Montagu and then, by some Indians, rejected altogether. His cautious policy towards unrest pleased neither the agitators nor the loyalists nor many of the officials. It is now possible to be more judicious. Alongside the undoubted failures—the indecisiveness over the Panjab, the general lack of tact, the tendency to be secret, formal and unyielding—must be placed the very considerable achievements of a remarkable period of progress and change.

What had happened during these years was that, because there had evolved a permanent articulate opposition, the government's policies were being judged and were having an effect as a whole. Failures in one area prejudiced success in another; and at the same time Indian demands and expectations constantly rose higher. Hardinge, after a grand gesture in ending the partition of Bengal, had been able to make do with little more than promises. Chelmsford had been expected to put the promises into effect. Hardinge, too, had managed to introduce repressive laws under cover of the war; Chelmsford had tried to retain them during the peace, as a last resort in dealing with internal hostilities. But the legacy he passed on to Reading was a virtual commitment to eschew such executive powers in future.

In 1916 when Chelmsford asked 'what is the goal of British rule?', his intention was to start enquiries on constitutional reforms. But his conclusions inevitably affected policies in other fields. Important though it is that the reforms did not anticipate an end to British dominion, it is even more significant that nonetheless, in the aim of self-government and in practical steps towards it, they did envisage a new kind of constitution for India, a new kind of role for Indians. If the goal were to be future transfers of power—not as a pious aspiration but as an active principle of policy embodied in immediate steps—then public opinion had to be scrutinized and attended to, political activity had to be seen in a generous light, the use of repressive powers had to be reconsidered. And each of these changes influenced or made necessary the others. The autocratic and bureaucratic had to take account of and begin to accommodate the future rulers of India; and this process was expressed partly in an increased awareness of interdependence between different spheres of government.

This awareness was one of the achievements of this administration. It sought coherence. It sought it in method by collective decision-making, and in policy by the enunciation of the goal. We too must assess all the policy. We see then that all the political moves—international changes, tactical non-interference, positive advances, publicity, repression, constitutional and secretariat reforms—were part of one whole, conceived as complementary, directed towards a deliberate goal. It is in this sense, not in any total abandonment of old methods or prejudices, that Chelmsford's viceroyalty marks a new starting-point.

Thus there was one way in which events between 1916 and 1921 markedly influenced the course of future government policy. All the participants in the reforms proposals (though with varying degrees of vehemence) had thought it obvious that India should not become 'a single autonomous Dominion'. But, though Lloyd George in 1921, as we have seen, or Hailey in a speech in 1924 might try to perpetuate this position, it was inevitably eroded. In 1929 Irwin's 'Dominion status' declaration agreed that India had been promised colonial self-government not only as it was in 1917 but also in any extended form it might subsequently take—a self-governing India could not be subordinate in standing to other partners in the Empire. Of course this was precisely the insight of William Marris as early as 1912, but under Irwin it had been officially and publicly endorsed. Now once more, as in 1917, there was no going back, whatever the private regrets of British administrators and politicians. What was the force which ensured this? It was the situation which such announcements created as they were put into practice; the more they were put into practice the more they became entrenched. Thus it was, I believe, Irwin's pressure which forced the 1929 statement: he was reacting to conditions in India which the previous decade had produced. And not the least potent of the forces then had been the revolutionary direction adopted during the first world war, in indianization, international relations, constitutional reforms and political tactics.[63]

True, progress in all spheres was too slow; true, the vision was limited, generally by belief in British suzerainty and specifically by policies towards the princes and separate electorates; true, the political approach had bypassed not solved the central dilemma of how to control an agitation which could neither be appeased nor permanently repressed. And true, finally, the policies of the Chelmsford administration were continued with varying and contradictory emphasis in later years—not least by Irwin himself under whom, for example, tactical non-interference briefly became a policy of treating with Gandhi as an equal, while consultation took the extreme form of Round Table conferences to decide constitutional questions which hitherto and later were reserved to the executive. The first world war period did not have all the answers; but it had taken steps which were interrelated and hence self-supportive. Of course there was throughout for the British a tension between the promise of advance and their need to hold on to power. This had been fought out in the 19th century over such issues as the indianization of the I.C.S.; and the battle was certainly not suddenly conceded in 1920. Dyarchy was still in one sense the old sort of compromise between Indian opportunity and executive control. But the avowed purpose was new—and it is here that we see the significance of the fact that in this viceroyalty political policy increasingly conformed to the constitutional goal. Though the same emphasis, the same conjunction between political policy and reform, did not continue uninterrupted under future administrations, yet the progress towards coherence in the postwar period could not be entirely forgotten: the liberal goal announced in Chelmsford's time gained authority from the administration as a whole, from both the prompt introduction of the reforms and the gradual accommodation to them of political policy in general.

At the same time the sins of omission under Chelmsford also had repercussions over the following decades. The rejection of the changes by nationalists illustrated that, because of the qualifications implicit in Chelmsford's and the British vision, the programme was unacceptable to the leaders of India; that alien and autocratic rulers would not be able to adapt themselves and would have no role to play in the new politics of a democratic state. Only one outcome was possible in the conflict between Indian self-determination and British supremacy.

APPENDIX I

Martial Law Sentences in the Panjab[1]

Chart I. No. of persons 1. tried; 2. convicted; 3. acquitted or discharged

A. Martial Law Commissions	852	581	271
B. Summary courts	1,437	1,179	258
(including area officers	564	495	69)
C. Ordinary Municipal Courts	13	11	2
D. Special D. of I. Tribunal	56	21	35

Chart II. Sentences under martial law

	by summary courts	by martial law commissions	by D. of I. tribunals	Totals
For 'waging war'	—	355	8	363
Other offences	1,179	226	13	1,418
Total	1,179	581	21	1,781
of whom:				
served sentences	630	83	1	714
released	189	16	—	205
pardoned (1/1/20)	36	—	—	36
released through proclamation (28/12/20)	232	288	9	529
(some conditionally	—	104	5	109)
released through reviewing judges	92	9	—	101
still in gaol (31/7/20)	—	80	6	86

Chart III. Conviction for murder or waging war

	by martial law commissions	by D. of I. tribunals
A. Sentence by court		
—death	104	—
—transportation for life	248	8
B. Sentence under government review		
—death	20	—
—transportation for life	25	—
—over 2 years' imprisonment	263	8
—under 2 years' imprisonment	40	—
C. Releases		
—by government review	8	—
—by proclamation (23/12/20)	248	6
—by reviewing judges	3	—
D. Still in gaol (31/7/20)	76	2

Chart IV. Comparative figures for

	Bombay	Delhi
Convictions during disturbances		
—total	123	21
—for 'waging war'	36	—
—for other offences	87	21
Subsequently pardoned	—	—
Sentences reduced	18	2
Released (31/7/20 Bombay; 2/8/20 Delhi)	72	9

APPENDIX II

Some Biographical Notes

THIS list gives additional information about persons mentioned in the text, in cases where the person may not be well known, or the information may be relevant to the discussion. There is no attempt to give comprehensive information.

ALI, Muhammad—Scholar and translator of the Quran; member, Central Khilafat Committee, 1920–4; Congress President 1923; leader, Civil Disobedience Movement (in opposition to Gandhi), 1930.

ALI, Shaukat—brother of Muhammad; civil servant for 15 years; Khilafat leader; representative of Muslim League, Round Table Conference; member ILA, 1934.

ANSARI, Dr. M. A.—1880–1936; Muslim League President 1920; Congress General Secretary 1920; Congress President 1927; imprisoned 1930 and 1932.

ARUNDALE, G. S.—1878–1945; Theosophist; Honorary Professor of History (1903) and later Principal, Central Hindu College, Banaras (founded by Annie Besant in 1898).

BARNES, Sir George Stapylton—barrister; comptroller with Board of Trade, 1904–13; member, various wartime financial commissions; Commerce and Industry Member, G/I, 1915.

BASU, Bhupendranath—Member, Bengal legislature, 1909–12, ILC, 1916, and S/S Council, 1917–24; Congress President 1914.

BEACHCROFT, C. P.—Acting Puisne Judge, Calcutta High Court.

BEATSON-BELL, Sir N. D.—ICS 1886; Member, G/Bengal, 1914–18; CC/Assam, 1918 (Governor, Jan.—March 1921).

BISHAMBER NATH—vakil; Government Pleader and Public Prosecutor, Ajmir; member, Ajmir Municipal Committee, 1896; famine worker, 1899–1900 and 1905–6; Government guest at Delhi coronation durbar.

BRUNYATE, Sir James—ICS 1889; FD Secretary 1914–17; Member, S/S Council, 1917, and committee on Indian exchange and finance, 1919.

BUTLER, Sir Spencer Harcourt—ICS 1888; Member, G/I, 1910–15; LG/Burma 1915; LG/United Provinces, Feb. 1918 (Governor, Jan. 1921).

CARMICHAEL, Baron, of Stirling—MP 1895–1900; G/Victoria, 1908–11; G/Madras 1911; G/Bengal, 1912–17.

CHAKRAVARTI, B.—barrister; Member, Bengal legislature; Minister 1927; founding member of National Party under Sapru (q.v.), 1926.

CHANDAVARKAR, Sir Narayan Ganesh—retired Bombay judge; pleader 1881; Editor, *Indu Prakesh*; Delegate to England 1885; Member, Bombay legislature, 1897–1900; Congress President 1900; High Court judge 1901–13; Vice-Chancellor, Bombay University 1909.

CHELMSFORD, Lord (Frederick John Napier Thesiger, 3rd Lord and 1st Viscount)—born 1868; educated Winchester, and Oxford (B.A. first class in law); Fellow of All Souls, 1892–9; barrister 1893; Member, London School Board, 1901–4, and London County Council, 1904–5; G/Queensland, 1905–9; G/New South Wales, 1909–13; officiating Governor General of Australia, Dec. 1909–Jan. 1910; alderman, London County Council, 1913; Privy Councillor 1916; V and Governor General of India, 4 April 1916–2 April 1921; First Lord of the Admiralty 1924.

CHEVIS, William—ICS 1883; District Judge 1899; Judge, Panjab Chief Court, 1914 (temporary from 1911).

CHIROL, Sir Valentine—onetime director, Foreign Department, *The Times*; correspondent of *Times* in India, 1905–6; Member, Public Service Commission, 1912; author of many books, chiefly on Middle East and India.

COBB, H. V.—ICS 1883; CC/Coorg, 7 April 1916–8 March 1920.

CRADDOCK, Sir R. H.—ICS 1882; CC/Central Provinces 1907; Home Member, G/I, 1912–17; G/Burma 1918.

DAS, Chittaranjan—prosperous lawyer; defender of Aurobindo Ghose in Alipore Bomb Case; Mayor of Calcutta; Congress President 1921; member, Swaraj Party (with Motilal Nehru and N. C. Kelkar).

DONOUGHMORE, Earl of (Richard Walker Hely Hutchinson)—1875–1948; Chairman of Committees (Lords), 1911–31; Privy Councillor 1918; on deputation to India, 1917–18; considered for viceroyalty 1915.

DU BOULAY, Sir J. H.—ICS 1887; PSV 1915; HD Secretary from 1916; temporary Home Member, G/I, 1917–1918; temporary Member, G/Bombay, 1918; member, Jails Committee, 1919.

DUFF, General Sir Beauchamp—Commander-in-Chief in India, 8 March 1914 to 1 Oct. 1916.

DUKE, Sir F. W.—ICS 1882; Member, G/Bengal, 1910–14; Member, S/S Council, 1914–19; on deputation to India, 1917–18; Under Secretary of State for India, Jan. 1920.

DYER, Brigadier-General R. E. H.—born Panjab 1864; transferred to Indian Army 1888; awarded decorations in Burma (1886–7), on the Northwest Frontier (Hazara, 1888; Waziristan, 1902; Zakka Kehl,

1908), and mentioned in despatches, 1914–18 War; Commander, Jullundur training brigade, 1917; injured in riding accident, 1917, invalided for one year, suffered increasing paralysis (paralysed 1921); responsible for Amritsar massacre 1919; invested as a Sikh by guardians in the Golden Temple for services to its protection; appointed to active service in Afghan War; forcibly retired.

GAIT, Sir E. A.—ICS 1882; Member, G/I, 1912; LG/Bihar and Orissa 1915.

GRANT, Sir A. Hamilton—ICS 1894; Assistant Secretary, FD, 1903; on mission to Kabul, 1904–5; Deputy Secretary, FD, 1912, and Secretary, May 1916; CC/Northwest Frontier Province, Sept. 1919.

HAILEY, W. M.—ICS 1894; Secretary, G/Panjab, 1907; with FD, 1908; CC/Delhi, 1913; on deputation with reforms committees 1918; Finance Member, Dec. 1919; G/Panjab, 1928–34; Baron 1936; Privy Councillor 1949; O.M. 1956.

HILL, Sir C. H. A.—ICS 1885; Member, Royal Commission on decentralization, 1907; Agent to Governor General, Kathiawar, 1908; Member, G/Bombay, 1912; Member, G/I, 1915–20.

HIRTZEL, Sir Arthur—joined India Office 1894; Assistant Under-Secretary of State 1917; Deputy 1921.

HOLDERNESS, Sir T. W.—ICS, 1870–1901; joined India Office 1901; Under-Secretary of State, 1912–19.

HOLLAND, Sir T. H.—ICS 1890, as Assistant Superintendent, Geological Museum and Laboratory; Professor of Geology, Manchester, 1909; President, Indian Industries Commission, 1916; President, Munitions Board, 1917; Member, G/I, 1920 (temporary, 1919).

HORNIMAN, B. G.—editor, *Bombay Chronicle*; formerly with the *Daily Chronicle*, *Morning Leader*, *Daily Express*, *Manchester Guardian*, and *Calcutta Statesman* (1906); correspondent of *The Times*.

ISLINGTON, Baron (Sir John Dickson-Poynder)—1866–1936; Conservative MP 1892 (became a Liberal over tariff reform, 1905); Member, London County Council, 1898–1904; Governor of New Zealand 1910; Privy Councillor 1911; Chairman, Public Services Commission, 1912; Parliamentary Under-Secretary of State for India, 1915–19. According to *The Times* obituary (8 Dec. 1936), he was 'unassuming without shyness, and able without a touch of intellectual aloofness'.

JAMNADAS DWARKADAS—Home Ruler; founder editor, *Young India*, 1916–19; Member, India Tariff Commission, 1923; Member, Congress and Bombay Municipal Corporation.

KELKAR, N. C.—editor, *Kesari* (1897–9 and 1910–31) and *Mahratta* (1897–1919); President, Poona Municipality, 1918 and 1922–4 (Councillor, 1898–1924); President, Bombay Provincial Congress, 1920; Member, Home Rule deputation, 1919; Member, ILA, 1923 and 1926; originally (until 1896) a pleader.

KHAN, Sardar Sahibzade Sultan Ahmed—Barrister; Member for Appeals, Gwalior State; Member, Hunter Committee.

KHAPARDE, Ganesh Shrikrishna—1854–1938; advocate; co-worker of Tilak; member, Home Rule deputation, 1919; Chairman, District Board, for 17 years; Member, ILC (re-elected 1925).

KITCHLEW, Dr. Saif-ud-din—German educated; barrister; Khilafatist; Muslim political leader, Amritsar.

LAJPAT RAI, Lala—1856–1928; lawyer; Arya Samajist; deported 1907; Congress President 1919 (Calcutta).

LLOYD, Sir G. A. (later Lord)—HM attache, Constantinople, 1905; MP, 1910–18 (war service, 1914–17); G/Bombay 1918.

LOWNDES, Sir G. R.—formerly a Leader at the Bombay Bar; Legal Member, after Dec. 1915.

LYTTON, Lord—Parliamentary Under-Secretary after 1920.

MACLAGAN, Sir E. D.—ICS 1883; career largely in Panjab—Chief Secretary, 1914; ED Secretary, G/I, 1915; LG/Panjab, 26 May 1919 (Governor, Jan. 1921).

MAFFEY, Sir John—ICS 1899; officiating Deputy Secretary, F&PD, 1915; PSV 1916; Chief Political Officer, Northwest Frontier Province, May 1919.

MALAVIYA, Madan Mohan—1861–1946; vakil; journalist; Congress President 1908 & 1918; Member, United Provinces legislature, 1902; Member ILC & ILA; a founder of the Hindu University, Banaras.

MARRIS, Sir W. S.—ICS 1895; Under-Secretary, HD, 1901; temporary appointments in India Office 1915, and as Inspector-General of Police, United Provinces, 1916, and as joint secretary, HD, 1917; drafter, Montagu-Chelmsford Report and on deputation with S/S to England, 1918; Secretary, HD, 1919; G/Assam, 1921. (On p. 122, above, Marris is mentioned as Officiating Secretary, HD, in 1913. The *India Office List* does not record this appointment; but the printed copy of the Secret Circular No. 89/100, 8 April 1913, in *H. Poll.*13, May 1913, and the type-written copy on the Press Act file, *IOR* J&P4468/19, are clearly signed W. S. Marris, Officiating Secretary etc., and from internal evidence must be correctly dated.)

MAJUMDAR, Ambika Charan—1851–1922; Lawyer 1877; Congress President 1916.

MESTON, Sir J. S. (later Baron)—ICS 1883; FD Secretary 1909; LG/United Provinces 1912; on deputation to Imperial War Conference and Cabinet 1917; Finance Member 1918; retired, Nov. 1919.

MEYER, Sir W. S.—ICS 1879; Member, Decentralization Committee, 1907; Finance Member, 1913–18; High Commissioner for India, London, 1920.

MITTER, B. C.—barrister 1897; Advocate, Calcutta High Court, 1893;

Standing Counsel, G/I, 1910; Officiating Advocate General, Calcutta, 1911.

MONRO, General Sir C. C.—commissioned 1879; Commander-in-Chief in India, 1 Oct. 1916—21 Nov. 1920.

MULLICK, B. K.—educated King's, Cambridge; ICS 1887; judge, Patna High Court, 1916.

NAIDU, Sarojini—1879–1949; poet, politician; first woman Congress President 1925; State Governor, Uttar Pradesh, 1947–9.

NAIR, Dr. T. M.—educated Presidency College, Madras, and Edinburgh University; surgeon; nominated (formerly elected) Member, Madras legislature; editor of a Madras medical journal; unsuccessful candidate for ILA; opponent of Home Rulers and Theosophists.

NARAYAN, Jagat—Member, United Provinces legislature and Hunter Committee.

PATEL, Vithalbhai—1873–1933; elder brother of Vallabhbhai; advocate; Congress General Secretary 1918; Member, ILC; became Swarajist and first elected President, ILA.

PENTLAND, Lord (John Sinclair)—commissioned 1879; Member, London County Council, 1889–92; MP, 1892–95; Secretary to Governor General, Canada, 1895–97; MP, 1897–1909; Secretary for Scotland, 1909–1912; G/Madras, 1912–19.

RAHIMTOOLA, Sir Ibrahim—Member, G/Bombay, 1 March 1918; reappointed Jan. 1921; declined pressing invitation to join G/I, 1919.

RAWLINSON, General Baron, of Trent—Commander-in-Chief in India, 21 Nov. 1920.

REED, Sir Stanley—editor, *Times of India*; accompanied Prince of Wales on tour, 1905–6; Western Indian representative, Imperial Press Conference, 1909; President, Publicity Board.

ROBERTS, Charles H.—MP since 1906; Parliamentary Under-Secretary of State for India, 1914–15; on deputation with S/S, 1917–18.

ROBERTSON, Sir Benjamin—ICS 1883–1920; C&ID Secretary, 1908–12; temporary Member, G/I, 1910; CC/Central Provinces 1912; on special duty in South Africa, Jan.–April 1914.

RONALDSHAY, Lord (Lawrence Dundas, later 2nd Marquess of Zetland)—born (as Lord Dundas) 1876; travelled in the East, 1897–1907; Conservative MP, 1907–17; G/Bengal, 1917–22; succeeded to Marquessate 1929; Secretary of State for India, 1935–40.

ROOS KEPPEL, Sir G. O.—commissioned 1886; commander, Khyber Rifles, 1903; CC/Northwest Frontier Province, 1908–19; Member, S/S Council, 1919.

ROY, K. C.—editor and journalist; Director, Associated Press of India; member, Reuter's Indian staff, British Institute of Journalists, and secretary, committee for organization of Indian Branch of Empire Press Union (see *IOR* J&P4468/19 for J&P1575/21).

SADLER, Sir Michael Ernest—1861–1943; Secretary, Extension Lectures Committee, Oxford, 1885; Member, Bryce Commission on Education; Director, 1895–1903; part-time Professor of Education, Manchester Vice-Chancellor of Leeds 1911; Chairman, Calcutta University Committee, 1917; Master, University College, Oxford, 1923. According to the DNB, he was known in 1903 as 'the greatest living authority in England on educational matters'.

SANKARAN NAIR, Sir C.—Government pleader 1899; Advocate-General, Madras, 1907; High Court judge 1908; Education Member, 1915–19; Member, S/S Council, 1919.

SAPRU, Sir Tej Bahadur—advocate, Allahabad High Court; Member, United Provinces legislature (1913–16) and ILC (1916–20); Law Member, G/I, 1920–23; onetime member, All-India Congress Committee; President, Indian Liberal Federation; delegate, Round Table Conference, 1930, 1931, 1932.

SARMA, Rao Bahadur Bayya Narasimheswara—pleader; member, Madras Legislative Council, 1914–16; deputation to England 1914; member, G/I, 1920.

SASTRI, Srinavasa—1869–1949; schoolmaster; member, Servants of India, 1907; Member, Madras legislature, 1907; represented India at Imperial Conference and League of Nations 1921; Leader of Liberal Party.

SATYA PAL, Dr.—assistant surgeon, and Hindu political leader, Amritsar.

SELBORNE, Earl of (William Waldegrave Palmer)—1859–1942; Liberal MP, 1885–95; Under-Secretary of State for Colonies under Joseph Chamberlain; First Lord 1900; accepted viceroyalty, 1904, but refused after Curzon's extended term, 1905; High Commissioner (later Governor-General) in South Africa, 1905; President, Board of Agriculture and Fisheries, 1915; Chairman, Joint Select Committee, Indian Reforms, 1919; offered viceroyalty by Lloyd George, 1920.

SETALVAD, Chimanlal Harilal—advocate, Bombay High Court; Vice-Chancellor, Bombay University, 1917; member, Hunter Committee, 1920; additional judge, Bombay, 1920; Member, G/Bombay, Jan. 1921.

SETON, Sir Malcolm C. C.—ICS 1895; India Office 1898; on deputation with S/S, 1917–18; assistant Under-Secretary of State, Dec. 1919 (acting, Dec. 1918).

SHAFI, Khan Bahadur Mian Muhammad—barrister; Education Member 1919.

SINHA, Lord, of Raipur (Sir Satyendra)—Advocate-General, Bengal, 1916; Member, Bengal legislature, 1916–19; on deputation to Imperial War Conference and Cabinet, 1917 and 1918; Parliamentary Under-Secretary of State, 1919–20; G/Bihar and Orissa, 1921.

SLY, Sir Frank George—member, Public Service Commission, 1912–1915; on deputation to England with reforms committee, 1919; CC/Central Provinces, Jan. 1920 (Governor, Dec.).

SOUTHBOROUGH, Baron (Francis John Stephens Hopwood)—1860–1947; civil servant; Permanent Secretary, Board of Trade; 1901; Under-Secretary of State for Colonies, 1907–10; Privy Councillor 1912; peer 1917; Chairman, Indian Reforms Committees, 1918; non-political in Lords.

SPOOR, Ben—1878–1928; member, Labour Party executive, after 1919; Chief Whip under MacDonald; pacifist; member, I.L.P.; Secretary British Committee of the Congress. (See Georges Fischer, *Parti travailliste et la décolonisation de l'inde*, Paris 1966, 113; he adds, with what seems to me, for 1919, a certain confusion of categories, 'Il [Spoor] était lié bien davantage aux milieux modérés du Congrès qu'avec Besant et ses amis. Cependant, en 1919, aux Communes, il mène la lutte avec Wedgwood pour amender le projet gouvernemental sur l'inde . . .'.)

STEVENSON-MOORE, C. J.—ICS 1885; magistrate and collector 1898; Inspector-General of Police 1904; officiating Director, Criminal Intelligence, 1907; Chief Secretary, G/Bengal, 1910; Member, Board of Revenue, 1914.

VINCENT, Sir W. H. H.—ICS 1885; judge, Calcutta High Court, 1909; LD Secretary, G/I, 1911; Member, G/Bihar and Orissa, 1915; Home Member, G/I from April 1917.

WACHA, Sir Dinshaw Edulji—1844–1936; Managing Agent, Morarji Gokuldas and Sholapur Mills; Bombay Presidency Association Secretary, 1885–1915, and President, 1915–18; Congress Joint Secretary, 1896–1907, and Secretary, 1908–13, and President, 1901; member, Bombay Corporation and Bombay legislature, 1915–16, and ILC, 1916–20.

WILLIAMS, L. B. Rushbrook—born 1890; Fellow of All Souls, Oxford, 1914–21; Professor of Modern Indian History, Allahabad, 1914–19; on special duty in connection with reforms (1918) and in HD (1919); Director, Central Bureau of Information, 1920–6.

WILLINGDON, Lord (Freeman Freeman-Thomas)—MP, 1900–10; G/Bombay, 1913–18; G/Madras after 1919; V and Governor General, 1931–6.

References and Notes

Introduction

1. *Social Change in Modern India*, Berkeley & Los Angeles 1968, 2.
2. I have also omitted, in the interests of brevity, most of my original references to the literature on this subject. Some relevent works are cited in the bibliography.
3. H. V. Hodson, *The Great Divide*, London 1969, 6.
4. R. C., with A. K., Majumdar, edd., *The History and Culture of the Indian People* Vol. XV, *Struggle for Freedom*, Bombay 1969, 8; Percival Spear, *The Oxford History of Modern India 1740–1947*, Oxford 1965, 323; Montagu to Chelmsford, 1 Jan. 1918, *CP4*; *Moral and Material Progress Report*, 1921, 54–6. See also *The Dictionary of National Biography* under Thesiger (Chelmsford). For another favourable view, see the Maharaja of Mysore (speech of 2 Dec. 1919) in *Speeches* II, 346; also below, pp. 284–9.
5. Sachchidananda Bhattacharya, *Dictionary of Indian History*, Calcutta 1967, 221–2.

Chapter One. The System

1. Most of this introductory material is discussed in detail later, and full references are not given at this stage. For Pentland's attitude to the press, however, see Lady Pentland, *The Right Honourable John Sinclair, Lord Pentland, G.C.S.I., A Memoir*, London 1928, 242–5; and for O'Dwyer's attitudes, see Sir Michael O'Dwyer, *India as I Knew It 1885–1925, passim.*
2. Willingdon to Hailey, 9 Sept. 1921, *Hailey Papers* 4b.
3. See Marris to Kerr, 25 Nov. 1920, *Lothian Papers* GD40/17/215a (on Willingdon); Willingdon to Montagu, 7 Feb. 1921, *MP21*, and Lloyd to Montagu, 24 July 1919, and also 1 and 26 Dec. 1918 and 25 Jan. and 17 Aug. and 2 Oct. 1919, *MP24*. See also O'Dwyer to Chelmsford, 27 Aug. 1916, *CP17*.
4. Asquith and Chamberlain considered proconsuls or parliamentarians—almost all peers and with impeccably conservative backgrounds, schooling and careers. They ruled out Islington (too little authority), the Duke of Devonshire ('slow-gaited' in intelligence), Sir Thomas Buxton (too old), Lord Crawford (inexperienced), Montagu (because a Jew) and Hardinge (vetoed by Crewe and Chamberlain). Only in Chelmsford did their choices coincide: he was Asquith's first choice with Viscount D'Abernon; Chamberlain thought him a 'better man' in the same type as Sir Arthur Lawley, that is among the proconsuls. See Chamberlain to Prime Minister, 24 Sept. and 30 Nov., and Asquith to Chamberlain, 25 Dec. 1915, *ACP15/1/5* and 7–8; and also S/S to V, 17 Dec. 1915

and 13 Jan. 1916, *ACP*45/2/8–9, and Hardinge of Penshurst, *My Indian Years 1910–1916*, London 1946, 122.

5. See S. D. Waley, *Edwin Montagu*, London 1964, 127–31; Islington to Chamberlain, 19 and 24 July, and Chamberlain to Prime Minister, 13 July 1917, *ACP*15/4/70, 72 and 82; and also Islington to Seton, 19 July 1917, *Seton Papers* 7. Montagu had been associated with liberal reforms as Under-Secretary of State—including the Public Services Commission and the idea of financing the India Office from Britain (see Montagu to Wilson, 26 Oct. 1911, *Wilson Papers* 8).

6. On the Mesopotamia Commission, see Chamberlain to Chelmsford, 18 July 1917, *CP*3. (He also earlier expressed anxiety; see Chamberlain to Hardinge, and to Willingdon, 24 Feb. 1916, *ACP*12/31–2.) On the army, see *Speeches* II, 480; Chelmsford to Chamberlain, 27 May, 29 July, 11 Aug., 18 Oct. and 10 Nov. 1916, *CP*2, and 7 and 30 June, and to Montagu, 18 Oct. 1917, *CP*3. Duff's capacity had long been in doubt: Fleetwood Wilson described him in 1913 as 'an impossible old fool', 'absolutely Gaga' and 'a danger' (to Lucas, PS to Crewe, 15 and 23 Jan. 1913, *Wilson Papers* 2b). Later Hill and Lowndes, feeling debarred from military matters under Duff, sought to enlist Meyer to try to present Munro with plans for complete reorganization; Chelmsford proved 'quite keen to take this up' (Hill to Seton, 24 Aug. 1916, *Seton Papers* 6). For other criticisms of the G/I, especially arguments for devolution, see Montagu to Lloyd, 2 Oct., *MP*22, and Lloyd to Montagu, 18 March 1919, *MP*24; Willingdon to Montagu, 30 July 1918, *MP*18; and Curtis to Kerr, 25 March 1917, *Lothian Papers* GD40/17/33. For Montagu's suspicion of the police, see Montagu to Lloyd, 8 Sept. 1919, *MP*22.

7. See Chelmsford's reply to a speech of welcome, 4 April 1916, *Speeches* I; and Chelmsford to Chamberlain, 5 May 1916, *CP*2.

8. For Chelmsford's interest in the development of Indian industries, see Chelmsford to Nair, 15 June 1916, *CP*17; for measures to expand wartime production, see Note by T. H. Holland, 20 Oct., with Chelmsford to Chamberlain, 26 Oct. 1916, *CP*2, and Chelmsford to Chamberlain, 26 Jan. and 14 June 1917, *CP*3; for postwar policy and the beginnings of state intervention to promote industry, see Chelmsford to Montagu, 19 July and 8 Sept. 1917, *CP*3; for a summary of the conclusions of the Indian Industrial Commission, see V(C&ID) to S/S, 26 Oct. 1918, *CP*9.

9. Subsequent delays in these reforms, caused by the Secretary of State's refusal to sanction a bill based on the Sadler Report, were later very nearly to lead to an open breach between Chelmsford and Montagu. See V(ED) to S/S, 18 May and 1 and 22 June 1920, S/S to V, 25 June, and V to S/S, 22 June, *CP*12, and 21 and 26 July and 12 Aug. 1920, *CP*13; Chelmsford to Ronaldshay, 22 July 1920, *CP*25; Maffey to Chelmsford, 18 Aug. 1920, *CP*20; and Ronaldshay to Montagu, 12 May 1920, *MP*31. The question was later transferred to the Bengal legislature; see V(ED) to S/S, 18 Feb. 1921, *CP*14. For Chelmsford's earlier interest in expediting matters, see V to G/Bengal (for Sadler), 2 April 1918, *CP*20; Sadler to Chelmsford, 22 Aug., and Chelmsford to Sadler, 28 Aug. and 5–6 Nov., 1918, *CP*21; and Chelmsford to Montagu, 8 Sept. 1917, *CP*3. In addition

to Aligarh (given university status) two new universities, Dacca and Banaras, were opened in this period, both after delays. H. Sharp, Educational Commissioner under Nair (whom he found 'quite good') believed that Bengal continued to 'boggle' at Dacca, 'the one really good university . . . yet . . . devised out here', because of the old policy of doing nothing which touched 'even remotely, the vested interests . . . in Calcutta' (to Seton, 11 Oct. 1916, *Seton Papers* 6). Chelmsford's other educational hope, to double the numbers in primary education in ten years (see Chelmsford to Montagu, 19 July 1917, *CP*3), was not to receive his full attention.

10. Chamberlain to Chelmsford, 13 Sept. 1916, *CP*2, and also 2 Feb. 1917, *CP*3.

11. Montagu to Chelmsford, 22 Oct. 1918, and Chelmsford to Montagu, 4 Dec. 1918, *CP*4. See also Chelmsford to Montagu, 5 Oct. 1917, *CP*3.

12. V(HD) to S/S, 21 June 1916, *H.Public* (*C*) 88, June 1916.

13. Montagu to Chelmsford, 1 Jan., 17 April, 10 Oct. and 23 Dec. 1918, *CP*4. See also Chelmsford to Montagu, 30 May 1918, *CP*4.

14. Chelmsford to Montagu, 23 April and 30 May 1918, *CP*4.

15. See Chelmsford to Montagu, 15 April 1918, *CP*4, and to Chamberlain, 11 Aug. 1916, *CP*2, and 23 Feb. and 20 April 1917, *CP*3.

16. *Speeches* II, 483–8.

17. Chelmsford to Chamberlain, 18 Aug. 1916, *CP*2, and to Montagu, 28 April 1918, *CP*4.

18. See E. S. Montagu, *An Indian Diary* (ed.: Venetia Montagu), London 1930, 41, 72 and 110–11.

19. See R. J. Moore, *Sir Charles Wood's Indian Policy*, Manchester 1966, 53–6.

20. S/S to G/I, No. 112, Public, 5 Aug. 1904, *Wilson Papers* 10.

21. To Fletcher, 10 Aug. 1909, *Wilson Papers* 3.

22. To Jenkins, 17 June and 6 July 1909, *Wilson Papers* 2a. His dissent from Minto's reforms despatch was influenced by his not having been consulted (note, [July 1909], *loc. cit.* 10).

23. Chelmsford to Montagu, 18 Oct. 1917, *CP*3, and to Chamberlain, 5 May, 18 and 25 Aug. 1916, *CP*2. Wilson to Jenkins, 6 July 1909, *Wilson Papers* 2a.

24. Chelmsford to Montagu, 18 Oct. 1917, *CP*3.

25. PSV to Departmental Secretaries, 29 April 1916, *CP*17, and 8 June 1917, *CP*18.

26. Chelmsford to Montagu, 18 Oct. 1917, *CP*3.

27. Collective decisions tended to increase paper work. One revised Rule of Business required that each important despatch should be signed by all members who had discussed it including those who dissented. Other despatches were to be signed by at least three members. A second revised Rule required that any member who wished to write a minute of dissent should confine himself to matters raised in discussion, and circulate his minute before the despatch was finally settled. It would then refer to the dissent, and if necessary include a statement on the majority view. See Rules 37A and 38A, *H.Public* 53–4, Nov. 1917.

304 REFERENCES AND NOTES (*Ch. 1*)

28. Chelmsford to Reed, 26 March 1919, *CP*22. The members were themselves thought by some to be weak, but this is common enough: Morley was told by everyone who could afford to that Minto's Council was 'mediocre or even a trifle below that' (Morley to Wilson, n.d., *Wilson Papers* 11).

29. Chelmsford to Chamberlain, 18 Oct. and 11 Nov. 1916, *CP*2, and to Montagu, 19 Oct. 1918, *CP*4.

30. Reed to Chelmsford, 23 March 1919, *CP*22.

31. Chelmsford to Reed, 26 March 1919, *CP*22.

32. V to S/S, 29 Nov. and 29 Dec. 1918, *CP*9; V(HD) to S/S, 30 May 1919, *H.Public* 326 and see 327–40, Jan. 1920; Memorandum (approved by Llewellyn Smith), *H.Public* 342–3, Dec. 1919.

33. *H.Public* 493–496, March 1921.

34. For attempts by Chelmsford to hurry local governments, see Chelmsford to Ronaldshay, 18 Feb. and 25 June, to Lloyd, and to Craddock, 18 Feb. 1919, *CP*22, but also Montagu to Ronaldshay, 26 June 1919, *MP*27; for Chelmsford's willingness to circumvent usual procedure (to hasten Lloyd's housing schemes in Bombay), see Lloyd to Montagu, 28 Feb., 18 July and 17 Aug. 1919, *MP*24; for the HD circular, 9 June 1919, urging local governments to consult only a limited number of interested parties when replying to enquiries, see *H.Public* 6–7, Feb. 1920. Under another rule, differences of opinion were to be resolved personally (between departments) without further noting, with only the agreement embodied in a joint note.

35. *H.Public* 73–4, Jan., and 85–6, May 1921.

36. PSV to Departmental Secretaries, with V to S/S, 3 Oct. 1917, *CP*22.

37. G/I despatch (FD), 3 June 1930, *H.Public* 102, Nov. 1920.

38. Rules 11 (1) and (2) and 19, May 1920, *H.Public* 991–2, Dec. 1920.

39. See *Report of the Secretariat Procedure Committee* 1919, or B. B. Misra, *The Administrative History of India 1834–1947*, Oxford 1970, 138–43. The report envisaged new or combined departments of Education and Public Health; Commerce and Industry; Ways and Communications; and Agriculture, Lands and Public Works. Commerce and Industry had not been joined, largely because of the work of the Munitions Board under Thomas Holland and his advocacy of a separate body to encourage Indian industry (see above, note 8).

40. Chelmsford to Reading, 3–4 March 1921, *CP*16, and see V to S/S, 2 tels., 6 May 1920, *CP*12. Emigration (within the Empire) had been transferred to Commerce in January 1920, but to Revenue and Agriculture in August. The Department of Education and Public Health was set up in April 1921. Emigration was moved so that it could be handled by an Indian.

41. The allocation was made provisionally on the eve of Chelmsford's departure, because Barnes was leaving as well. The effect was to abolish Hill's Revenue and Agriculture Department whose responsibilities were distributed as follows (marked by *) among three departments: (1) Commerce and Industry (Holland)—trade, commerce, industry, technical

education, *forests, *agriculture, railways, ports and docks (all matters associated with economic development); (2) Education (Shafi)—education, public health, medical services, local self-government, *land revenue, *famines, *civil veterinary, *co-operation, *surveys, *metereology, *excise, salt; (3) Public Works (Sarma)—*public works, posts, telegraphs, tramways, internal navigation, aviation, road traffic, emigration. Commerce and Industry had been separated with the intention of re-uniting them under Holland after Barnes's departure, but to do so without adjustment would have given one Member an intolerable burden. See Chelmsford's memorandum for Reading, *Reading Papers* (*private*) 104. Under Reading the departments were Foreign and Political; Army; Home; Finance; Legislative; Commerce; Railways; Industries; Public Works; Revenue and Agriculture; Education and Health. After the Inchcape Committee 1922, Industries and Public Works were joined as Industries and Labour, and Revenue and Education joined as Education, Health and Lands. A Central Board of Revenue was set up in 1924.

42. See *CP*17 *passim*, and Chelmsford to Meston, 7 April 1916, *Meston Papers* 1.

43. E. S. Montagu, *An Indian Diary*, 17 and 224–5.

44. See O'Dwyer, 2 Dec., Robertson, 6 Dec., and Ronaldshay, 6 Dec. 1918, to Chelmsford, *CP*21; Lloyd to Montagu, 10 Jan., and to Chelmsford, 25 Jan. 1919, *MP*24; Willingdon to Montagu, 7 and 21 Jan., but also 30 Jan. 1920, *MP*20.

45. See Willingdon to Montagu, 30 Jan. 1920, *MP*20, and also 21 July and 30 Oct. 1919, *MP*19. Hill blamed Chelmsford's overwork, bad health and inability to correspond readily: he and Willingdon were 'temperamentally poles apart' for Willingdon's 'rather irresponsible suggestions . . . get on the V's nerves, & rather than answer with a negative he leaves such proposals unanswered' (to Seton, 15 Jan. 1917, *Seton Papers* 7).

46. Montagu to Lloyd, 14 April 1920, *MP*22.

47. Lloyd to Montagu, 12 Feb. and 5 Sept. 1919, *MP*24. See also Lloyd to Chamberlain, 11 July 1919, *ACP*18/1/6: 'I . . . cannot understand why he had been so much criticised—He is certainly first rate to work with, prompt, sympathetic . . .'.

48. Chelmsford to Chamberlain, 25 March 1917, *CP*3. Hill's first reaction was that Chelmsford seemed 'sensible' and was 'very nice' (to Seton, 7 [May 1916], *Seton Papers* 22, marked '23').

49. Barnes to Chamberlain, 30 April 1916, *ACP*12/11; Meston to Chelmsford, 31 May 1919, and see Holland to Chelmsford, 14 June 1919, *CP*22.

50. Montagu to Lloyd, 30 Aug. 1919, *MP*22.

51. Chelmsford to Chamberlain, 15 Sept. 1916, *CP*2.

52. See Lloyd to Chamberlain, 13 June 1920, *ACP*18/1/9: ' . . . the machinery of Government is really vile . . . but the understaffing of the Civil Services has resulted in each individual from the Secretary of State downward being so over-worked that no-one has had time . . . to cope with the system'.

53. See Chelmsford to Chamberlain, 1 and 25 March 1917, *CP*3; Mary Eva Bell to Seton, 27 Jan. 1919, *Seton Papers* 9.
54. HD circular, 22 Feb. 1918, and replies, *H.Public* 600–6, May 1918.
55. *Speeches* II, 483.
56. Chelmsford to Montagu, 27 July 1918, *CP*4.
57. See for example Chelmsford to Chamberlain, 20 April 1917, *CP*3.
58. Chelmsford to Chamberlain, 25 March 1917, *CP*3.
59. Chelmsford to Chamberlain, 6 Oct. 1916, *CP*2.
60. See for example *Index to Home Department Proceedings 1919*, 325–7.
61. Chelmsford to O'Dwyer, 24 May 1919, *CP*22.
62. Willingdon to Montagu, 30 Jan. 1920, *MP*20.
63. Chelmsford to Montagu, 27 July 1918, *CP*4, and S/S to V, 15 and 25 Feb. 1921, *CP*14.
64. *Speeches* II, 249–281; *H.Poll.*253–254, May 1917; Memorandum on Press Legislation, 1 July 1920, *IOR* J&P1589 (4468/19); Chelmsford to Chamberlain, 1 March 1917, *CP*3.
65. Montagu to Lloyd, 25 June, *MP*22 and Lloyd to Montagu, 18 July 1919, *MP*24. The importance of speech-making is perhaps demonstrated by Lord Ronaldshay who arrived in Bengal to vehement opposition in the press, but before long was being congratulated on his speeches; see Ronaldshay to Montagu, 24 July 1917, *MP*29.
66. Montagu to Chelmsford, 1 Jan. 1918, *CP*4, and see Lascelles to Kerr, 24 Nov. 1920, *Lothian Papers* GD40/17/214.
67. Montagu to Chelmsford, 4 Oct. 1917, *CP*3.
68. Chamberlain to Chelmsford, 21 July 1917, *CP*3.
69. Montagu to Chelmsford, 3 Aug. 1917, *CP*3, and to Ronaldshay, 25 Sept. 1918, *MP*27. For a similar view, see Lloyd to Montagu, 26 Dec. 1918, *MP*24.
70. See E. S. Montagu, *An Indian Diary*, 349–57, and Montagu to Chelmsford, 10, 15 and 17 April 1918, *CP*4.
71. For the Delhi War Conference, including the exclusions and Gandhi's attitude, see Chelmsford to Montagu, 28 April and 15 May 1918, *CP*4, and to Willingdon, 15 May, and PSV to G/Madras and to G/Bombay, 18 April, and to Resident, Aden (for PS to Montagu), 29 April, and G/Madras to V, 22 April, and V to G/Madras, 11 May, and PS, G/Bombay to PSV, 21 April, and Gandhi to Chelmsford, 29 April 1918, *CP*20; and *Speeches* II, 82. A list of people in attendance is at *H.Poll.* Dep.14, May 1918. See also Gandhi to Chelmsford, 29 April, and to Maffey, 30 April, and Maffey to Gandhi, 21 May, and to Crerar, 17 May 1918, *CP*20. Willingdon criticized the Delhi conference as giving 'extremists' undue prominence; Chelmsford thought his reaction 'hysterical'. See Chelmsford to Montagu, 15 May 1918 (with enclosures, Willingdon to Chelmsford, 9 May, Chelmsford to Willingdon, 15 May, and Reed to Maffey, 11 May 1918), *CP*4, and Willingdon to Chelmsford, 11 June, Chelmsford to Willingdon, 17 June, and Maffey to Reed, 16

May 1918, *CP*20. Montagu was disappointed; see Montagu to Willingdon, 4 July 1918, *MP*18.

72. See *H.Public* 522–34, May, and 330–2, Aug. 1918 (including Proceedings of the Bombay War Conference, 10 June 1918); Willingdon to Montagu, 17 April and 8 June, and to Chelmsford, 21 June 1918, *CP*20; and also (for example) S. L. Karandikar, *Lokamanya Bal Gangadhar Tilak*, Poona [1957?], 505. Ronaldshay thought his conference a success; see Ronaldshay to Montagu, 10 June 1918, *MP*29.

73. V(HD) to S/S, 9 June 1918, *H.Public* 384–446, Aug. 1919.

74. Central Publicity Board to United Provinces War Board, 13 July, and S/S to V(HD), 11 July 1918, *H.Public* 402 and 404, Aug. 1919.

75. Chelmsford to Montagu, 13 June 1918, *CP*4. The work of the Board was allegedly held up by delays in the India Office; see Reed to Seton, 8 Feb. 1918 (*sic*=1919); and G. F. Adams to Seton, 21 March 1919, *IOR* J&P1530, 4287; *H.Public* 384–446, Aug. 1919. For lecture tours organized with mixed success, see *H.Public* 300–92a, July, 398, Aug. and 281–3, Nov. 1919.

76. HD Circular, 10 May 1918, *H.Public* 166, March 1919.

77. See V to S/S, 28 Jan. 1920, *CP*12; *H.Public* 65–8, July 1918, and 166–230, March 1919; G/I despatch (FD), 5 April, and S/S reply, 4 June 1918, *H.Poll.*369 and 372, June 1918. See also *H.Poll.*162, Sept. 1920; and, for use of the publicity papers, such as *Al Hakikat*, *H.Public(C)* 302–420, March 1918, and *H.Public* 171–258, April 1921.

78. A forerunner, in a sense, was the Press Commissioner set up under Lytton; see Margarita Barns, *The Indian Press*, London 1940, 289–93.

79. United Provinces War Board to Central Publicity Board, 28 Nov. 1918, *H.Public* 214, March 1919.

80. Seton to Hignell, 15 Nov., and to Reed, 7 Dec. 1918, and Reed to Seton, 8 Feb. 1918 (*sic*=1919), *IOR* J&P1530, 4287; Central Publicity Board to HD, 27 March 1919, *H.Poll.*543, Jan. 1920; and see also Bombay Publicity Department to G/Bombay, 19 Dec. 1918, *H.Poll.*92, Feb. 1919.

81. HD circular, 18 Feb. 1919, *ibid.*

82. Reed to Maffey, 20 March 1919, *CP*22.

83. See *H.Public* 301–33, Feb., and 151–81, Oct. 1919; and *H.Poll.* 454–71 and 473, Jan., and 374–5, Feb. 1920; and Chamberlain to Chelmsford, 14 Oct. 1917, *ACP*18/3/1a.

84. V to S/S, 28 Jan. 1920, *CP*12; and see *H.Poll.*127, 155 and 159, Sept. 1920.

85. See *H.Poll.*318, 320, 689 and 691–2, May 1919, and 241–61, July 1920. For criticism of a publicity board for buying copies of a book and trying to resell them instead of distributing them free, see Eva Mary Bell to Seton, 27 Jan. 1919, *Seton Papers* 9.

86. See *H.Poll.*689, May 1919; *H.Public* 58–67, May 1921; V(RD) to S/S, 9 Dec. 1920, *CP*13.

87. See Montagu to Ronaldshay, 28 June 1921, *MP*28, on publicity and propaganda: 'I believe we have still got to invent our system in India'. Local officers may have been losing influence (thus prompting the change

in rules) but of course they could not adopt a political form of leadership.
88. Seton to Hailey, 8 Jan. 1920, *Hailey Papers* 2b. The name in this letter is indecipherable, but it must be Nair: he had recently been appointed to the Council of India; he was on the Viceroy's Council 'that winter' (1917–18, when Seton visited for the reforms discussions); he had, since 1916 at least, the reputation of being influenced by politicians.

Chapter Two.   Public Opinion

1. Chelmsford to Chamberlain, 17 May 1918, *CP*15.
2. Carmichael to Chelmsford, 3 Aug. 1916, *CP*17.
3. See below, Chapter 9.
4. See *H.Poll.*175–177, 178 (Report by A. Montgomerie, 30 May 1916), 180A (*Kesari*, 30 May 1916), and 182–5, Jan. 1917, and 89 and 244–62, Oct. 1918, and 309 (Report by A. Montgomerie, 18 March 1919), Aug. 1919; and *H.Poll.*Dep. 50, June 1917; Willingdon to Montagu, 13 Aug. 1917, *MP*18; Chamberlain to Willingdon, 24 Feb. 1916, *ACP*12/32. Willingdon had put forward Chirol's claims for assistance to Hardinge who had been doubtful, though Chirol was an old friend, but had decided that the matter was 'highly political' and should be handled officially; see Hardinge to Lowndes, 14 Jan. and 5 Feb., and Chirol to Lowndes, 10, 11, 12, 19, 22 Feb., and 19 April 1916, *Lowndes Papers*.
5. V to S/S, 5, 6 and 9 April and 22 May, and (HD) 9 and 21 March, and S/S to V, 3, 8 and 11 April, and (HD) 2 April and 8 June 1918, *CP*9; Islington to Chelmsford, 12 April 1918, *CP*4; *H.Poll.*203, 207–8, and 212, June, and 244–62, Oct. 1918, and Dep. 35, May 1918, and also *Pioneer* (Allahabad), 3 April 1918 and *Amrita Bazar Patrika*, 25 March 1918. Montagu thought H.M.G. acted on a 'black picture' (of Tilak's possible activities) painted in the Home Department telegram (see Montagu's *Indian Diary*, 15 April 1917).
6. See Chelmsford to Montagu, 13 June 1918, *CP*4; V to S/S, 9 Sept. and (HD) 8 June, and S/S to V(HD), 11 and 24 June 1918, *CP*9; Montagu to Chamberlain, and Chamberlain to Montagu, 10 June 1918, *ACP*21/5/35 and 32; *H.Poll.*227, Oct. 1918.
7. See ILC Proceedings, 25 Sept. 1918, *H.Poll.*225, Oct. 1918; S/S to V, 3 and 18 Sept., and V to S/S, 9 Sept. and 3 Oct. 1918, *CP*9. For later assistance given to reforms deputations, see *H.Poll.*B173–81, July 1920.
8. Chelmsford to Hardinge, 1 March 1917, *CP*15.
9. *H.Poll.*323, July 1917.
10. See *H.Poll.*314–39, July 1917; V to LG/Bihar and Orissa, 22 May, and Chelmsford to Gait, 8 June, and Gait to Chelmsford, 21 May 1917, *CP*18. See also *The Collected Works of Mahatma Gandhi* Vol. XIII (Jan. 1915–Oct. 1917), Ahmedabad 1964, 362–446; K. K. Datta, *History of the Freedom Movement in Bihar* Vol. I, 1857–1928, Patna 1957, 167–280; B. R. Nanda, *Mahatma Gandhi*, London 1958, 156–62; M. K. Gandhi, *An Autobiography* or *The Story of My Experiments with Truth* (tr. Mahadev Desai), Ahmedabad 1940 (2nd ed.), 300–13; D. G. Tendulkar

Gandhi in Champaran, [Patna?] 1957; Rajendra Prasad, 'The Champaran
Agrarian Policy', *Hindustan Review*, Vol. XXXVIII, No. 227 (July 1918),
9–56; and particularly documents nos. 32, 35, 71, 77, 79, 81, 85, 95, 100,
104 and 111, in B. B. Misra, ed., *Select Documents on Mahatma Gandhi's
Movement in Champaran 1917–1918*, Bihar (Secretariat Press) 1963. The
Champaran Inquiry Committee recommended the abolition of com-
pulsory indigo cultivation; a bill providing for this was promptly
approved by Simla and passed in the Bihar legislature; see *H.Poll*.Dep.
5, April 1918, and also 47, Oct. 1917. See also the accounts of Girish
Mishra (in *Indian Economic and Social History Review* V, 3 (1968) and
II, 4 (1966)), Ravinder Kumar (*South Asia* 1, 1 (1971)), and Judith Brown,
Gandhi's Rise to Power, Cambridge 1972, 52–83.

11. See Chelmsford to Chamberlain, 20 Dec. 1916, *CP2*; *H.Poll*.178–
, April 1917, and also 335, Jan. 1918.

12. Note, 9 April 1918, *H.Poll*.Dep. 18, May 1918. On Kaira see
Kenneth L. Gillion, *Ahmedabad, A Study in Indian Urban History*,
Berkeley & Los Angeles 1968, 160–6.

13. Chelmsford to Chamberlain, 17 May, and to Archbishop, Brisbane,
March 1917, *CP15*; Montagu to Willingdon, 9 Aug. 1920, *MP18*, and
Willingdon to Montagu, 27 July 1920, *MP20*. See also Lloyd to Montagu,
Nov. 1920, *MP25*, and Grant to Chelmsford, 30 Oct. 1920, *CP25*.

14. Despatch 7, June 1916, *H.Poll*.Dep. 32, Feb. 1819; Islington to
Chelmsford, 15 March 1918, *CP4*; S/S to V, 17 Jan. 1917, *CP8*; V to
S/S, 12 Feb., and S/S to V(HD), 21 and 28 March 1918, *CP9*; [Kerr] to
Curtis, 24 April 1917, *Lothian Papers* GD40/17/33; *Extracts from Minutes
of Proceedings and Papers laid before the Imperial War Conference* (8th
day), 22–3, *ACP47/3/1*; ILC Proceedings, 19 March 1918; *H.Poll*.91–101,
June 1918. See also Chelmsford's report and reference to Borden's praise
of Sinha, *Speeches* I, 384–7; see also *ibid*. 244–5; and K. M. Panikkar,
His Highness the Maharaja of Bikaner, A Biography, London 1937, 177.
Earlier Lionel Curtis had suggested Indian participation (to Meston, 16
July 1915, *Meston Papers* 11) and Hill had seen Indian representatives
growing to be an accepted fact' (to Seton, 6 March [1916], *Seton Papers* 22).

15. See *Extracts from Minutes of Proceedings* . . . (Imperial War Conference, 15th day), 117–20, *ACP47/3/1*; Chamberlain to Kerr, 24 April,
and Kerr to Chamberlain, 27 April 1917, *Lothian Papers* GD40/17/34.
For an early suggestion or reciprocity, see *ibid*. GD40/17/3, p. 232; the
idea may have been Chelmsford's—he mentioned it to the Australian
High Commissioner who was discouraging, and discussed it with Curtis
who was more impressed (Curtis to Chelmsford, 2 Nov. 1916, *Meston
Papers* 11).

16. See Imperial War Cabinet, 'Report of Committee on Terms of
Peace (Territorial Desiderata) under Lord Curzon', *ACP20/9/33*.
Chelmsford appreciated the importance of the principle: see *Speeches* I,
184–7. For the antecedents of the change, see, for example, Lord
Islington, 'Speech to Conference of Representatives of Home and
Dominion Parliaments', 31 July 1916, *H.Poll*.259, Oct. 1916, and, for a
survey of the schemes into which India (like Ireland) had to be fitted,

J. E. Kendle. 'The Round Table Movement and "Home Rule A:
Round"', *Historical Journal*, XI, 2 (1968), 332–53.

17. Montagu, as Under-Secretary, had referred in the Commons to th
Governor-General as the 'agent' of the Secretary of State, and Minto ha,
agreed with J. L. Jenkins (note, 22 Aug. 1910) that they should 'stan
fast as a whole and that while not raising the main issue of their position a
a Government they should assert that position in respect to every concret
case' (Minto, note, 2 Sept. 1910, *Wilson Papers* 13).

18. S/S to V, 26 Jan. 1916, *ACP*21/1/14; Memorandum by Lor
Hardinge, with appended opinions, *ACP*21/2/1; and see Chamberlain t
Guy Fleetwood Wilson, 9 April 1913, *ACP*10/3/62—Chamberlai
approved of tariff reform, but only as part of a 'general Empire policy
to be undertaken after the war. George Lloyd agreed, and later urge
imperial preference (partly because it would please Indians and en
courage local industry)—see Lloyd to Chelmsford, 22 May 1919, *CP*22
See also Sinha's Congress presidential address, 27 Dec. 1915, *H.Poll.*358
Dec. 1916.

19. Chelmsford to Chamberlain, 14 June, and to Montagu, 5 Oct. 1917
*CP*3.

20. See India Office notes on contribution, *ACP*21/1/11 and 15–19
various correspondence, *ACP*21/1/21–3; G/I(AD) to S/S, 6 Oct. 1916
*ACP*21/1/25; V to S/S, 21 Oct., Chamberlain to the Chancellor, 23 Nov.
and S/S to V, 23 Dec. 1916, and draft, *ACP*21/1/27, 36, 40 and 41; an
S/S to V, 29 Nov. 1916, *ACP*21/1/32 (and *CP*7).

21. S/S to V, 5 Jan., and V to S/S, 6 and 7 Jan. 1917, *CP*8 (an
*ACP*21/1/43 and 44).

22. Fiscal independence was a long-standing Indian demand, arisin,
out of Naoroji's theory of the 'economic drain'. See Colin Forbes Adam
Life of Lord Lloyd, London 1948, 142, for an official endorsement of th
idea. Note also Chelmsford to Nair, 15 June 1916, *CP*17: 'Personally
wish to see *Indian* industries created on a large scale . . .'.

23. V to S/S, 11 March 1917, *CP*8 (and *ACP*21/2/14).

24. S/S to V, 2 Feb. 1917, *ACP*21/1/28.

25. Chamberlain to Hardinge, 10 Jan., Chamberlain, Cabinet mem
orandum, 25 Jan., Note by the Chancellor, 27 Jan., Statement by Mesto
before War Cabinet, 3 April 1917, *ACP*21/1/45, 59–60 and 69; House c
Commons questions and replies, *ACP*21/2/3 and 10.

26. Hardinge to Chamberlain, 10 Jan. 1917, *ACP*12/102; S/S to V,
Feb. and 10 and 15 March, and (F&PD) 13 March 1917, *CP*8.

27. V to S/S, 11 March 1917, *CP*8 and *ACP*21/2/14; and see *Speeches*
319 and 388, and II, 25–8. On Lloyd George's attitude, see Chamberlai
to Chelmsford, 10 and 15 March and 2 May 1917, *CP*3.

28. See Meston to Chelmsford, 15 March 1917, *Meston Papers* 1.

29. Hardinge to Chamberlain, 10 Jan. 1917, *ACP*12/102.

30. *Speeches* I, 388. Chelmsford later wrote to Reading to congratulat
him for 'a great coup being able to remove the cotton excise' (28 De
1925, *Reading Papers* (*private*) 104).

31. See B. R. Nanda, *Mahatma Gandhi*, London 1958, 116–17. Claud

Hill wrote: 'The point is that we are legalizing and perpetuating an abomination, and that, the indenture system being wholly wrong in principle, and stinking in its results, we cannot conscientiously . . . allow it to continue' (to Seton, 7 [May 1916], *Seton Papers* 22).

32. Chamberlain to Hardinge, 24 Feb. 1916, *ACP*12/31; Chelmsford to Chamberlain, 28 Sept. and 24 Nov. 1916, *CP*2.

33. See *Speeches* I, 46–9; Chelmsford to Chamberlain, 28 Sept. 1916, *CP*2; V to S/S, 6 Oct. 1916, S/S to V(C&ID), 12 Jan. and 1 Feb., & V(C&ID) to S/S, 20 March 1917, *CP*8. In refusing the second bill Chelmsford used the excuse that investigation was needed and that legislation, when it came, should be a government measure; see *Speeches* I, 226–8.

34. Chelmsford to Chamberlain, 9 Feb. and 10 March 1917, *CP*3. Meston also described the issue as a 'great worry' for it would be a bad case on which to revive the atrophied powers 'of squelching dishonest agitations' (to Seton, 16 March 1917) and Holderness concluded that 'resumption of recruitment of indentured labour would be impossible' (to Seton, 23 March 1917); Hill had written very strongly—the question was a 'moral one'; he thought it their 'business . . . to give a flat negative to any continuation' (to Seton, 17 Feb. 1917, *Seton Papers* 7). Stanley Reed blamed the agitation on lack of public confidence in Chelmsford 'in this and other matters' (to Hill, 10 Feb. 1917; copy at *loc. cit.*).

35. See Chelmsford to Chamberlain, 15 Feb., and Chamberlain to Chelmsford, 2 March 1917, *CP*3; V to S/S, 16 and 28 Feb., and 9 March, and (C&ID) 9 March 1917, *CP*8. Further delay was also due, according to Hill, to the incompetence of Barnes and Low, the latter 'a clever fellow and a shocking bad Secy.' (to Seton, 31 March [1917], *Seton Papers* 22).

36. See Chelmsford to Chamberlain, 6 Oct. 1916, *CP*2, and 9 and 15 Feb., 3 and 10 March, and Reed to Claude Hill, 28 Feb. 1917, *CP*3; V(C&ID) to S/S, 18 Sept. 1916, *CP*7. Bonar Law, in the Colonial Office, requested 12 months' delay for the most minor changes; Chelmsford objected strongly. See Chelmsford to Chamberlain, 6 Oct. 1916, *CP*2.

37. See *Speeches* I, 286–7 and 295–6; V(C&ID) to S/S, 20 March 1917, *CP*8; Chelmsford to Chamberlain, 3 March, and Chamberlain to Chelmsford, 16 and 29 March 1917, *CP*3.

38. *Speeches* I, 387–8; Chamberlain to Chelmsford, 2, 16 and 29 March, and Chelmsford to Chamberlain, 3 March 1917, *CP*3.

39. Chelmsford to Chamberlain, 28 April 1917, *CP*3. He had 'complete sympathy' with the Indian point of view: see Chelmsford to Archbishop of Brisbane, 5 March 1918, *CP*15.

40. V(C&ID) to S/S, 19 March 1917, *CP*8.

41. S/S to V(C&ID), 1 Feb. and 29 May, and V(C&ID) to S/S, 3 June 1917, *CP*8.

42. See, for example, S/S to V(CD), 7 and 25 Jan., and V(CD) to S/S, 5 Jan. 1921, *CP*14.

43. *Speeches* II, 242–5 and 453–6; Chelmsford to Montagu, 29 Jan., Feb. and 7 July 1920, *CP*6.

44. See V(CD) to S/S, 20 Dec. 1920, *CP*13, and 15 and 20 Jan., an*
S/S to V(CD), 7 Jan. 1921, *CP*14.

45. See Chelmsford to Montagu, 17 March (with enclosures: Shafi t
Chelmsford, 11 March, and Chitnavis, and Currimbhoy to Chelmsford
17 March) and 30 Oct., and Montagu to Chelmsford, 1 and 15 April an*
10 Nov. 1920, *CP*6; G/I(HD) to S/S, 7 Sept. 1917 and 16 July 1918
S/S to G/I, 14 Dec. 1917 and 30 Jan. 1919, and HD circular, 13 Oc*
1919, and replies, *H.Public* 88, Sept. 1917, 76–7, July 1918, 367–88
Oct. 1919, and 43–54, May 1920.

46. See *Speeches* I, 389.

47. Chelmsford to Montagu, 19 Nov. 1918, *CP*4.

48. Chamberlain to Chelmsford, 5 April, and 16 May 1916 (with
minute by Daljit Singh, 13 May), *CP*2; *H.Poll.*146–7, March 1916, an*
136–48, March 1917.

49. HD circular, 20 March 1917, *H.Poll.*149, March 1917.

50. *H.Police* 81–3, Aug. 1918.

51. HD circular, 26 July 1918, *ibid.*

52. *H.Police* 131–6, Feb., and 157–209, Dec. 1920. (They were read
to discuss details, but not the underlying objection that changes in polic*
had virtually disarmed the Europeans; see also below, note 55.)

53. See *H.Police* 131–56, Feb. 1920; V to S/S, 9 July, and (HD)
21 Oct. 1918, *CP*9. The immediate reason for the Act was to avoid ;
situation in which people no longer exempted would be breaking th
law.

54. The main provisions of the new regulations followed the earlie*
suggestions—a removal of any racial exemptions and a general curtail*
ment of persons formerly exempted by the discretionary powers allowe*
under section 27 of the Indian Arms Act 1878. The Arms Amendmen*
Act of 1919 provided an opportunity for the government to explain an*
gain approval for its new policy, but the Act's provisions merely substi*
tuted a new section 16 in the 1878 Act, to allow deposit and sale of arm*
by persons no longer exempted.

55. Chelmsford to Montagu, 13 Oct. 1920, *CP*6. (Chelmsford was re*
jecting the 'strain of antagonism' which underlay detailed criticisms o*
the new regulations.) Montagu was apprehensive and wrote: 'If th*
alteration ... makes it easier for wicked people to get arms for use i*
civil disturbances, it must give us furiously to think' (to Richards, 1
April 1921, *Richards Papers* 3).

56. See Chelmsford to Chamberlain, 12 Oct. 1916, *CP*2; *Speeches* I
381–3.

57. See Mary Kynynmond, Countess of Minto (ed.), *India, Mint*
and Morley, 1905–1910, London 1934, 265; Hardinge, Note on Grants o*
Commissions to Indians (with enclosures), *ACP*21/3/2; S/S to V
17 Nov., V to S/S, 24 Dec., Hardinge to Duff, 18 Dec., & Duff t
Hardinge, 21 Dec. 1915, *ACP*21/3/3. The demand had also been pu*
forward by Sinha in his Congress Presidential address, 27 Dec. 1915
see *H.Poll.*358, Dec. 1916.

58. Chelmsford to Chamberlain, 21 April 1916, *CP*2.

59. Chamberlain to Chelmsford, 5 April, and see also 22 Aug. 1916, *CP*2.
60. S/S to V(AD), 5 and 19 Feb. 1917, *CP*8. See also Chamberlain to Chelmsford, 14 Feb. 1917, *CP*3.
61. V(AD) to S/S, 8 March 1917, *CP*8.
62. S/S to V(AD), 28 March and 5 May, S/S to V, 29 March, and V(AD) to S/S, 17 April, *CP*8, and see S/S to V, 19 Oct. 1917, *ACP*21/3/7.
63. Chamberlain, Memorandum, 10 July, and Montagu, Note, 20 July 1917, *ACP*21/3/4.
64. Cabinet minute 203(1), *Curzon Papers* 588; Montagu to Chelmsford, 3 Aug. 1917, *CP*3; S/S to V, 2 Aug. 1917, *CP*8; Curzon to Chamberlain, 25 Aug. 1917, *ACP*14/1/5a. The agreement was announced; see S/S to V(AD), 16 and 18 Aug. 1917, *CP*8.
65. G/I(AD) to S/S, 3 Aug. 1917, *ACP*21/3/6.
66. S/S to V, 19 Oct., and V(AD) to S/S, 13 Nov. 1917, *ACP*21/3/7.
67. See Montagu to Chelmsford, 16 May and 15 June 1918, *CP*4; S/S to V(AD), 5 April 1918, *CP*9 (and *ACP*21/3/7).
68. Chelmsford to Chamberlain, 13 May, and see Chamberlain to Chelmsford, 11 April 1917, *CP*3.
69. Chelmsford to Montagu, 28 April 1918, *CP*4. A communique was issued on 21 June; see V(AD) to S/S, 13 July 1918, *CP*9.
70. S/S to V, 23, 24, 26 and 27 April, and (AD), 22 and 28 April 1918, *CP*9 (and *ACP*21/3/8); *ACP*21/3/9–11.
71. See Montagu to Chelmsford, 16 May 1918, *CP*4; Montagu, Cabinet Memorandum, 27 May 1918, *ACP*21/3/12. See also Stamfordham to Ronaldshay, 28 July 1918, *Ronaldshay Papers* 5b: 'His Majesty does not see how this principle could have been withheld especially after the way the Indian Army has fought in the war'.
72. V(AD) to S/S, 18 May 1918, *CP*9 (and *ACP*21/3/12).
73. Curzon, Cabinet Note, 3 June 1918, *ACP*21/3/13.
74. S/S to V, 13 June, and (AD), 12 June 1918, *CP*9; Montagu to Chelmsford, 15 June 1918, *CP*4.
75. *Speeches* I, 380–1.
76. *Ibid.*, 202–3.

Chapter Three. The Goal

1. Parliamentary Debates (Lords), 37, No. 109 (12 Dec. 1919), 1033.
2. Chelmsford to Chamberlain, 5 May, *CP*2, to Hardinge, 12 May 1916, to Frederick Guest, 8 April, and to Selbourne (*sic*), 17 Oct. 1918, *CP*15, and to Sinha, 25 March 1921, *CP*26; Curzon to Chamberlain 9 June 1915, *ACP*14/1/4; *Speeches* I, 389–93; Sinha, Presidential address 27 Dec. 1915, *H.Poll.*358, Dec. 1916. Lord Crewe confirmed Chelmsford's version: 'I know from personal knowledge that before Lord Chelmsford went out to India in 1915 [*sic*] he had become clearly convinced in his own mind, from conversations he had had with those competent to give opinions and from his own reflexions . . ., that it would be necessary at once to make an announcement of the character which was made in 1917 . . .' (*Parliamentary Debates* (Lords) 37, No. 109, 986). See below, notes 3 (Hardinge) and 93 (Round Table).

3. Chelmsford to O'Dwyer, 18 and 25 May, and see to Willingdon, 4 July, *CP*17, to Hardinge, 2 Sept., *CP*15, and to Chamberlain, 12 and 18 Oct. 1916, *CP*2. Hill claimed this procedure had 'curious' results (tc Seton, 22 May [1916], *Seton Papers* 6. See also Chirol to Chamberlain 13 Oct. 1915, *ACP*12/43; and 'Memorandum by H. E. the Viceroy upon Questions likely to arise in India at the end of the War'; Hardinge tc Heads of Governments and Members of his Council, 30 Aug.; Meston 7 Sept., Willingdon, 10 Sept., O'Dwyer, 13 Sept., Hailey, 17 Sept. 1915 to Hardinge; notes or letters by Sir Syed Ali Imam, 13 Sept., Sir W Clark, undated, Sir Reginald Craddock, 16 Sept., Sir W. Meyer, 5 Sept., C. H. A. Hill, 4 Sept. 1915, and Sir Benjamin Robertson, undated: *ACP*22/2. See also Chirol to Chamberlain, 13 Oct. 1915, *ACP*12/43.

4. Chelmsford to Chamberlain, 5 and 27 May and 16 June 1916, *CP*2; 'Formula', and notes by Home Member (Craddock), Finance Member (Meyer), Revenue and Agriculture Member (Hill), Legal Member (Lowndes), and Education Member (Nair), [26 or 27 May 1916], *CP*17.

5. Holderness, 'Memorandum on Viceroy's Formula', with Chamberlain to Chelmsford, 8 August 1916, *CP*2.

6. Chelmsford to Chamberlain, 27 May and 8 Sept. 1916, *CP*2.

7. Chelmsford to Chamberlain, 23 Sept. 1916, *CP*2.

8. 'Formula', 1 June 1916, *CP*17; HD despatch, 24 Nov. 1916, *H.Poll.* 358, Dec. 1916; Note, 26 June, with Hill to Chelmsford, 26 June 1916, *CP*18.

9. Chelmsford to Chamberlain, 7 July 1916, *CP*2.

10. See above, notes 2, 3 and 8. For a contemporary Indian suggestion on local government—wanting more power for panchayats—see M. S. Sesa Ayyangar, *Madras Village Panchayats*, Madura [1915].

11. Notes by Craddock, 3 and 10 June, Meyer to Chelmsford, and Meyer, Hill and Lowndes, 'Proposed formula *re* larger employment of Indians in the public services', 8 June 1916, and revised formula, undated *CP*17; Chelmsford to Chamberlain, 7 and 21 July 1916, *CP*2.

12. 'General Principles which should be observed in the Development of Local Self-Government', 30 June 1916, *CP*17; Memorandum circulated by Viceroy, *H.Poll.*358, Dec. 1916. See also, for the Secretary of State's approval, S/S to G/I, 19 Oct. 1917, *H.Poll.*337, March 1918.

13. Chamberlain to Chelmsford, 15 May 1917, *CP*3.

14. Montagu to Chelmsford, 15 April 1918, *CP*4.

15. Chelmsford to Montagu, 18 April 1918, *CP*4.

16. Chelmsford to Chamberlain, 23 Sept. 1916, *CP*2.

17. Memorandum by Craddock, 16 Sept. 1915, *ACP*22/2; Minute by Craddock on Provincial Legislative Councils, 26 June 1916, *CP*17.

18. See above, note 4; *H.Poll.*Dep.3, May 1917.

19. Hill to Seton, 7 [May 1916], *Seton Papers* 22, and 22 May [1916] and 24 Aug. 1916, *ibid.* 6. Hill's first minute on reforms had been largely inspired by Willingdon (who sent it to Crewe).

20. *Speeches* I, 85, 88–9 and 232.

21. See Chelmsford to Chamberlain, 6 Oct., and Zulfikar Ali Khan to Maffey, 30 Sept. 1916, *CP*2; V to S/S, 24 Oct. 1916, *CP*7; and also

memorandum of Ali Chaudhuri, and a review of the 19 Members' scheme by Raja Kushalpal Singh (member, United Provinces' Legislative Council), sent to Holderness, 18 May 1917, *H.Poll.*243, May 1917.

22. Meston to Chelmsford, 4 Sept. 1916, *CP2*.

23. *Speeches* I, 191.

24. Marris to Meston, 22 Sept., with Meston to Chelmsford, 22 Sept. 1916, *Meston Papers* 1.

25. Meston to Chelmsford, 22 Sept., and Chelmsford to Meston, 14–15 Oct. 1916, *Meston Papers* 1.

26. Chelmsford to Chamberlain, 25 Aug. 1916, *CP2*, and to Lowndes, 23 Oct. 1916, *Lowndes Papers*; Hill to Seton, 6 March [1916], *Seton Papers* 22. Lowndes had suggested stepping down in Sinha's favour, but Chelmsford also thought it 'all important that Carmichael's successor should have a man of Sinha's judgment to help him'.

27. HD despatch, 24 Nov. 1916, *H.Poll.*358, Dec. 1916; Chelmsford to Chamberlain, 24 Nov. 1916, *CP2*. Chelmsford asked Lowndes to persuade Nair to modify the language of his dissent (not 'withdraw any of his concrete proposals'): 'I absolutely decline to forward a despatch to which such a dissenting minute as his is attached'. Chelmsford thought the fault bad drafting, and believed—though 'sadly shaken of late'—that Nair was 'really sound at bottom' (to Lowndes, 20 Oct. 1916, *Lowndes Papers*). Hill wrote: 'the delay was . . . due to Sanky's Congress manifesto. The blighter had *agreed* to the whole thing and sprung his dissent (the result of confabs with the politicians) suddenly on us when the despatch was fully drafted. His dissent . . . is written largely by another (said to be Sinha!).' To Seton, 31 March [1917], *Seton Papers* 22.

28. Hardinge to Chamberlain, 10 Jan. 1917, *ACP*12/102.

29. See above, note 17.

30. See above, note 27; the Viceroy's memorandum was Appendix III of the November despatch.

31. Kitchener to Richards, 24 Sept. 1908, *Richards Papers* 2 (and see also Fleetwood Wilson's dissent, *Wilson Papers* 2a and 10). For earlier views see Minute by Dufferin, attached to G/I despatch, 6 Nov. 1888; Note by Lansdowne on Mandate of Parliament for Indian Councils Act 1892; G/I despatch, 26 Oct. 1892; Report of Committee considering Minto's proposals, 1906; G/I despatches, 21 March 1907 and 1 Oct. 1908: annexures to Craddock's minute of dissent to the November despatch (see above, note 27). Crewe later admitted that the need for a change had become clear, as 'events have moved fast', since his repudiation of 'misapprehensions' about Hardinge's despatch; see *Parliamentary Debates* (Lords) 37, No. 109 (12 Dec. 1919), 986.

32. Chelmsford to Meston, 20 July 1916, *Meston Papers* 1.

33. Georges Fischer, *Parti travailliste et la décolonisation de l'inde*, Paris 1966, 54–5.

34. See above, note 19.

35. Chamberlain to Chelmsford, 10 Jan. and 2 Feb. 1917, *CP3*; Meston to Chelmsford, 15 March 1917, *Meston Papers* 1.

36. Chamberlain to Chelmsford, 22 March 1917, *CP3*; Report on

G/I despatch, by F. W. Duke, A. A. Baig, M. Hammick, C. S. Bayley, W. D. Sheppard, T. W. Holderness and Lord Islington, 16 March 1917, *ACP*21/4/4.

37. Chelmsford to Chamberlain, 7 June 1917, *CP*3.

38. Marris to Seton, 21 Nov. 1916, *Seton Papers* 6; Chamberlain to Chelmsford, 2 May 1917, *CP*3.

39. *Ibid.*, and 15 May 1917.

40. S/S to V, 22 May 1917, *H.Poll.*305, July 1917.

41. V to S/S, 1 May 1917, *CP*8.

42. Chamberlain to Chelmsford, 22 March, and 2 and 15 May, *CP*3, and see S/S to V, 22 May 1917, *CP*8.

43. India Office Memorandum on Reforms, 24 May 1917, *ACP*21/4/5; Islington to Chamberlain, 11 May 1917, *ACP*21/5/10.

44. Chamberlain to Chelmsford, 8 May 1917, *CP*3; and see Meston to Chamberlain, 16 April 1917, *ACP*12/154.

45. Chamberlain to Chelmsford, 15 May, and also 29 March 1917, *CP*3. Chamberlain saw a commission as a conservative influence, a means of gaining authority to stand up to 'preposterous' demands from the Indian politicians, who had 'found out how to agitate'.

46. Chamberlain, Cabinet minute, 22 May 1917, *ACP*21/4/16.

47. V to S/S, 30 May 1917, *CP*8; Chelmsford to Chamberlain, 7 May 1917, *CP*3; *H.Poll.*Dep.3, May 1917. Hill's ideas reappeared; see below pp. 81–2. Meston had been advancing Marris's idea; see [Marris] to Seton, 28 Jan. 1917, *Seton Papers* 7.

48. Meston to Chelmsford, 5 April 1917, *Meston Papers* 1.

49. V to S/S, 30 May 1917, *CP*8.

50. Chelmsford to Chamberlain, 13 and 31 May, *CP*3, and V to S/S, 18 May 1917, *CP*8. See also G. N. Barnes to Chamberlain [June or July 1917], *ACP*12/10.

51. Chamberlain to Chelmsford, 14 and 27 June 1917, *CP*3.

52. Chelmsford to Chamberlain, 26 May 1917, *CP*3.

53. Willingdon to Chelmsford, 27 June and 8 and 18 July, and Pentland to Chelmsford, 16 July (plus Pentland to Chamberlain, 7 July) 1916, *CP*17.

54. Chelmsford to Willingdon, 25 May and 15 and 24 July, *CP*17, and 14 July 1916, *CP*2.

55. Chamberlain to Chelmsford, 8 and 16 Aug., and to Willingdon, 15 Aug. 1916, *CP*2.

56. S/S to V, 27 Nov., *CP*7, Chamberlain to Chelmsford, 27 Nov., *CP*2, and Chamberlain to Willingdon, 30 Sept. (with Crerar to Maffey, 28 Nov.) 1916, *CP*17.

57. V to S/S, 1 Dec. 1916, *CP*7.

58. Bombay Provincial Congress Committee, 'Congress Memorandum on Reforms', with Chelmsford to Chamberlain, 28 Dec. 1916, *CP*2. The Muslims involved seem to have been largely the U.P. 'Young Party'; see Francis Robinson, *Separatism among Indian Muslims*, Cambridge 1974, ch. 6.

59. Meston to Chelmsford, 11 and 12 Jan. 1917, *CP*18.

60. Chelmsford to Montagu, 28 Aug. 1917, *CP*3.
61. Chelmsford to Willingdon, 21 Jan. 1917, *CP*18.
62. V and V(HD) to S/S, 18 May 1917, *CP*8.
63. Chelmsford to Chamberlain, 19 May, *CP*3, and to Willingdon, 21 May 1917, *CP*18.
64. Chelmsford to Chamberlain, 7 May 1917, *CP*3.
65. Meston to Chelmsford, 5 May 1917, *Meston Papers* 1.
66. India Office Memorandum on Reforms, 24 May 1917, *ACP*21/4/5.
67. S/S to V, and Cabinet memorandum by Chamberlain, 22 May 1917, *ACP*21/4/16–17.
68. Meston, 'Note on Constitutional Reforms in India', and Meston to Chamberlain, 21 May, and Chamberlain to Meston, 19 June 1917, *ACP*21/5/24–6.
69. J. B. Brunyate to Chelmsford, 20 June 1917, *CP*15; Chamberlain to Chelmsford, 2 and 15 May 1917, *CP*3.
70. V to S/S, 11 June 1917, *CP*8.
71. Chelmsford to Chamberlain, 7 June 1917, *CP*3.
72. *Ibid.*, 7 July 1917. Earlier Du Boulay had been 'astonished at the advance made by Indian politicians in their overt demands' since his return to Britain six months before (to Seton, 10 Nov. 1916, *Seton Papers* 6).
73. See below, chapter 5.
74. Meston to Chelmsford, 25 July 1917, *CP*19. See also Meston, 20 June, *CP*18, and 7 July, and Robertson, 15 July, and J. B. Wood (Political Secretary, F&PD) to Chelmsford, 20 July, and Chelmsford to Robertson, 21 July, and to Meston, 23 July 1917, *CP*19.
75. Chelmsford to Montagu, 27 July 1918, *CP*4.
76. Chamberlain, Cabinet minutes, 12 and 26 June 1917: see *ACP*21/4/18–20. See also V to S/S, 21 June and 6 July 1917, *CP*8.
77. Chamberlain to Chelmsford, 5 July 1917, *CP*3. For this and subsequent Cabinet discussions, see also War Cabinet minutes, 161(1), 172(13), 176, 181(18) and 214(11), *Curzon Papers* 588.
78. V to S/S, 10 July 1917, *CP*8.
79. Chelmsford to Chamberlain, 7 July 1917, *CP*3.
80. See above, note 78.
81. V to Prime Minister, 16 July, and to S/S (Montagu), 18 July and 2 Aug. 1917, *CP*8.
82. Banerjea to Chelmsford, 7 Aug. 1917 (plus Resolution, Congress/League Joint Session, Bombay, 28–9 July 1917), *H.Poll.*638, Nov. 1917.
83. V(HD) to S/S, 12 Aug. 1917, *CP*8.
84. V to S/S, 8 Aug., *CP*8, and Chelmsford to Montagu, 7 Aug. 1917, *CP*3; Montagu, note, 9 Aug. 1917, *Curzon Papers* 439.
85. Montagu to Chelmsford, 3 Aug., *CP*3, and Montagu, Cabinet memo., 30 July 1917, *ACP*15/5/5.
86. Montagu to Willingdon, 3 Aug., *MP*16, and S/S to V, 1 Aug. 1917, *CP*8; Montagu to Curzon, 9 Aug. 1917, *Curzon Papers* 439. The 'Cabinet' was the Imperial War Cabinet, an inner group, supplemented from the

larger according to the subject discussed; see A. J. P. Taylor, *English History 1914–1945*, Harmondsworth 1970, 111–12, and Stephen Roskill, *Hankey, Man of Secrets*, London 1970, 334–75.

87. Montagu, Cabinet memorandum, 30 July 1917, *ACP*15/5/5; Chamberlain, draft terms of reference for a commission, *ACP*15/4/24; Chamberlain to Montagu, 8 Aug., *ACP*15/5/3, and S/S to V, 14 Aug. 1917, *CP*8. The full text, read in the Commons on 20 Aug. 1917, had this as its central passage: 'The policy of His Majesty's Government, with which the Government of India are in complete accord, is that of the increasing association of Indians in every branch of the Administration, and the gradual development of self-governing institutions, with a view to the progressive realisation of responsible government in India as an integral part of the British Empire'.

88. Curzon, note, 2 July 1917, *Curzon Papers* 439 and *ACP*21/4/23. For a fuller version of this argument, see my 'The British Cabinet and Indian Reform 1917–1919', *Journal of Imperial and Commonwealth History* 4, 3 (1976).

89. Montagu to Chamberlain, 15 Sept., *ACP*15/5/8, and Curzon to Chamberlain, 25 Aug. 1917, *ACP*14/1/5a.

90. 6 June 1918, *ACP*21/6/44 and *Curzon Papers* 438.

91. 5 Feb. 1918, *Curzon Papers* 439.

92. G. K. Gokhale, 'Memorandum on Political Reforms', with Crerar to Maffey, 6 Aug. 1917 (sent at Chelmsford's request), *CP*19; and *H.Poll.*Dep.5, Aug. 1917: Chelmsford and Vincent seem to have seen the Memo. first in Aug. 1917, when Willingdon sent a copy, and Vincent ordered extra copies printed.

93. 'Draft Round Table articles on India', [1912], and other papers, *Lothian Papers* GD40/17/3, 6, 7, 9, 15 and 16. See also *Meston Papers* 10, and S. R. Mehrotra, 'The Politics behind the Montagu Declaration of 1917' in C. H. Philips, ed., *Politics and Society in India*, London 1963. Both Meston and W. S. Marris had been seconded to South Africa during Milner's time and presumably met the Round Table group's founders there.

94. See *The Times*, 13 July 1974.

95. Curtis to Coupland, 19 May 1917, *Curzon Papers* 438.

96. Chelmsford to Meston, 5 May, *CP*17, and to Kerr, 1 July, and Kerr to Chelmsford, 19 May 1916, *CP*15; Curtis to Chelmsford, 8 Sept. 1917, *CP*19; Hill to Seton, 22 May [1916], *Seton Papers* 6.

97. Chelmsford to Chamberlain, 26 May 1917, *CP*3. In general, see also D. C. Ellinwood, 'The Round Table Movement and India', *Journal of Commonwealth Political Studies* 1971.

98. Chamberlain to Chelmsford, 8 May 1917, *CP*3; Kerr to Curtis, 23 April 1917, *Lothian Papers* GD40/17/33.

99. Basu to Wedderburn, 27 March 1917, *ACP*21/5/11; Basu to Sir Theodore Morison, 23 Dec. 1915, *ACP*14/1/9a.

100. Minute by Meston, [26 Oct. 1917], *H.Public* (*C*) 572, Oct. 1918; Kerr to Curtis, 9 and [12?] July and 2 Oct., and Curtis to Kerr, 28 Aug. 1917, *Lothian Papers* GD40/17/33.

101. 'The Problems of Indian Government', Oxford, 8 Aug. 1917, *ACP*15/5/4, and with Islington to Chelmsford, 9 Aug. 1917, *CP*15.
102. See above, note 97.
103. Hill to Chelmsford, 26 June 1917 (plus a note on the reforms), *CP*18. Hill had introduced the word 'responsible' in a letter of March 1916; see below, Chapter 6, note 23. (For the dating of this letter, by internal evidence, see *ibid.*, note 5, and Chapter 2, note 14.) Later he wrote of 'education in the wider responsibilities of admn.' (to Seton, 22 May [1916], *Seton Papers* 22).
104. Chelmsford to Montagu, 7 Aug. 1917, *CP*3.
105. Chelmsford to Chamberlain, 26 and 31 May 1917, *CP*3.
106. Chelmsford to Montagu, 7 Aug., and see also 28 Aug. 1917, *CP*3.
107. See Ronaldshay to Chelmsford, 13 Aug. 1917, *CP*19.
108. *H.Public* (C) 572, Oct. 1918; O'Dwyer to Chelmsford, 27 May 1917, *CP*3; and see above, note 24, and Marris to Seton, 21 Nov. 1916, *Seton Papers* 6.
109. At the conference in August (see above, note 107), the minority (13) succeeded in having the question referred to the Provincial Congress Committees; the next Congress gave it no support. See Robertson to Chelmsford, 8 Sept. 1917, *CP*19.
110. Chelmsford to Montagu, 28 Aug. 1917, *CP*3.
111. Meston to Chelmsford, 10 Oct. 1917, *CP*19.
112. Chelmsford to Meston, and to Robertson, 13 Sept. 1917, *CP*19.
113. *H.Public*(C) 567–75, Oct. 1918 (G/I circular, 8 Sept. 1917, with replies); Chelmsford to Montagu, 22 Sept. (plus Hill, 'Suggestions for change in the Constitution of, and Powers exercised by, Provincial Legislative Councils', 7 Sept.) 1917, *CP*3. See also Chelmsford to Curzon, 17 Nov. 1917, *CP*15.
114. 'Report of Second Special India Office Committee on Indian Reforms' (under Sir William Duke), 30 Sept. 1917, *ACP*21/4/27.
115. S/S despatch, 19 Oct. 1917, *H.Poll.*337, March 1918, and *ACP*21/4/28.
116. Chelmsford to Chamberlain, 20 Sept. 1918, *ACP*18/3/15.

Chapter Four.   First Steps

1. See Edwin S. Montagu, *An Indian Diary*, London 1930.
2. V to S/S, 29 Aug. 1917, *CP*8. The Bengal revolutionaries, however, had condemned it; see *Sedition Committee Report* 1918, Appendices, p. xxix (Proclamation of the Indian Revolutionary Committee), *IOR* L/Parl 444.
3. See *H.Public* A 451–95, May 1918.
4. S/S to V, 24 and 30 Aug. and 21 Sept., and V to S/S, 28 Aug. and 21 Sept. 1917, *CP*8.
5. Chelmsford to heads of provinces, 27 Sept. 1917, *CP*19.
6. HD circular, 14 Sept. 1917, *H.Public* 453, and see also 451–95, May 1918. One rule was that only constitutional matters might be discussed.

Ishrat Ali's *New Era*, in an article which cost it its security (8 Dec. 1917), recorded that a deputation was excluded when it refused to delete from its address a section about the Ali brothers; see *H.Poll.*455, Jan. 1918.

7. See Montagu, *Diary*, 7–8, 33–5, 64, 163, 283, 285, 287–8, and 310.

8. S/S to V, 24 and 29 Aug. 1917, *CP*8.

9. See Chelmsford to Curzon, 17 Nov. (with a collection of reforms schemes and departmental papers) and 1 Dec., to Chamberlain, 14 Dec. 1917, to Selborne, 3 Jan. 1919, and to Dawson, 17 May 1918, *CP*15.

10. See Chelmsford to Chamberlain, 20 Sept., and to Dawson, 17 May 1918, *CP*15. (Montagu's *Indian Diary* does not contradict this assertion.)

11. See Montagu and Chelmsford, *Report on Indian Constitutional Reforms*, 22 April 1918, Chapters 1 to 6. (The Report may be consulted in several collections, including Parliamentary Papers, Cmd. 9109. I have used the signed copy, *CP*42.) On the drafting, see Montagu, *Diary*, 338–46, 355, 358–9 and 362. See also the local government reports on the working of the Morley–Minto reforms, *H.Public* 600–6, May 1918.

12. Chelmsford to Curzon, 17 November 1917, *CP*15.

13. See Chelmsford to Selborne, 3 Jan. 1919, and to Guest, 8 April 1918, *CP*15.

14. Montagu and Chelmsford, *Report*, 71 and see 52; minute by Meston, *H.Public(C)* 572, Oct. 1918, quoted above, p. 83 (q.v.).

15. Chelmsford to Selborne, 3 Jan. 1919, *CP*15.

16. See Chelmsford to Chamberlain, 14 Dec. 1917, *CP*15; Report of Second Special Committee on Indian Reforms (Sir Wm. Duke) 30 Sept. 1917, *ACP*21/4/27; and S/S to V, 16 Oct. 1917, *CP*8. Montagu thought Duke was probably the inventor of 'dyarchy'; see Montagu, *Diary*, 377.

17. See *ibid.*, 12–14 (10 Nov. 1917); and Addendum to Duke Memorandum, in Montagu to Chelmsford, 26 Nov. 1917, *CP*3.

18. See Montagu and Chelmsford, *Report*, 116–19; Montagu, *Diary*, 11–12 and 54; Meston, Memorandum on Reforms Scheme, 20 Jan. 1918, *H.Public(C)* 590, Oct. 1918; Report of an informal committee appointed to consider the most suitable line of advance towards responsible government, Allahabad, 24 Oct. 1917, and Joint Memorandum from Europeans and Indians (of Bengal), *ibid.* 579.

19. See Montagu to Chelmsford, 26 Nov. 1917 (with enclosures), *CP*3; Montagu, *Diary*, especially pp. 49, 102–3, 141–2, 147 and 223–4; Montagu and Chelmsford, *Report*, 106–8 and 119–24. The recommendations of the Report, with paragraph references, are summarized in an appendix to that Report; descriptions are widely available, and no attempt is made here to give a comprehensive survey of the proposals.

20. Montagu and Chelmsford, *Report*, 110–15.

21. *Ibid.* 106–9.

22. See Montagu to Chelmsford, 1 Jan. 1918, *CP*4; Montagu, *Diary*, 179–83, 186–7.

23. See Chelmsford to Guest, 8 April, *CP*15, and to Ronaldshay, 30 May 1918, *CP*20, and V(HD) to S/S, 25 April 1919, *CP*10; Montagu and Chelmsford, *Report*, paragraph 218.

24. *H.Public(C)* 579, Oct. 1918; and see Chelmsford to Curzon, 1 Dec.,

to Chamberlain, 14 Dec., *CP*15, and to Islington, 30 Dec. 1917, *CP*3. Meston retained doubts about the adoption of Western forms; he wrote, in some speech notes (1919?), 'We gave OUR best gift. ?best for India.' (*Meston Papers* 25).

25. Montagu, *Diary*, 149, and see 65, 157 and 176–7.

26. *Ibid.*, 19 and 110; Montagu and Chelmsford, *Report*, 101–3; Chelmsford to Montagu, 8 Sept. 1917, *CP*3; Joint memorandum by Sir W. Meyer and Mr. Howard (13 Oct. 1917) and Memorandum by Mr. J. B. Brunyate (30 Sept. 1917), with HD circular, 11 Dec. 1917, *H.Public(C)* 579, Oct. 1918.

27. Memorandum by Sir L. Abrahams, *ibid.*; and see another copy of the same, and notes by T. W. Holderness, L. Currie and Sir L. Abrahams, *ACP*21/2/29–32.

28. *H.Public* 155–71, Sept. 1919.

29. Montagu, *Diary*, 306–8; Montagu and Chelmsford, *Report*, 105; Chelmsford to Curtis, 16 July 1918, *CP*15.

30. See Montagu, *Diary*, 48, 85, 90–3, 105, 116–17, 124, 165, 176–7, 194–7, 202, 271, 308–10, 312; Montagu to Chelmsford, *Report*, 129–35. Hill had suggested a second chamber for *provinces* on 26 June 1917; Duke (20 Aug. 1917) thought the idea should be encouraged (*Seton Papers* 7).

31. Montagu to Chelmsford, 15 March, and Chelmsford to Montagu, 16 March 1918, *CP*4; Montagu, *Diary*, 326–7 and 330; Montagu and Chelmsford, *Report*, 134, and see also 113 (on the provincial official *bloc*) and 44–6 (on the defects of the *bloc*).

32. *Ibid.*, 93–4.

33. Montagu, *Diary*, 96–7.

34. *Ibid.*, 16–17 and 59–60.

35. *Ibid.*, 363 and 369; Chelmsford to Curtis, 16 July 1918, *CP*15, and see also Chelmsford to Islington, 30 Dec. 1917, *CP*3.

36. Montagu, *Diary*, 41 and 363, and see also 16–17, 72, 248, 259–60, 264, 338–46, 356–7 and 359.

37. *Ibid.*, 110–11.

38. Chelmsford to Chamberlain, 17 May 1918, *ACP*18/3/11.

39. Montagu, *Diary*, 179–80 and 194–5.

40. *Ibid.*, 276. On this occasion Montagu was lobbying Nair. For Chelmsford's disagreement see pp. 269–71 and 274.

41. *Ibid.*, 338–46.

42. *Ibid.*, 10.

43. *Ibid.*, 248. My view differs from Shane Ryland, 'Edwin Montagu in India, 1917–1918: Politics of the Montagu–Chelmsford Report', *South Asia* 3 (1973).

44. Chelmsford to Montagu, 24 April 1918, *CP*4, and see Montagu, *Diary*, 374; Stamfordham to Ronaldshay, 24 July 1919, *Ronaldshay Papers* 5b.

45. Montagu to Chelmsford, 31 May 1918, *CP*4.

46. V to S/S, 15 and 24 May 1918, *CP*9; and Cmd. 176.

47. Montagu to Chelmsford, 16 May, and Chelmsford to Montagu, 30 May and 27 June, *CP*4, and S/S to V, 15 May 1918, *CP*9.

48. Montagu to Chelmsford, 16 and 31 May 1918, *CP*4.
49. S/S to V, 29 May and 7 June, *CP*9, and Montagu to Chelmsford, 15 June 1918, *CP*4.
50. Chamberlain, Cabinet note: 'Mr. Montagu's Report', 6 June 1918, *ACP*21/6/44; Chamberlain to Chelmsford, 20 June, *CP*15 and *ACP*18/3/ 13, and to Ronaldshay, 7 June 1918, *ACP*21/5/70; and *Curzon Papers* 438.
51. Curzon to Montagu, 26 July 1918, *Curzon Papers* 439. See also Montagu to Chelmsford, 3 and 26 July, 5 Sept., 22 Oct., 7 and 28 Nov. 1918, *CP*4; Montagu to Chamberlain, 6, 12 and 18 July, and 30 Oct., and Chamberlain to Curzon, 6 and 25 July, and to Montagu, 6, 15, 26 July, and Curzon to Chamberlain, 26 July 1918, *ACP*21/5/5–6, 48–57 and 64. For a fuller account see my 'The British Cabinet and Indian Reform 1917–1919', *loc. cit.*
52. See Montagu to Chelmsford, 15 June 1918, *CP*4, and to Curzon, 6 June 1918, *Curzon Papers* 439; Chamberlain, Cabinet note, 6 June 1918, *ACP*21/6/44; *Parliamentary Debates* (Lords) 31, No. 71, 865 (24 Oct. 1918); and also Lord Crewe and Donoughmore, *ibid.* 832–5 and 850–63, and Montagu, *Parliamentary Debates* (Commons) 116, No. 68, 343 (22 May 1919).
53. Chelmsford to Montagu, 31 Aug. 1918, *CP*4. See also Chelmsford to Selborne, 3 Jan. 1919, *CP*15, and note his wish to 'persuade the European Association to take a less extreme line' (to Ronaldshay, 4 Dec. 1919, *Ronaldshay Papers* 5a).
54. See *Meston Papers* 23.
55. S/S to V, 22 Aug., 2 and 14 Sept., and 2 and 8 Oct., and V to S/S, 23, 30 and 31 Aug., and 9, 12 and 16 Sept., *CP*9, and Chelmsford to Montagu, 19 Oct. and 6 Nov. 1918, *CP*4. The work of the Committees may be followed up in their Reports, Cmd. 141 (Franchise) and Cmd. 103 (Functions), and in the two despatches presenting the Government of India's views, Cmd. 176 and Cmd. 123. See *IOR* L/Parl409. In spite of Montagu, there seems to have been little contact between Southborough and Feetham's committee; see H. L. Stephenson to Seton, 7 Jan. 1919, *Seton Papers* 9 ('We are each too busy to worry about what the others are doing').
56. *H.Public* 1–130 and 153–67, Sept. 1919; PSV to Vincent, 17 Oct., V to G/Bombay, 16 Oct., Chelmsford to Willingdon, 18 Oct., and PSV to Resident, Aden (for Southborough), 24 Oct. 1918, *CP*21.
57. Robertson to Southborough, 11 Nov., Southborough to Chelmsford, 20 Nov. 1918, *CP*21; and see Harcourt Butler to Chamberlain, 12 Feb. 1919, *ACP*21/5/4.
58. Chelmsford to Pentland, 5 Jan. 1919, with Chelmsford to Montagu, 15 Jan. 1919, *CP*5.
59. V to S/S, 12 July 1918, *CP*9. Of other notable papers, the *Bombay Chronicle*, *Kesari* and *New India* found the Report unacceptable; the Lahore *Tribune* was disappointed; the Madras *Justice* deplored the lack of non-Brahmin representation, and the Bengali European papers the lack of European; the *Advocate of India* and two other Bombay papers (the Karachi *Daily Gazette* and *Samachar*) gave qualified approval. Thirty-

two papers were cited. See also, for details of Bengal newspapers as noted by the government, Ronaldshay to Montagu, 24 July 1918, *MP*29.

60. V to S/S, 8 Sept. 1918, *CP*9. The voting was 48 to 2. See also Wacha to Chelmsford, 12 July, and Bikaner to Chelmsford, 17 July 1918, *CP*21; and Ronaldshay to Montagu, 1 Sept. 1918, *MP*29.

61. V to S/S, 12 July, *CP*9, and Gandhi to Chelmsford, 12 July 1918, *CP*21. Nevertheless Tilak and his specially founded Congress Democratic Party were later to advocate working the reforms, in opposition to Gandhi's non-co-operation; see, for example, Stanley A. Wolpert, *Tilak and Gokhale*, Berkeley & Los Angeles 1962, 287–95.

62. See Annie Besant, 'National Home Rule League', Madras 1919, and 'Wounded to Death', 'The Coming Congress', 'The Parting of the Ways', 'The Reform Act . . .', 'Patriotism and Cooperation with the new Governments', 'Our Ministers', 'Organization for Freedom', 'Responsibility of the Press', 'The Joint Report—what we have gained' and 'The First Reform Conference', National Home Rule League pamphlets, Nos. 4–13, and 17, Madras 1920; see also G. S. Arundale, 'To the Youth of India', Madras 1924, V. G. Kale, 'The Reforms', Poona 1921, and V(HD) to S/S, 25 Feb. 1920, *CP*12.

63. Montagu to Chelmsford, 10 Oct. 1918, *CP*4.

64. Montagu to Chelmsford, 15 June, 8 and 26 July, *CP*4, and S/S to V, 6 and 15 July 1918, *CP*19; and Montagu to Kerr, 6 May 1921, *Lothian Papers* GD40/17/216.

65. Montagu to Chelmsford, 15 June, 3 and 8 July, 7 Aug., 10 Oct. and 7 Nov., and also 22 Aug. and 22 Oct. 1918, *CP*4; Curtis, 2 Sept., and Dawson, 5 Nov. 1918, *CP*15; *Curzon Papers* 439; and Indo-British Assoc. pamphlets, 'The Montagu-Chelmsford Report', another of the same title (extracts from Bombay criticism), 'Indian constitutional reforms' (speeches by Lansdowne, Macdonnel, Selborne, Sydenham and Curzon), London 1918, and 'Indian opposition to home rule' and '. . . the progress of political agitation in India, 1916–19', London 1919.

66. For a graphic account of the appointment, see W. M. Gourlay to Ronaldshay, 15 Jan. 1919, *Ronaldshay Papers* 5a.

67. Chelmsford to Pentland, 8 Sept., to Meston, O'Dwyer, Gait, Robertson and Earle, 6 Oct., and to Willingdon, 11 Nov., and to all heads of provinces except Burma, Assam and the United Provinces, 30 Nov. 1917, *CP*19. See also *ACP*22/1. The Madras Government had also protested against the form of the 1917 Declaration; see G/Madras to V, 19 Aug., and Pentland to Chelmsford, 31 Aug. 1917, *CP*19.

68. *H.Public(C)* 568–91, Oct. 1918; *H.Poll.*279, July 1917; *H.Public* 449–95A, May 1918 (450 is the HD circular, 8 Sept. 1917).

69. Montagu, *Diary*, 206–24.

70. See Willingdon to Chelmsford, 31 Jan. and 14 Feb. 1918, *CP*20.

71. LG/United Provinces to V, 11 Sept., Robertson to Chelmsford, 2 Oct., Meston to Chelmsford, 10 Oct., and Chelmsford to Willingdon, 12 Sept. 1917, *CP*19.

72. Ronaldshay to Montagu, 10 June, (and to Chelmsford, 26 April) 1918, *MP*24; Willingdon to Montagu, 5 Sept. and 23 Nov. 1918, *MP*18,

and 29 March and 2 Sept. 1919, *MP*19, and to Chelmsford, 30 June 1918, *CP*20; Butler to Chamberlain, 26 Aug., and see Chamberlain to Butler, 17 Dec. 1918, *ACP*21/5/2–3; Craddock to Chelmsford, 9 July 1918, *CP*21.

73. Chelmsford to Willingdon, 4 July 1918, *CP*21.

74. Hill to Chelmsford, 19 Nov., and Willingdon to Chelmsford, 12 Dec. 1918, *CP*21; Meston to Chelmsford, 19 Dec., *CP*21, and Lloyd to Montagu, 26 Dec. 1918, *MP*24.

75. Chelmsford to heads of provinces, 29 Dec. 1918, *CP*21; Montagu to Ronaldshay, 4 March 1919, *MP*27.

76. Chelmsford to Montagu, 15 Jan., 12, 19 and 26 Feb., and 5 March 1919, *CP*5.

77. V to G/Bombay, 8 Feb., and Lloyd to Chelmsford, 18 Feb. 1919, *CP*22.

78. S/S to V, 15 and 22 Feb. 1919, *CP*10, and Montagu to Chelmsford, 22 Jan., 4 and 18 Feb. and 4 March 1919, *CP*5.

79. V to S/S, 27 Feb. 1919, *CP*10.

80. Chelmsford to Montagu, 19 Feb., 5 March, 3 April, 25 Sept. and 18 Oct., and Montagu to Chelmsford, 31 March and 1 May, *CP*5, and S/S to V(HD), 22 Feb. 1919, *CP*10. See G/I despatch, 5 March 1919, Cmd 123.

81. Montagu to Chelmsford, 18 Feb. and 1 May (postscript, 14 May) 1919, *CP*5.

82. Montagu to Chelmsford, 28 May, 11 June and 17 July 1919, *CP*5.

83. S/S to V(HD), 14 and 17 June, *CP*10, and Chelmsford to Montagu, 31 July 1919, *CP*5. Marris was supported by Vincent, Barnes, R. A. Mant and H. F. Howard (note, 23 June 1919, and other papers, *Meston Papers* 27).

84. Meston to V, 26 Oct., and to Maffey, 5 Dec., and Maffey to Meston, 3 Dec. 1918, *CP*21. Meston himself had suggested that there should be such an appointment.

85. *Parliamentary Debates* (Lords) 37, No. 109, 1030; Chelmsford to Montagu, 4 June and 18 July 1919, *CP*5.

86. See Meston to Chelmsford, 24 July, 1, 12, 23 and 28 Aug., 13, 16 and 18 Sept., and 2 and 10 Oct. 1919, and see also Meyer to Chelmsford, 5 Sept. 1919, *CP*15. See also *Meston Papers* 23 and 25; and Sinha to Ronaldshay, 17 July 1919, *Ronaldshay Papers* 5b.

87. Meston to Chelmsford, 10 Oct., *CP*15; S/S (for Meston) to V, 10 Oct., V to S/S (for Meston), 15 Oct., and V(HD) to S/S, 2 Nov. 1919, *CP*11. The education controversy was characterized by Meston as a choice between quality before quantity, and quantity before quality; see Lord Meston, *India at the Crossways*, Cambridge 1920, 36–8. Perhaps Montagu's attitude may be discerned in his earlier reluctance when agreeing to leave compulsory education to local option; he had stressed that Indian intellectuals regarded illiteracy (because it was cited as an objection to liberal reform) as a stigma which had to be vigorously attacked. (See Montagu to Chelmsford, 21 Aug. 1917, *CP*3.) Presumably then it was a necessary token of good faith to transfer all education—to place the main instrument of Indian advance firmly in Indian hands.

Meston did not press the objections to the transfer at the meeting of Roberts' India Office reforms committee, 24 July 1919; *Meston Papers* 23.
88. Meston to Chelmsford, 11 Oct. 1919, *CP*15.
89. *Ibid.* 18 Oct.
90. Meston to Chelmsford, 2 Oct. 1919, *CP*15; Young to Hailey, n.d. [Oct, 1919], *Hailey Papers* 2b. (Details of Young's letter are rather confused, and it is perhaps not reliable).
91. Meston to Chelmsford, 24 and 31 Oct. 1919, *CP*15. There is a copy of the Joint Committee Report in the *Moral and Material Progress Report* of 1919 (financial arrangements at p. 220).
92. S/S to V(HD), 19 Nov. 1919, *CP*11.
93. Meston to Chelmsford, 8 Nov., 26 Sept. and 6 Dec. 1919, *CP*15. Meston wrote admiringly at times but more often critically of Montagu. For a similar view see W. M. Gourlay to Ronaldshay, 21 and 29 Jan 1919, *Ronaldshay Papers* 5a: 'He goes up and down in the most extraordinary manner' (whereas Sinha was 'very steady at all times'). For further praise of Montagu in the Commons, see Sadler to Ronaldshay, 26 Dec. 1919, *loc. cit.*
94. For the Government of India Act (9 and 10 Geo. V, c.101; 23 Dec. 1919), see C. H. Philips, ed., *Select Documents* . . ., 273–82, or *Moral and Material Progress Report* 1919.
95. See Lowndes to Chelmsford, 24 Dec., and Chelmsford to Lowndes, 28 Dec. 1919; and Sir Stanley Reed, *The India I Knew 1897–1947*, London 1952, 189.
96. V(FD) to S/S, 7 Jan. 1920, *CP*12. For Marris's work preparing rules with the staff of his Office and the legislature's Reforms Informal Advisory Committee; see *Meston Papers* 27 and 28. On the advisory committee (formed at Montagu's suggestion) see *HD, RO Proceedings (General)* A118–26, June 1920.
97. Willingdon to Montagu, 29 March 1920, *MP*20.
98. V to G/Bengal, Bombay, Madras, LG/Bihar and Orissa, United Provinces, CC/Central Provinces, 13 July, Chelmsford to Maclagan, 14 July, G/Bombay to V, 15 July, Ronaldshay, Maclagan, Sly to Chelmsford, 16 July, V to G/Madras, Bengal, Bombay, 10 Aug., Chelmsford to Maclagan, 12 Aug., and V to G/Bombay, 10 Sept. 1920, *CP*25; and Ronaldshay to Montagu, 17 and 21 July 1920, *MP*31.
99. V(RO) to S/S, 9 Jan., 25 Feb., *CP*12, and 9 Nov. 1920, *CP*13. The allocation of seats was as follows (by constituency and province):

	Ma.	Bo.	Be.	UP	Pa.	BO	CP	As.	Bu.	Total
General	10	7	6	8	3	8	4	2	3	51
Muslim	3	4	6	6	6	3	1	1	–	30
Landholder	1	1	1	1	1	1	1	–	–	7
European	1	2	3	1	–	–	–	1	1	9
Ind. commerce	1	2	1	–	–	–	–	–	–	4
Sikh	–	–	–	–	2	–	–	–	–	2
Total	16	16	17	16	12	12	6	4	4	103

100. V(RO) to S/S, 9 Jan., 4 Feb., 13 and 21 March, *CP*12, and 9 Nov.

1920, *CP*13. The revised numbers were as follows (by constituency and provinces):

	Ma.	Bo.	Be.	UP	Pa.	BO	CP	As.	Bu.	Total
General	4	3	3	3	1	2½	2	½	2	21
Muslim	1	2	2	2	1½	1	–	½	–	10
Sikh	–	–	–	–	1	–	–	–	–	1
Total	5	5	5	5	3½	3½	2	1	2	32

(*Note:* Halves indicate seats at alternate elections)

101. V to S/S, 26 Jan., *CP*12, and V(RO) to S/S, 9 Nov. 1920, *CP*13. For comparative Morley–Minto figures see *H.Public* 174–83, June 1918 (approximately: Madras 1700 electors, elected by 170,000; U.P. 1500 by 130,000; Bengal 1400 by 600,000; C.P. 900 by 130,000; Panjab 700 by 300,000; Bombay 570 by 17,000). The evolution of detailed provincial arrangements is an important subject, especially for provincial history, but one too large to be examined here.

102. Willingdon to Montagu, 20 May, 1 June, 4 Aug. 1919, *MP*19, 30 Jan., 8 and 26 Feb., 3 and 20 March, 7 June, 14 Aug., 27 Nov. and 9, 20 and 27 Dec. 1920, *MP*20. See *Meston Papers* 33, and Eugene F. Irshick, *Politics and Social Conflict in South India*, Berkeley and Los Angeles 1969, 112–30 and 159–70.

103. See *HD, RO Proceedings (General)* A11–13, May 1920 (notes by O'Donnell, 20 March, and Marris, 5 May 1920); *ibid.* (*Franchise*) A20–29, May 1920 (notes by Marris, 31 Dec. 1919, W. M. Hailey, 1 Jan., and O'Donnell, 28 Feb. 1920); and *ibid.* (*General*) A5, May 1920 (notes by O'Donnell, 28 Feb., Marris, 7 April and Chelmsford, 12 April 1920).

104. The Rules had to be approved in London. See *Meston Papers* 29, for meetings of another India Office Reforms Committee under Roberts and later Meston—with Basu very vocal and effective—and for proceedings of the Joint Select Committee, of which Meston was now a full member as a peer. See also Meston's earlier specimen draft rules and the Joint Committee's resolutions, *ibid.* 25. For an indication of the vast amount of work which had had to be done in India, see *HD, RO Proceedings (General)* A17–26A, Feb. 1920.

Chapter Five.   Tactical Non-interference

1. Anil Seal, *The Emergence of Indian Nationalism*, Cambridge 1968, 131–93.

2. S. Gopal, *British Policy in India 1858–1905*, Cambridge 1965, 224–49, 261, 266–7 and 271–2. 'Good' government, the orthodox and self-centred concentration on efficiency, rampant in the secretariats, is discussed, for 1857–1907, in Valentine Chirol, *India Old and New*, London 1921, 102–3.

3. See for example E. Maconochie, *Life in the Indian Civil Service*, London 1926, 251–2.

4. S. R. Wasti, *Lord Minto and the Indian Nationalist Movement 1905 to 1910*, Oxford 1964, 22–5 and 93.

5. Explanations are suggested in A. Besant, *India: Bond or Free*, Adyar,

Madras 1939, 176–208, and *Congress Speeches*, Adyar, Madras 1917, 50–77 (or see excerpts in C. P. Ramaswami Aiyar, *Annie Besant*, Delhi 1963, 11–45).

6. See Francis Robinson, *Separatism among Indian Muslims*, Cambridge 1974.

7. See for example D. D. Karve (tr.), *The New Brahmans*, Berkeley, Los Angeles and Cambridge 1963, 114 and 125–284.

8. See M. R. Palande, ed. (for G/Bombay), *Source Material for a History of the Freedom Movement in India* Vol. II (1885–1920), Bombay 1958, 333–540.

9. See Palande, *op. cit.*, 687–94; N. C. Kelkar, *Home Rule and the Home Rule League*, [Poona] 1917; H. F. Owen, 'Toward Nation-Wide Agitation and Organisation: the Home Rule Leagues, 1915–1918', in D. A. Low, ed., *Soundings in Modern South Asian History*, London 1968.

10. This subject may be pursued, in addition to standard commentaries and biographies, in Gopal Krishna, 'The Development of the Indian National Congress as a Mass Organization, 1918–1923', *Journal of Asian Studies* XXIV (1965–6), 413–30; Judith M. Brown, *Gandhi's Rise to Power. Indian Politics 1915–1922*, Cambridge 1972; N. R. Phatak, ed. (for G/Maharastra), *Source Material for a History of the Freedom Movement in India* Vol. III (*Mahatma Gandhi*, Part I: 1915–1922) Bombay 1965, 46–7, 71, 76–88.

11. D. Rothermund, 'Constitutional Reforms versus National Agitation in India, 1900–1950', *Journal of Asian Studies* XXI (1961–1962), 505–6: in the struggle with agitation, government 'veered away from unmitigated autocratic rule and tended toward a manipulative maintenance of power'.

12. D. A. Low, 'The Government of India and the First Non-cooperation Movement—1920–1922', *Journal of Asian Studies* XXIV (1965–1966), 241 and 247: a wish 'to stalk Gandhi, not martyr him' is seen to have evolved after 1920, replacing the earlier (Rowlatt; 1919) view that agitation was all seditious. See also his *Lion Rampant*, London 1973, 159–69: it will be noted that I also do not follow the emphasis there on the personalities of Craddock and Vincent.

13. For fuller treatment and references for this and later paragraphs, see my 'The Government of India and Annie Besant', *Modern Asian Studies* 10, 1 (1976).

14. Chamberlain to Chelmsford, 12 July 1916, *CP*2; and see *H.Poll.*299, July 1917. According to Seton, Meston wrote that he was being given a free hand by Chelmsford, implying a contrast with Hardinge whose intervention in the 'Cawnpore mosque affair' (1913), '(understood to be on the advice of Sir Ali Imam) . . . was generally regarded as inflicting a public slur on Sir James Meston' (Seton to Chamberlain, 16 Aug. 1916, *Seton Papers* 6).

15. Chelmsford to Willingdon, 25 May and 15 July 1916, *CP*17; Montagu to Chelmsford, 17 April 1919, *CP*4.

16. HD circular, 8 April 1913, *IOR* J&P1589(4468/19). According to Fleetwood Wilson, the moderation (which ensured Hardinge's subse-

quent popularity) was secured only by his (Wilson's) efforts, in the face
of 'demands . . . which . . . will, I hope, never be made public' (to
Stamfordham, 10 June 1921, *Wilson Papers* 2b).

17. See *H.Poll.*A299–313, July 1917.

18. See A. Besant, *India a Nation*, London [1915], ix–x and 19.

19. Minute, 26 Oct. 1917, *H.Poll.*572, Oct. 1917.

20. See *H.Poll.*Dep.8, Sept. 1916, and 32, Feb. 1918. Bombay had
predicted Tilak's failure, in their fortnightly report in mid-August.

21. 20 March 1917, *H.Poll.*299, July 1917. Craddock was no friend of
even a modest Home Rule goal, unlike his successor, Vincent, whom
Cleveland (to his amazement) found looking upon Home Rule as legitimate and practical; Cleveland to [Seton?], 29 Jan. 1917, *Seton Papers* 7.

22. 27 June 1917, *H.Poll.*A310, July 1917.

23. See V(HD) to S/S, 18 May and 12 Oct. 1917, *CP*8.

24. Chelmsford to Chamberlain, 16 June and 24 July 1917, *CP*3.

25. Meston to Chelmsford, 20 June, *Meston Papers* 1, and 20 Aug. 1917,
*CP*19.

26. *New India*, 15 June 1917, *H.Poll.*Dep.14, March 1918. Reed was
strongly critical of the 'abdication' and 'negation' of the Government of
India, allowing Besant's arrest and making no encouraging statements: to
Hill, 30 June 1917—seen in the India Office by Seton and Holderness
(August 1917)—*Seton Papers* 7.

27. Chelmsford to Montagu, 8 Aug. 1917, *CP*3.

28. Chelmsford to Pentland, 14 Sept. 1917, *CP*8.

29. Chelmsford to Montagu, 22 Sept. 1917, *CP*3. Curtis wrote: 'I have
reason to believe that he [S/S] had as little to do with Mrs Besant's
release as with the rebuke administered to Sir Michael O'Dwyer': to
Meston, 15 Oct. [1917] *Meston Papers* 11.

30. Chelmsford to O'Dwyer, 14 Sept. 1917, *CP*19.

31. *H.Poll.*14, and A305–32, k.w., Sept. 1917.

32. Holderness to Chamberlain, 3 Nov. 1917, *ACP*12/109. Chamberlain
criticized Madras for not consulting the centre before arresting Besant, and
hence did not criticize the Government of India for her release; but he
strongly objected to the O'Dwyer incident as 'derogatory to the dignity of
the Government of India & destructive of the authority of the Lieutt.
Governor. . . . I fear that Chelmsford made a serious mistake . . .' (to
Ronaldshay, 9 Nov. 1917, *Ronaldshay Papers* 5a). The European Association held a protest meeting in Calcutta; see *H.Poll.*B43–5, Nov.
1917.

33. Chelmsford to Chamberlain, 17 May 1918, *CP*15.

34. *H.Poll.*Dep.29 and k.w., Feb. 1918, and see also *H.Poll.*A408–10,
July 1917.

35. See Besant to PSV, 27 and 27 Sept., Maffey to Besant, 2, 9, 10 and
21 Oct., Vincent to Chelmsford, 17 Oct., Cleveland to Maffey, 18 Oct.,
Maffey to Vincent, 18 Oct., and to Cleveland, 21 Oct., Willingdon to
Chelmsford, 28 Oct., and Chelmsford to Willingdon, 18 Oct. and 8 Nov.
1917, *CP*19. See also Chelmsford to Montagu, 18 Oct. 1917, *CP*3, on the
Ali brothers: 'Many of us came to . . . the case . . . with an open mind; but

when the causes of their internment were shown, we felt that from every point of view it was undesirable to release them.' For C.I.D. reports see *H.Poll.*247, March 1918. Cleveland's hostility to Besant persisted (see note, 3 Jan., *H.Poll.*B184, Feb. 1918). See also Willingdon to Chelmsford, 9 May 1918, *CP*20.

36. *H.Poll.*328, Sept. 1917, and 133–4, Jan. 1918. On Besant in Madras, see Eugene F. Irshick, *Politics and Social Conflict in South India*, Berkeley and Los Angeles 1969, 25–38 and (on the release) 62–7.

37. See *H.Poll.*Dep.2, Nov. 1917.

38. Chelmsford to Montagu, 5 Oct. 1917, *CP*3.

39. See *Amrita Bazar Patrika*, 19 April, *New India*, 5 May, G/Madras fortnightly report, 1 May, notes by Hignell, 20 April and 11 May, and Vincent, 21 April 1918: *H.Poll.*Dep. 48, May 1918.

40. See *Indian Social Reformer*, 31 March, *Amrita Bazar Patrika*, 8 April, *Observer*, Lahore, 6 April 1918, *H.Poll.*Dep.36, Feb. and 25, April 1918.

41. S/S to V, 22 May, and V to S/S, 5, 7 and 22 June 1918, *CP*9; Chelmsford to Montagu, 13 June 1918, *CP*4; Montagu to Pentland, 13 Aug. 1918, *MP*15; A. Besant, *An Abominable Plot: a Memorandum containing Sir Subramaniam's letter to Dr. Wilson* (of 24 June 1917), Adyar, Madras [1918]. (The question of proscribing this pamphlet provided another example of the policy in action—the Home Dept. recommended not, and Chelmsford noted, 'Leave it alone'; see *H.Poll.*Dep.55, July 1918.)

42. *H.Poll.*29–33, and Dep. 37, May 1918.

43. See *H.Poll.* 26, Nov. 1917, and 23–8 and 43, Sept. 1918, and 695, June 1919; and Dep.14, Jan. 1918; and *H. Police* 74–5, Oct. 1917. The Panjab Government were permitted to instruct magistrates to curb rumours using the Defence of India rules; see *H.Poll.*303, April 1919. See also the formal warning given to Sadasiva Aiyar of the Madras High Court for his involvement in politics while practising as a judge; *H.Poll.* 160, Feb. 1919. The existing rule on pensioners stated that pensions might be withdrawn for 'seditious propaganda or the expression of disloyal sentiments'.

44. See Bombay Secret Abstract no. 27, Poona, 6 July, and Vincent note, 19 July 1918, *H.Poll.*Dep.54, July 1918.

45. See *H.Poll.*3, Sept. 1918; and G/Bombay to HD, 8 Aug. 1918, *CP*9. Later, in April and May 1919, the G/I twice agreed to executive measures in Sind, but so insisted on discretion as to give their consent almost the force of a refusal; see *H.Poll.*307, 308, 314–17, April, and 235, May 1919; and Lloyd to Montagu, 6 April 1917, *MP*24.

46. He expressed his fears to O'Dwyer on 24 Feb. 1918; see Chelmsford to Montagu, 4 Sept. 1919, *CP*5.

47. V to HD, 8 April 1919, *CP*22. See *H.Poll.*A455–72, k.w., May 1919.

48. Vincent note, 9 April 1919, *ibid.*

49. See *H.Poll.*455–8, 462, 463, 465, 467, 469 and 471, May, and 452, Aug. 1919; HD to PSV, 9 April 1919, *CP*22; Lloyd to Montagu, 6 April, and 2 and 15 May 1919, *MP*24; Chelmsford to Montagu, 9 and 16 April

and 23 July 1919, *CP*5. Gandhi reported: 'The two days detention was no detention. . . . The officials . . . were all attention and kindness. . . . I was afforded greater comforts that I am used to when free'; Gandhi to Maffey, 15 April 1919, *CP*22. See also M. K. Gandhi, *An Autobiography* . . . (tr. Mahadev Desai), 2nd ed. Ahmedabad 1940, 342–3; and *The Collected Works of Mahatma Gandhi* Vol. XV, Ahmedabad 1965, 86–243—notably, for instructions to obey police orders and eschew violence (3 and 5 April 1919), pp. 174–8, for his interview with Chelmsford in March and later telegrams, pp. 126, 129–30, for his reaction to the Delhi shooting, pp. 173, 179, and 184–7, and for his arrest, pp. 208–10.

50. See Willingdon to Chelmsford, 5 Oct. 1917, *CP*19; Chelmsford to Willingdon, 24 June 1918, *CP*20; Meston to Chelmsford, 19 Dec. 1918, *CP*21; Lloyd to Montagu, 26 Dec. 1918, *MP*24. Willingdon was anxious because of profiteering, near-famine conditions and the influenza epidemic; Meston thought his nerves 'rather in rags'. Lloyd would have been prepared to prosecute, but dared not risk failure; he did not want to use the Defence of India Act after the armistice. The rules had been amended in July 1918 to give a clear right of deportation; see *H.Poll.*64, Sept. 1918.

51. See G/Bombay to V, 16 April 1919, *CP*22; Lloyd to Montagu, 6 April, and 2 and 15 May, and 12 June 1919, *MP*24; Willingdon to Montagu, 5 Oct. 1918, *MP*18; and *H.Poll.*20–2, June 1918, and 619–634, and 638, May 1919. Lloyd's proposal for deportations seems to have grown out of a HD suggestion in May that a warning might be given to the *Bombay Chronicle*, Horniman's paper; after the Bombay War Conference the G/Bombay had suggested 'strong measures', including internments, precensorship and outlawing of speeches on certain subjects, against the *Chronicle*, *Mahratta*, *Kesari*, Horniman, Tilak, Annie Besant and others. Lloyd had found Willingdon's predictions borne out. For an office summary on Horniman's 'swift and secret deportation', 'fully justified by results', see *H.Poll.*Dep. 63, May 1921. For earlier actions against Horniman, see *H.Poll.*B333–4, Sept. 1917; for Vincent's wish to deport him for fallacious reports of the Delhi riots in 1919, see *H.Poll.* B192–5, April 1919. On Gandhi, see *Pioneer*, 9 May, *H.Poll.*B705, July 1919.

52. *H.Poll.* 2–32, Aug., and see 406–23, Sept. 1919.

53. See *ibid.*, 218–25, 228–29, 236 and 250; Gandhi to Maffey, 14 and 15 April, and Maffey to Gandhi, 7 May 1919, *CP*22; Chelmsford to Montagu, 16 April and 18 July 1919, *CP*5.

54. Cleveland letter, 23 May, and Marris note, 24 May 1919, etc., *H.Poll.*A.261–72, k.w., Aug. 1919.

55. Lloyd to Montagu, 23 May 1919, *MP*24.

56. Lloyd to Chelmsford, 12 June 1919, *CP*22, and to Chamberlain, 11 July 1919, *ACP*18/1/6, and to Montagu, 31 May, *MP*24, and 12 June 1919, *MP*26. See also Lloyd to Chamberlain, 13 June 1920, *ACP*18/1/9. For his policy, July to August, see G/Bombay to V, 6 July, and Lloyd to Chelmsford, 27 July 1919, *CP*23; for Chelmsford's opposition to measures except in the courts, see Chelmsford to Lloyd, 22 June 1919, *CP*22.

57. Panjab demi-official, 27 May, and Marris note, 6 June 1919, *H.Poll.*A261–72, k.w., Aug. 1919.

58. Marris note, 18 June, and Vincent, 20 June 1919, *ibid.*

59. *H.Poll.*B705, July 1919, and A261–72, k.w., Aug. 1919.

60. Vincent, 28 June (2 notes), *ibid.*

61. See HD to G/Bombay, 28 June 1919, *H.Poll.*261, Aug. 1919; see also *ibid.* 262 and 270, Lloyd to Chelmsford, 27 July, and Chelmsford to Lloyd, 2 Aug. 1919, *CP*23.

62. Montagu to Lloyd, 18 July 1919, *MP*22, and Lloyd to Montagu, 24 July 1919, *MP*24.

63. *H.Poll.*Dep.36, Aug. 1919.

64. See *H.Poll.*Dep.43, May 1921.

65. See *H.Poll.*426 and 437, Oct. 1919, A261–72, Aug. 1919 (including Lloyd to Chelmsford, 6 July, V to S/S, 23 July and 5 Aug., S/S to V, 30 July and 12 and 15 Aug.), and Dep. 36, Aug. 1919 (Lloyd to S/S and V(HD), 30 July, and V(HD) to S/S, 5 Aug.); B. R. Nanda, *Mahatma Gandhi*, London 1958, 197–8.

66. See *H.Poll.*B493–502, Jan. 1920, and also Dep.40, June 1918.

67. Chelmsford to Lloyd, 1 May 1920, *CP*24; and *IOR* J&P 1530 (4597/18). (An almost exactly parallel scenario occurred over Khilafat 'one rupee' notes issued in Bengal in November 1920; see *H.Poll.*Dep.2, Feb. 1921.)

68. Vincent note, 16 Feb. 1918, *H.Poll.*Dep.10, March 1918.

69. See Willingdon to Montagu, 18 July 1917, *MP*16, and 30 April, 13 and 25 May, 16 and 29 June, 11 and 30 July, 11 Aug., and 5 Sept. 1918, *MP*18. Compare with Lloyd to his wife (1916), in Colin Forbes Adam, *Life of Lord Lloyd*, London 1948, 106—maintaining that obvious persecution merely helped agitators 'to enlist . . . sympathies . . . which they claimed before but never had'. For Willingdon's opposition to the Alis' release, predicting trouble, see Willingdon to Seton, 2 Jan. 1920, *Seton Papers* 9.

70. *New India*, 12 and 14 Nov. 1918, G/Madras to HD, 23 Jan., and Chelmsford note, 30 Jan. 1919, *H.Poll.*B150–9, Feb. 1919. The new Governor being Willingdon, ill-feeling persisted: Hill wrote that Madras struck him as 'an entirely closed borough, purposely shutting itself off from the interests and politics of the rest of India . . . in some respects in a childish manner.' (to Seton, 24 Aug. 1916, *Seton Papers* 6.)

71. *H.Poll.*295–319, Feb. 1920, and also 446, June 1919. Chelmsford called the government's letter 'unfortunate and ungracious', and Maclagan apologized; see Chelmsford to Maclagan, 15 Nov., and Maclagan to Chelmsford, 17 Nov. 1919, *CP*23.

72. *H.Poll.*B215–25, Sept. 1918.

73. 13 June 1919, *H.Poll.*Dep.56, Aug. 1919. See also *H.Poll.*A452–3, Aug. 1919.

Chapter Six. Repression

1. The main enactments of these powers were Regulation III of 1818, the Press Act 1910, the Code of Criminal Procedure and the Indian Penal

Code as last amended under Hardinge, and the Defence of India Act 1915.

2. For this and earlier paragraphs, see *H.Poll.*A9–13 and k.w., and A72–5 and k.w., May 1913, and B40–3, July 1918; Vincent to Ronaldshay, 30 Aug. 1917 and 17 April 1918, and Ronaldshay to Vincent, 3 Oct. 1917, *Ronaldshay Papers* 5b. For the sympathetic treatment of Carmichael's policy, see J. H. Broomfield, *Elite Conflict in a Plural Society*, Berkeley and Los Angeles 1968, 73–81. See also below, note 68.

3. Hardinge of Penshurst, *My Indian Years 1910–1916*, London 1948, 14.

4. Chamberlain to Chelmsford, 5 May 1916, *CP*2. In 1910 there were 9 revolutionary crimes in Bengal with one fatality and loot of Rs.78,607, while in 1915, in Calcutta alone, there were 11 incidents, 6 fatalities and loot of Rs.84,850. See *Secret Report of the Sedition Committee 1918*, 23–58, *IOR* L/Parl444.

5. See Chelmsford to Chamberlain, 14 April, *CP*2, and Carmichael to Chelmsford, 16 April, and Minute by H. E. the Viceroy on the situation in Bengal, 27 April 1916, *CP*17. See also Chelmsford to Chamberlain, 11 Jan. 1917, *CP*3. The attitude was not new: Guy Fleetwood Wilson called Carmichael's government 'the worst in India' (to Lucas, 23 Jan. 1913, *Wilson Papers* 2b); and earlier Morley ascribed the trouble to 'past slackness', 'Police difficulties', and Fraser's 'ill-health and want of energy' (to Wilson, *loc. cit.* 11).

6. Hignell, notes, 11 Feb. and 2 March 1918, *H.Poll.*B40–3, July 1918. Hill to Seton, 6 March [1916], *Seton Papers* 22.

7. *H.Poll.*A302–11, k.w., Nov. 1916. The government did approve the use of Regulation III against *specific* prisoners: *H.Poll.*198–201 and 234–40, Oct. 1916. The offence of possessing seditious literature was limited to wartime, but only because the second Rowlatt Bill was abandoned.

8. See V to S/S, 9 July 1916, *CP*7, and Chamberlain to Chelmsford, 20 June 1917, *CP*3; Sedition Committee *Report*, 23–8 and 59–60; *H.Poll.* 192–9, Jan., 144, Feb., 316–17, April, and 424–5, June 1917, and 308, May, and 480–1, June 1918. Other early initiatives were the consideration of proposals to use the Criminal Tribes Act, by redefining a tribe as any single criminal, and to take powers to detain habitual criminals after the expiry of their sentence; the government rejected these schemes. See Chamberlain to Chelmsford, 24 May, and Chelmsford to Chamberlain, 7 July 1916, *CP*2.

9. *Speeches* I, 60 (5 Sept. 1916); Chelmsford to Chamberlain, 15 Sept. 1916, *CP*2, and to Ronaldshay, 24 May 1917, *CP*18; *ED(C)Proceedings* 28–9, Oct. 1917.

10. See Ronaldshay to Montagu, 24 July 1917, *MP*21; Chelmsford to Chamberlain, 14 April, 15 Sept. and 28 Dec. 1916, *CP*2; Carmichael to Chelmsford, 3 Sept. 1916, *CP*17; Hornell (Director, Public Instruction, Bengal) to Maffey, 13 Sept. 1916, *CP*17.

11. See Sedition Committee *Report*, 75.

12. See HD to G/Bengal, 6 May, *H.Poll.* 172, May 1916, and G/Bengal to HD, 21 Sept. 1916, *H.Poll.*229, Aug. 1917. In 1920 Ronaldshay was to

suggest a separate education board for the Dacca area; see Ronaldshay to Montagu, 2 Dec. 1920, *MP*31.

13. See *H.Poll.*140, May, and 298, June 1916, and 118, April 1917; and *H.Public* 364–78, April, 44–5, July 1918, and 482–502, Dec. 1919.

14. *H.Police* 1–5, Feb. 1917. See also discussions of the Public Services Commission and measures for the indianization of the police, in *H.Police* 1–29, July 1919, and 247–335, June 1921; and, for a reorganization in the 24-Parganas district, see *H.Police* 1–3, Feb. 1919.

15. *H.Poll.* 39–40, Aug. 1916; *H.Police* 80–1, Sept. 1916, and 124–5, March, and 95–8, April 1917.

16. *H.Poll.* 44, 45, 47–49, Aug. 1916; *H.Police* 100–5, March, and 66–8, Aug. 1918, and 30–4 and 317–34, April 1919, and 217–19, Feb., and 126–7 and 174–6, April 1920.

17. See *H.Police*(*C*) 50–53, Aug., 88, Sept., and 91, Oct. 1916; *H.Police* 93–7, July, and 156–7, Oct. 1919, 96, March, and 257–8, June 1920, and 136–7, April 1921. See also G/Bengal to HD, 28 July 1916, *H.Poll.* 228, Aug. 1917. Islington thought Carmichael had made out 'a good case for a substantial increase'—which helped overcome India Office qualms about cost; notes by T. W. H.[olderness], 6 May 1916, and I[slington], 9 May [1916], *Seton Papers* 6.

18. ILC Proceedings, 6 Feb. 1919, *IOR* J&P1571(2539/19).

19. 6 May 1916, *H.Poll.*A172, May 1916; and 17 July 1916, A225–32, Aug. 1917.

20. *H.Poll.*230, Aug. 1917, and B40–3, July 1918.

21. *H.Poll.*302, 304–8, Nov., and 493–4, Aug. 1916.

22. *H.Poll.*A225–32, Aug. 1917.

23. Chelmsford to Chamberlain, 14 April 1916, *CP*2.

24. See G/Bengal to HD, 17 July 1916, *H.Poll.*227, Aug. 1917; and Chelmsford to Montagu, 19 July 1917, *CP*3.

25. G/Bengal to HD 17 and 28 July 1916, *H.Poll.*227–8, Aug. 1917. The Bengal proposal was in response to the Government of India's request which in turn was a reaction to the urging of the Secretary of State; see HD to G/Bengal, 6 May, *H.Poll.*172, May 1916, and 20 July 1916, *H.Poll.*226, Aug. 1917, and S/S despatch, 21 April 1916, followed up by S/S to V(HD), 17 July 1916, *H.Poll.*225, Aug. 1917.

26. *H.Poll.*230–2, Aug. 1917; Ronaldshay to Chamberlain, 27 June, *ACP*21/5/66 (replacement copy sent 26 April 1918, *ACP*26/4/18); Zetland, '*Essayez*', London 1956, 77.

27. CID Director to HD, 15 Dec. 1916, *H.Police* 126–31, March 1917, and J. C. Ker, *Political Trouble in India 1907–1917*, Calcutta 1917.

28. ILC Proceedings, 8 Feb. 1917, *H.Poll.*463 and 463a, May 1917, and Dep.9, June 1917.

29. *H.Poll.*A472–503, May 1918.

30. *H.Poll.*B40–3, July 1918, and see B292–316, k.w., July 1918 (containing about 400 pages of local government representations for the Rowlatt Committee).

31. See Chamberlain to Chelmsford, 22 Feb., *CP*3, and V(HD) to S/S, 16 Aug. 1917, *CP*8 (or *H.Poll.*232, Aug. 1917); G/Bengal to HD, 21

June 1917, *ibid.* 231. For evidence laid before the Committee, see *H.Poll.*
B40–3, July 1918.

32. See HD resolution, 10 Dec. 1917, and note by Holderness, 6 July
1918, *IOR* J&P1517(2404/18); Rowlatt to HD, 15 April 1918, and
Sedition Committee *Report*. The Committee members were Sir Basil
Scott, C. J. (Bombay), Rai Bahadur C. V. Kumaraswami Sastri, J.
(Madras), Sir Verney Lovett, member of the United Provinces' Board of
Revenue, and Provash Chandra Mitter, vakil, Calcutta High Court. Their
Report was unanimous.

33. See Sedition Committee *Report*, *passim*, especially 11–60, and for
the classification of evidence, 19–21, on education, 76, on rules and
ceremonies, 61, 63 and Appendices, lxiii–lxvi, on conspiracy and inter-
connection between societies, 68–74, on the Panjab, 99–113, and on other
provinces, 1–10, 87–97 and 115–22.

34. Sedition Committee *Report*, 53–6, 63–7 and Appendices, lxxxv and
lxxxix–xc.

35. The dual flavour is captured in a note-book uncovered from the
Ghose brothers' secret training school, Calcutta: 'Morning, get up at
4 am., Wash face, 4.30, Meditation, 4.30 to 5.30, Physical exercises, 5.30 to
6.00, Study in class, 6 to 9 (to begin with singing *stotras* in class), Cooking
or *shikar* ['apparently means shooting at the tree . . . or at crows'], Bath, 11
to 11.30, Meditation, 11.30 to 12' and so on. *H.Poll.*Dep. 17, May 1908.

36. See in particular the judgment, pp. 1–104, and the evidence (829pp.)
in the Supplementary Lahore Conspiracy Case (trying members of the
Ghadr conspiracy in the Panjab), *H.Poll.*221, May 1916. See also other
trial proceedings, *H.Poll.*264 and 403–10, Sept. 1916, 55–7, 63, 69 and
183, Sept. 1918; of these the first (264, Sept. 1916) and the last (183, Sept.
1918) are especially interesting, the last including prosecution evidence
from one Bibhuti Bhusan Haldar on organization and revolutionary
intentions in Benares, and the first, an appeal case, upholding the existence
of a conspiracy in Barisal. See also Leonard A. Gordon, 'Portrait of a
Bengal Revolutionary', *Journal of Asian Studies* XXVII, 2 (Feb. 1968),
197–216, and *Bengal. The Nationalist Movement*, Delhi 1974, ch. 5. Lists
of suspects detained under executive orders bear out at least that the
majority of detenus were Brahmin or Kayastha; see *H.Poll.*345 and 405,
Jan., 167, 172, 240, 251, 258, 428, 538, Feb., 479, 488, 596, 607, March,
129–34, April 26–30, 35–9, 40–4, 153–60, May, 128–31, June, 1–5, 6–10,
59–63, 479 and 492, July, 120–6, 201–7, 250–3, Aug., 28–31, Sept., 12–20,
639, 644 and 651, Nov., 318–27, 336–40, 343–59, Dec. 1917, and 339,
Jan. 1918.

37. See Sedition Committee *Report*, 81–5, 99–115 and 123–7. Japan
was also suspected of having been involved in arms shipments to India,
and of having ambitions in the area; see India Office and War Committee
memoranda, 16 and 19 May 1916, *ACP*21/6/20 and 20A.

38. See Sedition Committee *Report*, 19–21, 23–58 (increase in revolutionary crime 1906–1919), 131–2 and 139 (criticisms of the courts) and
142; *H.Police* 100, Oct. 1918; ILC Proceedings 7 Feb. 1919, *IOR*
J&P1571 (2539/19).

39. *Ibid.*; and Sedition Committee *Report*, 105–6.

40. See Sedition Committee *Report*, 141–52. For the striking similarity of these proposals to those of the Secretary of State (April, July and Oct. 1916), the Government of Bengal (July 1916), and the Government of India (Aug. 1917), see *H.Poll.*225, 227, and 230, Aug. 1917, and V(HD) to S/S, 17 Aug. 1917, *CP*8.

41. V(HD) to S/S, 23 Nov. 1919, *CP*9.

42. ILC Proceedings, 6 Feb. 1919, *IOR* J&P1571(2539/19). Corroborating this view is that of S. R. Hignell that 'With reforms, the Committees, Council & Rowlatt bills—everyone in the Govt. of India just at present seems on edge' (to Seton, 16 Feb. 1919, *Seton Papers* 9). In particular there may have been a weakening in the liberal influence of Hill, who 'will, I think, take 6 months leave home this summer, which he needs' (C. W. Waddington, principal of Mayo College, 13 Feb. 1919, *loc. cit.*).

43. See Chamberlain to Ronaldshay, 7 June 1918, *ACP*21/5/70; and Vincent's speech, 12 March 1919, ILC Proceedings, *IOR* J&P1571(2539/19).

44. ILC Proceedings, 23 Sept. 1918, and Seton, note, 8 April 1918, *loc. cit.*

45. Bengal Legislative Proceedings, *Calcutta Gazette*, 5 Feb. 1919, *IOR* J&P1577(3132/19); and *H.Poll.*B661–3, June 1919: Akhil Chandra Datta had moved for the release of D. of I. detenus (21 Jan.) but was the only speaker in favour.

46. Chelmsford to Montagu, 19 Feb., 12 and 28 March, *CP*5, and V to S/S, 28 March 1919, *CP*10. Perhaps the Council could have been handled better. Chelmsford had wished Vincent could have been more of a conciliator—he had remarked in 1918, on Vincent's performance at the Delhi War Conference, that 'if only he would keep calm, his usefulness would be increased a hundredfold'—and he must have had similar feelings over Vincent's heated exchanges with Malaviya and Banerjea at the end of the committal debate on the Rowlatt Bill. See Chelmsford to Montagu, 28 April 1918, *CP*4, and ILC Proceedings, 7 Feb. 1919, *IOR* J&P1571(2539/19).

47. Chelmsford to Montagu, 19 Feb. 1919, *CP*5. Cumming, in charge of the investigation of political crime in Bengal, told Chelmsford that Bengalis were 'heartily tired of the present unrest' and would welcome restrictions; see Chelmsford to Chamberlain, 15 Sept. 1916, *CP*2. In their letter of 17 July 1916, the G/Bengal echoed this assessment (*H.Poll.*227, Aug. 1917).

48. ILC Proceedings, 12 March 1919, *IOR* J&P1571(2539/19).

49. The Bill contained provisions punishing possession of a seditious document, giving magistrates some power to order preliminary inquiries, allowing promises of protection to witnesses, admitting evidence of previous convictions, and providing for restrictions after release; see *IOR* J&P1567(2278/19), and also below, p. 278.

50. See *H.Public* 602, May 1918. The bill which was abandoned was the Calcutta and Suburban Police (Amendment) Bill of 1910.

51. V(LD) to S/S, 22 May 1920, *CP*12.

52. HD circular, 16 March 1918, *H.Poll.*275 (and see also 272-4), April 1918. See also *H.Poll.*440-5, Aug. 1916: the Act was applied to Patna District in 1916 for the flimsiest of reasons—for the speedy trial of a clerk charged with distributing seditious literature, and because 'it was not impossible that other sedition cases' might arise.

53. Vincent note, 27 Aug. 1919, *H.Poll.*B70-5, Nov. 1919 (the ban was lifted on 1 Sept.); Gwynne, 29 Nov., and Marris, 1 Dec. 1919, *ibid.* Dep. 24, Jan. 1920.

54. See Montagu to Chelmsford, 10 Oct. and 23-4 Dec. 1918, *CP*4, and 8 and 26 March and 1 May 1919, *CP*5; S/S to V, 19 March and 2 May 1919, *CP*10; and Montagu to Ronaldshay, 25 Sept. and 24 Oct. 1918, *MP*27.

55. *Speeches* II, 174-5 (6 Feb.) and 208 (21 March 1919); Chelmsford to Montagu, 19 Nov. 1918, *CP*4, and 21 Feb. 1919, *CP*5; ILC Proceedings, 7 Feb. 1919, *IOR* J&P1571(2539/19).

56. ILC Proceedings, 6 Feb. and 18 March 1919, *IOR* J&P1571(2539/19).

57. 20 March 1919, *H.Poll.*B82, June 1919.

58. Fleetwood Wilson warned against 'handing over India to . . . Cleveland who . . . is unsuitable for special purposes' (telegram for S/S, 28 Jan. 1913, *Wilson Papers* 8).

59. Bengal Legislative Proceedings, *Calcutta Gazette*, 5 Feb. 1919, *IOR* J&P1577(3132/19)—Statement by Sir Henry Wheeler.

60. ILC Proceedings, 7 Feb. 1919, *IOR* J&P1571(2539/19)—Vincent and Lowndes.

61. See Holderness, note, 14 Feb., Basu, 4 March, and Sinha, 6 March 1919, *loc. cit.*; and above, note 54.

62. See *Speeches* I, 60 and 200 (5 Sept. and 23 Dec. 1916).

63. *H.Poll.*A472-503, May 1918; Hignell, note, 2 Feb., and discussion, 3 Feb. 1918, *H.Poll.*B40-3, July 1918.

64. See above, note 43; Chamberlain to Chelmsford, 18 Dec. 1916, *CP*2; and *H.Poll.*225, 227 and 230, Aug. 1917.

65. V(HD) to S/S, 23 Nov., *CP*19, and Chelmsford to Lloyd, 8 April 1919, *CP*22.

66. Question, Sir J. D. Rees, 23 Oct., and other questions (Commons), 17, 22, 24 and 28 Oct., and (Lords), 15 Oct. 1918; S/S to V(HD), 17 Oct. 1918; note by Seton, 10 Oct. 1918: *IOR* J&P1529(4189/19).

67. HD circular, 28 Aug. 1918, *H.Poll.*45, Jan. 1919. The spurious nature of this argument was emphasized when Vincent pointed out that it had been the government's awareness of the 'revolutionary' threat which had made them appoint the Committee; see ILC Proceedings, 23 Sept. 1918, *IOR* J&P1571(2539/19).

68. *H.Poll.*229, Aug. 1917; Lyon to Seton, 15 Aug. 1917, *Seton Papers* 7; Broomfield, *op. cit.*, 92-3.

69. HD to G/Bengal, 6 May 1916, *H.Poll.* 172, May 1916; *ibid.* 227, Aug. 1917.

70. Ronaldshay to Montagu, 13 Oct. 1918, *MP*29; *H.Poll.*493, Aug. 1916; ILC Proceedings, 6 Feb. 1919, *IOR* J&P1571(2539/19).

71. ILC Proceedings, 12 March 1919, *IOR* J&P1571(2539/19).
72. *Ibid.*, 14 and 18 March; *Speeches* II, 207–8 (21 March 1919); V to S/S, 11 Feb. 1919, *CP*10.
73. Ronaldshay to Chelmsford, 21 Feb. 1919, *CP*22; G/Bengal to HD, 28 Jan. 1919, *H.Poll.*B38–47, June 1919. They wanted powers to arrest absconders without warrant, and to impose detention as an alternative to confinement. Du Boulay regarded it as impossible to tighten up the Bill once published.
74. Report of Select Committee, 27 Feb. 1919, *IOR* J&P1571(2539/19).
75. 4 Dec. 1918, *H.Poll.*B82, June 1919.
76. Anarchical and Revolutionary Crimes Act (as amended), *ibid.* There is a copy of the Act (No. XI of 1919) in the *Moral and Material Progress Report* 1919.
77. Indian Criminal Law (Amendment) Bill, *IOR* J&P1571(2539/19); V(HD) to S/S, 2 March 1919, *CP*10.
78. *H.Poll.*B447–8, Aug. 1919, and Dep.33, April 1919.
79. ILC Proceedings, 18 March 1919, *IOR* J&P1571(2539/19).
80. *Ibid.*, 7 Feb. 1919.
81. *Bhavishya* (Allahabad), 25 April 1919 (govt. translation).
82. *H. Poll.* 339, Jan., 91–103, May 1918, and Dep. 43, July 1919.
83. *H.Poll.*639–44, Nov. 1917, 7–19, 21–2 and 30a and 339, Jan. 1918.
84. *H.Poll.*649, Nov. 1917, and 478, June, and 226, July 1918.
85. *H.Poll.*1, Sept., 125, Oct. 1918, 379–80, Feb. 1920; Sir Henry Wheeler (of Bengal Government), 20 Oct., and Ronaldshay, 21 Oct. 1919, to Chelmsford, *CP*23.
86. See S/S to V, 16 Aug. 1917, *CP*8; *H.Poll.*310–13, 316, 318–23, 327–31, Sept. 1917, and 57, 60–9, 72 and 80, Feb. 1918. See also Chelmsford to Carmichael, 24 March 1917, *CP*18; and above, Chapter 5; and HD circular, 14 Sept. 1917, *H.Poll.*14, Sept. 1917—Vincent had given an undertaking that wartime restrictions would be lifted from persons who guaranteed to abstain from violence for the duration (reply to Jinnah, ILC, 5 Sept. 1917).
87. See *H.Poll.*662–4, May 1918, and 440–91 and 518–23, June 1919.
88. See *H.Poll.*423, 440, 445–6, 450–2, 455, 458, 464–5, 468, 470–2, 474–6, and also 60–70, May 1920; V(HD) to S/S, 4 and 11 Jan. and 4 Feb., and V to S/S, 11 and 20 Jan. 1920, *CP*12; Ronaldshay to Chelmsford, 8 and 27 Jan. 1920, *CP*24; Montagu to Ronaldshay, 8 April, *MP*27, and Ronaldshay to Montagu, 5 Feb. 1920, *MP*31. For Montagu's views on the reinternment of Shaukat Ali and a general resumption of a strong line, see Montagu to Ronaldshay, *MP*27, and to Willingdon, *MP*16, 9 Sept. 1920; see also below, pp. 254 and 256–7.
89. See *H.Poll.*156–60, March, and 265–6, April 1920; Ronaldshay to Montagu, 8 April, 12 May, 9 June and 6 July 1920, *MP*31, and 6 Jan. 1921, *MP*32, and to Chamberlain, 26 April 1918, *ACP*21/5/71—even in 1918 Ronaldshay was enunciating a principle of maximum possible releases. See also *H.Poll.*B38–49, Feb. 1920.
90. See ILC Proceedings, 19 March 1918, *H.Poll.*Dep.1, and 21 Feb. 1917, *H.Poll.*799, April 1917.

91. See *H.Poll*.1–8, May, and 14–17, 319–20 and 324–6, June, 79–81, Aug., 202–14, Sept., 108–18, Oct., and 105–6, Nov. 1918, and 3–5 and 206, Jan. 1919; Chelmsford to Montagu, 19 July 1919, *CP*3. The Bengal objections were not in principle—the local government had suggested a limited sort of advisory council as early as July 1916; see *H.Poll*.227, Aug. 1917. For visiting committees in Bihar and Orissa, see *H.Poll*.B6, Sept. 1916.
92. *H.Poll*.18, Oct. 1918 (Beachcroft-Chandavarkar memorandum, 31 Aug. 1918), and 206, Jan. 1919 (Rauf-Lindsay report, 16 Dec. 1918).
93. *H.Poll*.149 and 151, Sept. 1918; and Dep.63, April 1918, and Dep.29 and 45, March 1918 (for Besant's accusations); Ronaldshay to Montagu 10 June and 24 July 1918 (with copy of Stevenson-Moore—Mitter report, 6 June 1918), *MP*29, and to Chamberlain, 26 April 1918, *ACP*21/5/71.
94. See *H.Poll*.154–5, 161–2 and 165, July 1919; *H.Police*, 133–58, Dec. 1917, and also 217–39, Aug. 1918. (The Government of India were fully informed after the event: these very extensive proceedings include official reports from all levels and trial transcripts.) See also *Bihar and Orissa District Gazetteers—Shahabad* (revised ed., 1924); Gait to Chelmsford, 14 Oct. 1917, *CP*19; and Montagu to Chelmsford, 3 July 1918, *CP*4.

Chapter Seven.   Disturbances

1. Barron to Du Boulay, 23 April 1919, *H.Poll*.Dep.5, May 1919.
2. *H.Poll*.Dep.33, April 1919.
3. 27 March 1919, *H.Poll*.B141–7, May 1919.
4. Chelmsford to Montagu, 8 Sept. 1917, *CP*3. For general background see Ronaldshay to Montagu, 13 Oct. 1918, *MP*29, and 19 May 1919, *MP*30; G/Bombay to V, 23 April, and Ronaldshay, 22 May, and Craddock, 24 May 1919, to Chelmsford *CP*22; *Report of the Disorders Inquiry Committee* 1920, pp. 64–71, *CP*47 (or Cmd. 681). On influenza deaths (Panjab 42·2 per 1,000, C.P. 56·8, Delhi 55·6, Bombay 45·9, Bengal 4·7) see also V(ED) to S/S, 21 Feb. 1919, *CP*10. For Panjab publicity see *H.Poll*.B447–8, Aug. 1919, and tax-defaulters see Appendices to *H.Poll*. B373, Feb. 1920.
5. Sinha, *Parliamentary Debates* (Lords) 36, No. 76, 498 (6 Aug. 1919); on Bolshevism, F&PD Secy. to General Officer Commanding, Egypt, 28 April 1919, *H.Poll*.B679, May 1919; on Cleveland, B. R. Nanda, *The Nehrus. Motilal and Jawaharlal*, London 1962, 166, and *H.Poll*. B673–85, May 1919, and A261–72, and k. w., Aug. 1919; on G/I view, V to S/S, 13 April 1919, *CP*10, and *Report of the Disorders Inquiry Committee*, 71 and 109–14. See also O'Dwyer to Chelmsford, 21 Aug. 1919, *CP*5: the Afghans had 'counted on the internal troubles . . . favouring their plans'.
6. Willingdon to Montagu, 15 April and 4 May, *MP*19, and Montagu to Lloyd, 1 May and 11 June 1919, *MP*22; Montagu to Chelmsford, 1 and 28 May and 8 Aug., and Chelmsford to Montagu, 16 April and 4 Sept. 1919 (reference to Chelmsford to O'Dwyer, 24 Feb. 1918) *CP*5; O'Dwyer to Chelmsford, 27 Aug. 1916, *CP*17 (while declining appoint-

ment as Home Member), 4 March 1918, *CP*20, and 4 May, and to
Maffey, 17 April 1919, *CP*22. See also Montagu, 22 May 1919, *Parliamentary Debates* (Commons) 116, No.
68, 328–9; draft answers to parlia-
mentary questions, 13 May, and note by Seton, 22 July 1919, *IOR*
J&P3132/19. For the earlier outbreak over recruiting see G/Panjab to
HD, 23 Feb. 1918, *H.Police* 100, April 1918. On Sikhs (and denial of a
rumour that the Golden Temple had been bombed), see *H.Poll.*B184,
May 1919. On the press see, for example, *H.Poll.*B370–89, April 1919, and
471–84, June 1920: the Panjab proscribed 83 publications, the centre
500, C.P. 380, Bombay 216, Bengal 170 and Assam 92.

7. No attempt is made here to duplicate the information and findings of
Ravinder Kumar, ed., *Essays on Gandhian Politics. The Rowlatt Satyagraha of 1919*, Oxford 1971.

8. V(HD) to S/S, 17 April 1919, *CP*10; Roos-Keppel to Maffey, 21 and
27 April, and to Chelmsford, 28 April, and Chelmsford to Roos-Keppel,
3 May 1919, *CP*22.

9. Ronaldshay to Chelmsford, 11 and 14 April 1919, *CP*22; G/Bengal
to G/I, 29 April 1919, *IOR* J&P1566(2200/19); Ronaldshay to Montagu,
14 and 22 April, 14 May and 20 Aug., *MP*30, and see Montagu to Ronaldshay, 22 April and 20 May 1919, *MP*27; *H.Poll.*Dep.33, Oct. 1919.

10. Report of Acting Commissioner of Police, Bombay, 19 April 1919,
*H.Poll.*54, July 1919, and *IOR* J&P1566(2200/19); and see *H.Poll.*354,
Sept. 1919. On Gandhi's arrest and Bombay policy, see above pp. 129 ff.

11. Report of Assistant Collector, Viramgam, 5 May, *IOR* J&P1566
(2200/19) and Report of District Magistrate, Ahmedabad, 12 April 1919,
ibid. and *H.Poll.*451–2, Sept. 1919; V(HD) to S/S, 11 April 1919, *CP*10.
See also descriptions of riot and arson in trial judgments, *H.Poll.*Dep.399–
410, Jan. 1920.

12. Report of Deputy Commissioner, Delhi, 20 May 1919, *H.Poll.*452,
Aug. 1919; Reports of Chief Commissioner, Delhi, 31 March and 17
April 1919, *IOR* J&P1566(2200/19); Inquest Proceedings, 28 and 29
[April 1919], *H.Poll.*452, Aug. 1919; *H.Poll.*Dep.5, May 1919, and 34,
Oct. 1919. Similarly troops were ordered to stay out of Delhi city between
14 and 18 Jan. 1920 during receptions for the Ali brothers: *H.Poll.*B37–38,
April 1920. See also *H.Poll.*Dep.42, Oct. 1919.

13. Note for Hunter Committee, 12 Dec. 1919, *H.Poll.*B513, Jan. 1920.

14. For this and following paragraphs, see V(HD) to S/S, 10, 11, 13, 14,
15, 17, 20, 20 and 23 April and 7 May, and V to S/S, 14, 16, 17 and 21
April 1919, *CP*10; O'Dwyer to Chelmsford, 21 April 1919, *CP*22; press
communique on Amritsar riots, 30 May 1919, and 'Punjab Disturbances'
(reprints from *Civil and Military Gazette* and list of Lahore Martial
Law Notices), *IOR* J&P1566(2200/19); and *H.Poll.*74–85, May 1919.
For the Panjab reports, very brief at first, see their telegrams of 10, 11, 13,
14, 14, 15, 15, 16, 17, 19, 20, 21, 23, 23, 24 and 30 April 1919, *H.Poll.*
B148–78, May 1919. For a chronology of events, a list of offences on railways and a statement of damage to property, see *Report of the Disorders
Inquiry Committee* 1920, Appendices I–III, pp. 167–91, *CP*47. See *ibid.*,
37–43 and 104–5 on Lahore, 19–36 and 104 on Amritsar, 44–7 on Kasur,

and 48–56 on Gujranwala. The fullest account of the disturbances is the Govt. House War Diaries and local reports, with J. P. Thomson's secret memo., *H.Poll.*B373, Feb. 1920; or the files of immediate reports at *H.Poll.*B551–605, May 1919, and 342–52 and 408–31, June 1919.
    15. *H.Poll.*A74–108, May 1919.
    16. *H.Poll.*B551 and Dep.20, May 1919. The significance of the Delhi incident was lost on the Commissioner who did not report it until it appeared in the *Mahratta*. See also V(HD) to S/S, 13 April 1919, *CP*10; *H.Poll.*B284–6, April 1919, and Dep.51, May 1921—there were no outbreaks anywhere during the *hartal* of 6 April. See also Robertson to Chelmsford, 19 April 1919, *CP*22, for an account of the *hartal* in the Central Provinces. For another example, in an area where Gandhi had been active, of disturbances as a result of his arrest, see the Kaira wire cutting case (3 of 1919), *H.Poll.*Dep.399–410, Jan. 1920. Telegraph wires were apparently cut at Gujrat as a result of Gandhi's arrest; see Prakash Tandon, *Punjabi Century 1857–1947*, Berkeley and Los Angeles 1968, 121.
    17. See *Civil and Military Gazette*, 13 April 1919, reprinted in 'Punjab Disturbances' (see above, note 14); and *H.Poll.*326, March 1920.
    18. See *H.Poll.*B134–5, March 1920, and Dep.50, May 1921.
    19. Chelmsford to Montagu, 30 April 1919, *CP*5.
    20. G/I communique, note by Hose, and Gazette Extraordinary, 14 April 1919, *IOR* J&P1566(2200/19)); *H.Poll.*146, April 1919; V to S/S, 5 May, *CP*10, and 14 July 1919, *CP*11.
    21. Chelmsford to Montagu, 25 Sept. 1919, *CP*5. Nair later made his opposition seem more general; see Willingdon (who largely agreed) to Montagu, 21 July 1919, *MP*19. On the approval of extra powers, see *H.Poll.*74–85, 91–101 and 114–18, May 1919, and *IOR* J&P1566(2200/19); the Seditious Meetings Act was applied to Lahore and Amritsar on 13 April, Multan and Jullandar on 16th, Delhi on 17th, Lyallpur on 20th, and to Sind after 29th. Defence of India rules were applied, mainly to expedite trials, to Bombay province in April, Delhi in May, and two Panjab districts in June. Martial law was approved for the Panjab progressively after 13 April with retrospective effect in respect of trials for offences relating to the disturbances; the authorities were also able to arrest without warrant persons assisting or promoting the 'rebellion'.
    22. Willingdon to Montagu, 28 April 1919, *MP*19. Willingdon (and many Europeans) were influenced by the Besant release and the O'Dwyer incident in 1917.
    23. 15 April 1919, *H.Poll.*B223 and 225, April 1919.
    24. Chelmsford to O'Dwyer, 26 April 1919, *CP*22.
    25. V(HD) to S/S, 14 June 1920, *CP*12 and *H.Poll.*228, June 1920.
    26. *H.Poll.*86–7, May 1919; O'Dwyer to Chelmsford, 16 April 1919, *CP*22; Chelmsford to Maffey, 16 June, *CP*16, and V(HD) to S/S, 15 June 1920, *CP*12 and *H.Poll.*229, June 1920.
    27. *H.Poll.*103–5 and 108, May 1919; Chelmsford to O'Dwyer, 15 April 1919. *CP*22.
    28. *H.Poll.*436–46, and B169–91, Aug. 1919; O'Dwyer, 13 and 21

May, and Maclagan, 21 May, to Chelmsford, *CP*22, and V to S/S, 8 June
1919, *CP*10; Nehru to Vincent, 20 May and 3 June, V(HD) to S/S, 8
June, and S/S to V(HD), 9 June 1919, *H.Poll.*291, 294, 300 and 302,
June 1919.

29. Gandhi to PSV, and Andrews to Maffey, 21 April, V to LG/Panjab,
and Maffey to Andrews, 23 April, *CP*22; and see S/S to V, 28 April
1919, *CP*10.

30. Johnson, report, *H.Poll.*Dep.35, Oct. 1919; *H.Poll.*Dep.139–42,
Nov. 1919, and B33, Jan. 1920.

31. Chelmsford to O'Dwyer, 30 April, *CP*22, and to Montagu, 7 May
1919, and V(HD) to S/S, 30 Aug. 1919, *CP*5; *H.Poll.*405, Sept. 1919.

32. *H.Poll.*A74–108, May 1919, and Dep.4, June 1919; V to S/S, 27
Jan. 1920, *CP*12.

33. Chelmsford to O'Dwyer, 30 April 1919, *CP*22.

34. O'Dwyer to Chelmsford, 1 May 1919, *CP*22.

35. O'Dwyer to Chelmsford, 27 May 1919, *CP*22. Contrast Maclagan
to Chelmsford, 2 June 1919, *CP*22: 'As I have now been a week in charge
here you may like to hear . . . how things seem to me to be going on.'

36. Chelmsford to Montagu, 25 Sept. 1919, *CP*5; and see draft answer
to parliamentary question, 30 June 1920, *IOR* J&P3132/19.

37. Chelmsford to Montagu, 30 April, *CP*5, and O'Dwyer to Chelmsford, 23 April 1919, *CP*22; *H.Poll.*Dep.57 and k.w., Oct 1919, and 85,
Nov. 1920; note for Hunter Committee, 12 Dec. 1919, *H.Poll.*B513, Jan.
1920, and O'Dwyer to Chelmsford, 21 April 1919, *ibid.* 148–78, May 1919.

38. O'Dwyer to Chelmsford, 13 May 1919, *CP*22; *H.Poll.* 146–52,
June 1919, and B373, Feb. 1920, and Dep.85, Nov. 1920.

39. *H.Poll.*Dep.33, Oct. 1919.

40. Chelmsford to Maclagan, 15 Nov. 1919, *CP*23.

41. Chelmsford to O'Dwyer, 12 May, O'Dwyer to Chelmsford, and
Thompson to Maffey, 15 May, *CP*22, and Chelmsford to Montagu, 21
and 28 May 1919, *CP*5; *H.Poll.*23–31, June, and 295, March 1919, and
B169–91, Aug. 1919.

42. V(HD) to S/S, 28 Aug. and 5 Sept., V to S/S, 20 Sept., and S/S to
V, 7 Aug., *CP*11, and Montagu to Chelmsford, 2 Oct., and Chelmsford
to Montagu, 1 Oct. 1919, *CP*5; *H.Poll.*14, Aug., 289–95, Nov., and 58,
Dec. 1919, and A1–16 and k.w., Aug. 1919 (for A. Caruana, note, 30
June 1919).

43. See *H.Poll.*128–35, May 1919, and Dep.42, Aug. 1919; S/S to V, 2
May 1919, *CP*10.

44. V to S/S, 4 May 1919, *CP*10; *H.Poll.*109, Sept. 1919. Appendix I
shows sentences under martial law and subsequent remissions (see
below).

45. *H.Poll.*425, Jan. 1920; HD to G/Panjab, 23 Sept., and G/Panjab to
HD, 27 Sept. 1919, *H.Poll.*59–60, Dec. 1919.

46. Maclagan to Chelmsford, 7 Aug. 1919 *CP*23; *H.Poll.*A187–97,
Oct. 1919.

47. Meston to Chelmsford, 12 Aug. 1919, *CP*15.

48. *H.Poll.*Dep.44, May 1919, and 133, Nov. 1919.

49. *H.Poll.*323–8, March 1920, and 425, 430, 434–5 and 438, April 1920, and Dep.123, March 1921.

50. *H.Poll.*B283–4, Sept. 1919.

51. V to S/S, 27 Jan., and (HD) 10 April 1920, *CP*12; *H.Poll.* 49–53, 185 and 190, June 1920.

52. Chelmsford to Ronaldshay, 17 May 1919, *CP*22; S/S to V, 2 May, and (HD) 11 and 18 June, *CP*10, and to V, 23 July, *CP*11, and Montagu to Chelmsford, 1 and 28 May 1919, *CP*5; *Parliamentary Debates* (Commons) 116, No. 68, 338, and (Lords) 36, No. 76, 502.

53. Banerjea to PSV, and to Maffey (telegram and letter), 3 April, *CP*22, and V to S/S, 5 May 1919, *CP*10; *H.Poll.* 1–14, Aug. 1919, B141–7, May 1919, and Dep.3, July 1919.

54. Seton to Hailey, 8 Jan. 1920, *Hailey Papers* 2b; Lloyd to Montagu, 30 Dec., *MP*24, and Montagu to Lloyd, 8 Aug. and 2 Oct. 1919, *MP*22; Chelmsford to Montagu, 31 July, and Montagu to Chelmsford, 11 June and 31 July 1919, *CP*5; Harcourt Butler to Chelmsford, 25 July 1919, *CP*23; Marris note, 1 July 1919, *H.Poll.*A1–16, k.w., Aug. 1919.

55. HD circular, 21 June, and Vincent notes, 3 June and 2 July 1919, *ibid.*; Chelmsford to Montagu, 31 July, *CP*5, and V to S/S, 2 Sept. 1919, *CP*11.

56. V(HD) to S/S, 12–13 July 1919, *H.Poll.*14, Aug. 1919; V to S/S, 11 Aug. 1919, *CP*11. In view of the local government's opposition, Bengal was excluded from the scope of the inquiry; see *IOR* J&P3132/19 and *H.Poll.*A1–16 and k.w., Aug. 1919. No Bengal member supported an ILC resolution for its inclusion (by Kamini Kumar Chanda, 12 Sept.); *H.Poll.* Dep.300–5, Nov. 1919. But Bengal did make its own inquiries; for example, *H.Poll.*B407, June 1919.

57. *H.Poll.*A425, Oct. 1919.

58. V(HD) to S/S, 1 July 1919, *H.Poll.*15, Aug. 1919; *ibid.* A1–16 and k.w.; *H.Poll.*188, Oct. 1919.

59. *H.Poll.*Dep.43, Aug. 1919, B53–4, Feb. 1920, and A1–16, k.w., Aug. 1919 (Chelmsford note, 7 July 1919), and also, for subsequent instructions to local governments, B266–72, Dec. 1919.

60. *H.Poll.*A187–216, and 425 (ILC Proceedings, 10 and 12 Sept. 1919), Oct. 1919; Chelmsford to Montagu, 13 Sept. 1919, *CP*5; V to S/S, 12 June 1919, *CP*12.

61. Chelmsford to Montagu, 3 Dec. 1919, *CP*5; draft reply to parliamentary question, 7 June 1920, *IOR* J&P3132/19; Malaviya to PSV, 13 Nov. 1919, *CP*23 and *H.Poll.*473, Feb. 1920; *ibid.* 474–80. For G/ Panjab to Malaviya, see *Pioneer*, 19 and 20 Nov. 1919 (reports which were the HD's first intimation of the texts), *H.Poll.*Dep.49, Nov. 1919. Hunter concluded that 'no further concession was necessary to give the Congress Committee the fullest opportunity for placing before us any evidence relevant to the enquiry'—Hunter to HD, 8 March 1920 (with Hunter Report), *CP*47. On the appearance of counsel, see *H.Poll.*469–471, Feb. 1920. Gandhi also requested the withdrawal of the restrictions on him in view of the enquiry; see Gandhi to PSV, 2 Oct. 1919, *CP*23.

62. *IOR* J&P3132/19; and see *Report of the Disorders Inquiry Committee*

1920, *CP*47—especially, for general approval by the majority, pp. 1–18 (Delhi, Ahmedabad, Viramgam, Kaira, Bombay city), 72–86 (introduction and continuance of martial law) and 87–99 (martial law administration); for substantial agreement by the minority, pp. 103–4; for criticisms by the majority, pp. 30–6 (Amritsar), 55–6 (Gujranwala), 94–8 (exclusion of counsel, various orders and 'fancy punishments'); and for further criticisms by the minority, pp. 104 and 115–30 (introduction of martial law), 131–8 (Dyer) 139–50 (objectionable orders), 151–9 (armoured cars and aeroplanes), and 160–6 (courts and punishments).

63. *Baisakhi* day. The Seva Samiti claimed that visitors had come from as far as Peshawar and Srinagar; see *H.Poll*.Dep.31, Oct. 1919.

64. *Report of the Disorders Inquiry Committee* 1920, 30–6 and 131–8; *The Times*, 15 Dec. 1919; *Daily Express*, 13 Dec. 1919.

65. Panjab Police Rules, p. 55, *IOR* J&P1566(2200/19). Compare those of the U.P., ch.VI, para. 66, *loc. cit.*, and the C.P., Bengal, Bombay and Madras, *H.Poll*.B282–3, April 1919.

66. Note by Holderness, *IOR* J&P3132/19; *H.Poll*.B552, May 1919, and 513, Jan. 1920.

67. Statement of evidence by Capt. F. C. C. Briggs, 11 April–8 May 1919, *IOR* J&P3132/19. The Hunter Committee saw this statement but did not include it in the evidence appended to the Report, as Briggs had died on the Northwest Frontier before being cross-examined.

68. See above, note 64.

69. Holderness to Montagu, 30 June 1920, *IOR* J&P3132/19; V to S/S, 2 July 1920, *CP*13.

70. Lloyd to Chamberlain, 13 June 1920, *ACP*18/1/9.

71. Chelmsford to Hardinge, 25 Nov. 1916, *CP*15. Nonetheless Dyer was awarded C.B. for his part in this campaign. For his record, see Appendix II.

72. Marris to Meston, 26 June 1919, *Meston Papers* 27; Banerjea to PSV, 29 April 1919, *CP*19; *H.Poll*.A1–16 and k.w., Aug. 1919; *IOR* J&P3132/19. There were Commons questions relating to the disturbances, on 28 May (2), 17 and 23 (3) and 30 (3) July; the AICC meeting was at Allahabad.

73. *H.Poll*.Dep.23, Sept. 1919, and B257–65 and k.w., Dec. 1919.

74. *The Times*, 19 April 1919; V(HD) to S/S, 18 March 1920, *CP*12; *H.Poll*.347–53, Feb., and 317–18, April 1920, and B328–9, Sept., and Dep.46–7, Nov. 1919; *IOR* J&P3132/19 and 1566(2200/19). The Samiti estimate of 530 dead, 200 wounded, was claimed to include visitors to Amritsar missed in official accounts, but the government were unaware of this when Vincent made his announcement, and unable to verify it later as V. N. Tivary, the Samiti secretary, failed to supply his lists although he had promised to and had been shown the government ones; see *H.Poll*. Dep.31, Oct. 1919.

75. Ronaldshay to Montagu, 21 Oct. 1919, *MP*30; Holderness, 3 notes, O'Dwyer to Montagu, 30–1 Dec. 1919, Holderness to Montagu, 30 June 1920, *IOR* J&P3132/19; *H.Poll*. B513, Jan. 1920; O'Dwyer to Maffey, 31 Dec. 1919 (with a copy of his letter to Montagu, for Chelmsford), *CP*23.

76. See above, note 75; *Parliamentary Debates* (Commons) 130, 2147–57, and 131, 412–17, 1023–8 and 1111–19 (23 and 30 June, and 5 and 7 July 1920); S/S to V, 5 June, *CP*10, and 17 Sept., *CP*11, and Montagu to Chelmsford, 17 July and 18 Dec. 1920, *CP*5.
77. V to S/S, 2 July 1920, *CP*13.
78. V to S/S, 8 June 1919, *CP*10; *H.Poll*.A1–16 k.w., Aug. 1919.
79. Craddock to Chelmsford, 23 Dec., and Chelmsford to Craddock, 31 Dec., and to Harcourt Butler, 21 Nov. 1919, *CP*23.
80. V to S/S, 21 March 1920, *CP*12, and 23, 24 and 30 Dec., and S/S to V, 30 Dec. 1919, *CP*11; Chelmsford to Montagu, 4 and 25 Sept., and Montagu to Chelmsford, 29 Aug. and 11 Sept. 1919, *CP*5. See also Chamberlain to Chelmsford, 3 Aug. 1916, *CP*2.
81. *Amrita Bazar Patrika* 7 Aug. 1919, *H.Poll*.Dep.23, Sept. 1919.
82. Note by Basu, 8 Dec. 1919, *IOR* J&P1566(2200/19).
83. V(HD) to S/S, 25 March, 5 and 7 April, 24 May, 1 and 19 June 1920, *CP*12; *H.Poll*.376–81, Aug. 1920, B118–20 and k.w., April, and also 134–5, March 1920, and Dep.51, July 1919 (G/Panjab fortnightly report, 15 July 1919).
84. V to S/S, 21 March, and draft resolution of G/I, week of 10 April, *CP*24, and Maffey to Vincent, 19 March 1920, *CP*24. The government's attitude was no doubt influenced by a report that the King entertained 'a great . . . admiration for O'Dwyer'; see Meyer to Chelmsford, 5 Sept. 1919, *CP*15.
85. S/S to V(HD), 6 May, and V(HD) to S/S, 11 May 1920, *CP*12; *H.Poll*.126–61, June 1920; G/I(HD) to S/S, 3 May, and S/S to G/I, 26 May 1920, *H.Poll*.162–3, June 1920. There were Commons questions on the publication of the Hunter Report, on 17 and 24 (2) March and 26 April 1920. The Government of India sent H. W. Williamson, a United Provinces police officer who had been secretary to the Hunter committee, on deputation to London to assist the Secretary of State and express the government's view; see *H.Poll*.18–35, Aug. 1920. Rushbrook Williams also prepared summaries of the report for publicity purposes: *H.Poll*. Dep.91, April 1920. For references in the following paragraphs to criticisms by the committee, see the descriptive analysis, above, note 62.
86. V(HD) to S/S, 8 June 1919, *CP*10, and also 6 June and 30 Aug., and S/S to V(HD), 2 June and 18 July 1919, *H.Poll*.400–5, Sept. 1919.
87. V to S/S, 20 May 1920, *CP*12; *H.Poll*.Dep.74 and appendices, May 1921.
88. Montagu to Hunter, 29 Aug., to Chelmsford, 2 Oct. 1919, *CP*5, to Ronaldshay, 20 May, *MP*27, and to Lloyd, 9 Sept. 1920, *MP*22.
89. See *H.Poll*. 8, June 1920. The *Pioneer, Englishman, Civil and Military Gazette, Statesman, Madras Mail, Rangoon Times, Rangoon Gazette, Empire*, and *Advocate of India* (all English-owned) were sympathetic to Dyer. The *Times of India* would have supported Dyer if he had not used excessive force. The *Indian Daily News, Amrita Bazar Patrika, Bombay Chronicle, Independent, Leader, Tribune, Bandematram, Bengali* and *Hindu* (all Indian-owned) called for more severe punishment of Dyer and criticized the majority Hunter Report. The *Indian Daily*

Telegraph and *New India* supported the Report; the *Indian Mirror* argued that Montagu had sacrificed Dyer.

90. S/S to V, 10 July, *CP*13, and Maffey to Chelmsford, 10 July and 18 Aug., and Meyer to Chelmsford, 15 July 1920, *CP*16; Hilton Young to Hailey, n.d., *Hailey Papers* 2b.

91. Chelmsford to Reed, 11 Jan. 1921, *CP*26; *H.Poll.*414–16, July 1920.

92. V to S/S, 14 Aug., and (HD) 12 Sept. 1920, *CP*13; *H.Poll.*85–8 and 93–6, Sept. 1920, and Dep.85, Nov. 1920, and 41, Dec. 1920, and 45, 50 (Gwynne note, 12 May 1921) and 74, May 1921. Note the delay in awarding honours for service during the disturbances: L. French (for G/ Panjab) to Hignell (PSV), 7 May 1920, *CP*24.

93. *H.Poll.*Dep.85, Nov. 1920, and also 41, Dec. 1920, and 50, May 1921.

94. Montagu to Chelmsford, 22 April 1919, *CP*5; S/S to V, 15 and 23 Sept., and (HD) 22 Sept. 1920, *CP*13; Willingdon to Montagu, 15 July and 18 Sept. 1920, *MP*20. By May 1921 those officers who had not resigned were all in their same posts, except for Colonel O'Brien who had been appointed Political Agent at Bahawalpur; see S. K. Brown to Hignell, 25 May 1921, *Richards Papers* 3.

95. V to S/S, 18 Sept., and also (HD) 6 Oct. 1920, *CP*13; Chelmsford to Reed, 28 Nov. 1920, *CP*25. In 1921 the Panjab gave Johnson an oil-prospecting licence for Attock district; Montagu and then Reading expressed disapproval but the matter was dropped; V to S/S, 23 April and 4 May 1921, *Reading Papers* 10. Bosworth Smith's 'good record' included showing 'the greatest courage and resolution' in 1899 during a cholera outbreak in Hissar when over 800 died; *Revenue and Agriculture Dept. (Famine) Proceedings C1*, May 1908.

96. *H.Poll.*Dep.50, May 1921, and 79, April 1920 (Vincent to Maclagan, 24 April 1920).

97. V(HD) to S/S, 7 Jan., 4 Feb., 19 and 26 June 1920, *CP*12; Chelmsford to Reed, 11 Jan. 1921, *CP*26; Lloyd to Chelmsford, 12 Nov. and 10 Dec. (proposals by Setalvad) and Chelmsford to Lloyd, 16 Dec. 1920, *CP*25.

98. Chelmsford to Lloyd, 4 Dec. 1920, *CP*25, to Reed, 11 Jan., and to Sly, 26 Jan., and see Sly to Chelmsford, 1 Jan., and Chirol to Chelmsford, 5 Jan. 1921, *CP*26. Chirol considered only 'mild censure and even milder penalties' had been applied for 'humiliation and terrorism' and 'things . . . repugnant to . . . justice' (to Hailey, n.d. [1921], *Hailey Papers* 4b). On the refusal of amnesty, see *H.Poll.*Dep.6, March 1921.

99. *H.Poll.*Dep.45, July 1919, and 50, May 1921. For this and the next paragraph see also V(HD) to S/S, 29 Jan., 6 Feb. & 6 March 1920, *CP*12; & *H.Poll.*231–4, April 1920.

100. *H.Poll.*B139–40 and 280–1, April 1919, and 179–87c and k.w., Jan. 1920.

101. V(HD) to S/S, 17 Feb. 1921, *CP*14; *H.Poll.*Dep.50–1, May 1921; and see also *H.Poll.*B179–87c and k.w., Jan. 1920. In May 1921, 31 Indians (mainly Amritsar piecegoods merchants) had received Rs. 11,61,004, almost all for property; 32 Europeans had received Rs. 4,84,767

346   REFERENCES AND NOTES (Chs. 7-8)

for injury or death, and Rs. 1,64,556 for property; Bagh victims in Amritsar had received Rs. 13,800 for deaths and Rs. 5,000 for injuries.
102. V to S/S, 14 Sept. 1920, *CP*13; Chelmsford to Reed, 11 Jan. 1921, *CP*26; Montagu to Lloyd, 9 Sept. 1920, *MP*22, and to Ronaldshay, 21 Nov. 1918, *CP*27; *H.Poll*.181-2, Nov. 1919, and B94-7, April 1920. To Montagu's suggestion that they should use Regulation III of 1818, Chelmsford had repeated the rationale of the Rowlatt Act as a special and necessary reserve power to meet emergency situations; see V to S/S, 6 May 1920, *CP*12.
103. See above, note 101; Reed to Chelmsford, 15 Feb. 1921, *CP*26; Vincent speech, 8 March 1921, *H.Poll*.Dep.50, May 1921, and see 6, March 1921: privately the government considered more releases would not be safe, but they were prepared to place before the reviewing judges the 14 cases not already examined.
104. Judgment of L. Leslie Jones, 31 May 1919, *H.Poll*.Dep. 40, Oct. 1919.
105. Bishamber Nath to Chelmsford, and to the editor of the *Leader*, 20 April 1919, *CP*22. For Bishamber Nath, see Appendix. Compare his attitude with Prakash Tandon, *Panjabi Century 1857-1947*, Berkeley and Los Angeles 1968, 122: '. . . this Sarkar was different; it had been kind and benign. . . . Why this sudden change?'.

Chapter Eight. Against *Satyagraha*

1. See Hardinge to Meston, 4 Sept., and Meston to Hardinge, 6 Sept., 1914, *H.Poll*.Dep.2, April 1916; Chelmsford to Chamberlain, 7, 14 and 21 July, and O'Dwyer to Grant, 26 June 1916, *CP*2; V(F&PD) to S/S, 4, 5, 7, 8, 10, 15 and 27 July 1916, *CP*7; Chelmsford to Carmichael, 24 July, and Communique, 31 July 1916, *CP*17; Ronaldshay to Chelmsford, 8 July, and V to G/Bombay, 25 July 1919, *CP*23. For newspaper comments on the Sherif's revolt see *H.Poll*.Dep.20, Dec. 1916. On the Russian treaty, see V(F&PD) to S/S, [Aug. 1916] (2 telegrams), and 28 Dec., and V to S/S, 19 Nov. 1916, *CP*7. See also for example, G. Minault, 'Islam and Mass Politics . . .' in D. E. Smith, *Religion and Political Modernization*, New Haven 1974; P. Hardy, *The Muslims of British India*, Cambridge 1972; Gopal Krishna, 'The Khilafat Movement in India; the First Stage', *Journal of the Royal Asiatic Society* 1968; and Francis Robinson, *Separatism among Indian Muslims*, Cambridge 1974.
2. See *H.Poll*.164-73, 180-94 and 199-201, Nov. 1918; ILC Proceedings, 19 Sept. 1918, 292-3, *IOR* J&P1589(4468/19); Chelmsford to Montagu, 17 Sept., *CP*4, V(HD) to S/S, 3 Sept., *CP*9, and Ronaldshay to Montagu, 1 and 18 Sept. 1918, *MP*29; Lawrence, Second Marquess of Zetland, *'Essayez'*, London 1956, 108-16; and J. H. Broomfield, 'The Forgotten Majority: The Bengal Muslims and September 1918', in D. A. Low, ed., *Soundings in Modern South Asian History*, London 1968.
3. See Chelmsford to Montagu, 26 June, 31 July, 7, 8, and 20 Aug., 18 and 28 Oct., and 24 Dec. 1919, *CP*5, and 4 March, 12 April, 23 and 30 June, and 4 Aug. 1920, and 12 Jan. 1921, *CP*6; Montagu to Chelmsford, 11 Sept., 31 Oct. and 28 Nov. 1919, *CP*5, and 13 March 1920, *CP*6;

Speeches II, 228–30; Chief British Representative, Indo-Afghan Peace Conference (Sir Hamilton Grant) to V, 8 Aug. 1919, *CP*24; V(F&PD) to S/S, 9 June 1919, *CP*10.

4. V to S/S, 10 May, and (HD) 3 and 18 May, *CP*10, and 17 Nov. 1919, *CP*11, and 2 Feb. 1920, *CP*12; *H.Poll.*529, May 1919; Ronaldshay to Montagu, 14 May and 20 Nov., *MP*30, Willingdon to Montagu, 6 Sept., *MP*19, and Lloyd to Montagu, 21 and 28 Nov. 1919, *MP*24. For Hardinge see *H.Poll.*Dep.2, April 1916; and for the Sindhi pamphlet *ibid.* 30, July 1919.

5. See A. J. Balfour, 4 Oct. 1916, 'The Peace Settlement in Europe', and Report of Lord Curzon's Committee of Imperial War Cabinet on Terms of Peace (Territorial Desiderata), *ACP*20/9/9 and 33. On policy in general see Briton Cooper Busch, *India, Britain and the Arabs*, Berkeley etc. 1971, *passim*.

6. Curzon to Kerr, 12 March 1920, *Lothian Papers* GD40/17/208; Meston to Chelmsford, 23 March 1917, *Meston Papers* 1; Montagu to Lloyd, 14 April 1920, *MP*22; see 'An Appreciation of Lord Hardinge on the Note by Chief of Imperial General Staff dated March 29, 1917' (12 April 1917), *ACP*20/9/37; 'Minute by Political Department, India Office, The War with Turkey' (25 May 1916), probably by Sir Arthur Hirtzel, and Lord Islington, 'The War with Turkey' (13 June 1916), *ACP*/21/6/22–3; Montagu, Cabinet Memorandum, 24 Oct. 1918, in Montagu to Chelmsford, 7 Nov. 1918, *CP*4; and see Montagu to Chelmsford, 20 May and 3 June 1920, *CP*6, and to Willingdon, 16 April 1919 and 20 May 1920, *MP*16.

7. See Ronaldshay to Chelmsford, 15 and 22 May, and O'Dwyer to Chelmsford, 27 April 1919, *CP*22; V(HD) to S/S, 3 May 1919, *CP*10, and 28 Jan. and 2 Feb. and V to S/S, 8 and 20 Jan. 1920, *CP*12; *H.Poll.*98–113, 363, 368, 373, 524–7, and 532, May, and 362, 364, 372–5, June 1919, 413–16. Feb. 1920, and also 193–4, Sept. 1916; *Speeches* II, 388–94. For later private exhortations, see Chelmsford to Lloyd, 9 Feb., and V to G/Bombay, 25 April 1920, *CP*24. The course had been urged by Gandhi; see Gandhi to Hignell, 27 July, and Hignell to Gandhi, 5 Aug. 1919, *CP*23.

8. V to S/S, 10 May, and (HD) 18 May 1919, *CP*10, and 2 Feb., 19 May (*Gazette Extraordinary* 15 May), and 29 June 1920, *CP*12; *H.Poll.* 101, Sept. 1920; *Speeches* II, 224–5. The Turks did retain Constantinople, and this was represented in a draft notification as a victory for the Indian Muslim view, strongly urged by the Government of India and the Secretary of State, against those who wanted the Turks expelled from Europe; see *H.Poll.*Dep.59, July 1920. For an account of the Turkish peace negotiations up to Montagu's resignation in 1922, see S. D. Waley, *Edwin Montagu*, London 1964, 239–51 and 271–84.

9. *H.Poll.*368–73, May 1919. See also Muhammad Ali's demand for the exclusion of non-Muslim troops and control from every inch of Arab land; Speech at Lucknow, 26 Feb. 1921, Oudh Khilafat Conference: *H.Poll.*Dep.3, May 1921.

10. See Ronaldshay to Montagu, 8 April 1920, *MP*31; V(HD) to S/S, 7, 12 and 17 March, *CP*12, and Chelmsford to Montagu, 17 March

1920, *CP*6. The local government consensus was that any announcement was likely to do more harm than good.

11. *H.Poll.*B109, July 1920.

12. See *H.Poll.*B279–82 and k.w., Jan. 1920.

13. *H.Poll.*101, Sept. 1920; Gandhi to Chelmsford, 22 June 1920, *CP*24.

14. V(HD) to S/S, 19 June 1920, *CP*12.

15. See notes by Vincent, 2 and 6 May, and Marris, 6 May, and HD circular, 12 May 1919, *H.Poll.*A235, May 1919.

16. A Khilafat meeting in April had approved 4 stages for *satyagraha*: (1) boycott of titles, war loans and Councils; (2) resignation of civil posts; (3) resignation of police and military posts; (4) non-payment of taxes. These were described as the 'progressive abstention from cooperation with Government'. See *Justice* (Madras) 19 April, and *Searchlight* (Patna) 29 April 1920; *H.Poll.*100, Sept. 1920. In *Young India* 5 May 1920, Gandhi explained that stage (3) was a 'distant goal'; in the event the campaign was not to develop beyond an elaboration of stage (1). Interesting suggestions about the programme are made in Richard Gordon, 'Non-cooperation and Council Entry, 1910 to 1920', *Modern Asian Studies* 7, 3 (1973).

17. *H.Poll.*100, 102 and 147, Sept. 1920.

18. V(HD) to S/S, 10 July and 3 Sept. 1920, *CP*13.

19. Ronaldshay to Montagu, 26 May 1920, *MP*31.

20. Chelmsford to Montagu, 3 and 30 June, *CP*6, and V to S/S, 24 Oct., and (HD) 16 Oct. 1920, *CP*13.

21. Chelmsford to Montagu, 6 and 27 Oct., *CP*6, and V to S/S, 24 Oct. 1920, *CP*13. See also V to S/S, 17 July 1920, *CP*13: 'repressive action would only stimulate' the movement.

22. Chelmsford to Montagu, 25 Aug. 1920, *CP*6.

23. Chelmsford to Montagu, 4 Aug. 1920, *CP*6.

24. Lloyd to Montagu, 26 March 1920, *MP*25; V(HD) to S/S, 21 and 25 March 1920, *CP*22. The Home Department had requested a general assessment of the *hartal*: see *H.Poll.*B134, April 1920.

25. V(HD) to S/S, 23 April 1920, *CP*12.

26. V(HD) to S/S, 6 Aug. 1920, *CP*13.

27. V(HD) to S/S, 23 and 30 April, 7 May, and also 26 June 1920, *CP*12. For an example of optimistic reporting—too much so to convince the Home Department—see a C.I.D. report by S. C. Banerjea and a note by H. W. B. Hare-Scott suggesting that the elections might discredit Gandhi and cause a split with the Alis, *H.Poll.*Dep.51, Oct. 1920.

28. V(HD) to S/S, 11 June 1920, *CP*12.

29. V to S/S, 19 May 1920, *CP*12.

30. V(HD) to S/S, 11 and 19 June 1920, *CP*12. For the later programmes see V(HD) to S/S, 3 Sept. 1920, *CP*13.

31. V to S/S, 17 and (HD) 11 June 1920, *CP*12, and also 7 Dec. 1920, *CP*13.

32. V(HD) to S/S, 14 and 20 May 1920, *CP*13.

33. V(HD) to S/S, 7 May 1920, *CP*13.

34. *H.Poll*.B165–6, June 1920, and see Jawaharlal Nehru, *An Auto-biography*, New Delhi etc. 1962, 50–1. For a summary of Home Department policy see V(HD) to S/S, 28 May 1920, *CP*12.

35. *H.Poll*.A341–54 and k.w., Feb. 1921; Chelmsford to Maffey, 9 Sept. 1920, *CP*16.

36. *H.Poll*.Dep.72, June 1920; V to S/S, 17 June 1920, *CP*12. The army did not have much need for alarm; combatants numbering 15,500 and a total of 20,000 were recruited in 1913–14, and 61,500 and 157,000 in 1919–1920 (see Chelmsford to Montagu, 13 Oct. 1920); Chelmsford suspected military judgments in political matters (see Chelmsford to Montagu, 23 Nov. 1920, *CP*6). There were 30 recorded attempts to tamper with troops in 1920, 82 in 1921 and 59 in 1922, mostly affecting Sikhs; Muslim recruitment was not adversely affected: V to S/S, 22 Jan. 1923, *Reading Papers* 12.

37. *H.Poll*.A341–54 and k.w., Feb. 1921, especially notes by Jacob, 26 May, Monro, 2 June, McPherson, 11 June, and Chelmsford, 11 and 18 June 1920.

38. V(HD) to S/S, 25 April, *CP*2, and Chelmsford to Maffey, 9 Aug. 1920, *CP*16.

39. Note by McPherson, 24 Sept. 1920, *H.Poll*.B353, Sept. 1920. The circular is at *H.Poll*.A100–3, Sept. 1920.

40. Note by Gwynne, 12 May 1920, *H.Poll*.B172–6, May 1920 and *H.Poll*.29–33 and 172–7, May 1918, and 128, Aug., and 273, Nov. 1920. Willingdon did not expect the India Government to agree, but he thought Shaukat 'a pestilential brute', and expressed 'hate' for central policy. He also objected when he was not allowed to 'scupper Gandhi'. See to Ronaldshay, 8 and 18 Aug. 1920, *RP*56.

41. *H.Poll*.71 and 72, Aug. 1920; V to S/S, 17 July 1920, *CP*13. Earlier Maclagan's government had followed Chelmsford's policy and refrained from prosecuting for violent speeches at the Amritsar Congress; see Maclagan to Chelmsford, 3 Jan. 1920, *CP*24.

42. See Lloyd to Chamberlain, 17 Sept., *ACP*18/1/13, and to Montagu, 23 July, 27 Aug. and 17 Sept. 1920, *MP*25; V(HD) to S/S, 9 and 16 Aug., *CP*13, and Chelmsford to Montagu, 11 and 19 Aug. 1920, *CP*6.

43. F&PD to CC/Northwest Frontier Province, 6 Aug., CC to PSV, 10, 24, 28 and 30 Aug., Grant to Chelmsford, 7 Aug. and 2 Sept. 1920, *CP*25; CC to V, 7 May 1920, *CP*24; *H.Poll*.195–204, Aug. 1920; *H.Poll*.B133, Nov. 1920.

44. See Chelmsford to Montagu, 11, 19 and 25 Aug. 1920, *CP*6. For an eyewitness statement on conditions in Afghanistan, see *H.Poll*.B20, Sept. 1920.

45. Chelmsford to Grant, 12 Aug. 1920, *CP*25. See also CC/Northwest Frontier Province to V, 7 May, and PSV to CC, 8 and 10 May 1920, *CP*24.

46. V to S/S, 17 July 1920, *CP*13.

47. See *H.Poll*.Dep.38, Aug. 1920.

48. See V to S/S, 24 Oct. 1920, *CP*13.

49. V(HD) to S/S, 10, 18 and 26 Sept. 1920, *CP*13; Ronaldshay to

Montagu, 15 and 22 Sept. 1920, *MP*31. For an admirable account see Francis Robinson, *op. cit.*, 289–325. (If I have not entirely followed it, here and elsewhere, it is firstly because I record mainly the government's view of events, to understand their policy, and secondly because I would give rather more weight to Gandhi and less to his Muslim allies over the decision on non-co-operation, and in general more to the persuasiveness of issues and less to the needs of 'professional' politicians in explaining upsurges of agitation.)

50. Ronaldshay was a little surprised at the number of withdrawals; see Ronaldshay to Montagu, 22 Aug. 1920, *MP*31.

51. See V(HD) to S/S, 9 and 26 Aug. and 30 Oct. 1920, *CP*13; and D. G. Tendulkar, *Mahatma* Vol. II (1920–9), Bombay 1951, 18–19.

52. *H.Poll.*Dep.112, June 1920, and 43, Jan. 1921.

53. V(HD) to S/S, 16 Oct. 1920, *CP*13.

54. Montagu to Ronaldshay, 9 Nov. 1920, *MP*27.

55. V(HD) to S/S, 24 Oct. 1920, *CP*13.

56. *Ibid.*; and see below, note 64. The Volunteers also bore a similarity to the *melas* organized by Tilak for Ganpati festivals. On receipt of replies it was decided that general legislation would not be politic or perhaps necessary; but the question was raised again in February 1921 after volunteers armed with daggers and swords had created a disturbance and been condemned for rowdyism by Gandhi while he was visiting Fyzabad. In March the Legislative Department were instructed to prepare a draft ordinance in case of need, though for the time being the Home Department were still content to point out to local governments the danger of allowing these volunteers to become armed. See *H.Poll.*Dep.89, March, and 67, April 1921. A bill to deal with volunteers was later prepared: V(HD) to S/S, 28 April 1921, *Reading Papers* 10.

57. *H.Poll.*Dep.53, Oct. 1920. The new aims were drafted by the Joint General Secretaries, Umar Sobani, Jawaharlal Nehru and Rajagopala-chariar; see below p. 236.

58. Speech (translation), 15 Oct., DCI report, 1 Nov., and note by McPherson, 2 Nov. 1920, *H.Poll.*Dep.5, Jan 1921.

59. See Chelmsford to Montagu, 19 Oct. 1920, *CP*6; V to S/S, and *ibid.* (HD), 24 Oct. 1920, *CP*13; Lloyd to Montagu, 15 Oct. 1920, *MP*25.

60. V to S/S, 24 Oct. 1920, *CP*13; Chelmsford to Reed, 28 Nov., *CP*25, to Montagu, 2 and 23 Nov., *CP*6, and also to Maffey, 9 Nov. 1920, *CP*16.

61. S/S to V, 19 Nov., V to S/S, 23 Nov., and (HD) 24 Nov. 1920, *CP*13.

62. V(HD) to S/S, 16 and 30 Oct. and 12 Nov. 1920, *CP*13.

63. *H.Poll.*Dep.65, Oct. 1920.

64. V to S/S, 23 Nov. 1920, *CP*13. At this time action was taken against volunteer groups in Delhi, where they had prevented the burial of Khan Bahadur Maulvi Abdul Ahad, a prominent Muslim who had refused to renounce his titles before his death. Chelmsford decided this was a good moment to act—when public opinion would be with the government—and had the leaders arrested and their organizations out-

lawed. In all, four out of twelve political volunteer groups were proscribed. See Chelmsford to Montagu, 23 Nov. 1920, *CP*6; V(HD) to S/S
13 Dec. 1920, *CP*13; and *H.Poll*.Dep.67, April 1921. This last contains a
full account of volunteer activities in Delhi.

65. See Chelmsford to Montagu, 27 Sept., *CP*6, and to Maffey, 9
Sept. 1920, *CP*16.

66. V to S/S, 24 Oct., *CP*13. Perhaps to encourage this, Chelmsford
strongly urged Ronaldshay to hurry with the opening of Dacca University
(to allay suspicion that Calcutta Hindus were causing a delay); see
Chelmsford to Ronaldshay, 19 May and 9 June 1920, *CP*24.

67. V(HD) to S/S, 12 Nov. 1920, *CP*13. See above, note 57.

68. Willingdon to Montagu, 15 Nov. 1920, *MP*20.

69. V(HD) to S/S, 8 and 29 Nov. 1920, *CP*13.

70. Butler to Vincent, 4 Aug. 1920, and HD circular, 25 Aug. 1920,
H.Poll.B333–5, Aug. 1920. Butler's suggestion also proposed 'not to
interfere with the people so long as they do not molest loyal citizens whom
we are bound to protect' and that 'force must be ready in the background,
where there is any expectation of trouble, but it should be hidden as far as
possible. If the people want *hartals*, let them have them.'

71. *H.Poll*.B40–3, Jan. 1921. Other papers blacklisted were *Hindustan*,
Muhammadi, Nayak, Hitavadi, Hindu Patriot, Dainik Basumati (Calcutta);
Hindustan, Praja Mitra, Parsi, Sanj Vartaman (Bombay); *Swadesamitran*
(Madras); *Democrat, Abhudaya* (Allahabad); *Maharatta* (Poona);
Zamindar, Bande Mataram (Lahore); *Vakil* (Amritsar); and 18 other
Panjab papers; and *Haqiqat* and *Hindustani* (Lucknow). *Tribune* was
removed from an earlier list by Gwynne and McPherson.

72. V to S/S, 24 Oct. 1920, *CP*13.

73. V(HD) to S/S, 8 Nov. 1920, *CP*13; *H.Poll*.273, Nov. 1920 (HD
resolution, 6 Nov. 1920).

74. V(ED) to S/S, 10 Dec., and (HD) 30 Oct. 1920, *CP*13.

75. V(ED) to S/S, 1 and 4 Nov. and 10 Dec., and (HD) 27 Nov. 1920,
*CP*13.

76. V(ED) to S/S, 20 Nov. 1920, *CP*13.

77. V(HD) to S/S, 4, 8 and 11 Nov. 1920, *CP*13; Ronaldshay to Montagu, 18 Nov. 1920, *MP*31.

78. V(ED) to S/S, 20 Nov. 1920, *CP*13.

79. V(ED) to S/S, 4 Nov. 1920, *CP*13.

80. V(HD) to S/S, 5 Dec. 1920, *CP*13.

81. See, for example, V to S/S, 23 Nov., *CP*13, and Montagu to
Ronaldshay, 18 Nov. and 8 Dec. 1920, *MP*27.

82. V to S/S, 5 and 17 Jan. 1921, *CP*14, and (RO) 31 Dec. 1920, *CP*13.

83. V(HD) to S/S, 23 Nov. and 13 and 22 Dec. 1920, *CP*13.

84. Lloyd to Montagu, 19 Nov. and 3 Dec., *MP*25, and Ronaldshay
to Montagu, 16 Dec. 1920, *MP*31.

85. Gandhi explicitly refuted this view in *Young India* 24 Nov. 1920;
see *The Collected Works of Mahatma Gandhi* XIX (Nov. 1920–April 1921),
Ahmedabad 1966, 21, and also 183.

86. V to S/S, 23 Nov. 1920, *CP*13; see also Chelmsford to Montagu,

21 Dec. 1920, *CP*6. Of 5186 titles held in August 1920, only 24 had been resigned by February 1921; see *H.Poll*.B222–3, March 1921.

87. See V(HD) to S/S, 5–7 and 12 Jan. 1921, *CP*14; Chelmsford to Montagu, 28 Dec. 1920, *CP*6; Lloyd to Montagu, 3 Dec. 1920, *MP*25.

88. V(HD) to S/S, 29 Dec. 1920, *CP*13. (By end of 1920 total receipts to the Khilafat funds of Central Khilafat Committee were Rs.6,43,766 and expenditure Rs.4,73,688, compared with receipts of Rs.20,99,789 for 1921. See *H.Poll*.741, May 1922.)

89. See V(HD) to S/S, 5–7 and 15 Jan. 1921, *CP*14; and *The Collected Works of Mahatma Gandhi* XIX (Nov. 1920–April 1921), Ahmedabad 1966, 158–68, 182–200, 206–9 and 217–20.

90. See Report of the Chief Commissioner, Delhi, 20 Dec. 1920, *H.Poll*.Dep.43, Jan. 1921.

91. See C.I.D. reports, *H.Poll*.Dep.26, Jan. 1921; and Ronaldshay to Montagu, 20 Jan. 1921, *MP*32.

92. V(HD) to S/S, 15 Jan. 1921, *CP*14; compare Chelmsford to Lloyd, 16 Jan. 1919, *CP*22.

93. V(HD) to S/S, 13 and 23 Jan. and 24 Feb. 1921, *CP*14; W. F. Crawley, 'Kisan Sabhas and Agrarian Revolt in the United Provinces 1920 to 1921, *Modern Asian Studies* 5, 2 (1971); M. H. Siddiqi, 'The Peasant Movement in Pratabgarh 1920', *Indian Economic and Social History Review* 9 (Sept. 1972).

94. V(HD) to S/S, 17 and 24 Feb. 1921, *CP*14.

95. See also the handling of a railway strike in the Jamalpur workshops; *H.Poll*.366–72, Feb. 1920.

96. V(HD) to S/S, 20, 21 and 23 Jan. and 8 Feb. 1921, *CP*14; Chelmsford to Ronaldshay, 21 Jan. 1921, *CP*26.

97. V(HD) to S/S, 24 Feb. 1921, *CP*14.

98. V(HD) to S/S, 21 Jan. and 8 Feb. 1921, *CP*14.

99. V(HD) to S/S, 29 Jan. 1921, *CP*14.

100. On CP see V(HD) to S/S, 23 Jan. 1921, *CP*14, and Sly to Chelmsford, 14 Jan. 1921, *CP*26. In Panjab, there were two parties of Sikhs, the reformers (with an extremist branch, the Akali party) and the old Sikhs (the Sanatan party). The latter were in possession of virtually all shrines, whose Mahants (or guardians) regarded themselves as hereditary tenants enjoying the income in return for performance of religious duties. The reformers wanted common ownership of the shrines and use of the revenues for the benefit of the community. After a meeting of the Sikh League (at which Gandhi was present) in October 1920, the reformers had begun to take possession of the shrines. There were riots at Tarn Taran shrine, and a terrible massacre at the Nankana near Lahore. The local government decided to introduce legislation after an enquiry by a legislative committee; they also called a meeting to discuss the situation. A committee was placed in charge at Nankana; for the time being the government undertook to protect shrines against attacks. Gandhi blamed the British for the tragedy. See V(HD) to S/S, 8 and 17 Feb., 4, 6 and 17 March 1921, *CP*14, and *The Collected Works of Mahatma Gandhi* XIX (Nov. 1920–April 1921), Ahmedabad 1966, 396–402, 407 and 421–5.

101. V(HD) to S/S, 8 Feb. 1921, *CP*14.
102. V(HD) to S/S, 17 Feb. 1921, *CP*14.
103. V(HD) to S/S, 29 March 1921, *CP*14.
104. V(HD) to S/S, 15 Jan. 1921, *CP*14.
105. V(HD) to S/S, 24 Jan. 1921, *CP*14. On prohibition, see P. D.
Kaushik, *The Congress Ideology and Programme 1920–1947*, Bombay etc.
1964, 177–9.
106. V(HD) to S/S, 24 Feb. 1921, *CP*14.
107. Speech at National School, Aminabad, Lucknow, 27 Feb. 1921,
translation at *H.Poll.*Dep.16, May 1921; V(HD) to S/S, 24 Jan. 1921,
*CP*14.
108. V(HD) to S/S, 23 Jan. and 17 Feb. 1921, *CP*14.
109. V(HD) to S/S, 23 Jan. 1921, *CP*14.
110. *H.Poll.*Dep.13, Feb. 1921.
111. V(FD) to S/S, 19 and 21 Feb. and (HD) 29 March 1921, *CP*14.
112. V(HD) to S/S, 23 and 29 Jan. and 8 and 24 Feb. 1921, *CP*14;
Ronaldshay to Montagu, 20 and 27 Jan. 1921, *MP*32; G/Madras to V,
1 Jan, and G/Bombay to V, 23 Feb. 1921, *CP*26.
113. V to S/S, 19 Feb. 1921, *CP*14.
114. Lady Blanche Lloyd to Chamberlain, 31 Dec. 1920, *ACP*18/1/17;
The Collected Works of Mahatma Gandhi XIX, Ahmedabad 1966, 310–12.
115. V(ED) to S/S, 20, 24 and 27 Jan. and 8 and 10 Feb. 1921, *CP*14;
Ronaldshay to Chelmsford, 19 and 25 Jan. 1921, *CP*26.
116. V(ED) to S/S, 2 Feb. 1921, *CP*14.
117. V(HD) to S/S, 17 Feb. and (ED) 21 Feb. 1921, *CP*14.
118. V(HD) to S/S, 24 Feb. 1921, *CP*14.
119. V(HD) to S/S, 29 Feb. and 8 Feb. 1921, and (HD) 5 Feb. 1921,
*CP*14.
120. V to S/S, 14 and 19 Feb. 1921, *CP*14. Agitation among the masses
was expected to be sporadic, hampered by lack of funds; see V(HD) to
S/S, 23 Jan. 1921, *CP*14.
121. V to S/S, 14 Feb. and (ED) 24 Feb. and 3 March 1921, *CP*14.
122. V(HD) to S/S, 8 Feb. 1921, *CP*14.
123. V to S/S, 6, 19 and 20 Feb. and (HD) 26 Jan. 1921, *CP*14.
124. See Maffey to McPherson, 21 Jan. 1920, and other notes and
letters, *H.Poll.*B.411–16, Jan. 1920; *ibid.*, 39–45, April 1920; *H.Poll.*Dep.
105, March 1921.
125. V to S/S, 25 Feb. 1921, *H.Poll.*Dep.49, March 1921.
126. V(HD) to S/S, 2 Feb., and S/S to V, 4 Feb. 1921, *CP*14; and see
Lord Cromer to V, 6 Feb. 1921, *CP*26.
127. See above, note 126, and V to S/S, 8 Feb. 1921, *CP*14.
128. V(HD) to S/S, 23 and 29 Jan. 1921, *CP*14.
129. V to S/S, 29 Jan. 1921, *CP*14.
130. V(HD) to S/S, 8 and 24 Feb. and 17 and 29 March 1921, *CP*14.
131. V to S/S, 24 Feb. 1921, *CP*14.
132. V(HD) to S/S, 6 and also 29 March 1921, *CP*14.
133. *Ibid.*, and V(HD) to S/S, 24 Feb. 1921, *CP*14.
134. V(HD) to S/S, 6 March 1921, *CP*14.

135. V(HD) to S/S, 17 March 1921, *CP*14.
136. Chelmsford to Montagu, 14 Feb. 1921, *CP*6; *H.Poll.*Dep.12, May 1920.
137. Willingdon to Montagu, 15 Nov. 1920, *MP*20.
138. See *H.Poll.*Dep.14, March 1921.
139. Chelmsford to Lord Reay, 2–3 Feb. 1921, *CP*16; *H.Poll.*Dep.29 Feb. 1921; Horace Williamson to Seton, 21 Dec. 1921, *Seton Papers* 9.
140. See Willingdon to Montagu, 27 June, 8 Aug., 8 and 28 Sept. 1920 *MP*20, and 3, 6, 20 and 27 Jan. and 6 and 31 March 1921, *MP*21, but also (for some less condemnatory moments) 4 and 22 Aug. 1920, *MP*20.
141. See Lloyd to Chamberlain, 15 Oct. 1920, *ACP*18/1/5, and to Montagu, 26 March, 3 April, 23 July, 13 Aug., 15 Oct., 19 Nov. and 3 Dec. 1920, *MP*25; Montagu to Lloyd, 9 Sept. 1920, *MP*22.
142. Ronaldshay to Montagu, 9 and 23 June, 6 and 21 July, 1–3 and 17 Aug. and 20 Oct., *MP*31, and Montagu to Ronaldshay, 20 April and 16 Aug. 1920, *MP*27. Willingdon had tried to enlist his support, and also later against Reading; see above, note 40, and Willingdon to Ronaldshay 11 July 1921, *RP*56.
143. Chelmsford to Ronaldshay, 9 March, and Ronaldshay to Chelmsford, 11 March 1921, *CP*26.
144. Chelmsford to Craddock, 18 Nov. 1920, *CP*25; Minute by Craddock, 22 Jan. 1920, *H.Poll.*134, July, and see also 46, May 1920.
145. *H.Poll.* 266, July 1920.
146. See Harcourt Butler, *India Insistent*, London 1931, 84.
147. See V to S/S, 24 Oct. 1920, *CP*13.
148. Montagu to Chelmsford, 15 and 27 July, 9 and 16 Sept., and 7 20 and 28 Oct., but also 2 Dec. 1920, *CP*6; S/S to V, 15 and 22 July 1920 *CP*13.
149. See Montagu to Ronaldshay, 17 Nov. 1920, *MP*27, to Willingdon 16 Feb., *MP*17, and to Chelmsford, 16 Feb. 1921, *CP*6.
150. Chelmsford to Craddock, 13 March, *CP*26, and to Montagu 9 March 1921, *CP*6.
151. See V(HD) to S/S, 29 March 1921, *CP*14.
152. Curtis to Chamberlain, 10 Nov. 1920, *ACP*23/10/12.
153. See above, note 91; and report of a secret meeting with Mohani 28 Dec. 1920, *H.Poll.*Dep.26, Jan. 1921.
154. Gandhi to Chelmsford, 22 June 1920, *CP*24.

Chapter Nine. Coherence

1. See V to S/S, 23 Nov. 1918, *CP*9; Chelmsford to Curtis, 13 Jan., to Meston, 26 Jan., *CP*18, and to Chamberlain, 15 and 20 April and 16 March 1917, *CP*3; *H.Poll.*132, June 1917; Marris to Seton, 19 Dec. 1916, *Seton Papers* 6, and 28 Jan. 1917, and Hill to Seton, 17 Jan. 1917, *ibid.* 7 and 31 March and 29 April [1917], *ibid.* 22; Curtis to Kerr, 13 Jan., and to Meston, 31 Jan. 1917, and copy of Meston's statement, *Meston Papers* 11. A Round Table moot met later and asked Curtis to be careful not to associate the group with his private opinions; Kerr to Curtis, 9 July 1917 *Lothian Papers* GD40/17–33. Marris, who had not seen the letter, com-

lained that rumour portrayed him as a vile colonial (he was from New Zealand) who had 'corrupted the just & lenient Meston' (to Seton, 9 Dec. 1916, *Seton Papers* 6). J. H. Broomfield seems to have confused his incident; see *Elite Conflict in a Plural Society*, Berkeley and Los Angeles 1968, 97. See also Lionel Curtis, *Dyarchy*, Oxford 1920.

2. Chelmsford to Bryce, 3 June 1919, *CP*16, and to Chamberlain, 20 Sept. 1918, *CP*15.

3. Chamberlain to Chelmsford, 20 June 1918, *ACP*18/3/13, and Montagu to Chelmsford, 1 Jan. 1918, *CP*4.

4. Montagu, *Diary*, 55, 107, 118–19, 144, 163, 177, 311, 320 and 337: support from Besant, Jinnah, Sankaran Nair, Setalvad, Chandavarkar, Ramaswami Aiyar (then Congress Secretary) and Rahimtoola. Montagu had also expressed himself as more and more anxious about reforms, because events, such as the ban on Tilak's deputation to England, and Willingdon's row with Home Rulers at the Bombay War Conference, were going to create 'an important hostile section' (to Chamberlain, 2 July 1918, *ACP*21/5/44).

5. Willingdon to Montagu, 31 July 1918, *MP*18.

6. Willingdon to Montagu, 11 and 30 July, 11 and 24 Aug., 5 and 17 Sept. and 8 Nov. 1918, *MP*18.

7. Montagu to Ronaldshay, 13 Aug., 25 Sept., 24 Oct. and 29 Nov. 1918, and 17 Feb., 4 March and 22 Aug. 1919, *MP*27.

8. Chelmsford to Montagu, 13 and 27 July, 16 Aug. and 17 Sept. 1918, *CP*4.

9. See Montagu to Willingdon, 13 Aug., *MP*16, and to Ronaldshay, 3 Aug. and 24 Oct. 1918, *MP*27.

10. Chelmsford to Montagu, 27 July, *CP*4, and V to S/S, 3 and 19 July, and S/S to V, 2 and 24 July 1918, *CP*9.

11. See Chelmsford to Montagu, 13 and 27 July, 16 Aug. and 17 Sept., *CP*4, and V to S/S, 3 and 19 July and 7 Aug., and S/S to V, 2, 15 and 24 July, and 1 and 7 Aug. 1918, *CP*9. Chelmsford passed on Montagu's propaganda suggestions to local governments but, while calling for every effort to ensure the reforms were properly understood, he stressed the need for delicacy and circumspection and did not give the suggestions his personal support; see Chelmsford to Pentland, Willingdon, Ronaldshay, Butler, O'Dwyer, Gait, Robertson, Bell and Beadon, 18 Aug., and also V to G/Madras, 4 and 12 Aug. 1918, *CP*21. But he did urge Pentland to call a meeting of his legislature to discuss the reforms scheme; see Chelmsford to Pentland, 16 Sept. 1918, *CP*21.

12. Lloyd to Chelmsford, 6 May, and Craddock to Chelmsford, 6 May 1917, *CP*22; Montagu to Ronaldshay, 17 Feb. 1919, *MP*27; Willingdon to Montagu, 28 Oct., 6, 14 and 19 Nov., 16 and 24 Dec. 1919, *MP*19, but also 7 Jan. 1920, *MP*20.

13. See Central Provinces Moderate Party leaders to *Times of India*, 4 Oct., with Chelmsford to Montagu, 19 Oct. 1918, *CP*4; and Report of committee of non-official ILC members on the Report, with V to S/S, 31 Oct. 1918, *CP*9; and B. L. Mitter, quoted in V. Chirol, *India Old and New*, London 1921, 160–1. Montagu thought even moderates wanted

more than was possible; see Montagu to Ronaldshay, 29 Nov. 1918 *MP*27.

14. Chelmsford to Chamberlain, 19 Jan. 1917, *CP*3, and to Montagu 16 March 1918, *CP*4; Chamberlain to Chelmsford, 28 Nov. 1917, *CP*1!

15. The typical attitude could reasonably have been expected to be that something was better than nothing, a philosophy embraced by A Rangaswami Aiyangar, an opponent of dyarchy, in 'The "Coming Re forms" in India', *Hindustan Review* Vol. XXXVIII, No. 227 (July 1918)

16. For this argument see Francis Robinson, *Separatism among India Muslims*, Cambridge 1974, 291 and 317–18.

17. Chelmsford to Chamberlain, 17 May 1918, *CP*15 and to heads c governments, 11 Feb. 1919, *CP*22. Reportedly the ICS were discontente before the Public Service Commission sat, and animosity to the reform was growing: shelving the PSC report was 'a fatal mistake', as th reforms were not launched on a contented service. Immense annoyanc had also been caused by the decision to cut the exchange compensatio formerly paid. Moreover 'All the other services are grumbling, as wel including the Indian. . . . The official Indian is a big political force & was a mistake to alienate him. After all he . . . exercises a wider influenc than the professional politician': M. S. D. Butler (Attock District) t Seton, 15 Jan. 1917, *Seton Papers* 9.

18. See Montagu to Chelmsford, *Report*, chapter X; and *Speeches* I 148–65 and 268–81. Chiefs' conferences were held in Feb. 1918, and Jan and Nov. 1919, to inaugurate the system. See also Montagu, *Diary* 116–17 and 124: Montagu suggested an upper chamber designed fc future development, in the Government of India, and wanted to associat the princes with it; Chelmsford, presumably seeing the practical diff culties rather than the future necessities, objected, and Montagu did ne insist.

19. See J. H. Broomfield, *op. cit.*, 102–5, for a rather different view.

20. Beatson-Bell to Chelmsford, 17 Dec. 1920, *CP*25.

21. Lloyd to Chelmsford, 24 Dec. 1920, *CP*25, and 13 March, an G/Bombay to V, 19 March, and V to G/Bombay, 24 March 1921, *CP*26 and S/S to V, 2 March 1921, *CP*14. Compare Willingdon's and Chelms ford's willingness to appoint Chaubal Vice-President in Bombay in 1916 Willingdon to Chelmsford, 20 April, and Chelmsford to Willingdon, 2 April 1916, *CP*17. On the other hand, Montagu refused to interfere, o constitutional grounds, when Harkishen Lal, convicted in 1919, wa appointed a minister in the Panjab, and this was criticized in the House c Commons; see S/S to V, 24 Feb., and S/S to V(RO), 20 Jan., 8 and 1 Feb. 1921, *CP*14.

22. See Majority Report, *Reforms Enquiry Committee* 1925, Cmd. 236 Governors may also have undermined ministers' influence by consultin them individually; see R.C. (with A.K.) Majumdar, *op. cit.*, 278–9.

23. For 'satanic' see *The Collected Works of Mahatma Gandhi* Vol. XI (Nov. 1920–April 1921), Ahmedabad 1966, 15, 28, 43, 49, 412 and 41 (for example).

24. See Ronaldshay to Montagu, 17 Feb., 24 and 31 March, 8 and 2

April 1921, *MP*32; Chelmsford to Ronaldshay, 27 March 1921, *CP*26; and Broomfield, *op. cit.* 177–83. For later budget cuts in Madras, see Reading to Montagu, 23 Feb. 1922, *Reading Papers* 4; in U.P., see Butler memo., 5 May 1923, and in Burma, *ibid.*, 26 July 1924, *Butler Papers* 76.

25. H. Gordon Milburn, *England and India*, London 1918, 72–3.

26. See Montagu and Chelmsford, *Report on Indian Constitutional Reforms*, 22 April 1918, *CP*42, pp. 142–56.

27. See V to S/S, 8, 9, 10, 12 and 17 Aug., and S/S to V, 3 (2 tels.), 10, 11, 15 and 16 Aug. 1922, *Reading Papers* 16; Kaye to Seton, 16 Feb. 1922, *Seton Papers* 10. Orders issued in 1920 had stated that the proportion of Europeans in the I.C.S. should be reduced to 52 per cent. See also Vincent to Seton, 30 Aug. 1922, *ibid.*: 'we . . . now feel we are in the cart. It is difficult indeed to reconcile some of L.G.'s statements with the Act and quite impossible to do this as far as the previous speeches of S of S . . .'; and [Vincent] to Seton (fragment), 24 April 1923, *ibid.* 22: 'what really annoys me is Lloyd George's message to Europeans. . . . If he means it . . . why did HMG go so very much further than the G of I wanted. Now when we are making desperate efforts to carry out generously and loyally your policy we are . . . let down'.

28. M. S. D. Butler to Seton, 15 Jan. 1919, *ibid.* 9; Du Boulay to Seton, 27 Aug. 1917, *ibid.* 7; *Meston Papers* 10 and 23; and see above, ch. 3, note 25.

29. *H.Poll.*Dep.39, Aug. 1919; *Tribune*, 2, 3, 8, 9, 10, 11 and 12 April, *Punjab Press Abstracts* 5 and 12 April 1919 (Vol. XXXII, 14 and 15), and Andrews to Montagu, 11 June, and note by Lord Sinha, 11 June 1919, and G/I telegrams, 30 June and 31 July 1919, *IOR* J&P1594 (4799/19). This file also contains later enquiries and notes, including an India Office despatch, G/I and local government replies. The proposal was finally refused by the G/I in a despatch of 31 March 1921, but continued to be discussed at least until 1924.

30. See D. A. Low, 'The Government of India and the First Non-cooperation Movement—1920–1922', *Journal of Asian Studies* XXIV (1965–6).

31. Lloyd to Chamberlain, 24 March and 11 April 1922, *ACP*18/1/25 and 27; V to S/S, 14 Feb. 1922, *ACP*14/1/57; Chamberlain to Lloyd, 31 Dec. 1920, *ACP*18/1/16; Lloyd to Seton, 13 Jan., and Kaye to Seton, 16 Feb. 1922, *Seton Papers* 10; Chelmsford to Reading, 30 March 1922, *Reading Papers* (*private*) 104.

32. See V to S/S, 28 April, 20 Oct., 2 Nov. and also 17 Dec. 1921, *Reading Papers* 10.

33. Landon to Kerr, 23 Feb. 1921, *Lothian Papers* GD14/17/213; Montagu to Willingdon, 16 Feb. 1921, *MP*17 (and also to Chelmsford, same date, *CP*6).

34. Motilal Nehru, *The Voice of Freedom*, London 1961, 16–17.

35. See *H.Poll.*242, 244, 246, 247, 249, March 1919, and 366–72, Feb. 1920; *H.Police* 359–60, June 1921; G/Bombay to V, 11 Jan., and Chelmsford to Lloyd, 14, 16 and 28 Jan. 1919, *CP*22; V to S/S, 23 April 1919, *CP*13; Willingdon to Montagu, 23 April 1919, *MP*19, and 23 and 28 May

1920, *MP*20; Lloyd to Barnes, 25 Jan., and to Montagu, 25 and 31 Jan. and 14 Feb. 1920, *MP*25; and Montagu to Ronaldshay, 9 Nov. 1920, *MP*27.

36. See above, chapter 6, note 54; ILC Proceedings 10 March 1921, *H.Poll.*B172, July 1920.

37. *H.Poll.*376, 379, 381, 382–3 (=377–8?), April 1920.

38. See V to S/S, 20 and 25 Jan., and V(FD) to S/S, 30 Jan. and 17 Feb., and V(AD) to S/S, 22 Jan. and 10 March, and S/S to V, 24 Jan. and 11 and 19 Feb. 1921, *CP*14; Chelmsford to Montagu, 26 Jan. and 16 March 1921, *CP*6; and Appendix (4 Oct. 1917) to Meyer and Howard, memorandum, *H.Public*(*C*) 579, Oct. 1918. See also Chelmsford to Hailey, 14 Sept. 1921, *Hailey Papers* 4b; V to S/S, 28 April and 3 Aug. 1921, *Reading Papers* 10, and (AD) 23 Jan. and 5 Feb. 1922, and S/S to V(AD), 14 Feb. 1922, *ibid.* 11; R.C. (with A.K.) Majumdar, *The History and Culture of the Indian People* XI. *Struggle for Freedom*, Bombay 1969, 800–2; and Philip Mason, review article, *Pacific Affairs* 46, 3 (1973).

39. *H.Public* 40–1, March 1921.

40. *Speeches* II, 576–7.

41. *Ibid.*, 249–81; *H.Poll.*253–4, May 1919, and 111–52, July, 423, 458 and 464–5, May 1920, and A121, Jan. 1919 (Hignell note, 31 July 1918), and Dep. 10, May, and 3 and 63, July 1919; *IOR* J&P1589 (4468/19); V to S/S, 8 Oct. 1918, *CP*9, and 2 June 1920, *CP*12; Montagu to Chelmsford, 10 Oct., and Chelmsford to Montagu, 19 Nov. 1918, *CP*4, and to Chamberlain, 1 March 1917, *CP*3, and to heads of governments, 29 Aug. 1917, *CP*19; and Gait, 12 Sept., Butler, 15 Sept., Ramsey, 19 Sept., Roos-Keppel, 22 Sept., Pentland, 13 Oct., Ronaldshay, 20 Oct., Robertson, 24 Oct., Earle, 7 Nov., Willingdon, 12 Nov., Meston, 16 Nov. 1917, *CP*19, and O'Dwyer, 20 Feb., and Hailey, 14 March 1918, to Chelmsford, *CP*20; Willingdon to Chelmsford, 2 and 8 July, G/Madras to V, 4 July, and V to G/Madras, 3 and 9 July 1919, *CP*23; and Montagu to Lloyd, 6 Nov., *MP*22, and Lloyd to Montagu, 7 Oct. and 20 and 30 Dec. 1919, *MP*24; and Willingdon to Montagu, 7 and 13 July 1919, *MP*19, and 30 Jan. and 3 March 1920, *MP*20. On the use of the Press Act, see also *H.Poll.*373–88, Nov. 1916, 446–63, April 1917, 103, Feb. 1918, and 274 and 278, July 1920. For the committee idea, see above, chapter 7, note 103; and G/I circular, 1 July 1920, and *Proceedings of the Imperial Legislative Assembly* 22 Feb. 1921, p. 341, *IOR* J&P1589 (4468/19); and V to S/S, 16 Dec. 1920, *CP*13.

42. See V(HD) to S/S, 10 March and 5 July 1921, *Proceedings of the Imperial Legislative Assembly* 22 Feb. 1921, and *Gazette of India* 21 March 1921, *IOR* J&P1589 (4468/19); *H.Poll.*B172, July 1920, and Dep.16, May 1921.

43. Reading to Montagu, 18 Oct. 1921, *Reading Papers* 3; S/S to V, 28 May and 16 June, and V to S/S, 19 May, and (HD) 11 June, 5 July, 11 and 27 Sept. 1921, *ibid.* 10. For the full report see *Moral and Material Progress Report* 1921, Appendix II.

44. V(HD) to S/S, 9 Nov., *Reading Papers* 10, and Montagu to Reading, 10 Nov. 1921, *ibid.* 3; *H.Poll.* File 379-I and k.w., 1924.

45. *Proceedings of the Imperial Legislative Assembly* 22 Feb. 1921, pp. 242–3, *IOR* J&P1589 (4468/19).

46. Chelmsford to Montagu, 28 April 1920, *CP6*.

47. Chelmsford to Butler, 25 March 1921, *CP26*. Montagu also found accounts of Indian debates 'very encouraging' (to Richards, 12 April 1921, *Richards Papers* 3). Chelmsford believed, however, that the second session would 'be an even greater test that the first, for the awe of the novelty will have worn off' (to Hailey, 14 Sept. 1921, *Hailey Papers* 4b).

48. J. H. O[ldham] to Kerr (?), 31 Dec. 1921, *Lothian Papers* GD40/17/19. See also S/S to V, 24 Jan. 1920, *CP12*: Montagu noted that the Reform Act was being misrepresented in the Indian press and that the 'great powers it gives are not understood'.

49. Hailey to H. F. Howard, 9 June 1921, *Hailey Papers* 4b. The deliberate nature of the policy towards the Assembly is hinted at in Chelmsford's later letter to Hailey: 'I have been thinking of you all this month with your debates in the Legislature. . . . I am longing to hear how the second Session goes off' (14 Sept. 1921, *loc. cit.*).

50. See V(HD) to S/S, 20 Jan. 1920 (reporting Sinha's speech), *CP12*; Sinha, 26 Jan., Meston, 31 Jan., Basu, 15 and 31 Jan., and Besant, 9 Feb. 1921, to Chelmsford, *CP26*. See also V. Chirol, *India Old and New*, London 1921, 151 and 301; and, for a contrary view, disapproving of the Report, Sir Reginald Craddock, *The Dilemma in India*, London 1929.

51. Lloyd to Chamberlain, 15 Oct. 1920, *ACP18/1/15*, and to Montagu, 18 March 1921, *MP26*; Ronaldshay to Montagu, 1 March 1921, *MP32*.

52. Willingdon to Montagu, 24 April 1921, *MP21*.

53. *Speeches* II, 576 and 588. The contrast between Chelmsford and Reading was shown, for example, in Reading's greater openness, holding 'firm and frank' discussions with Malaviya about interviewing Gandhi (V to S/S, 5 and 6 May 1921, *Reading Papers* 10)—and this style was crucial to popularity.

54. See above, p. 19 ff.; and Chelmsford to Montagu, 22 Sept. 1917, *CP3*: 'We must both remember that the day of honeyed phrases is past'— 'some portion of these promises' now had to be redeemed. Cleveland had written, similarly, 'Indian politicians are crying for the moon, and Lord Hardinge's trick of giving them promises . . . is played out' (to [Seton?], 29 Jan. 1917, *Seton Papers* 7).

55. Holderness, note, 11 Aug. 1917, in Montagu to Chelmsford, 21 Sept. 1917, *CP3*.

56. Craddock to Chelmsford, 15 March 1920, *CP24*.

57. See Chelmsford to Montagu, 22 April 1918, *CP4*, and to Lloyd, 1 May 1920, *CP24*, and also Willingdon, 17 Sept. 1918, *CP21*.

58. Meston to Chelmsford, 2 Oct. 1919, *CP15*.

59. Maffey to Chelmsford, 27–8 April and 17 May 1920, *CP16*.

60. *Speeches* II, 94–5 (4 Sept. 1918).

61. Willingdon to Montagu, 24 April 1921, *MP21*, and also 28 May 1920, *MP20*.

62. Chelmsford to Curzon, 23 April, *CP15*, and to Montagu, 28 April, and Montagu to Chelmsford, 23 April 1918, *CP4*.

63. See R. J. Moore, *The Crisis of Indian Unity, 1917–1940*, Oxford 1974. (I have discussed these ideas more fully in a review of this book, *Modern Asian Studies* 10, 3 (1976).) For a related argument—seeing declarations in response to the threat of agitation as forming the basis of future policy—see also D. A. Low, *Lion Rampant*, London 1973, 168–71 (though, I believe, the India Government is characterized too simply there, as a constant opponent of change).

Appendix I.   Martial Law Sentences in the Panjab

1. The sources for these charts are *H.Poll.*492, Jan., and 122–5, Aug. 1920; and ILC Proceedings, 10 Sept. 1919.

BIBLIOGRAPHY

THE manuscript and documentary sources listed here are those cited in the notes and references. Descriptive summaries are given for the more important or numerous collections, to assist the location of documents to be found in more than one collection. (In the notes only one reference is normally given, where possible to the Chelmsford Collection unless the document may be more usefully consulted elsewhere among other papers on similar subjects.)

The list of published and other sources is not limited to works mentioned in the notes, but includes some supplementary and illustrative material which has been of assistance.

(A) PRIVATE PAPERS

Butler Papers Collection of Sir Harcourt Butler, India Office Library London; MSS.Eur.F.116.

Austen Chamberlain Papers Collection of Sir Austen Chamberlain, University of Birmingham Library.

AC2/2/25–61. Notes.

AC12/1–227 & 15/1/1–35. Correspondence, 1914–1918 and 1911–1924.

AC13/1/1–104. The War, 1914–1918.

AC13/5/1–7 and 15/4/1–147. Letters on appointment and resignation as Secretary of State, 1915 and 1917.

AC14/1/1–72, 15/5/1–13, and 21/4/1–36. On India, 1915–1918.

AC18/1/1–46. Correspondence with Lloyd.

AC18/3/1–19. Correspondence with Chelmsford.

AC21/1/1–69. War Loan, 1915–1917.

AC21/2/1–18. Cotton duties, 1917.

AC21/3/1–13. Commissions.

AC21/5/1–75. Correspondence in India, 1917–1918.

AC21/6/1–45. India Office Memoranda, 1915–1916.

AC22/1 and 2. Memoranda on goal of Indian government.

AC23/3/1–16. Paris Conference.

AC34/1/1–154. Cabinet memoranda.

AC45/2/1–26. Private telegrams with India, 1915–1917.

AC47/3/1. Imperial War Conference, 1917.

Chelmsford Papers Collection of Lord Chelmsford while Viceroy of India, 55 vols., India Office Library; MSS.Eur.E.264.

1. Correspondence with King-Emperor.

2–14. Correspondence with Secretary of State.

15 and 16. Correspondence with persons outside India.

17–26. Correspondence in India.

27 and 28. Speeches.

29–39. Despatches.
40. Mesopotamia Commission Report.
41. Indian Industrial Committee Report, 1918.
42. Montagu–Chelmsford Report, 1918.
43. Sedition Committee Report, 1918.
47. Disorders Inquiry Committee Report, 1919.
48. Proceedings of Military Requirements Committee (II), 1921.
50. Index to pending departmental cases, 1916–1921.
51. 'Goal of British Rule in India'—correspondence and memoranda on self-government.
Curzon Papers Collection of Lord Curzon, Marquis of Kedlestone, India Office Library; MSS.Eur.F.111.
especially. War Cabinet papers, 438, 439, 442, 444 and 588.
Hailey Papers Collection of Lord Hailey, India Office Library; MSS. Eur.E.220.
Lothian Papers Newbattle Muniments—Papers of Philip Henry Kerr, Marquis of Lothian, Scottish Record Office, Edinburgh, GD40/17.
2–16. Round Table and other papers on India, 1910–1915.
19. Oldham on the constitutional struggle in India, 1921.
32. Kerr on Morley–Minto reforms, 1917, and commissions, 1918.
33. Kerr to Curtis on Indian affairs.
34. Indian emigration, 1917.
35–36. Montagu's Indian diary.
206–220. Alphabetical volumes of correspondence, 1918–1921.
Lowndes Papers Papers of Sir George Lowndes, India Office Library; MSS.Eur.C.224.
Meston Papers Collection of Sir James (Baron) Meston, India Office Library; MSS.Eur.F.136.
1. Correspondence with Chelmsford, 1916–1917.
10. Round Table.
11. Correspondence with Curtis.
16–33, 51 and 53. Reforms papers.
Montagu Papers Private Correspondence of E. S. Montagu, India Office Library; MSS.Eur.D.523.
1–11. Correspondence with Chelmsford, 1917–1921.
15. Correspondence with Pentland.
16–21. Correspondence with Willingdon.
22–26. Correspondence with Lloyd.
27–32. Correspondence with Ronaldshay.
33. Reforms correspondence, 1916–1917.
34–44. Papers relating to the visit to India, 1917–1918.
47. Montagu–Chelmsford Report, 1918.
Reading Papers Collection of Lord Reading while Viceroy of India, India Office Library; MSS.Eur.E.238.
Reading Papers (*private*) Private papers of Lord Reading, India Office Library; MSS.Eur.F.118.
Richards Papers Collection of Erle Richards, India Office Library; MSS.Eur.F.122.

Ronaldshay Papers Collection of Lord Ronaldshay, India Office Library; MSS.Eur.D.609.
Seton Papers Collection of Sir Malcolm Seton, India Office Library; MSS.Eur.E.267. 3–10, 19 and 22. Correspondence dated and undated.
Wilson Papers Collection of Sir Guy Fleetwood Wilson, India Office Library; MSS.Eur.E.224.

(B) OFFICIAL RECORDS

Government of India Proceedings, India Office Library and Records, London (A series), and National Archives, New Delhi (A, B and Deposit series), chiefly 1916 to 1921. (See note above, p. xii.) Those consulted include:
Confidential Proceedings.
Home Department Police Proceedings.
Home Department Political Proceedings.
Home Department Public Proceedings.
India Office Proceedings, India Office Library and Records, London, including:
Judicial and Political Department Records (L/P&J series—J&P files).
Parliamentary Department Records (L/Parl series):
394. Calcutta University Committee Report, 1919 (8 vols.).
404. Indian Industrial Committee Report, 1918 (5 vols.).
405. Government of India Bill and Joint Select Committee Report, 1919 (2 vols.).
409. Franchise and Functions (Reforms) Committees' Reports, and Government of India letters, 1919 (4 vols.).
444. Sedition Committee Report, 1918.
Speeches by Lord Chelmsford, Simla 1919 (Vol. I) and 1921 (Vol. II), India Office Library, London.

(C) PUBLISHED AND OTHER SOURCES

Colin Forbes Adam, *Life of Lord Lloyd*, London 1948.
Afzal Iqbal, ed., *My Life, a Fragment. An Autobiographical Sketch of Maulana Mohamed Ali*, Lahore 1946 (1942).
C. F. Andrews and Girija K. Mookerjee, *The Rise and Growth of Congress in India 1832–1920*, Meerut, Delhi, Calcutta 2nd ed. 1967 (1920).
G. S. Arundale, 'To the Youth of India' (pamphlet), Madras 1924.
M. S. Sesa Ayyangar, *Madras Village Panchayats*, Madura [1915].
K. K. Aziz, *Britain and Muslim India*, London 1963.
Christopher Baker, 'Non-cooperation in South India', in C. J. Baker and D. A. Washbrook, *South India: Political Institutions and Political Change 1888–1940*, Delhi etc. 1975.
Surendranath Banerjea, *Nation in Making*, Bombay, Calcutta, Madras 1963 (1925).
Margarita Barns, *The Indian Press*, [London] 1940.
S. C. Bartarya, *The Indian Nationalist Movement*, Allahabad 1958.

Annie Besant, *An Abominable Plot: a Memorandum containing Sir Subramaniam's Letter to Dr. Wilson*, Adyar, Madras [1918].
—— *Congress Speeches*, Adyar, Madras 1917.
—— *India a Nation*, London [1915].
—— *India: Bond or Free*, Adyar, Madras 1939.
—— *Under Sentence of Death* (reprints from *New India*, 29 and 30 Aug. 1916), Madras 1916.
Sukumar Bhattacharya, 'Lord Curzon and the Indian National Congress', *Calcutta Review* 131, 1 (April 1954). (Correspondence between Curzon and the Secretary of State.)
V. C. Bhutani, 'Some Aspects of the Administration of Lord Curzon', *Bengal Past and Present* LXXXV, ii, 160 (July–Dec. 1966).
Brian Bond, 'Amritsar, 1919', *History Today* 13 (Oct. 1963).
Joan V. Bondurant, *Conquest of Violence. The Gandhian Philosophy of Conflict*, Princeton 1958.
Michael Brecher, *Nehru. A Political Biography*, London 1959.
F. S. Briggs, 'The Indian Hijrat of 1920', *Moslem World* 20, April 1930.
J. H. Broomfield, 'The Vote and the Transfer of Power. A Study of the Bengal General Election, 1912–1913', *Journal of Asian Studies* 21 (Feb. 1962).
—— *Elite Conflict in a Plural Society*, Berkeley and Los Angeles 1968.
D. MacKenzie Brown, 'The Philosophy of Bal Gangadhar Tilak. *Karma* vs. *Jñāna* in the *Gītā Rahasya*', *Journal of Asian Studies* 17 (Feb. 1958).
Giles T. Brown, 'The Hindu Conspiracy 1914–1917', *Pacific Historical Review* 17 (Aug. 1948).
Judith M. Brown, *Gandhi's Rise to Power. Indian Politics 1915–1922*, Cambridge 1972.
Briton Cooper Busch, *Britain, India & the Arabs*, Berkeley, Los Angeles and London 1971.
Harcourt Butler, *India Insistent*, London 1931.
Lord Carmichael of Skirling. A Memoir prepared by his wife, London [1929]. (India chapter by W. A. J. Archbold.)
Al Carthill, *Madampur*, Edinburgh and London 1931.
Margaret H. Case, *South Asian History 1750–1950. A Guide to Periodicals, Dissertations and Newspapers*, Princetown 1968.
Austen Chamberlain, *Down the Years*, London 1935. (Reminiscences, but not dealing with India.)
Dilip Kumar Chatterjee, *C. R. Das and Indian National Movement. A Study in his Political Ideals*, Calcutta 1965.
Benarsidas Chaturvedi and Marjorie Sykes, *Charles Freer Andrews*, London 1949.
G. S. Chhabra, *The Advanced History of the Punjab* II, Ludhiana (no date).
Sir Valentine Chirol, *India*, London 1926.
——*Indian Unrest*, London 1910.
——*India. Old and New*, London 1921.
R. Coupland, *The Indian Problem 1833–1935*, London, New York, Toronto, Bombay 1942.

Reginald Craddock, *The Dilemma in India*, London 1929.
W. F. Crawley, 'Kisan Sabhas and Agrarian Revolt in the United Provinces 1920–21' *Modern Asian Studies*, 5,2 (1971).
Sir John Cumming, ed., *Political India*, London 1932.
L. Curtis, *Papers relating to the application of the principle of Dyarchy to the Government of India*, Oxford 1920. (Including an introduction, the Duke Memorandum, Curtis' letters to the People of India and to Bhupendranath Basu, the Joint Address from Europeans and Indians to the Viceroy and Secretary of State, a Memorandum of Evidence before the Joint Select Committee, other papers, and appended copies of the Select Committee Report and the 1919 Act.)
D. Dalton, 'Mahatma Gandhi: The Shaping of Satyagraha', *Asian Review* 2, 2 (Jan. 1969).
——'M. N. Roy and Radical Humanism', in Edmund Leach and S. N. Mukherjee, *Elites in South Asia*, Cambridge 1970.
Richard Danzig, 'Common Ground. The Early Stages of the Montagu–Chelmsford Reforms', Oxford B.Phil. thesis, June 1967.
——'The Announcement of August 20th, 1917', *Journal of Asian Studies* 28, 1 (Nov. 1968).
——'The Many-Layered Cake: A Case Study in the Reform of The Indian Empire', *Modern Asian Studies* 3, 1 (Jan. 1969).
M. N. Das, *India under Morley and Minto*, London 1964.
K. K. Datta, *History of the Freedom Movement in Bihar* I (1857–1928), Patna 1957.
A. R. Desai, *Social Background of Indian Nationalism*, Bombay 2nd ed. 1954.
H. H. Dodwell & R. R. Sethi, *The Cambridge History of India* VI, Delhi 1964. (See especially L. F. Rushbrook Williams, 'India and the War', 476–88; Sir Richard Burn, 'Political Movements 1909–1917' and 'The Reforms of 1919', 574–603; H. R. C. Hailey on war currency and problems, 330–4; and Sir Verney Lovett on the 1918 scarcity, 311–12.)
Jamnadas Dwarkadas, *Political Memoirs*, Bombay 1964.
'An Englishwoman', 'Amritsar', *Blackwood's Magazine* 207 (April 1920).
Georges Fischer, *Le Parti travailliste et la décolonisation de l'Inde*, Paris 1966.
Louis Fischer, *The Life of Mahatma Gandhi*, London 1951.
Rupert Furneaux, *Massacre at Amritsar*, London 1963.
M. K. Gandhi, *An Autobiography or The Story of My Experiments with Truth* (tr. Mahadev Desai), Ahmedabad 2nd ed. 1940.
——*The Collected Works of Mahatma Gandhi* XIII–XIX (Jan. 1915–April 1921), Ahmedabad 1964–1966.
——*Satyagraha in South Africa* (tr. Valji Govindji Desai), Ahmedabad 2nd ed. 1950.
——*Self-Restraint v. Self-Indulgence*, Ahmedabad 3rd ed. 1947.
Martin Gilbert, *Servant of India. A Study of Imperial Rule from 1905 to 1910 as told through the correspondence and diaries of Sir James Dunlop Smith*, London 1966.
Kenneth L. Gillion, *Ahmedabad. A Study in Indian Urban History*, Berkeley and Los Angeles, 1968.

Ram Gopal, *Indian Muslims*, Bombay 1964.
——*Lokamanya Tilak*, London 1956.
S. Gopal, *British Policy in India 1858–1905*, Cambridge 1965.
——*The Viceroyalty of Lord Ripon 1880–1884*, Oxford 1953.
Leonard A. Gordon, 'Portrait of a Bengal Revolutionary', *Journal of Asian Studies* 27, 2 (Feb. 1968).
——*Bengal: the Nationalist Movement 1876–1940*, Columbia 1974.
Richard Gordon, 'Non-cooperation and Council Entry, 1919 to 1920', *Modern Asian Studies* 7, 3 (1973) (also published separately as John Gallagher, Gordon Johnson and Anil Seal, edd., *Locality, Province and Nation*, Cambridge 1973).
B. J. Gould, *The Jewel in the Lotus. Recollections of an Indian Political*, London 1957. (Assistant PSV under Chelmsford.)
Government of India, *Moral and Material Progress Reports*, 1915–1921.
Atulchandra Gupta, ed., *Studies in the Bengal Renaissance*, Jadarpur, Calcutta 1958.
Karl Reinhold Haellquist, 'The Socio-Political Development in the Punjab 1907–1919', unpublished paper (read at the Conference on Modern South Asian Studies, St. John's College, Cambridge, 5–9 July 1968).
Gerald A. Heeger, 'The Growth of the Congress Movement in the Punjab 1920–1940', *Journal of Asian Studies* XXXII, 1 (1972).
P. Hardy, *The Muslims of British India*, Cambridge 1972.
——*Partners in Freedom and True Muslims*, Lund 1971.
W. S. Holdsworth, 'The Indian States and India', *Law Quarterly Review* 46, 184 (Oct. 1930).
B. G. Horniman, *Amritsar and our Duty to India*, London 1920.
H. J. N. Horsburgh, *Non-violence and Aggression. A Study of Gandhi's Moral Equivalent of War*, Oxford 1968.
Indo-British Association, pamphlets opposing home rule, London 1918 and 1919 (see above, chapter 4, note 65).
'Indigo Plantation—A Source of Oppression', *Bengal Past and Present* LXXXII, 154 (July–Dec. 1963) and 154–60 and LXXXIII, I, 155 (Jan.–June 1964).
Eugene F. Irshick, *Politics and Social Conflict in South India*, Berkeley and Los Angeles 1969.
Z. Islam and L. Jensen, 'Indian Muslims and the Public Service 1871–1915', *Journal of the Asiatic Society of Pakistan* IX, 1 (1964).
Gordon Johnson, *Provincial Politics and Indian Nationalism*, Cambridge 1973.
——'Chitpavan Brahmins and Politics in Western India' in Edmund Leach and S. N. Mukherjee, *Elites in South Asia*, Cambridge 1970.
Kenneth W. Jones, 'Communalism in the Punjab. The Arya Samaj Contribution', *Journal of Asian Studies* 28, 1 (Nov. 1968).
Vijaya Chandra Joshi, *Lala Lajpat Rai, Writings and Speeches* II (1920–1928), New Delhi 1966.
V. G. Kale, 'The Reforms' (pamphlet), Poona 1921.
S. L. Karandikar, *Lokamanya Bal Gangadhar Tilak*, Poona [1957].

D. D. Karve, tr., *The New Brahmans. Five Maharashtrian Families*, Berkeley and Los Angeles; Cambridge 1963.

Manmohan Kaur, *The Role of Women and the Freedom Movement 1857–1947*, Delhi and Jullundur 1968.

P. D. Kaushik, *The Congress Ideology and Programme 1920–1947*, Bombay etc. 1954.

Dhananjay Keer, *Veer Savarkar*, Bombay 2nd ed. 1966.

N. C. Kelkar, *Home Rule and the Home Rule League* (Indian Home Rule League Pamphlet No. 1), [Poona] 1917.

J. E. Kendle, 'The Round Table Movement and "Home Rule All Round"', *Historical Journal* XI, 2 (1968).

James Campbell Ker, *Political Trouble in India, 1907–1917*, Calcutta 1917 (Government of India: confidential.).

Stephen E. Koss, 'John Morley and the Communal Question', *Journal of Asian Studies* 26, 3 (May 1967).

Krishna Kripalani, *Rabindranath Tagore. A Biography*, London 1962.

Gopal Krishna, 'The Development of the Indian National Congress as a Mass Organization, 1918–1923', *Journal of Asian Studies* 24 (1965–1966).

——'The Khilafat Movement in India: the First Phase (September 1919–August 1920)', *Journal of the Royal Asiatic Society* 19 (1968).

Ravinder Kumar, 'Class, Community or Nation', *Modern Asian Studies* 3, 4 (Oct. 1969).

——ed., *Essays in Gandhian Politics, The Rowlatt Satyagraha of 1919*, Oxford 1971.

Mary Kynymond, Countess of Minto, *India, Minto and Morley, 1905–1910*, London 1934.

Lajpat Rai, *The Political Future of India*, New York 1919.

Sir Verney Lovett, *A History of the Indian Nationalist Movement*, London 1920.

D. A. Low, 'The Government of India and the First Non-cooperation Movement—1920–1922', *Journal of Asian Studies* 21 (1961–1962).

——*Lion Rampant*, London 1973.

Evan Maconochie, *Life in the Indian Civil Service*, London mcmxxvi.

Bihambehari Majumdar, *Indian Political Associations and Reform of Legislature 1818–1917*, Calcutta 1965.

——*Militant Nationalism in India and its Socio-Religious Background 1897–1917*, Calcutta 1966.

—— and Bhakat Prasad, *Congress and Congressman in the Pre-Gandhian Era, 1885–1917*, Calcutta 1966.

R. C., with A. K., Majumdar, edd., *The History and Culture of the Indian People* XI, *Struggle for Freedom*, Bombay 1969.

Nicholas Mansergh, *The Commonwealth Experience*, London 1969.

R. P. Masani, *Dadabhai Naoroji*, Delhi 1960.

S. R. Mehrotra, 'The Early Organization of the Indian National Congress, 1885–1920', *India Quarterly* 22, 4 (1966).

V. P. Menon, *The Transfer of Power in India*, Bombay, Calcutta, Delhi, Madras 1957.

H. Gordon Milburn, *England and India*, London 1918.

G. Minault, 'Islam and Mass Politics . . .' in D. E. Smith, ed., *Religion and Political Modernization*, New Haven 1974.

B. B. Misra, ed., *Select Documents on Mahatma Gandhi's Movement in Champaran 1917–1918*, Bihar (Secretariat Press) 1963.

Girish Mishra, 'Indigo Plantation and the Agrarian Relations in Champaran during the Nineteenth Century', *Indian Economic & Social History Review*, 4.

——'Socio-Economic Background of Gandhi's Champaran Movement', *loc. cit.* V, 3.

E. S. Montagu, *An Indian Diary* (ed. Venetia Montagu), London 1930.

H. C. Mookerjee, 'Gandhiji's First Arrest and its Repercussions', *Calcutta Review* 86, 1 (April 1943).

——'Indian Leadership and the Awakening of the Masses', *Calcutta Review* 77, 1 (Oct. 1940).

——'The War of 1914–1918 and the Appearance of Discontent', *Calcutta Review* 83, 3 (June); 84, 1 (July) and 2 (Aug.) and 3 (Sept. 1942).

R. J. Moore, *Sir Charles Wood's India Policy*, Manchester 1966.

——*The Crisis of Indian Unity, 1917–1940*, Oxford 1974.

Morris Day Morris, *The Emergence of an Industrial Labor Force in India. A Study of the Bombay Cotton Mills*, Berkeley and Los Angeles 1965.

M. Mujeeb, *The Indian Muslims*, London 1967.

H. and U. Mukherjee, *Bipin Chandra Pal and India's Struggle for Swaraj*, Calcutta 1958.

Panchanadas Mukherji, *Indian Constitutional Documents* I (1600–1918) and II (Government of India Acts 1915 and 1916), Calcutta and Simla 1918.

P. J. Musgrove, 'Landlords and Lords of the Land: Estate Management and Social Control in Uttar Pradesh 1860–1920', *Modern Asian Studies* 6, 3 (1972).

B. R. Nanda, *Mahatma Gandhi. A Biography*, London 1958.

——*The Nehrus. Motilal and Jawaharlal*, London 1962.

Gopi Nath, 'The Home Rule Movement in India', Agra Ph.D. thesis 1962.

Jawaharlal Nehru, ed., *A Bunch of Old Letters*, London 1960.

——*The Discovery of India*, London 1926.

Motilal Nehru, *The Voice of Freedom*, London 1961.

Arthur H. Nethercot, *The First Five Lives of Annie Besant*, London 1961.

——*The Last Four Lives of Annie Besant*, London 1963.

Sir Michael O'Dwyer, *India as I Knew It 1885–1925*, London 1925.

L. S. S. O'Malley, *The Indian Civil Service 1601–1930*, London 1931.

B. C. Pal, *The New Policy*, Madras [1918].

——*Writings and Speeches* I, Calcutta 1958.

M. R. Palande, ed. (for G/Bombay), *Source Material for a History of the Freedom Movement in India* II (1885–1920), Bombay 1958.

K. M. Panikkar, *His Highness the Maharaja of Bikaner. A Biography*, London 1937.

Kewal L. Panjabi, *Rajendra Prasad*, London 1960.
——*The Indomitable Sardar*, Bombay 1962.
Narhari D. Parikh, *Sardar Villabhbhai Patel* I, Ahmedabad 1953.
T. V. Parvate, *Bal Gangadhar Tilak*, Ahmedabad 1958.
——'Tilak and Gokhale', *Gandhi Marg 44* II, 4 (Oct. 1967).
Lady Pentland, *The Right Honourable John Sinclair, Lord Pentland, G.C.S.I. A memoir*, London 1928.
Urmila Phadnis, *Towards the Integration of the Indian States, 1919–1947*, New York 1968.
N. R. Phatak, ed. (for G/Maharashtra), *Source Material for a History of the Freedom Movement in India* III, *Mahatma Gandhi* I (1915–1922), Bombay 1965.
C. H. Philips, ed., *Politics and Society in India*, London 1963.
——*The Evolution of India and Pakistan 1858–1947* (*Select Documents on the History of India and Pakistan* IV), London 1962.
H. S. L. Polak, H. N. Brailsford and Lord Pethick-Lawrence, *Mahatma Gandhi*, London 1949.
Sri Prakasa, *Annie Besant*, Bombay 2nd ed. 1954.
C. P. Ramaswami Aiyar, *Annie Besant*, Delhi 1963.
A. Rangaswami Aiyangar, 'The "Coming Reforms" in India', *Hindustan Review* 38, 227 (July 1918).
R. Gundu Rao, *The Panjab Atrocities*, Mysore 1922.
M. V. Krishna Rao and C. S. Halappa, *History of the Freedom Movement in Karnataka* II, Bangalore 1964.
Rajat K. Ray, 'Masses in Politics: the Non-cooperation Movement in Bengal, 1920–1922', *Indian Economic and Social History Review* XI, 4 (1974).
Sir Stanley Reed, *The India I Knew 1897–1947*, London 1952.
Peter D. Reeves, 'The Politics of Order', *Journal of Asian Studies* XXV (Feb. 1966).
Peter Robb, 'The Government of India and Annie Besant', *Modern Asian Studies* 10, 1 (1976).
——'The British Cabinet and Indian Reform 1917–1919', *Journal of Imperial and Commonwealth History* 4, 3 (1976).
——'Officials and Non-Officials as Leaders in Popular Agitations: Shahabad 1917 and other "conspiracies"', in B. N. Pandey, ed., *Leadership in South Asia* (forthcoming).
Francis Robinson, *Separatism among Indian Muslims*, Cambridge 1974.
Lord Ronaldshay (Lawrence Dundas, later 2nd Marquess of Zetland— qv), *India, a Bird's Eye View*, London 1924.
——*The Heart of Aryâvarta*, London 1925.
——*The Life of Lord Curzon* III, London [1928].
Kenneth Rose, *Superior Person. A Portrait of Curzon and his Circle in late Victorian England*, London 1969.
Stephen Roskill, *Hankey, Man of Secrets* I (1877–1918), London 1970.
Indira Rothermund, 'The Individual and Society in Gandhiji's Political Thought', *Journal of Asian Studies* 28, 2 (Feb. 1969).

Tej Bahadur Sapru, ed., *Encyclopedia of the General Acts and Codes of India*, 14 vols., Calcutta 1935–1945.

Sir George Schuster and Guy Wint, *India and Democracy*, London 1941.

Anil Seal, *The Emergence of Indian Nationalism. Competition and Collaboration in the Later Nineteenth Century*, Cambridge 1968.

Bernard Semmel, *Imperialism and Social Reform*, London 1960.

Padmini Sengupta, *Sarojini Naidu*, London 1966.

Jagdish Saran Sharma, *Indian National Congress. A Descriptive Bibliography of India's Struggle for Freedom*, Delhi, Jullundur, Lucknow 1959.

M. H. Siddiqi, 'The Peasant Movement in Pratabgarh 1920', *Indian Economic and Social History Review* 9 (Sept. 1972).

Ray T. Smith, 'The Role of India's "Liberals" in the Nationalist Movement, 1915–1947', *Asian Survey* VIII, 7 (July 1968).

Percival Spear, *The Oxford History of Modern India 1740–1947 (The Oxford History of India*, III), Oxford 1965.

——'Mahatma Gandhi', *Modern Asian Studies* 3, 4 (Oct. 1969).

D. V. Tahmankar, *Lokamanya Tilak*, London 1956.

——*Sardar Patel*, London 1970.

Prakash Tandon, *Punjabi Century 1857–1947*, Berkeley and Los Angeles 1968.

A. J. P. Taylor, *English History 1914–1945*, Harmondsworth 1970.

D. G. Tendulkar, *Gandhi in Champaran*, [Delhi] (Government of India) 1957.

——*Mahatma* I and II (1869–1929), Bombay 1951.

Edward Thomson and G. T. Garratt, *Rise and Fulfilment of British Rule in India*, London 1934.

S. J. Thomson, *The Silent India. Being Tales and Sketches of the Masses*, Edinburgh and London 1913.

B. G. Tilak, *Letters of Lokamanya Tilak (1884–1920)*, Poona 1966.

A. T. Yarwood, 'The overseas Indians as a problem in India and imperial politics at the end of world war one', *Australian Journal of Politics and History*, V, 14 (Aug. 1968).

S. D. Waley, *Edwin Montagu, A Memoir and an Account of his Visits to India*, London 1964.

Syed Razi Wasti, *Lord Minto and the Indian Nationalist Movement 1905 to 1910*, Oxford 1964.

Stanley A. Wolpert, *Tilak and Gokhale*, Berkeley and Los Angeles 1962.

Philip Woodruff, *The Men Who Ruled India* II, *The Guardians*, London 1954.

Trevor Wilson, ed., *The Political Diaries of C. P. Scott 1911–1928*, London 1970.

Lawrence, 2nd Marquess of Zetland (formerly Lord Ronaldshay—q.v.), *'Essayez'*, London 1956.

Index to the text and notes